LEARNING AND EMOTION:
A Biological Synthesis

Volume 1
EVOLUTIONARY PROCESSES

LEARNING AND EMOTION:
A Biological Synthesis

Volume 1
EVOLUTIONARY PROCESSES

Peter J. Livesey
The University of Western Australia
Nedlands, Western Australia

LEA LAWRENCE ERLBAUM ASSOCIATES, PUBLISHERS

1986   Hillsdale, New Jersey   London

Lawrence Erlbaum Associates, Inc., Publishers
365 Broadway
Hillsdale, New Jersey 07642

Library of Congress Cataloging-in-Publication Data

Livesey, Peter J.
   Learning and emotion.

   Bibliography: p.
   Includes index.
   1. Learning—Physiological aspects.   2. Emotions—
Physiological aspects.   3. Nervous system—Evolution.
4. Physiology, Comparative.   I. Title.
QP408.L58   1986   156′.315   85-27540
ISBN 0-89859-552-5

Printed in the United States of America
10 9 8 7 6 5 4 3 2 1

Table of Contents

Preface

This work elaborates my conviction that an understanding of the biological basis of our behavior is essential for an adequate view of the nature of learning processes. As Schneirla (1966) put it, considerations of probable evolutionary relationships in mechanisms underlying behavior are fundamental guides for those investigating such behaviors. A knowledge of the organization and functioning of the nervous system, and of how that system evolved in response to the demands imposed for survival, is of particular significance in this context. It is this system that organizes and controls our behavior.

The views of such people as Lashley, Harlow, and Hebb who argued for unity of process between behavior (mind) and neural function, played a significant part in shaping my thinking. In this regard, a statement of Lashley's at the conclusion of his paper on "Cerebral Organization and Behavior" intrigued me when I first read it and has lived with me ever since. Lashley (1958) said:

> Mind is a complex organization, held together by interaction of processes and by the time scales of memory, centered about the body image. It has no distinguishing features other than its organization. The mental phenomena must be subjected to an analysis as complete and detailed as that which is being made of neural activities. Only as progress is made in such an analysis, and as the picture of the brain's activities is completed, will it be possible to make significant correlations between the two organized systems. Meanwhile, there is no logical or empirical reason for denying the possibility that the correlation may eventually show a complete identity of the two organizations. (p. 18)

During the past 25 years this question of the relationship between the two systems has been of particular interest to me. Over that period I have come to the view that, although separate analysis of both behavior (mind in action) and neural organization has been a necessary pre-requisite for a bettter understanding of how we function, more and more it is becoming clear that these two areas of study are essentially two facets of a single system and need to be considered as such. Evolutionary history reveals that the nervous system evolved in its particular form in the pursuit of survival. The system functions in various ways to ensure that the animal will remain alive and will reproduce itself. One outcome of this functioning is what we call *mind*.

This volume has a long evolutionary history in itself, the first seeds being planted when, having to spend Christmas of 1957 confined to a hospital bed, I read and became entranced by Thorpe's *Learning and Instinct in Animals.* This proved to be the beginning of a rich and rewarding period with the appearance of Harlow and Woolsey's *Evolution of Brain and Behavior,* Roe and Simpson's *Behavior and Evolution* and the collection of Lashley's works under the editorship of Beach, Hebb, Morgan, and Nissen. These books exerted a strong influence on my thinking at the time. To these must be added Olds' work on the reward systems of the brain and Pribram's (1960) review of his theory of brain function in the *Annual Review of Psychology.* It was however, not until after my return from year's study leave at the Wisconsin Regional Primate Center with Harry Harlow and Jerry Schwartzbaum that I first commenced to write.

It became apparent to me quite early that emotion, or more particularly the affects or feelings of emotion, must have played a significant part in the evolution of learning. Olds' work was a major factor in shaping this view. The necessity to lecture on and discuss with my students the concept of emotion and to present a logical account of this function within an evolutionary framework forced me to focus on this aspect of behavior. As a consequence I became convinced that emotion was of crucial importance for the evolution of the more advanced learning processes that became evident along the path that led to the emergence of man.

Since then the work has undergone many transformations shaped by my own work, by the demands of my students and in particular by study leave periods spent with colleagues in various parts of the world during which discussion, reading and writing proceeded apace. The present publication is the culmination of these activities.

ACKNOWLEDGMENTS

Over the years during which this book has been in preparation, I have received considerable assistance and encouragement from many sources. The students with whom I have worked provided much of the inspiration for the project by raising questions that demanded answers. Seeking those answers provided an important part of the challenge that led to both the preparation and the direction of this work.

Study leave periods spent in various and widely differing university environments yielded extensive opportunities for updating my knowledge, for research, reading, and writing and for discussion with colleagues. I am indebted to the following institutions for providing these opportunities: University of Bergen, Duke University, University of Hong Kong, University of Michigan, and Stanford University.

A number of colleagues at these universities or during visits to the University of Western Australia read parts or all of the manuscript at various stages over the years and I am deeply indebted to them for their many helpful comments and criticisms. These include Don Baer, Jeff Bitterman, Charles Butter, Irving Diamond, John Dawson, Dorothy Eichorn, Karl Pribram, John Staddon, Holger Ursin, and Elliot Valenstein. I owe a particular debt of gratitude to Bill Uttal for maintaining a pipe line with my publisher at a time when communication problems developed.

At the University of WA I am indebted firstly to Jenny Bell for her invaluable assistance in the search for information and the referencing of that information, for her work on the subject index, and finally for her review of the draft material, then to Ron Davidson for his critical reading of the final draft, to John Watson for his proof reading skills when the page proofs arrived, to Peter Meyer for preparation of the histology figures, and to Herb Jurkiewicz for photography. The preparation of the manuscript would not have been possible without the typing skills of various Departmental Secretarial staff including, Pat Edwards, Pam Basden, Lisa Chitty, Romana Kopp, and in particular, Chris Pfaff who put the whole manuscript onto the word processor and thereby made life much easier for all of us. I express my appreciation to the Psychology Department for providing the facilities that made preparation of the mauscript possible.

I am deeply indebted to the authors and publishers whose figures and words I have drawn on extensively throughout this work. Acknowledgment of the individual sources is given in the text.

Finally, my heartfelt thanks to my wife who time and again over the years, at home and abroad, translated my handwriting and converted it into readable typescript.

Prologue

An amoeba, a minute single-celled animal, moving through its freshwater habitat, encounters a small object, makes contact, then moves on. Seconds later it contacts another particle of similar size and shape but this time its pseudopods engulf it and incorporate the particle into the protoplasmic mass of the amoeba. Shortly thereafter, upon encountering a third particle, the amoeba does not make contact but exhibits an active withdrawal of the pseudopod and then reverses direction away from the object. The first particle was a small piece of cork, inert and non-nutritive, the second a speck of protoplasm, highly nutritive for the small animal, and the third an acid crystal which, if engulfed, would have been lethal.

Amoeba's interaction with its environment in these instances exhibits selective behaviors that enable it to survive in that environment. Furthermore, the behaviors may be classed as cognitive in that amoeba sensed the nature of each of the three particles and responded differentially to them. Cognition denotes the capacity of the organism to know something of its environment and involves some form of registration of relevant stimuli leading to a response that is appropriate for survival.

A small crab is dangled into a tank of water. An octopus rushes out of its rocky cave, seizes the crab and devours it. A short time later another crab is lowered. This time it is accompanied by a white disc. Again the octopus moves forward to take the crab but stops suddenly, blanches and retreats. It has learned that crab with white disc means that if it attacks the crab it will suffer a painful experience, an electric shock.

A large female mantis waits for her prey. She holds her posture for many minutes without the slightest movement and blends perfectly with her sur-

1

roundings. A fly approaches and settles near her. Suddenly she explodes in a blur of speed and, with a lightning fast movement, secures the fly with her specially equipped forelimbs and consumes it. A small male mantis approaches from the rear, mounts her and begins copulation. However, he is not cautious enough and the female grasps him and begins to devour him head first. Nonetheless the copulation proceeds to a successful completion despite the fact that, by this time, the male's head and thorax have been consumed.

A hungry rat patrolling its domain encounters a novel nutritive substance. It surveys the food, sniffs it vigorously and then retreats. Another rat from the same colony, more hungry or less cautious, eventually samples the food. Should that rat become sick or die then the substance will be ignored and the rats could even leave the area. If, however, the animal continues to prosper this food will be incorporated into the colony's diet. This phenomenon, in fact, posed a major problem for rodent control in British granaries during World War II and led to the development of the slow anti-coagulant poisons that have proved so effective against these animals.

A chimpanzee squats beside a termite nest threading a piece of branch, from which it has stripped the leaves, down one of the holes in the nest. It withdraws the stick and eats, with obvious relish, the ants adhering to it.

A man sits quietly at a desk, almost immobile. After some 15 minutes of seeming inactivity he then takes a pen and begins writing vigorously.

These are but a minute sample of the vast array of behaviors exhibited by living organisms in their interactions with the environment, interactions that are undertaken to preserve their integrity and thus ensure their survival.

The effectiveness of such behaviors depends upon the animal receiving appropriate stimuli to enable it to interpret events in the environment and to respond adaptively to those events so that it can gain its needs and avoid harm. For these signals to be of value to the organism they must be matched or compared in some way with patterns or images or representations held in the organism. These may be images of relevant objects in the environment, established relationships between events, fixed patterns of response that are triggered by appropriate stimuli, or complex representations of the outcomes of past organism-environment interactions that are utilized to modify or change behavior.

How are these representations laid down and modified? How are they utilized? The evolution of behavior is tied to the increasing capacity of the organism to receive and interpret relevant signals and to anticipate environmental events to its benefit. This capacity is inexorably bound to the evolution of the central nervous system. It defines the essential nature of the nervous system and the prime thrust or direction of behavior.

In the chapters to follow I am thus concerned with systems that link the organism to its environment through knowledge of that environment. In particular I examine the aspects of cognition that we call learning. These are the processes by which an animal is able to acquire and modify its representations of the environment through information from its interaction with the environment. Such modifications result in adaptive processes with changes in subsequent behavior resulting from the earlier experience.

To further this objective I explore the evolution of the nervous system and the evolution of learning to see what links may be established between the two, i.e., between the system and its product. In this analysis my concern is to trace man's evolutionary background in both neural and behavioral terms.

Following consideration of these links between the evolution of the nervous system and of learning I examine how this relationship may have come about, paying particular attention to the nature of emotion and of the significance of emotion for the evolution of learning.

These relationships between the evolution of the nervous system and of emotion and learning return us to the organization of neural mechanisms and in particular the limbic structures of the brain and the functioning of this system in the mediation of learning. In Volume 2, I will examine in some detail the neural systems that enable external or environmental events and internal states, needs, drives, rewards and punishments, to become associated. In particular, I will consider those processes that direct the animal's attention to stimuli that have relevance for it and enable it to utilize these relevant occurrences for the organization of behavior on future occasions.

Our knowledge of man's evolutionary history, together with a growing understanding of how the nervous system is organized and functions, opens new vistas for our theorizing about the nature of learning. Such knowledge also sets significant constraints on the form which such theorizing may take. An examination of the implications of this biological, evolutionary approach for the understanding of learning is my ultimate objective in this work.

I | AN OVERVIEW: OBJECTIVES AND PLAN OF ATTACK

1 An Evolutionary Approach to Learning

INTRODUCTION

Individual self preservation through adjustment or accommodation to a changing and unstable environment is one reliable criterion for distinguishing the living from the non-living. As Young put it: "A living thing maintains an improbable steady state, by which it is prevented from diffusing into its surroundings" (Young, 1957, p. 25). To maintain this steady state animals engage in activities or behaviors that are classed as adaptive, i.e., that enable them to accommodate to changes, both internal and external. For these behaviors to be effected cognitive processes must intervene between stimulus and response.

By cognition I am not implying any self-conscious appreciation by the organism but simply some knowledge of the environment; an awareness of the significance of stimuli or events that enables the organism to make behavioral adjustments necessary for its survival. Such processes would encompass what Cyril Burt (1955) defined as "the directive, adaptive or cybernetic aspects of conscious behavior," a definition of cognition also proposed earlier by Franz and Gordon (1933).

We entertain the belief that animals, including man, "know" something of their environment because our observations tell us that, in response to certain changes in the environment, consequential changes of a consistent nature occur in the behavior of the individual animal. From the nature of these changes we deduce that not only immediately current events, but also past experiences influence the resultant behavior. From this we postulate intermediate or intervening processes such as memory and learning that influence the responses to current stimuli.

In their attempts to establish theories of cognition and to study the nature of cognitive processes, philosophers and psychologists have, for perhaps obvious reasons, tended to concentrate on the currently behaving organism and particularly, though not exclusively, to concern themselves with observations of this behavior in terms of the stimuli impinging on the animal and of its responses to those stimuli. With human subjects the use of introspection has been favored or condemned, depending on the theoretical position taken by the investigator. The psychologist who adopts an S–R approach is thus concerned with environmental events, i.e., the observed stimuli (S) and responses (R), and learns about the prime object of the enquiry, the behaving organism, only indirectly from these environmental relationships. The animal thus becomes, as it were, a mediator, a black box that gives rise to the observed relationships. These relationships are then explained in terms of constructs or intervening variables. These theoretical constructs, elaborated on the basis of such S–R relationships, have often proved less than satisfactory in accounting for the observed behaviors.

Many observations of man's interactions with the environment have been made and many theories developed to give a parsimonious account of these findings. Quite frequently such theories have been developed with little consideration for how man is structured or how these structures actually function. Another major source of error is that such approaches have, not infrequently, ignored the biological history of the animals being studied or the origins or evolutionary development of the behaviors under consideration.

The analysis of behavior presented by such molar psychologists may vary substantially from the pattern that appears to be evident from comparative and evolutionary studies of behavior on the one hand and comparative studies of the nervous system or of neural development in ontogeny on the other. As we see in later chapters, the definition and the role assigned to emotion by S–R psychologists is one example. Accounts of cognitive structures and the arbitrary divisions of the learning process are others.

Razran (1971) in an analysis of the development of this approach in American psychology traced it back to Thorndike and his view that all learning consists of trial and error connections of action and result through the law of effect. Two antithetical approaches, said Razran, consolidated the American viewpoint, namely that of the behaviorists led by Watson and supported by the Russian work on classical conditioning and, in particular, the writings of Pavlov, on the one hand and the Gestaltists and the influential works of Koffka's *The Growth of Mind* (1924) and Kohler's *The Mentality of Apes* (1925) on the other.

Razran pictured present day American psychology as sharply divided into two camps both of which ignored man's evolutionary heritage. One group, the "unevolutionary conditioners," said Razran, saw "the minds of worms and men as the minds of rats" while the other was comprised of "unevolutionary cognitionists" to whom "the minds of worms and rats are the minds of men" (p. 5).

Bitterman has made a similar point. In a comment on the Hodos and Campbell (1969) paper in which they ask the question "Why is there no theory in comparative psychology?" Bitterman observed that the question is the wrong one, at least as it relates to learning, long the principal concern of animal psychologists. A better question, he suggested, is "Why has there been so little comparative research?" The answer, said Bitterman, "is that work on learning has been dominated almost from the outset by a powerful theory which denies that learning has undergone any fundamental change" (viz. the comparative analysis of learning begun by Edward L. Thorndike) (Bitterman, 1975, p. 699.) Bitterman's observations also apply to Lockard's (1971) controversial paper "Reflections on the Fall of Comparative Psychology." In that paper Lockard sets up a straw man of comparative psychology, epitomized by the animal learning theorists referred to by both Razran and Bitterman, and then proceeds to tear that straw man to shreds.

THE ROLE OF BEHAVIOR IN EVOLUTION

In fact man is not "ready made" but has been developed by a long and continuing process over a period of probably more than 3000 million years. The process itself has been far from parsimonious, with countless millions of trials failing to survive the test of time. The primary "purpose" of living organisms is to survive, to maintain their integrity in the face of a changing and hostile environment, which has a limited capacity to meet the essential needs for survival. Purpose in this sense is an active process but does not necessarily involve, in fact in almost every instance would not involve, any conscious awareness of such an objective. As Koestler has expressed it,

> the term "purpose" in its biological context implies neither a Purposer nor a cut-and-dried image of the ultimate goal to be achieved . . . . Purposiveness means goal-directed instead of random activity, flexible strategies instead of rigid mechanisms and adaptive behavior but on the organism's own terms . . . . *The Purposer is each and every individual organism, from the inception of life, which struggled and strove to make the most of its limited opportunities* (Koestler, 1967, p. 152).

Lorenz (1969) also addressed himself to the question of purpose in evolutionary change and development. "This molding through evolutionary change," said Lorenz, "is called adaptation and we have a pretty good idea of the mechanisms achieving it." He continued:

> These insights not only justify but demand our asking a question unknown to physics and chemistry, the question "What for?" This is not the teleological

question concerning the ultimate aims and reasons of creation — it is just short-hand for the Darwinian question "Which is the function whose survival value exerted the selection pressure *causing* the species to evolve the characteristics that our question concerns?" (p. 13).

These "efforts to survive" have led to an evolutionary process that has resulted in the development of very complex organisms indeed, capable of processing many and varied inputs of information and of utilizing this information to adjust their activities to cope with the perturbations of the world around them. Adjustment of activities involves the behavior of the organism — its behavior provides the key to its survival, a point not overlooked by biologists but one that has been sadly neglected by many psychologists. It is noteworthy, however, that one of the great theorists of American psychology, Clark L. Hull, adopted a natural science approach to behavior theory (Hull, 1945).

Darwin pointed to the important role of behavior in natural selection and some groups of biologists, the Lamarkians and neo-Lamarkians, went so far as to argue that the behavior of individual organisms could be impressed on the germ plasm and thus be transmitted to or influence the behavior of succeeding generations. Although this particular view has been largely, if not completely, discredited, there is no doubt that both the Darwinian and Lamarkian approaches were primarily concerned with the behaving organism, the chicken rather than the egg. The modern synthetic view as expressed by Simpson (1958) sees the genetic mechanisms as the medium of evolution, providing an essentially random or nondirectional combining of elements. Direction is then given by selective pressure, with behavior at the core of this process.

The basic tenets of current evolutionary theory can be summarized in the view that evolutionary change or "progress" has been and is being achieved by the directing of random gene mutation by the processes of natural selection. These processes enable the adaptation of a particular population of organisms to their environment, one which is almost invariably a changing one. The emphasis, then, is on variation; on individual differences within a population. Any genetic change that would confer a selective advantage, i.e., in the final analysis would improve the prospects of an organism reproducing itself, would increase in the population and would help to change that population. "Natural selection always favors reproductive success and nothing else" (Simpson, 1958, p. 20).

Thus we can differentiate between evolution seen as a population phenomenon, with change in populations over time, and adaptation, which relates to the individual's capacity to adjust to its environment. The change in populations that we call evolution is the outcome of individual attempts to adapt. Selection relates to the relative survival of these individuals and their capacity to produce offspring. If the differential survival of such individuals reflects genetic differences, then selection will result in a changing population, i.e., evolutionary change.

While this expresses, in simplest terms, the concept of the genetic basis for evolution, it says nothing about the manner in which a genetic blueprint is converted into a living organism or the implications of gene changes for such a developmental program.

Modern genetic theory pays considerable attention to what is called the genetic environment, namely the interaction between genes and the effect of modifiers and what happens within that environment as a result of gene recombination or the more disruptive and dramatic events of gene mutation. Thus the genetic "environment" can modify the message carried by individual genes. Of equal importance is the environment provided by the developing organism.

In ontogeny the first cell, the fertilized ovum, has the potential to develop all the cells of the adult organism. As soon as the cell divides the two daughter cells start to exert an influence on each other. However, if these two cells fail to adhere then they will develop into two separate individuals, to wit, identical twins. If, as is normal, the two cells adhere and continue to divide, a hollow blastula is formed followed by the gastrula. The location of each dividing cell, the environment of that cell, puts more and more constraints on the ultimate form that that dividing cell can take. Early cells have almost complete docility, i.e., may take part in the development of any structure within the whole. Later cells become more and more precisely determined by the developing cell environment so that after a given stage has been reached the decision becomes irreversible. Within each morphogenic field, however, "each organ primordium displays the holistic character of an autonomous unit, a self-regulating holon" (Koestler, 1967, p. 121). Thus if a developing field has a section removed the remainder will form, not a half organ, but a complete unit and even if cells of a tissue are scrambled and filtered they may reform again. Thus, said Koestler,

> these autonomous, self-regulating properties of holons within the growing embryo are a vital safeguard; they ensure that whatever accidental hazards arise during development the end product will be according to norm . . . . The self-regulating mechanisms which correct deviations from the norm and guarantee, so to speak, the end result have been compared to the homeostatic feedback devices in the adult organism—so biologists speak of "developmental homeostasis" (p. 121).

A major problem with the particulate theory of evolution is raised by the question: How can single gene mutational changes resulting in single specific structural or functional changes confer a selective advantage, or, more particularly, lead to the sequences of changes that have been evidenced many times in evolutionary history? Koestler gives as an example the problem of how the change from the amphibian to the reptilian egg was effected. Mechanisms had to be provided for a waterproof shell, adequate food and water supplies, a means for eliminating or storing waste products, an oxygen supply and a way for the young animal to get out of the egg at the appropriate time. It is inconceivable, said Koestler, that discrete isolated random changes could have put these changes together in the right sequence to allow for survival of the young at each stage.

Waddington, in considering the problem, claimed that the difficulty would largely disappear if it was borne in mind that organs and structures of the body are not just a collection of elements but are gradually formed as the animal develops with different parts influencing each other. Thus, if by some experimental means the retina and eyeball are made larger than usual, that in itself will cause a larger lens to appear of at least approximately the appropriate size for vision. Thus, said Waddington,

> there is no reason, therefore, why a chance mutation should not affect the whole organ in a harmonious way, and there is a reasonable possibility that it might improve it . . . . A random change in a hereditary factor will, in fact, not usually result in an alteration in just one element of the adult animal. It will bring about a shift in the whole developmental system, and may thus alter a complex organ as a whole (Waddington, 1952[1]).

A flexible developmental program, in which the influences of the individual discrete genes interact to facilitate the building of an organized structure, conforming to a laid down plan or pattern of representations, allows for the incorporation of modification or change in individual genetic components. The changes so incorporated will result in a unique structure, an individual different from all other individuals. This concept of development or unfolding through a flexible developmental program has been advanced by Schneirla in a number of papers (e.g., Schneirla, 1949, 1957, 1966). Schneirla argued that development in ontogeny of an individual is composed of a complex and gradual set of changes involving interrelated biochemical, physiological, and other functional events. The patterns of organization, evident at each stage, are, said Schneirla, reorganizations of previous patterns evident in earlier stages (Schneirla, 1966). He supported Waddington's (1959) view that both the individual "genetic" system and the "epigenetic" system (i.e., including a whole range of events active during the developmental sequence) must be considered as an indissoluble complex in the ontogeny of each individual.

These individual differences, then, may result in a greater or a lessened chance of survival in a particular environment. If more individuals with a

---

[1]Waddington, C. H. In *The listener,* London, 13.11.1952 (from Koestler, 1967).

particular sort of "difference" survive and reproduce and if their total genetic structure is such that those differences are perpetuated, an evolutionary change will be effected. This then depends on reproductive success.

Clearly reproductive success involves all the processes of interaction between organism and environment but, as Simpson pointed out, this effect will be favored by the individual capacity for adaptation to the environment. Thus behavior becomes a central element in factors that produce or guide evolutionary change.

Koestler has underlined the significance of behavior in evolutionary change. He argued that, according to orthodox theory,

> we would have to believe that some random mutation, by modifying the shape of the bird's beak, *caused* it to develop its ingenious way of hunting insects . . . . Let us rather agree with Hardy[2] that "the emphasis in present day view must be false" and that the main causative factor of evolutionary progress is *not* the selective pressure of the environment but the initiative of the living organism, "the restless exploring and perceiving animal, that discovers new ways of living, new sources of food" . . . . It is adaptations which are due to the animal's behavior, to its restless exploration of its surroundings, to its initiative that distinguishes the main diverging lines of evolution . . . . One might call this "progress by initiative" or do-it-yourself theory of evolution (Koestler, 1967, p. 154).

Koestler's approach is polemic, thus appearing to see the "current" view and his own as occupying extreme positions when both in fact acknowledge the significance of behavioral interaction with the environment and both, the impact of genetic change. The value of Koestler's approach is that it does underline the significance of the active, exploring, behaving animal and his conclusion on this topic is one that must be kept in the forefront of our thinking about evolutionary change. Koestler quoted Ewer (1960)[3] to note that, "Behavior will tend to be always a jump ahead of structure and to play a decisive role in evolutionary progress" (Koestler, 1967, p. 156). Here Koestler would seem to be arguing that many evolutionary pressures are on what the animal does, i.e., its behavior, and that selection pressures would thus relate to those systems that influence a particular behavior. In these terms, increased exploratory behavior would provide the animal with more information relevant to its survival. Any genetic changes that would sustain or increase such exploration would be selected out and enhanced. Thus to understand the evolution of animals we need to gain insight into the evolution of behavior.

The study of the evolution of behavior is, however, faced with a major problem. Since behavior can be observed only in living animals the unraveling of the evolution of behavior must rely heavily on studies of existing spe-

---

[2]Hardy, A. C. *The living stream,* London, 1956 (from Koestler, 1967).
[3]Ewer, R. F. Natural selection and neotony. *Acta Biotheretica,* 1960 (from Koestler, 1967).

cies. As living organisms represent the current end points of many lines of evolutionary development rather than any continuum along some main stream, such evidence must be treated with due circumspection. This in fact provides one of the main thrusts of attack by such writers as Hodos and Campbell, Lockard, and Warren on current work in comparative psychology and is also closely examined by Bitterman in his 1975 paper. Be that as it may such comparative studies form an indispensable element of research into the evolution of behavior and must provide the basis for any theoretical developments in this area.

While a primary source of data for evolutionary theory, the geological record can provide no direct evidence on the behaviors of the animals so preserved; it can yield valuable indirect evidence. That there is a close relationship between morphology and behavior should be apparent and Colbert (1958) discussed how a study of fossil remains, which give a fairly adequate picture of morphology, may be used to reconstruct an outline of the likely behaviors of such animals. Much more recently Hodos (1976) stressed the importance of the morphological basis of behavior in his discussion of the principle of homologous behavior. Structural correlates are, he said, the bases of an animal's behavioral heritage.

A fertile line of approach to a better understanding of the evolution of learning is through the study of the evolution of the nervous system. Here an area of morphological change that appears to be of particular significance is that of relative brain size.

The capacity of an animal to make adaptive changes in behavior is dependent on the neural mechanisms available to it. As Lashley (1949) expressed it, "the evolution of mind is the evolution of nervous mechanisms." A study of the evolutionary development of this system should therefore yield valuable data on the development of the cognitive processes of animals. If, at the same time, we can get an index that enables us to compare across species in terms of degree of neural organization, this would provide us with a further asset. Von Bonin's work provided such an index.

Von Bonin (1937) considered the relationship between brain weight and body weight and developed a coefficient of cephalization for various species. He pointed out that the value of this cephalization coefficient differs from species to species but "whether or not this is an indication of the intelligence of animals must be left to the psychologist to answer" (p. 388). If this index can then be employed to compare existing species with those known from the geological record to be at, or near, the main line of evolutionary development then this should be a tool of inestimable value. Jerison has provided us with a technique that enables us to exploit such a measure.

Thus, before I embark on an examination of comparative studies of learning in Chapters 6, 7 and 8, I explore evidence relating to the evolution of the nervous system. In so doing I consider findings from both living animals and the fossil record to establish a basis for interpretation of the behavioral data.

Lashley (1949), discussing the evolution of mind, pointed out that radical changes in structure, such as the advent of the nerve net in the primitive coelenterate or the development of the neocortex in mammals, did not seem to have introduced anything new in behavior when they first appeared but that these changes probably opened the way for later advancement. The evolutionary processes by which these neural changes may have been effected is examined further later. However, in the light of what I have said already it seems more likely that initial advantages existed for the genetic change to persist and develop and that the advantages became stronger with further development. On the basis of his studies of behavior and of neurology, Lashley then concluded that:

> The only neurological character for which a correlation with behavioral capacity in different animals is supported by significant evidence is the total mass of tissue or rather, the index of cephalization, measured by the ratio of brain to body weight, which seems to represent amount of brain tissue in excess of that required for transmitting impulses to and from the integrative centers. We must seek the clue to behavioral evolution in the number of interconnections of the nerve cells or in their biochemical characteristics, not in their gross structural arrangement (p. 463).

Later views would seem, in the main, to support Lashley's hypothesis. Pribram (1958), in an examination of comparative behavior of vertebrates, followed Lashley when he stressed the need to consider the overall development of the brain and the interrelations of the various parts. He saw increasing brain complexity as resulting primarily in an increase in multiple determination of action in these vertebrates, the ability to collect more diverse information at one time, and to integrate this information so that action is more adaptive.

That this is the sort of relationship that has evolved is not really suprising since the evolution of behaviors that facilitate survival dictate selection for those changes in neural organization that mediate such behaviors. Increasing size and complexity within the nervous system will enable more intricate processing and integration of data, permitting the animal to cope more adequately with a changing and variable environment.

On the other hand, behavioral scientists have divided the activities of animals into a set of constructs such as learning, memory, perception, motivation, and emotion, to make for ease of classification and clarification of observed behavior. That there should be a direct relationship between specific brain structures and these arbitrary constructs seems unlikely. However, we might expect to find the logic for these processes embedded in the organizational structure of the brain.

Luria (1966) expressed the same point of view when, in a criticism of work on localization of brain function, he observed that psychological processes are abstractions that are unlikely to be matched by specific brain systems but may be mediated by the brain in many different ways in many different locations.

In order to come to grips with the essential nature of behavior neither brain research nor behavioral research on its own is likely to provide a satisfactory solution. Rather, we need an understanding of the relationships between the two separate lines of research interpreted in the light of the evolutionary processes by which the current state of our development has been achieved.

RELATING THE EVOLUTION OF THE BRAIN AND THE EVOLUTION OF LEARNING

Harlow (1958) when looking at the evolution of learning, was impressed by the fact that animals were able to perform, in the laboratory, feats of learning and discrimination that, so far as he could see, would not have been called into play in their struggle for existence. In themselves, he said, it would appear that they conferred no relative advantage to the animals possessing these abilities. He concluded that these demonstrated capacities must be the expression of capabilities that animals had developed as a concomitant of increased resolving powers of receptors. He then went on to point out that any development of receptors would be likely to endow the organism with a selective advantage and that any such development demands the development of increasingly complex neural systems within the central nervous system, even in the receptor system itself. "Thus," said Harlow, "as long as increasingly complex receptor systems provide the organism with slight survival advantages, one can be assured that increasingly complex nervous systems will develop" (p. 275).

Lorenz (1969) made the point that the major difference between living organisms and inorganic systems lies in the ability of the former to gain energy, to exploit highly specific sources of energy, and that any relevant information that an animal acquired concerning its environment improves its chances of increasing this energy supply. He argued that,

It is the economic advantages of having more knowledge about environment that, since the very beginning of life, have exerted the selection pressure responsible for the progressively higher evolution of all knowledge-acquiring structures and functions. The general trend to more complex, "higher" organization, discernible in most evolutionary processes, is explicable on this principle . . . .
In fact, the levels of what, in living creatures we call "lower" and "higher" or-

ganization cannot be better or more objectively defined than by the amount of relevant, teleonomically organized information they possess — and this applies as well to information contained in the genome as to that which an individual or, for that matter, a human culture has acquired in its life span (p. 15).

Lorenz defined his use of the word "teleonomy" as a "shorthand for the Darwinian question 'which is the function whose survival value exerted the selection pressure *causing* the species to evolve the characteristics which our question concerns?' " (Lorenz, 1969, p. 13).

Lending support to Harlow's position is the well-established observation that many lines of descent show successive increase in body size, accompanied by a proportional increase in brain size. Rensch (1956) has noted a special progressive evolution of the brain by which relative brain size is sometimes also increased. This process, Rensch observed, is most evident in the highest centers in the species concerned, which show not only an increase in the quantity of neurons but also improved neuronal properties with much richer interconnections. He claimed, as did Harlow, that this increase in interconnections could confer a selective advantage.

How might this increased neural tissue lead to increased adaptability to a changing environment? For adaptive behavior to be effected, cognitive acts must occur. The basis of all cognition is the capacity for the development, within the nervous system, of representations of relevant external elements and of relationships between external elements and events within the organism. These representations enable the organism to act in the light of experience. The cornerstone of cognition is the learning process, which enables new elements and relationships to be incorporated into representational patterns already stored in the nervous system.

What then is the nature of this learning process and what is its evolutionary history?

Lockard has claimed that "learning is not the key to animal behavior because most behavior is not acquired" (Lockard, 1971, p. 174). In a restricted sense Lockard may be right, but not in the sense that I am emphasizing. If learning is viewed in its biological context as the process or rather the multiplicity of processes by which representations of the environment are formed and reformed within the nervous system, then this must be a characteristic of all living organisms. For the animal to be able to utilize any information from its environment it must hold patterns or representations of essential components of that environment with which to compare the current input.

Lashley in 1949 pointed out that, "A sharp distinction has often been made between instinct and intelligence, with the implication that these represent divergent lines of evolutionary development." He went on to say: "Analysis of behavior included under the two categories does not, I believe, justify the distinction. The differences are in degree only, not in kind" (p. 458). More recently Thorpe discussed the evolution of cognitive mechanisms while examining the relationships between learning and instinct. If, said Thorpe, we agree that "the very act of recognition involves something of the nature of insight which is essentially perception of relations (for the external stimuli to which higher metazoan sense organs react are all in some degree patterned), it seems to follow that the distinction between inborn and acquired responses has now become one of degree rather than kind" (Thorpe, 1956, p. 130), i.e., in degree of rigidity and plasticity in perception and response.

He then went on to say, and this links closely with Harlow's concern about the possible evolutionary significance of the very limited learning capacities of the more primitive phyla, that

> individual learning alone, coupled with such inborn faculties as depth perception and constancy relations will not, for an animal of very limited brain size, be a very efficient means of ordering life in the complex world in which it must survive. Accordingly, the more responses to oft recurring stimuli and situations can be stereotyped, the more the limited neural equipment for plasticity can be reserved for situations where it is indispensable" (p. 132).

For animals with limited neural tissue available to them, the development of inherited or instinctive response patterns to a set of releaser stimuli, with or without modifications through learning or experience, would thus be the most economical way by which the organism could adjust to common features of the environment. These patterns would be built into the nervous system through genetic mechanisms (e.g., Thorpe, 1956). Thus the representation or model would be recoded in successive generations to fit the changing environment.

Views on the nature of these inbuilt actions vary. Lorenz (1969) saw them as a form of action specific potentials whereas Lashley viewed the representation more as a perceptual pattern or organization, regarding instinctive behavior as plastic and adaptive (Lashley, 1949). Miller, Galanter, and Pribram (1960) developed a notion of the inbuilt plan and image which appears to be not far distant from Lashley's concept. Be that as it may, it is evident that, as the environment changed, providing the changes were slow enough, natural selection could result in changes in the response patterns.

This "learning" through genetic variation only occurs at one point in time with new "learning" taking place with each new generation and being determined by the characteristics of those members of the earlier generation that are able to reproduce. In the face of even moderate selection pressure there would likely be a very considerable loss of members of the species, i.e., those who were not equipped to cope with the change. With short lived species that breed rapidly this method of coping with change is quite evidently very efficient. Even severe selective pressure from a fairly rapidly changing environment might not wipe out the species before its better equipped genetic variants were selected out to meet the changed situation. The continued survival and proliferation of the arthropods and, in particular, the insects is a prime example of this.

For larger animals with a longer life cycle and consequently a longer time before reproduction, the species would be more likely to disappear in a rapidly changing environment as evidenced by the extinction of the amphibia, the reptiles, and the archaic mammals. Here then some mechanism that would enable the organism to develop and modify its neural representations of the environment during its own lifetime through processes of learning and memory would have strong survival value. The mutational changes resulting in the development of the plastic neural networks found within the nervous systems of the more advanced species would appear to have provided this system.

Thus the development of larger and more complex brains would seem to be characterized by increasing number, size, and complexity of interdependent neural networks. Ursin (1984) has argued that the brain may in fact be regarded as a complex system of such self-regulating networks.

Marcus Jacobsen (1970) has described specificity and diversity in neurons in the following terms:

> Some neurons may become different as a result of genetic control of their development, whereas others may diversify because they are released from genetic constraints. In other words, differentiation of the first class of neurons is deterministic; in the second class, it is probabilistic. Transitional and intermediate classes are also supposed to develop.

> Neurons of Class II remain unspecified until late in ontogeny. It is postulated that these neurons are produced in excess and in great diversity. From this diverse population, only those neurons, or their connections, that are functionally most fitted to survive to maturity do so. Many types of interneurons are supposed to belong to Class II or have transitional characteristics. Their con-
> types of large neurons with long axons and invariant connectivity are believed to exhibit similar characteristics.

> Neurons of Class II remain unspecified until late in ontogeny. It is postulated that these neurons are produced in excess and in great diversity. From this diverse population, only those neurons, or their connections, that are functionally most fitted to survive to maturity do so. Many types of interneurons are supposed to belong to Class II or have transitional characteristics. Their connections may be modified or may be maintained by function and experience of an appropriate type. One of the requirements for functional validation of connections of Class II neurons may be coincidence of patterns of impulses in convergent afferents. Evidence of this kind of requirement has been found in binocular connections in the visual cortex of newborn kittens. The cutaneous afferent neurons of the frog tadpole have characteristics intermediate between those of Class I and those of Class II, but after metamorphosis they clearly develop into neurons of Class I (p. 127).

For the development of modifiable representations through the processes of learning and memory it appears that a particular neural arrangement is required. This system is rich in Class II neurons, which form a densely packed and richly interconnected network of cells and fibers, a complex of interconnecting circuits that would provide for a maximum distribution of information within that system. This type of neural structure seems to have evolved independently along at least three widely divergent evolutionary lines, namely molluscs, arthropods, and vertebrates. It may be observed, for example, in the lobus verticales of the supra oesophageal ganglion of the cephalopod molluscs and in the corpora pedunculata or mushroom bodies of insects as well in the reticular system, limbic formation, and cerebral cortex of vertebrates.

The development of a larger and more complex brain with increasing size and complexity of neural nets available for learning would, however, scarcely provide an adequate mechanism for survival on its own. At least three further requirements would need to be met: (1) time in which to develop the representations; (2) a drive to acquire the information of which the representations are composed; and (3) a mechanism to allow discrimination between relevant and irrelevant experience.

The organism, if it does not have the inbuilt patterns of behavior necessary for survival, must have time in which to develop its own representations. A protracted growth period is therefore necessary during which the young animal is protected from its environment and is actively engaged in learning about that environment. In conjunction with this there must be an active seeking out of relevant information. Evidence that such a process exists comes from a number of sources. Russian work on the orienting reflex points to a general controlling role and function of this reflex that is not unlike cognition (Razran, 1961, p. 114). The significance of manipulative and visual exploratory rewards as a motivating force has been demonstrated in a variety of species, including rats and monkeys (Butler, 1953, 1965; Harlow, Harlow, & Meyer, 1950; Harlow & McClearn, 1954).

Diamond, Balvin, and Diamond (1963) saw the capacity for exploration as a "bright new band in the spectrum of choice and one that may well have been a more important step in the evolution of adaptive behavior than the appearance of learning" (p. 140). Glickman and Schiff (1967) also noted a broad relationship between brain organization and curiosity in different species.

Koestler, too, emphasized the significance of exploratory activity in the evolution of animals. In doing so he drew attention to Coghill's findings, and observed that:

> Coghill has shown that the moment it [the embryo] is hatched or born the creature lashes out at the environment, be it liquid or solid, with cilia, flagellae or contractile muscle fiber; it crawls, swims, glides, pulsates; it kicks, yells, breathes, feeds on its surroundings for all it is worth. It does not merely adapt to

the environment, but constantly adapts the environment to itself—it eats and drinks its environment, fights and mates with it, burrows and builds in it, it does not merely respond to the environment but asks questions by exploring it. The exploratory drive is now recognized by the younger generation of animal psychologists to be a primary biological instinct, as basic as the instincts of hunger and sex; it can on occasions be even more powerful than these. Countless experimenters, starting with Darwin himself, have shown that curiosity and the seeking of thrills is an instinctual urge in rats, birds, dolphins, chimpanzees and man, and so is what Behaviorists call "ludic behavior," known to ordinary mortals as playfulness (p. 153).

Thorpe developed the idea that all perception may be seen as a comparison of relations and that an animal might well be regarded as primarily something which perceives, something endowed with the "will to perceive." He then developed Thacker's (1950) notion that "motivation for learning is central and neural. An organized and proliferated cognitive structure is itself a goal towards which learning moves" (Thorpe, 1956, p. 132). This concept links closely with Pribram's picture of the "search by an information hungry organism" (Pribram, 1960, p. 18). Thus again we are confronted with the evolutionary implications of the active behaving organism, with those behaviors that support survival directing the selective processes that design and modify the underlying neural mechanisms.

This leads us to the third essential element for the laying down of these representations during the lifetime of the animal, i.e., a mechanism that will enable it to differentiate between relevant and irrelevant events and relationships and to incorporate these findings into its system of representations. In primitive systems this is done genetically, i.e., where the neural mechanisms generate relevant reactions to critical stimuli the organism survives and multiplies, but when the response is inappropriate it is likely to perish and thus fail to, or cease to, reproduce this inadequate mechanism.

If response patterns are to be generated and modified on the basis of representations within the nervous system that are built up and changed during the lifetime of the animal, the relevance of its response must be signaled in a manner more appropriate to such a system. That is, there must be some way of eliminating irrelevant relationships and of reinforcing relevant ones. The nature of this reinforcement mechanism is examined in Chapter 11.

If I have appeared to paint a dichotomy here of one set of animals that have only inbuilt patterns of behavior and another set that builds its own representations during its lifetime, this is because I have been emphasizing the two different aspects. In fact, all animals, even the simplest, have some capacity to learn, i.e., to change their responses in the light of continued interaction with the environment. All animals, even the highest, have some instinctive response patterns, however subject to modification they may be through the processes of learning. What concerns us is the shift in emphasis from one system to the other. It seems to follow that the distinction between inborn and acquired responses becomes one of degree rather than kind, i.e., in degree of rigidity and plasticity in perception and response (Thorpe, 1956).

My first objective in the following chapters is to explore the evidence relating to the evolution of the human nervous system. This I do in Part II of this volume. In this I am concerned primarily with the increase in mass and complexity of the brain. For our examination of changes in brain mass with evolutionary development, we have access to data from the geological record as well as evidence from living species. I also consider the phylogenetic development of various parts of the brain, and in particular, the organization of the forebrain. To achieve this I must rely much more heavily on the comparative data available from existing animals.

Having established the nature of the evolutionary sequence in neural development, I turn, in Part III, to evidence on behavioral evolution to see if neural and behavioral evolution can be linked in any compelling manner. Here we are constrained to depend on comparative studies across living species.

Razran did not include emotions in his study of learning because he considered emotion to be additive to but not intrinsic of learning. Thus he believed emotion modified learning, buoying or masking its stimuli, evoking or suppressing its participatory reactions, but not constituting the essence of its mechanism. He concluded, *"The basics of the learning mind would not be different, according to the view, in a hypothetical Martian wholly devoid of emotions"* (p. 326). My approach differs from Razran's in this regard. I contend that emotion evolved as an instrument for effective associative learning, that the two are inexorably bound together, that "emotion" evolved as a system that enables registration of what is relevant or not relevant to the organism and hence what will or will not be incorporated in its store of representations. In this view, then, the basics of the learning mind must be different in "the Martian wholly devoid of emotion." In fact, it is highly unlikely that such a being could evolve without the equivalent of emotion.

The failure of psychologists to come to grips with emotion stems largely from the failure to understand the biological and neural implications of the concept. In Part IV I explore the notion that emotion in fact forms the very basis of associative learning, that it has evolved as the process that enables the organism to differentiate the relevant from the irrelevant in its struggle for survival, thus enabling relevant information to be incorporated into its representations.

Finally, in Part V I review the current position in our studies of the evolution of learning, and of its mechanisms.

My first task then is to outline the evolution of the nervous system, and as a preliminary to this, I briefly describe, in Chapter 2, what the geological record can tell us about our evolutionary history, enabling us to view neural evolution within the geological perspective.

2 The Geological Record of Evolution

The following account is but a brief thumbnail sketch of findings from a massive volume of research that relates to our evolutionary history. For those wishing to explore this topic futher such works as F. H. Colbert's (1955) *Evolution of Vertebrates,* B. Rensch's (1959) *Evolution Above the Species Level,* A. S. Romer's (1966) *Vertebrate Paleontology* and G. G. Simpson's (1953) *The Major Features of Evolution,* and (1967) *The Meaning of Evolution,* give an excellent background. E. Olson's *Vertebrate Paleozoology* (1971) is well worth examination, in particular for his detailed consideration of the patterns of evolution and Pearson's (1964) *Animals and Plants of the Cenozoic Period* introduces readers to "the age of mammals." For a brief overview, but more particularly for the excellent pictorial reconstructions, Z. V. Spinar's *Life Before Man* (1972) with illustrations by Z. Burian merits attention. Lillgraven, Kielan-Jaworowska, and Clemen's (1979) volume on *Mesozoic mammals* provides a very useful summary of information on mammalian life prior to the extinction of the great reptiles. This work details the systematics and geographical distribution of fossil finds, and citations to original descriptions of all formally named taxa.

The geological record is comprised of the fossilized remains of animals and plants, preserved in the sediments deposited in oceans, lakes, and rivers over the ages and of specimens trapped in preservative substances such as the tar pits of North America or the deposits in caves in various parts of the world.

From the point in time when the weathering of the earth's surface began, these weathering products or sediments have been laid down in successive layers. One estimate of the total thickness of these sedimentary rocks from the bottom of the remote pre-Cambrian era to the top of the most recent sediments is 253,000 feet covering a possible time span in excess of 2,000,000,000 years (Dobzhansky, 1955). On the basis of studies of these various strata, geologists have divided the earth's history into four major geological eras, namely, pre-Cambrian, Palaeozoic, Mesozoic, and Cenozoic. These eras have been further divided into periods of varying duration. These studies of stratification provided the base for the geological time scale that Kulp (1961) defined as "the absolute calendar to which the progressive development of animals and plants may be related" (p. 1105).

Placing the fossilized remains accurately in this time scale posed a major problem until the discovery of radioactivity. Kulp (1961) observed that the use of isotopic chronometers with substances such as uranium 235 and rubidium 87 provided accurate dating of deposits with an error probably less than 3%. In examining the method, Pearson (1964) concluded that, given that decay rates have been constant for geological time and that, when incorporated within the closed systems of deposits, their concentration decreases with time according to their decay constants then "the concentration of a radio isotope contained in a deposit bears a direct relation to the time before the present that the material in the deposit was laid down" (p. 91). An account of dating methods is given in Buettner-Janusch's (1966) *Origins of Man*. For a more detailed technical examination of some of these dating techniques and their implications, the reader is referred to Bishop and Miller's (1972) *Calibration of Hominoid Evolution*.

A key factor in the shaping of our evolutionary history has been our changing environment, changes in flora and fauna responding dramatically to changes in temperature, climate, and land mass.

The evolution of our physical environment itself forms a fascinating study and one that is intimately tied to that of organic evolution. The cooling of the earth's crust and the development of atmosphere and hydrosphere through processes that are still continuing and still changing the distribution of the earth's elements were the precursors to the generation of life. The fact that for much of the time, for much of the earth's surface, the temperature has been in the range of 5°-95°C, i.e., within the range between which water freezes or boils and within which protoplasm could form and survive, was and is, also crucial.

The presence, for long periods of time, of warm moist climates convivial to the proliferaton of living organisms has been of prime significance. Equally significant have been those major structural and climatic changes that occurred from time to time. These have been associated with the upheaval and shifting of land masses, with the development of vast plateaux and mountain ranges and the formation of new continents. It is now believed that variability in the sun's radiation has led to increased heating or cooling of the surface of the earth and associated expansion and contraction of polar ice caps. This has resulted in successive glacial and interglacial or warm tropical periods.

There were long periods, i.e., many millions of years, when the world was in the grip of harsh dry climatic conditions or when much of it was frozen waste.

The value of attempts to estimate these changes as accurately as possible is clear. Methods include study of the evidence relating to rise and fall of oceans, linked with changes in the mass of water held in polar ice caps, evidence for glaciation, the types of sedimentary deposits, e.g., indicating dry or wet climatic conditions, and study of the nature and density of flora and fauna. For example, Pearson (1964) has shown a close congruence between three different techniques in determining the onset and termination of glacial periods throughout the Cenozoic era. The first of these made use of the fact that the ratio of two isotopic variants of oxygen $^{18}O/^{16}O$ in oceans is temperature dependent and that the carbonate skeletons of marine organisms are produced in equilibrium in sea water. Thus estimates of the changing temperature of sea water in a given region could be made by determining the $^{18}O/^{16}O$ ratios in marine fossils (e.g., Emilliani, 1961). Pearson claimed that, using this method, the temperature of the ocean at that time could be determined to within 1°C. The second method, developed by Durham (1950), used the occurrence and significance of reef building corals in Cenozoic marine deposits. He chose the 18°C February isotherm as the parameter for defining tertiary climate. This temperature was chosen because this sets the minimum sea water temperature where reef building hermatypic corals occur today. Shifts in the northern limits of coral building would thus coincide with temperature changes. The third technique was Van Der Hammen's (1957)[1] use of pollen counts in deposits in Columbia, South America.

On the basis of these data, said Pearson, it seems clear that there was a very significant temperature drop worldwide in the middle of the Cretaceous period, another at the beginning of the Cenozoic era and, finally, a series of rises and falls in the course of the repetitive glacial periods from Pliocene to recent. The evidence suggests that

> during the period in which Cenozoic fauna and flora were evolving there were climatic cycles with periods of 30 and 60 million years and probably minor cycles of 6 million and 2 million years . . . .it is highly probable that they represent extensive worldwide climatic oscillations and that these probably lie at the base of faunal replacement rhythms of geological time (p. 108).

Examination of deep sea cores including biostratigraphic studies of plankton deposits (Bandy, 1972) have provided further evidence of worldwide temperature fluctuations in the late Cenozoic. These showed major cold periods

---

[1]Hammen, T. Van Der Climatic periodicity and evolution of the South American Maestrichtiae and tertiary floras. *Bogota Bol. Geol.,* 1957, *5*, 49–91 (from Pearson, 1964).

in the upper Miocene and Pliocene and culminated in four cold or glacial and four interglacial periods in the Pleistocene.

A table of geological time based on Kulp's (1961) analysis and showing the various geological eras subdivided into periods, together with the principal flora and the dominant animal species of each period is presented in Table 2.1, which also gives an estimate of the climatic state and land dispositions of that period.

Perhaps the most outstanding characteristic of the geological record is that, from the time of the first observed fossil until now, the record has been, in a sense, a continuous one and tells a story of ever increasing complexity and diversity of organisms. However, this has not been a steady advance but has taken the form of a series of waves with each wave advancing further up the beach front of evolutionary history. Another striking feature of the paleontological story is that the inhabitants of any one period were descended, not from all the varied species of an earlier period but only from a small number of them. Furthermore, each new class of animal would seem to have evolved, not from the most successful and specialized representatives of the earlier groups, but from species that had to struggle hardest to survive. These ancestors almost inevitably proved to be seemingly insignificant and unspecialized representatives of that earlier period.

In the evolution of the land-dwelling vertebrates, for example, the first move to land appears to have taken place in the swamps and marshes of the Devonian period. The fossil evidence points to the first amphibians originating from a small freshwater fish with a primitive or lobed fin structure that enabled it to move through the mud banks that lined the shores, and with a swim bladder that had become modified for airbreathing. These modifications would have high survival value in oxygen deficient inland lakes. Two separate groups of fish are considered as likely ancestors of the amphibia. The group considered by most authorities as the more likely was the crossopterygian or lobe finned fish of which the coelacanth Latimeria is a living representative, literally a living fossil. The other group, the Dipnoi or Lungfish also has living representations in Neoceratodus, Protopterus, and Lepidosiren, the Lung Fish and the Mud Skippers. It has even been proposed that there is a dual origin of amphibia, one branch originating from the Dipnoi and the rest from the crossopterygian ancestor.

While one of the major features of evolutionary history has been ever increasing species diversification with the passage of time, it is also true that almost all living creatures have left no descendants at all — they finished in blind alleys of specialization. "The most probable fate of any group of plants or animals in the course of time is extinction" (Dobzhansky, 1955, p. 289).

The processes of evolution had almost certainly been in progress for vast periods of time before the beginning of the Palaeozoic era, but there is little record available of life until the beginnings of the Cambrian when the fossilized remains of living organisms with a hard body covering were first observed.

It was during the pre-Cambrian period that protoplasm first evolved and gave rise to living cells. Another major step forward, the evolution of cells containing chlorophyll and capable of utilizing sunlight to synthesize further proteins, the blue green algae, or most primitive of plants, also occurred during this period. With the evolution of plants the release of free oxygen to the air was accelerated and the food supply for animals was established.

Some of the oldest fossils were bacteria-like organisms found in South Africa with an estimated age of about 3,200,000,000 years. Some micro fossils or spheroids, four microns in diameter were recently discovered by J. Dunlop in a Barite deposit near Marble Bar in Western Australia and have been estimated to be some 3.5 thousand million years old. Further examples of life were found dating back between 1000 and 2700 million years. The existence of larger organisms was also deduced from evidence of the burrowing marks of worms (Spinar, 1972). There are a number of factors contributing to the sparseness of the evidence from this era. Firstly, the absence of skeletal structures that would be subject to fossilization dramatically reduced the probability that specimens would be preserved; secondly, the tremendous pressures to which these lowest layers would be subject would lead to obliteration of many of the deposits that were established and, lastly, the domain to be sampled is so large and samples so sparse and so minute in size that the probability of finding one becomes remote.

Until Devonian times all fossils appear to have been generated by water dwelling animals, most of them from the sea. Indeed there is a convincing body of evidence that life began in the sea and was the primary abode for all but about the last 10% of the fossil record (Olson, 1971).

During the pre-Cambrian period the foundations for evolutionary development of life were laid down. The basic unit, the cell, was accomplished. Single celled protozoa were proliferating and had developed into multicelled organisms with bodies of increasing complexity. The two-layered colenterates, or jellyfish, and the earliest of the more complex three-layered organisms, the annelids, the segmented or true worms, were probably already in evidence.

The Palaeozoic era, the primary era or era of ancient life, started, in Spinar's words, with tremendous oceanic floods that followed the lifting up of continents at the end of the pre-Cambrian. Animals were now developing a protective skeleton, which led to a rapid increase in the fossil record. This may well have related to increasing concentration of oxygen in the sea and the atmosphere above and to the development of the ozone layer that absorbed harmful ultraviolet radiation. The increased oxygen supply may, in itself, have triggered the much more vigorous proliferation of life in this period. The earliest period, the Cambrian, saw the evolution of the invertebrates

TABLE 2.1
The Geological Time Scale

Era	Period	Duration 000,000 yrs	Climate and Vegetation	Vertebrate Sequence
CENOZOIC	Recent	0.25	Warmer with	x--Hominids
	Pleistocene	1.0	periods of continental glaciation	x--Anthropoids
	Pliocene	12	Cold and barren	x--Primates
	Miocene	12	Warm tropical / Cool	x--Mammals
	Oligocene	10	Warm tropical / Cool	Age of Mammals
	Eocene	22	Warm tropical	
	Palaeocene	5		
	Total	62		
MESOZOIC	Cretaceous	72	Cold with glaciation extensive. Gymnosperms dominant	Extinction of most Reptiles
	Jurassic	45	Wetter and warmer. Luxuriant forests of gymnosperms and ferns	Age of Reptiles
	Triasic	50	Very dry – vegetation sparse and only around lakes	
	Total	167		

Era	Period	Duration	Environment	
PALEOZOIC	Permian	50	Violent change. Deserts replace forests. Parched and dry.	Extinction of most Amphibia
	Carboniferous	65	Surface folding. Luxuriant swamp forests of ferns and mosses. Extensive lakes.	Age of Amphibia
	Devonian	60	Wet and warm. Herbaceous marsh plants.	The Age of Fishes
	Silurian	20	Aquatic marine algae and marsh plants.	
	Ordovician	75		
	Cambrian	80		
	Total	350		
PRE-CAMBRIAN				

Organism ranges:
```
--------------------------------------------Reptiles---------- x------
-------------------------------------------Amphibia------------ x----
----------------------------------------Jawed Fishes-------- x---
--------------------------------------------Agnatha------------ x---
----------------------------------------Invertebrates---------------- x---
```

Information from:
Kulp, J. L. (1961) *Science, 133*, pp. 1105–1114.
Olsen. (1971) *Vertebrate paleozoology.*.
Spinar, Z. V. (1972) *Life before man.*

with the arthropods the most advanced animal of the period (Spinar, 1972). A pictorial representation of such life, one of Burian's illustrations from Spinar, is shown in Figure 2.1.

The earliest of the vertebrates became evident in the Ordovician period as Agnatha or jawless fish. There was then a great gap between these Ordovician fragments and the rich records of the upper Silurian. In this period both

FIG. 2.1.   A pictorial representation of Cambrian life forms. Seabed dwellers depicted here include three species of trilobite – *Paradoxides gracilis* (foreground), *Conocoryphe sulzeri* (middle larger specimen) and *Ptychoparia striata* (left two specimens). Sea lillies or crinoids, which channeled food along their waving arms to their mouths are anchored to the bottom by their long stalks (right). A group of brachiopods, marine animals that have two valves, occupy the foreground, right.

A Burian illustration from Spinar, Z.V. *Life before man,* 1972, p. 58.

the Agnatha and the first of the jawed fish were evident with representatives living both in the oceans and in fresh to brackish waters. Olson (1971) pointed out that even at this early stage in the vertebrate record some temporal sequencing was possible, and identified one such sequence in Europe, which, "passing from essentially marine to nonmarine deposits has been traced in a single section along with accompanying changes in the contained vertebrate faunas" (p. 31). However, the total Silurian record is far from complete and fails to anticipate the tremendous expansion evident in the Devonian period, the "Age of Fishes." This record, while still far from complete, allowed the first detailed study of adaptive radiation throughout the oceans, lakes, and rivers of the world. It also marked the beginnings of the land dwelling vertebrates.

The emergence of the amphibia from sea to land during the Devonian period was discussed briefly earlier. This period was characterized by increasing density and richness of vegetation, providing food sources on the land. At about this time, too, insects were occupying the terrestrial habitat. Thus as the Crossopterygian ancestors became more capable of moving on land, fins were evolved into limbs and radiation into the land habitat began. The picture in Figure 2.2 depicts an emergent amphibian Ichthystega.

Amphibia were still tied to the water in many ways, but the firmest tie was the reproductive one; eggs were laid in water and fertilized there. The larval stage also was water dwelling. The next major class, the reptiles, were liberated from this bondage through the evolution of internal fertilization and the development of the young through the larval stage to the fully formed animal while protected in its own special environment, namely the amniotic egg. The first reptilian remains were located in deposits of the upper Carboniferous period, the Pennsylvanian division. The Carboniferous period was characterized by very rich vegetation with the "trees" of this period consisting mainly of huge club mosses and ferns, pterigosperms or ferns bearing seeds, giant cordaites, tall gymnosperms with leaves a yard long, and primitive conifers. In and around the lakes and rivers created by the giant folded mountain ranges masses of vegetable matter accumulated and were transformed into the vast coal beds that characterize the deposits of this period. These coal beds have yielded a wealth of fossil material. A fine representaton of the likely appearance of the vegetation at this time is given in Spinar (1972, pp. 71–74). Many amphibian forms evolved during the Carboniferous period, the peak of their adaptive radiation taking place in the Pennsylvanian subdivision. Towards the end of this period great climatic changes were evident with droughts lasting for long periods of time and with massive uplifts of continental areas. This was associated with rapid extinction of all but a few of the amphibia during the Permian period and the commencement of the age of reptiles, with successive waves of increasingly large and complex reptilian forms. Towards the end of the Permian the therapsid reptiles, precursors of the mammals, were evident.

FIG. 2.2. A representation of the amphibian *Ichthyostega*. Bones of various stego-
cephalians, the first dry land quadrupeds, have been found in upper Devonian strata in
the eastern part of Greenland. The picture shows *Ichthyostega,* an amphibian that grew
to a length of about three feet and had a fish-like body and well-developed limbs. The
flora of that time were very varied and included the tall-trunked club moss (*Cyclostigma*),
Pseudobornia (the horsetails in front of the nearer amphibian), *Sphaeno phyllum* (the
creeper on the stump) and *Archaeopteris* (the ferns near the water).

   An illustration by Z. Burian from Spinar, Z. W. *Life before man,* 1972, p. 70.

The next major era, the Mesozoic, saw the dominance of reptiles and the first evidence of mammals and birds. The early Triassic period was characterized by a harsh dry climate with limited vegetation.

This was followed, in the upper Triassic, by a change in climate leading to luxuriant forests and an amenable climate with connected land masses which facilitated widespread distribution of reptiles throughout what is now America, Europe, Asia, and Africa. Stegocephalian amphibia were still extant and the predecessors of present day frogs became evident. The climate became wetter and warmer and luxuriant vegetation continued into the Jurassic and thence into the early Cretaceous. This period, through the Jurassic and into the Cretaceous saw the heyday of the largest of all reptiles, the dinosaurs, with animals such as Brontosaurus, up to 90 feet in length and estimated at over 50 tons in weight. The giant carnivorous dinosaurs, of which the most well known is Tyrannosaurus rex, up to 40 feet long and standing 17 feet high, evolved during the later stages of this period. A reconstruction of these and other reptiles may be seen in Spinar (1972, pp. 128-140).

The giant aquatic reptiles, the Plesiosaurs, together with the crocodiles and the winged reptiles, also became evident.

During the later Cretaceous period, there occurred dramatic geographical and climatic changes. According to Spinar a tremendous buckling of the earth's crust in a mountain forming process together with, it is believed, continental movement, restructured the geography of the world. At about this time, too, there is evidence of an ice age. Most of the old Mesozoic world inhabitants on land and in the sea died. The era of dinosaurs came to an end as the great reptiles who had dominated the land for more than 100 million years failed to survive the changes from Mesozoic to Cenozoic times. Others to disappear at this time were the marine reptiles, ichthyosaurs, plesiosaurs, and monosaurs. The pterosaurs also became extinct. The only reptilian survivors were turtles, crocodiles, lizards, and snakes (Dobzhansky, 1955). Also to vanish were the giant ammonites. As well there was a dramatic change in the microfauna or surface plankton of the oceans. "The end of the Cretaceous witnessed the ousting of existing foraminiferans and chalk-forming plankton, while at the base of the Tertiary blossomed foraminiferans of a totally different type" (Desmond, 1975, p. 216). The change was from warm water to much cooler water plankton types. This worldwide destruction appears to have coincided with a dramatic reduction in temperature, but what could have led to this cataclysmic change in environment? Many theories have been proposed including the explosion of a supernova in proximity to the earth. Discussion of some of these theories may be found in Desmond's (1975) The Hotblooded Dinosaurs, in various papers by Russell including his review in the Annual Review of Earth Planet Sciences (1979), and in papers in Science by Gartner and McGuirk (1979) and Alvarez, Alvarez, Asaro, and Michel (1980), and most recently by Pollack, Toon, Ackerman, McKay, and Turco (1983).

The final period, the Cenozoic, or recent life era, has lasted some 65–70 million years and is divided into two geological sub-eras, the Tertiary of some 65 million years, and the Quarternary of some 2 million years. Spinar, summarizing the geological events of the time, noted that this era began, as had most others, with marked movements of the earth's crust. The sea invaded Europe as far as the Russian plateau and engulfed the outlying parts of both the Americas and large parts of Africa. The end of the Oligocene was marked by new continental rifts which again altered the coastline. During the Miocene, new mountain ranges and chains were formed, with the Alps, the Pyranees, the Carpathians, and the Himalayas acquiring their present forms. The end of the Tertiary was characterized chiefly by a rapid worsening of the climate, a drop in temperature and the gradual formation of an ice sheet. During the final stage, the Quarternary, there was a rapid succession of ice ages and warmer interglacials.

Mammals that had first appeared as tiny mouse-like animals at the end of the Triassic had evolved from the mammal-like reptiles of the late Permian period. A reconstruction of one such early mammal, Triconodon, is shown in Figure 2.3.

Olson, (1971) in examining the geological record for the evolution of mammals observed,

> as for each of the earlier major radiations for which we have records, that of the mammals reaches deep into the earlier radiations for its beginnings. The first records of mammals, or very mammal-like creatures, is from the latest Triassic. The roots are clearly within the therapsid reptiles, and the transition is such that definitions of class relationships are blurred. Representatives of these first mammals are found at approximately the same time in the British Isles, East Africa, Central Europe and China. Somewhat similar remains have been found in the southeastern United States. This remarkable distribution for small animals whose skulls are little more than a centimeter in length is an expression of the excellence of the upper Triassic [record] (p. 48).

The descendants of these early mammals, the marsupials and the insectivores, became evident late in the Cretaceous period and continued to evolve in the Cenozoic era. From the early insectivores there was an explosive evolution of placental mammals throughout the Cenozoic period. These successive waves of mammalian radiation throughout this period may be correlated with the dramatic climatic changes already referred to. Another factor of probably major significance has been referred to by Pearson (1964) in the following terms:

> However, the predominant feature of this mammalian evolution, and more especially the succession of comparable and related genera, is the interaction of predator and prey . . . the evolution of the anatomy and nervous system of carnivores is intimately related to that of the herbivores upon which they prey. This situation will result in a more or less constant change in the characters of both (pp. 197–198).

FIG. 2.3.   A reconstruction of the early mammal *Triconodon*. This was a primitive mammal known only from its fossil teeth and jaws, that evolved from advanced "mammalian" reptiles at the end of the Triassic. Up to two feet in length, it was probably a carnivore and lived on small reptiles like *Sapheosaurus,* the prey shown here. A warm-blooded animal, it had a hair coat that must have helped to protect it from extremes of hot and cold. Although *Triconodon* may have laid eggs like its reptilian ancestors did, it probably suckled its young.

Drawn by Z. Burian, in Spinar, Z. V. *Life before man,* 1972, p. 124.

The primitive insectivores, surviving from the Cretaceous, have persisted through to modern times and their remains are strikingly similar to those of the earliest primates, pointing to a common origin. The primate line from this common origin may be followed from the fossil remains right through to the great apes. Towards the end of the Oligocene a branch separated off from the old world monkeys and evolved into the anthropoid apes and man. The path of evolution of man from the Oligocene to the present, while evident to the beginning of the Pliocene with either Proconsul or Dryopithecus as likely candidates, then presents a great gap over a 10 million year period before being picked up again in the Pleistocene with the Australopithecines.

The more conventional view of this period is that man was shaped from the more primitive man-like apes of the Pleistocene in the crucible of the Pleistocene deserts of Africa. An alternative view, proposed by Sir Alister Hardy and elaborated by Elaine Morgan (1973), suggests that the period was spent on the shores of Africa with man becoming semi-aquatic.

The path from Australopithecus to *Homo habilis, Homo erectus* to *Homo sapiens,* while still by no means confirmed, forms at least a relatively continuous line with the final ice age, and its aftermath, seeing the rise of *Homo sapiens.*

In discussing the vertebrate record, Olsen (1971) drew attention to the nature of the sampling of that record on which we have to depend. It is, of course, unlikely that samples of all species were ever preserved and it is even less likely that, even if preserved, they can now be located. The sample is, of course, being improved all the time and the record updated. In this regard Olsen observes that:

> One can hardly doubt that vertebrate evolution followed a course from shallow aquatic environments to the open waters of the seas to the lakes and streams of continents, over the strandline onto the land, to the uplands of the continents, into the air, and, many times, back to the water once more. Many of these steps were taken over and over again by different groups with the different levels of organization at different times. This is the clear picture that has emerged from paleontological studies.

> Yet many facets of this story are not supported by positive first order proof from the fossil record. Strong but secondary support, which brings many details into a common fold, rests on the fact that the major steps in the occupation of environments by successive radiations can be accounted for by the evolutionary sequences outlined in the last paragraph (p. 26).

Against this background then, let us return to consider, in more detail, the evolution of the nervous system.

II

THE EVOLUTION OF THE NERVOUS SYSTEM

The focus of the next five chapters is on the evolution of the human brain. Divergent paths are therefore considered only in terms of the light they may shed on the course of this evolutionary "mainstream" leading to man. As a corollary of this aim, I seek to establish the most likely animals, among living species, to represent the neural organization of now extinct "stem" animals along that evolutionary pathway.

I begin, in chapter 3, with a general overview of the origins and evolution of the nervous system leading to the emergence of the vertebrate brain. In Chapters 4 to 7, I examine in some detail the evolution of the vertebrate nervous system, culminating in the brain of man.

A primary endeavor in this book is to trace the evolution of learning leading up to man. This is a frankly anthropocentric approach, the basis for which was outlined many years ago by Hobhouse (1926). In his *"Mind in Evolution,"* he drew attention to the many branching pathways that were followed in the evolution of species with many different directions and specializations. Such directions were, he said, not necessarily, nor even mainly, "upwards." Evolution is not linear but rather like a tree. Once a species has branched then it sets out on a separate pathway with whatever leads to increased survival of that species being enhanced. Furthermore, he pointed out, "there is nothing in the physical condition of Evolution to imply the necessity for perpetual change" (p. 4), the tendency being not to produce the "highest type" but rather to produce as many types as will fill the various niches available.

Is there then any "upward" line in the evolutionary tree, asked Hobhouse, and if so, what do we mean by higher and lower? He answered this by saying "Evolution 'upwards' — Orthogenic or, as it has been called Aristogenic Evolution — is the growth of Mind or of the conditions which make Mind possible. Evolution in any other direction is the growth of any qualities whatever that assist survival" (Hobhouse, 1926, p. 5).

It is in essence then orthogenic evolution, the growth of mind, or more essentially the evolution of the brain that supports the growth of mind, that concerns us here. Another name for this particular view is anagenesis, i.e., the study of biological improvement, with the brain being the particular structure in which improvement is explored. Such an anthropocentric approach will, if clearly recognized as such, enhance rather than invalidate our approach because we set out with a particular perspective. With this clearly stated we are less likely to be lost in futile argument about what is progress in evolution in the broader sense. Both Hodos and Campbell (1969) and Lockard (1971) raise this issue in relation to comparative studies of behavior and rightly so, I believe, in the sense that the direction and objectives of many comparative studies are not spelt out clearly. Theirs becomes an even more valid criticism where comparative studies, so called, are undertaken without any consideration of the evolutionary history of the species under consideration.

Two approaches are available to us in the study of evolution of the vertebrate nervous system, namely, a consideration of living species — a strictly comparative approach — and a study of the fossil record. The major problem with the former method is that we are considering the few living representatives that have survived the test of time and each is an end product of the evolutionary process with continuing change from the stem stock from which it originated. The second approach, an examination of the fossilized endocasts of various vertebrate brains, provides us with information on size and outline of the brain. The information, however, varies considerably in quality from specimen to specimen and provides no detailing of internal organization. It does provide us with a record that, although sparse and far from complete, is different from that obtained from comparative studies and thus supplements, or rather, complements it. For these latter studies we are indebted to two people in particular, Jerison and Radinsky, and their work is subject to close scrutiny in subsequent chapters.

3 Origins of the Vertebrate Brain

THE INVERTEBRATE NERVOUS SYSTEM

In the single celled protozoan there is no nervous system. Amoeba, for example, exhibit the property of irritability, with stimulation at one point resulting in change at that point followed by a slow spread of irritation to neighboring areas. Even so, the behavior of amoeba is far from being random. Amoeba will engulf and digest a food particle but will withdraw from a noxious stimulus.

The evolution of specialized structures, even within the single cell, is evident as in the ciliate protozoan, paramecium (see Figure 3.1).

The major direction of evolution was, however, towards multicellular organisms with specialization of groups of cells within such organisms.

One such specialization was related to this need to transmit information about the outside environment throughout the system and to enable coordinated responses to these stimuli, a need met by the evolution of nerve cells. With cells organized in more than one layer and structured as a sphere or a tube, the inner cells are isolated from the environment. Outer cells could transmit information by extension of their membranes through the inner cell layers. Calvin (1967) pointed out that what was needed then was the evolution of a device for transmitting, without decrement, any chemically or physically sensed environmental changes and of repeating stations to rebuild the signal. The electrically active membrane is used by living cells in just this fashion.

Early evolution saw the arrival of such primitive multicellular animals as the coelenterates. These generally small, water-dwelling organisms consist

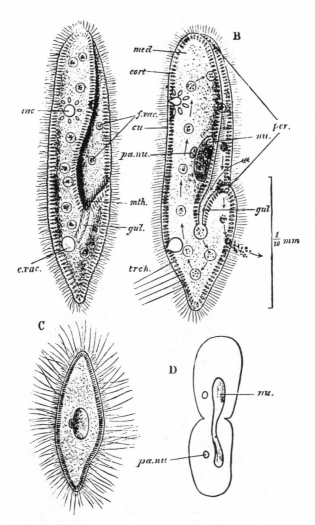

—**Paramecium caudatum.** *A*, the living animal from the ventral aspect ; *B*, the same in optical section : the arrow shows the course taken by food-particles ; *C*, a specimen which has discharged its trichocysts ; *D* diagram of binary fission ; *cort.* cortex ; *cu.* cuticle ; *c. vac.* contractile vacuole ; *f. vac.* food vacuole ; *gul.* gullet ; *med.* medulla ; *nu.* macronucleus ; *pa. nu.* micronucleus ; *per.* peristome ; *trch.* trichocysts. (From Parker's *Biology*.)

FIG. 3.1.   The ciliate protozoan *Paramecium caudatum* showing specialized organelles (from Parker, J. J. & Haswell, W. A. *A Textbook of Zoology.* London: Macmillan & Co., 1949, p. 88).

40

basically of two cell layers, an outer ectoderm and inner endoderm. The small sessile hydra, the sea anemones, and the many free swimming jellyfish are typical living examples of this class.

Certain of the outer cells move inward during development to form a loose, interconnecting network of nerve cells, each with one or several fibers. This ectodermal origin of nerve cells can be observed throughout all species from coelenterates to man (Bullock & Horridge, 1965).

In coelenterates the concentration of these nerve cells varies according to the needs of the particular region, e.g., there is a heavy concentration around the mouth area. Nerve cells in this network receive stimuli from specialized receptor cells and transmit these stimuli to specialized contractile cells. Nerve cells in the coelenterate network are separate units, thus the discontinuity of neural units is clearly established at this stage. While this arrangement resembles the synaptic system of higher vertebrates, the characteristic one-way transmission through synapses is not yet evident and responses are graded ones, i.e., incrementing in stepwise fashion as a result of intensity and frequency of stimuli (Bullock & Horridge, 1965). Habituation of responsiveness to repeated non-noxious stimuli may be observed in these simple organisms, e.g., decline in responsiveness in the sea anemones to repeated electrical stimulation.

As Hodgson (1977) has pointed out, it is likely that the most significant experiments on brain organization took place in the evolution of these early phyla, millions of years before the appearance of the first vertebrates. It has been argued that the earliest evolution of brains may have arisen as concentrations of neurons around the statocyst or balance organ in the coelenterates and flatworms, or platyhelminthes. By the time the annelid worms had evolved, the brain had become firmly established in the head region with two ventral nerve cords and a ganglion in each segment. There are many living examples of this class, e.g., the sea worm, Nereis and the land-dwelling annelid, the earthworm, Lumbricus.

With increasing complexity of cell organization in organisms moving freely in a liquid environment, a lengthening of the body together with bilateral organization provided for more rapid movement. This was accomplished by a structural repetition of identical segments. Each segment contained its own neural ganglion and nerve fiber structure with segments connected by a set of longitudinal fibers. With movement along a longitudinal axis the concentration of sense organs at the forward end became evident. With this, the process of cephalization, the forming of a head, became a dominant feature with increased neural capacity to serve the sense organs located there. This increase would appear to have been brought about initially by the coalescence of two or more segments.

Thus, in the annelids, the process of cephalization is well under way with major receptors, e.g., rudimentary eye spots sensitive to light, tentacles, sensitive to touch, and chemoreceptors all in the anterior segment. The head ganglia, the supra and suboesophageal ganglia, have resulted from the fusion of the three anterior segments. The organization of a typical annelid nervous system is shown in Figure 3.2.

In the annelids synaptic transmission is well established and, in some species, there is differentiation in control of function within the organism. Gan-

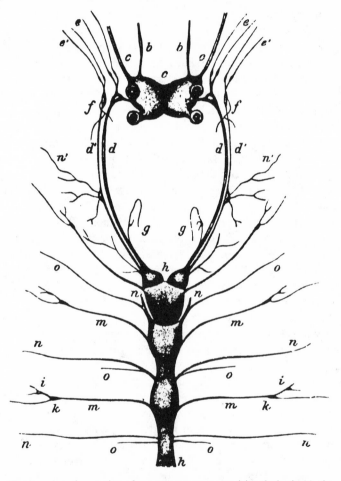

Nereis. – Anterior portion of nervous system, comprising the brain (*c*), the oesophageal connectives (*d*), and the anterior part of the ventral nerve-cord (*h*). (After Quatrefages.)

FIG. 3.2.   A typical annelid brain from *Nereis dumerilii* showing the segmental division of the nervous system and cephalization with fusion of 3 anterior segments to form the head ganglion. (From Parker and Haswell, 1949, p. 315).

glia serve not only as relay and coordination centers but also initiate action, e.g., complicated adaptive movements may be carried out that involve timed relationships and inhibitory processes.

In the invertebrates nerve fibers are unmyelinated and transmission is relatively slow. Where rapid transmission is required very thick fibers, up to 1 mm in diameter, are found and there are very few synapses to delay transmission. Such giant fibers are found in the lobster to activate the quick and violent tail flip for escape and in the squid, to activate the mantle, again for escape.

Razran (1971) has drawn attention to the almost incredible improvement in the efficiency of the neural transmission system that has taken place during evolution. To attain a transmission velocity of 25 meters per sec the giant fibers in the squid are 650 micrometers in diameter. In the frog a fiber diameter of 1.0 micrometer will achieve this transmission speed and in the cat fibers of 0.35 micrometer: as Razran observed, a truly fantastic economization in biological material for equal work.

So far we have traced the development of the nervous system from a diffuse nerve net to a complex set of ganglia and nerve fibers. In the invertebrates the process of cephalization, the development of the head ganglion then becomes the most striking feature of further development. This ganglion assumes the role of master regulator with inhibitory and coordinating roles.

Among the invertebrates, the cephalopod molluscs and the arthropods, in particular the hymenoptera, form significant end points with highly developed sense organs, a complex nervous system and well differentiated ganglia. In the cephalopod molluscs, e.g., octopus, a very elaborate eye with striking similarity to the vertebrate eye has been evolved by a process of parallel evolution. In the brain of these animals the supra oesophageal ganglion, of which the lobus verticalis is a key structure, has become a control center of major significance. This complex ganglion enables the animal to modify its behavior quite readily. For example, the octopus can be conditioned effectively and learns a maze with ease, as has been shown by such studies as those of J. Z. Young (1960, 1962) and of Sutherland (1960), Sutherland, Mackintosh, and Mackintosh (1963) and Wells (1961).

In the insects very complex behavior is evident though this appears to be largely stimulus bound. Edwards (1977) for example, has pointed out that insect behavior is dominated by patterns or sequences of behavior initiated by the release of central neural programs. Thus he said, "Instructions for elaborate and prolonged behavior patterns [such as flight, stridulation, echolocation, and copulation] which are housed in the ventral ganglia, may be activated by commands from brain centers but they can also be elicited from beheaded insects, even from isolated ganglia" (p. 59). In the insects, sense organs are very well developed, the animals have good manipulative ability, and the brain is capable of organizing the wealth of sensory information received so that meaningful action follows. The major coordinating centers in the insects are the paired corpora pedunculata or mushroom bodies (Rensch, 1956; Vowles, 1961; Young, 1957). Among the insects color discrimination learning and orientation learning have been demonstrated in bees (Thorpe, 1956; Von Frisch, 1950, 1967), location learning in wasps (Thorpe, 1943, 1950, 1956) and maze learning in ants (Schneirla, 1929, 1943; Thorpe, 1956). In some recent studies (Bitterman, 1976; Couvillon & Bitterman, 1980, 1982), striking similarities in learning performance of honey bees to that of vertebrates have been demonstrated. Bitterman (1976) showed an incentive-contrast-like effect using 20% and 40% sucrose solutions. However, this effect was a short term one (less than 20 minutes) and Bitterman argued that it could be understood in terms of sensory adaptation and did not require learning about reward. In other studies (Couvillon & Bitterman, 1980, 1982), free flying honey bees in a classical Von Frisch learning situation were reinforced with drops of sucrose solution presented on distinctly colored and scented targets. The measure of learning effects was the number of responses (contacts with a drop of water) given during extinction. A number of effects, typically observed in vertebrate conditioning, were reported including the overlearning-extinction effect (wherein resistance to extinction of the response following non-reward is reduced with overlearning of the association) and increased resistance to extinction following a partial (or short) delay between response and reinforcement. Stimulus control through the use of compound stimuli (color plus scent) was also examined with evidence for summation of components within the compound being more effective than the individual stimuli. Overshadowing (i.e., dominance of one member of the compound over the other) was also demonstrated with scent (jasmine) overshadowing color (orange). Other vertebrate-like phenomena such as compound stimulus uniqueness (in which the associative strength of a particular compound is greater than that of other compounds comprised of individual units from the initial compound that had been linked with reinforcement) and within compound association (i.e., the development of associative strength between two components of the compound) were also demonstrated.

In discussing these various results the authors observed that similarity of results of honey bees and vertebrates may be surprising considering the evolutionary remoteness of insects and vertebrates and the very different nervous systems. They suggested that similar synaptic mechanisms might offer a possible explanation. Bitterman also stressed the dangers of mistaking what are likely to be superficial similarities for common underlying mechanisms.

It is noteworthy that in both the lobus verticalus of the octopus and the corpora pedunculata of insects there are many nerve cells with short interconnecting fibers forming a complex neural network. This also characterizes the mammalian cortex and appears to be a critical arrangement of neural tissue for learning.

This does not mean, however, that one can interpret the vertebrate nervous system as a larger version of the invertebrate system, a point which Vowles (1961) emphasized in his penetrating analysis of the question. While starting from a common base these systems have had a very long history of separate evolutionary development. A major problem for insect nervous system evolution was that of number and size of units, as the total size of the animal is limited by the nature of the respiratory system and of its skeletal support, namely an exoskeleton. Vowles pointed out that the insect nervous system differs from that of vertebrates at all functional levels including the structure of its individual cells. Insect neurons have a small cell body, almost entirely nucleus, and axon termination is confined to the dendrite surface and does not invade the cell body. The receptive area of dendrites is also much less than in vertebrates. Another critical factor is the slow speed of neural conduction and this is especially relevant where successive integrations are called for, particularly in feedback control systems. The slowing down of processes in one channel would also delay other activities unless enough neurons are available and the insect system is limited by its size in this respect. Some compensation appears to have been achieved here by the small size and very dense packing of insect neurons.

With the capacity of the nervous system limited in this way one would anticipate neurologically simple receptors but this does not seem to be the case with insects, with the complex visual receptor system of the compound eye, the mass of sensory hairs or setae over the body and complex auditory and olfactory organs.

Vowles then examined how the complex sense organs are utilized by the relatively limited nervous system and suggested that physical and neural factors in sense organs may be inversely related in the case of insects, information conveyed to the CNS being more restricted than one might expect from the superficial structure. Integration of information appears to take place at the receptor itself and, in many cases, fused fibers convey information only of pressure and strength of a stimulus.

In the coordination of sensory and motor systems, the execution of complex acts appears to be organized in terms of a temporal sequence, each act triggering the next step with neural control at the sequential level and with absence of feedback. Vowles gave such examples as egg laying, antenna cleaning in the cricket, and attacks by the praying mantis.

While much more recent accounts of insect nervous systems are now available (e.g., Edwards, 1977; Ewert et al., 1983), Vowles' conclusion is worthy of reproduction in full. Biologically, he said, the insects are probably the most successful group of animals, particularly in the tropics. It has always been a wonder to mankind that animals which are so small should have a repertoire of behavior which is so varied and so adequate. Even recently an eminent zoologist (Patin, in the Croonian Lecture to the Royal Society, 1952) has suggested that perhaps insects have mechanisms for nervous integration different from vertebrates, and as yet undiscovered. If the evidence put forward in this chapter can be accepted, it shows the dangers of equating behavioral complexity — which may itself be only apparent — with complexity of neural mechanism. It shows too the risk of homologising vertebrate and insect behavior mechanisms, for different animals may use different neural devices to solve the same problems of adaptation. The properties of the insect neuron and the small size of the insect nervous system render necessary a functional organization of behavior far simpler than is often supposed. What should arouse our wonder is the success with which simplicity has been crowned (pp. 28–29).

This economy of organization is again exemplified in studies by Wine and his group of the mechanisms involved in escape behavior in another of the arthropods, the crayfish.

A major, though certainly not the only escape mechanism in this animal is a rapid and violently executed tail flick and in this the giant axon system plays a crucial part.

The giant fiber system is comprised of four giant axons, one pair medially and the other laterally located on the ventral nerve cord. These fibers are up to 200 mm in diameter. The medial fibers originate from cell bodies in the brain, with incoming fibers from the anterior sensory systems synapsing on these cells. The lateral pair consist of partly fused segments originating from cell bodies in each segmental ganglion and organized so that an impulse into one of the lateral giant fibers will fire the other (Wine & Krasne, 1972). These authors go on to point out that: "Both pairs of giant interneurons make a complex set of efferent connexions which are responsible for the coordinated patterns of muscle contractions that produce tail flips and various adjustments of appendages which accompany them" (p. 3).

Wine and his associates have shown that, with this basic system, escape behavior in the crayfish can be effected in different ways depending on the nature of the triggering stimulus and may involve either the lateral or the medial giant fiber system or a third non-giant system. For example, the lateral giant system can be activated by a light tap in the caudal region and results in a tail flip that pitches the animal forward, i.e., avoids a threat from the rear. The medial giant system is triggered by stimuli from the rostral region, e.g., a touch to the antennae, and this leads to a tail flip that causes the animal to dart backwards from the source of stimulation.

A third tail flip response involves the non-giant system and appears to be a much more flexible response to a variety of more slowly appearing stimuli including visual stimuli or gradually increasing pressure. The latency of this response is always much greater than that exhibited by responses activated by the giant fiber systems. The animal may be directed backward or upward depending on the source and nature of the stimulation. "In contrast to the giant fiber reactions, which are properly considered as reflexive," say Wine and Krasne, "non-giant reactions seem to be essentially voluntary in nature. Animals very much appear to choose their own moments to respond . . . . In fact, these responses are frequently entirely spontaneous" (pp. 14–15).

These developments in the ceophalopod molluscs, and in insects and crayfish, represent some of the more outstanding of many lines of parallel and convergent evolution of the nervous system with specialization to cope with particular evolutionary problems. Study of such developments reveals that similar functions may be achieved by different mechanisms and that, as Vowles has pointed out, attempts to directly relate the neural organization and functioning of that organization in the invertebrates to vertebrate neural organization should be undertaken with considerable caution.

This is clearly demonstrated in the recent work of Couvillon and Bitterman on learning in the honey bee, discussed earlier. Here we see what is likely to be the evolution of special processes for dealing with a limited range of stimuli (some odors and colors) in relation to a highly specific food (nectar or equivalents). If the processes involved (extinction, overshadowing, stimulus compounding and the like) are the most effective for dealing with the relevant stimuli in the search for nectar, then convergence of two very different systems to produce seemingly similar behavioral effects would not be unexpected. The honey bees, with a small compact nervous system, achieve this level of efficiency with reference to a very restricted range of stimuli while vertebrates with a much larger and more complexly organized nervous system exhibit a much more generalized effect. How these two disparate nervous systems achieve these common behavior effects is a question of major interest.

THE VERTEBRATE BRAIN

The Emergence of Vertebrates

There is no clear paleontological evidence by which to trace the evolutionary transition from invertebrates to vertebrates. It is highly likely that the reason for this is that the organisms involved were small larvae or larva-like forms that had no hard structures to leave their imprint on the geological record. This process, whereby what was initially a larval form retains its developmentally immature structure but develops to sexual maturity, has been given a special name, viz. neotony.

The origin of the vertebrate brain has been described by Jollie (1977) as "an 'enigma wrapped in a mystery.' The enigma is the origin of the tubular nervous system and its associated sensory organs and the mystery its subsequent history (functional and anatomic) to the level of complexity common to both agnatha and gnathostomes" (p. 74).

At this stage in our knowledge it is considered most probable that this major evolutionary step was effected by a form not unlike the larval stage of living sea urchins or echinoderms. Olsen (1971) has pointed out that there is general agreement that the chordates and echinoderms should be grouped together to form one of the major lines of descent within the animal kingdom. A common ancestor probably diverged before the beginning of the Ordovician period. This common ancestral line is presumed to have passed through a coelenterate level of organization but the nature of such animals is largely conjectural.

A small fish-like animal, Amphioxus, is the most vertebrate-like of any of the known chordates. This small animal has a body organized segmentally and has a hollow dorsal nerve cord supported by a notochord. This is in striking contrast to the invertebrate organization where the nervous system consists of a number of solid ventral nerve tracts with ganglia or masses of nerve cells arranged segmentally. The structure of Amphioxus is depicted in Figure 3.3.

Both Amphioxus and the tunicates are filter feeders and the mouth and pharangeal structures of some of the earliest vertebrates, the Agnatha, suggest a similar mode of feeding (Olsen, 1971).

With the evolution of the vertebrates, the restriction on size noted particularly in the arthropods was to a considerable extent removed by the development of an internal skeleton for support. Associated with this was a process of rapidly increasing cephalization with increase in the size of the brain and centralization of the various controlling and coordinating functions of the nervous system. This fact of increasing brain size together with a remarkable improvement in speed/volume relationships in impulse transmission referred to earlier and resulting from insulation or myelination of the nerve fiber, became aspects of critical significance when considering the increasing capacity of these animals to organize information and to increase the range and complexity of responses in coping with the environment.

In Amphioxus, there is a very simple brain consisting of an anterior enlargement, the prosencephalon or primary brain vesicle. The segmental organization of the body is still clearly evident with a pair of nerves serving each segment. The paired nerves show the basic vertebrate structure of dorsal and ventral roots with the dorsal root carrying sensory inflow and the ventral root motor outflow. This distinction between dorsal and ventral structures is evident throughout the whole vertebrate division.

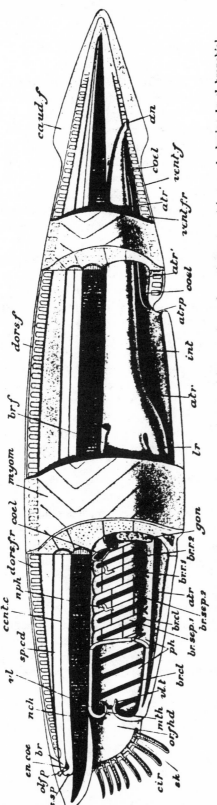

—Diagram of the anatomy of **Amphioxus**. *an.* anus; *atr.* atrium; *atr'.* its posterior prolongation; *atrp.* atriopore; *br.* brain; *br. cl.* branchial clefts; *br. f.* brown funnel; *br. sep. 1,* primary, and *br. sep. 2,* secondary branchial lamella; *br. r. 1,* primary, and *br. r. 2,* secondary branchial rod; *caud. f.* caudal fin; *cent.* c. neurocele; *cir.* cirri; *cœl.* cœlome; *dors. f.* dorsal fin; *dors. f. r.* dorsal fin-ray; *en. cœ.* encephalocele; *e. sp.* eye-spot; *gon.* gonad; *int.* intestine; *lr.* liver; *mth.* mouth; *myom.* myomers; *nch.* notochord; *nph.* nephridia; *olf. p.* olfactory pit; *or. f. hd.* oral hood; *ph.* pharynx; *sk.* skeleton of oral hood and cirri (dotted); *sp. cd.* neuron; *vent. f.* ventral fin; *vent. f. r.* ventral fin-ray; *vl.* velum; *vl. t.* velar tentacles.

FIG. 3.3.   The chordate *Amphioxus lanceolatis* showing the dorsal nerve cord. (From Parker and Haswell, 1930, Vol 2, p. 47).

The spinal nerves do, however, differ in several ways from those of the vertebrates. In Amphioxus the dorsal and ventral roots alternate. This is a primitive condition, the sensory fibers coming in at the intra muscular divisions from the skin, while the dorsal root fibers penetrate to the middle of the myotomic or muscle mass that they innervate. Thus the fibers from the two roots, ventral and dorsal, never combine into a single nerve tract. A further anomaly, is evident in that the dorsal roots emerge alternately on the right and left sides as also do the ventral roots. This is due to the shifting of the myotomes as the left side of the body has shifted with respect to the right, a secondary characteristic enhanced in Amphioxus (Ariens-Kappers, Huber, & Crosby, 1960).

Nieuwenhuys (1977) also drew attention to the fact that practically all the nerve cells in Amphioxus are situated in the immediate vicinity of the central canal. This central aggregation of nerve cells he regarded as a primitive condition and added that in certain generalized groups of gnathostomes, such as the dipnoid fish and urodele amphibia as well as in the agnathan lamprey a similar periventricular zone harbors the bulk of the nerve cells.

The agnatha, or the jawless fishes, are the first true vertebrates. In the living representatives, the lampreys and hagfish, the basic brain structure for all the higher vertebrates may be observed. Here the brain consists of three major divisions, the hind brain or rhombencephalon, the midbrain or mesencephalon, and the forebrain or prosencephalon. Anterior to the forebrain, as outgrowths from it, are the paired cerebral hemispheres with large olfactory lobes. The presence of 10 cranial nerves indicates that the process of cephalization is well advanced.

The organization of an agnathan brain, that of the lamprey Petromyzon, is shown in Figure 3.4.

Stahl (1977) cautioned against any sweeping generalization from the brain of living agnathans to those of higher vertebrates, pointing to the very long period of separate evolution since the armored ostracoderms first became evident in the fossil record some 500 million years ago. She also drew attention to the highly specialized way of life of the lampreys and hagfish that have led to regressive changes.

Against this she pointed to Stensiö's[1] studies of the cranial anatomy of the ostracoderms which indicated that the major regions of telencephalon, diencephalon, midbrain, and hindbrain were already well established in those animals. This work also revealed that the extinct agnatha, like the modern lamprey, had two rather than three semicircular canals, i.e., this was not a degenerative change.

[1]Stensiö, E. A. The brain and cranial nerves in fossil, lower craniate vertebrates. *Skr. Nor. Vidensk, Akad. Oslo,* 1963, No. 13.

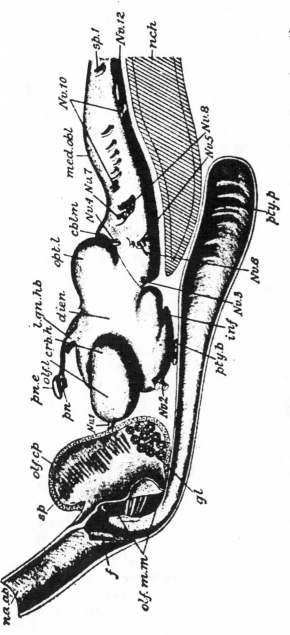

—**Petromyzon.** Side view of brain with olfactory and pituitary sacs, in section. *cblm.* cerebellum; *crb. h.* olfactory lobe; *dien.* diencephalon; *f.* fold in nasal tube; *gl.* nasal glands; *inf.* infundibulum; *l. gn. lb.* left ganglion habenulæ; *med. obl.* medulla oblongata; *na. ap.* nostril; *nch.* notochord; *Nv. 1,* olfactory nerve; *Nv. 2,* optic; *Nv. 3,* oculomotor; *Nv. 4,* trochlear; *Nv. 5,* trigeminal; *Nv. 6,* abducent; *Nv. 7,* facial; *Nv. 8,* auditory; *Nv. 10,* vagus; *Nv. 12,* hypoglossal; *olf. cp.* olfactory capsule; *olf. l.* olfactory bulb; *olf. m. m.* olfactory mucous membrane; *opt. l.* optic lobe; *pn.* parapineal organ; *pn. e.* pineal eye; *pty. b.* pituitary body; *pty. p.* pituitary pouch; *sp.* median septum of olfactory sac; *sp. l,* dorsal root of first spinal nerve. (Combined from figures by Ahlborn and Kaenische.)

FIG. 3.4. The organization of the brain in the Agnathid: *Petromyzon marinus.* (From Parker and Haswell, 1930, Vol 2, p. 127).

Stahl then concluded that, by the time vertebrates entered the fossil record, the brain had evolved its present fundamental vertebrate design. She further concluded that there appeared to be no way by which we could close the gap between the protochordates and Amphioxus and the primitive agnathan vertebrates.

In his comprehensive examination of the anatomy and the comparative relationships of the brain of lamprey, Nieuwenhuys (1977) gave strong grounds for believing that this living agnathan can be viewed as a significant link in the evolutionary chain. He referred to Ebbesson and Northcutt's (1976) extension of Jerison's work on brain-body ratios in which they show that the lamprey has a brain-body ratio considerably lower than any gnathostome vertebrate. He further pointed out that the brain of lamprey is "generalized," i.e., does not show any "group-specific sense organ-based 'hypertrophies' " (p. 128), and that this condition is also evident in the dipnoids and urodeles. It is with these species that, he claimed, the greatest "gross morphological similarity" is shown.

Nieuwenhuys examined in some detail the neural organization of specific categories of nerve cell and the segregation of the cells of the periventricular gray matter in lamprey. He then compared these findings with those relating to the cephalochordates and the anamniotic gnathostomes.

His conclusions, which he regarded as tentative, warrant quotation in full. They were:

(1) Although the present day cephalochordates did not give rise to the present day lampreys, the central nervous system of the former has more features in common with that of the latter, than with that of any group of gnathostomes.

(2) Although the present day lampreys have not given rise to any of the present day groups of gnathostomate anamniotes, their nervous system shares a strikingly large number of features with all of these groups.

(3) The central nervous system of the lamprey is smaller and in many respects more simply organized than that of any group of gnathostomes.

(4) It follows from the second and third conclusions mentioned that the central nervous system of the lamprey does not embody the "prototype" or the "morphotype" of the craniote brain; however, it offers an optimal starting point for the study of the development and differentiation of the vertebrate neuraxis (p. 138).

The acanthodians, the first jawed fishes to become evident in the geological record, appeared in late Silurian times. The elasmobranchs, the sharks and rays, have usually been cited as the closest living representatives of these early ancestors. There are, however, good reasons to doubt this. Ebbesson and Northcutt (1976), using Jerison's (1973) technique of comparison of min-

imal convex polygons for brain-body ratios, concluded that the living elasmobranchs yield comparatively very high brain-body ratios. Their analyses
of forebrain to body ratios showed a strong similarity to the gross brain-body
ratios. They therefore proposed that, for living vertebrates, there were three
quite distinctive groups. The lampreys have by far the smallest forebrain-
body ratios. The bony fish, amphibia and reptiles, form a middle group. The
group with the highest ratios is comprised of the birds and mammals and with
these they included the living elasmobranchs. This would argue strongly for a
substantial parallel evolution of the brain in elasmobranchs that must be
taken into account in any comparative studies involving that class. The use of
living elasmobranch species as representative of basic gnathostome ancestors
thus becomes highly suspect. This view is strengthened by Hotton (1976).
Hotton agreed that the acanthodians are the most likely common ancestors
for the main vertebrate line. These were small fish-like animals (2 to 8 cm in
length) that lived in fresh water. They had a fusiform shape, well developed
paired fins, well developed jaws for predation, and large eyes. These animals
are now believed to have been ancestors of the bony fish including the lobefin
fish—the Crossopterygii and the Dipnoi—that gave rise to the amphibia.
They may have also given rise to the Chrondrichthyes, the sharks and rays.
However, there is evidence that the Chrondrichthyes more likely evolved
from another group of primitive gnathostomes, the Placodermi, fish characterized by heavy dermal bony armor and grasping jaws. Their characteristics
suggest that the Placodermi evolved separately from some earlier form common both to the Placoderms and the Acanthodians. In fact, in the light of
Schaeffer's (1969) analysis, it may well be that elasmobranchs, placoderms,
acanthodians, and holocephalons (rat fishes) all evolved separately from a
common ancestor. This ancestor, suggested Hotton, "must have been less
specialized than any known agnathan and presumably very old. On theoretical grounds such an animal may have had an unossified skeleton and no teeth
or scales, which partially accounts for it being unknown" (Hotton, 1976, p.
9). If this is so, then all elasmobranchs came from a form that had already diverged from our main line before the first animals of the class became
evident.

   The Osteichthyes or bony fishes first became evident in the early Devonian
period. According to Hotton (1976) the most likely line of evolution of these
animals was from the acanthodians. From the earliest record the bony fishes
divided into two major subclasses. These were the Actinopterygii or rayfin
fishes which later gave rise to the vast bulk of the teleosts inhabiting the world
today and the Sarcopterygii or lobefin fish. This latter group was dominant
early but was quickly surpassed by the rayfins. The lobefins, however, gave
rise to the Crossopterygii and Dipnoi, the most likely ancestors of the amphibia. Schaeffer argued for the possibility that the crossoptergyians, in-

cluding the rhipidistians and coelacanths evolved independently from the Dipnoi, with amphibians evolving from rhipidistian stock.

Most living teleosts therefore diverged early from the main line of mammalian evolution. The Sarcopterygii or lobefin fishes, of which the coelacanth, Latimeria and the dipnoids, Neoceratodus, Protopterus, and Lepidosiren, are the living representatives, have the greatest claims to fill the gap between the agnatha and amphibia.

The amphibia or first land-dwelling vertebrates, are represented by the frogs, toads, newts, and salamanders. The basic neural organization of the frog is not markedly different from that observed in the elasmobranchs or the coelacanth, Latimeria, and the Dipnoi. The main changes that are evident are those associated with the move to the land, including the adaptation of the lateral line system of the fish to the auditory system of the land vertebrate and also changes in the visual and olfactory systems. The organization of an amphibian brain, that of Rana, is shown in Figure 3.5.

The living reptiles show a major advance in brain organization in that, for the first time, nerve cells may be observed on the walls of the pallium or roof of the forebrain. This is the beginning of the cerebral cortex.

In the mammals there has been a tremendous development of the neopallium from the earliest mammals to man. In the primitive vertebrates behavior is controlled largely by the sense of smell from which taste can hardly be separated. This compound sense enables the animal to find and determine the nature of food, recognize a mate or discover and avoid enemies. It has a quality of direct meaning that is not evident in the distance receptors. In these animals anticipation and consummation are linked together by smell and taste, giving the basis for associative memory. The cerebral cortex is derived from that part of the brain that was concerned primarily with smell and, unlike all other senses, the olfactory tracts reach the cerebral cortex directly.

The development of vision as a primary sense enabled the animal to steer a direct course, e.g., in the search for food. As the eye developed in size and importance the optic region of the brain, the optic tectum, established increasing control over motor action. In all vertebrates except mammals this visual dominance appears to have been attained only at the expense of other brain development with dominance of the midbrain over the forebrain as evidenced particularly in the avian species.

In mammals the central receptors for vision and the other main senses became established in the forebrain thus adding a further powerful stimulus to cortical development. We later examine how such neocortical dominance might have been established in mammals.

From the evidence considered to date we may plot the most likely line of the stream of evolution leading to the mammals as set out in Figure 3.6.

A more detailed examination of the changing structure and organization of the vertebrate brain follows. In the next chapter I examine the paleonto-

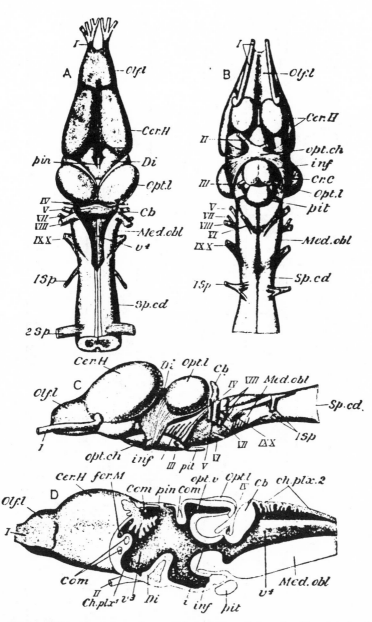

—Brain of **Rana.** *A*, from above; *B*, from below; *C*, from the side; *D*, in longitudinal vertical section. *Cb*, cerebellum; *Cer. H*, cerebral hemispheres; *ch. plx¹*, anterior, and *ch. plx²*, posterior choroid plexus (removed in *A*); *com*, commissures, the two in front the *anterior* and *hippocampal*, the two above the *superior* or *habenular* and the *posterior* ; *Cr. C*, crura cerebri; *Di*, diencephalon; *for. M*, foramen of Monro; *i*, iter, or aqueduct of Sylvius; *inf*, infundibulum; *Med. obl*, medulla oblongata; *Olf. l*, olfactory bulb; *opt. ch*, optic chiasma; *Opt. l*, optic lobe; *opt. r*, optic ventricle; *pin*, stalk of pineal body; *pit*, pituitary body; *Sp. cd*, spinal cord; *r³*, third ventricle; *r⁴*, fourth ventricle; *I—X*, cerebral nerves; *1Sp. 2Sp.* spinal nerves. (From Parker's *Practical Zoology.* *A—C*, after Gaupp; *D*, from Wiedersheim's *Comparative Anatomy*, after Osborn.)

FIG. 3.5. The brain of the amphibian *Rana temporaria*. (From Parker and Haswell, 1930, Vol 2, p. 277).

EVOLUTION OF MAMMALS

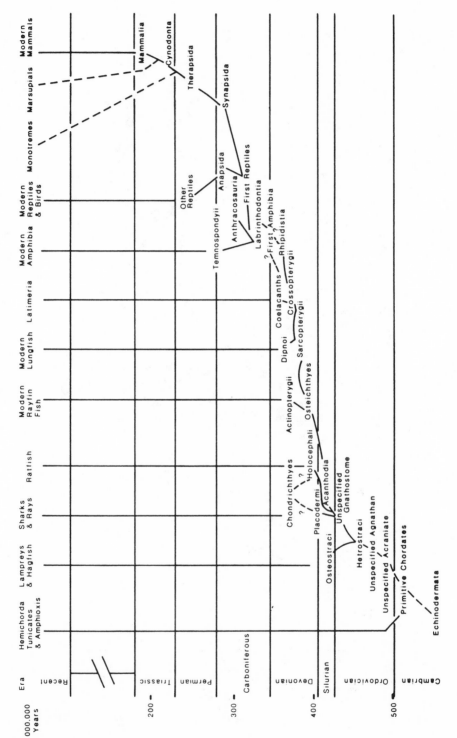

FIG. 3.6.   A likely line of evolutionary development from chordate to mammal.

56

logical evidence for vertebrate brain evolution. This work relies heavily on the use of brain endocasts which reveal the shape and volume of the brain contained within the cranium. These studies then, are largely confined to evidence relating to the total size and shape of the brain. For information about the changing structure of specific brain regions we have to rely on comparative studies across living species. This evidence is examined in chapters 6 and 7.

4 The Fossil Record of the Vertebrate Brain

BRAIN/BODY RATIOS AND BRAIN ENDOCASTS

The paleontological evidence considered in this chapter comes largely from the study of brain endocasts and from estimates of brain/body ratios derived from these endocasts. The work of Jerison and Radinsky dominates this field of enquiry so I rely heavily on their material. I begin with a discussion of the use of endocasts and of brain/body ratios. This leads to a consideration of the emergence of the mammals as a dominant class followed by examination (in Chapter 5) of the evolution of the primate brain. In this I call on evidence from both the fossil record and that provided by a series of comparative studies of primate brains by Stephan, Bauchot, and Andy.

Jerison, who has made extensive use of brain endocasts, has described the formation of these fossil remains in some detail. He pointed out that, under normal circumstances, when an animal dies it will disappear completely over a period of several months, firstly from attacks by scavengers and finally through the action of microorganisms consuming what remains of the skeleton. He continued:

> In order to be preserved as a fossil, the animal must usually be entombed under circumstances that will permit its skeleton to become mineralized, with all of the original organic material replaced by minerals. The process is discussed in the introductions to most texts on paleontology (Romer, 1966). During the period of fossilization the soft tissues in the cavities of the body, including the brain and its supporting tissue in the endocranial cavity, will decay and may be replaced by a "matrix" of sands, mud, clays, and pebbles that can be washed or blown into open holes. If these remains are buried for long enough a period the

matrix will become hardened sedimentary rock. A skull that is uncrushed, or not too badly crushed, may then contain a natural "endocast" which can be a nearly perfect "positive" for which the endocranial cavity, as the mould, is the "negative" (Jerison, 1973, p. 27).

Jerison took as the starting point for his work on evolution of brain and behavior Lashley's statement that "the only neurological character for which a correlation with behavior in different animals is supported by significant evidence is the total mass of tissue, or rather the degree of cephalization measured by ratio of brain weight to body weight" (Lashley, 1949, p. 33). His principle tool was Von Bonin's formula derived from the measurement of brain weights and body weights in various species. This formula expressed the ratio between brainweight and body weight in the form $E = kS^r$ where E = brain weight and S = body weight, both in grams. Von Bonin plotted the log of brain weight against the log of body weight for 115 mammals. He obtained a linear relationship with a correlation between brain weight and body weight of 0.835. The solution of this plot yielded the values $E = 0.185S^{0.655}$.

Von Bonin observed that the value for k varied from species to species and went on to speculate that, given the value of the exponent r (0.655) as a constant for mammals, then various species could be classified in terms of the coefficient k. However, he said, "Whether or not this is an indication of intelligence of animals must be left to the psychologist to answer" (Von Bonin, 1937, p. 388).

Almost 20 years after this challenging statement, Jerison confirmed and extended Von Bonin's findings. Using an independent set of 163 measurements, Jerison found a correlation of 0.92 between log E and log S with $k = 0.16$ and $r = 0.67$. The plot for these points is shown in Figure 4.1.

Assuming r to be a mammalian constant as did Von Bonin then, said Jerison, k will be the parameter for a family of parallel lines with slope r. The value of k for a given mammal can then be used as an "index of cephalization." This, he said, would give a numerical statement about the level of evolution of that mammal's brain (Jerison, 1955).

In a further study Jerison (1961) compared fossil animals from Oligocene and Eocene with a sample of recent mammals selected for similarity in adaptive niche and body configuration to the fossil forms. He demonstrated that the value of the exponent $r = 0.67$ held for Oligocene and Eocene as well as recent mammals but that k varied with $k = 0.12$ for the recent group, 0.06 for the Oligocene and 0.03 for the Eocene specimens. He concluded that

perhaps the most important aspect of the results is that they give simple, yet mathematically precise, statements about the evolution of the brain. The same general rule that describes brain-to-body relationships in contemporary mammals was found in the earlier evolutionary stages sampled here, and the parameter, k, differentiated those stages (Jerison, 1961, p. 1014).

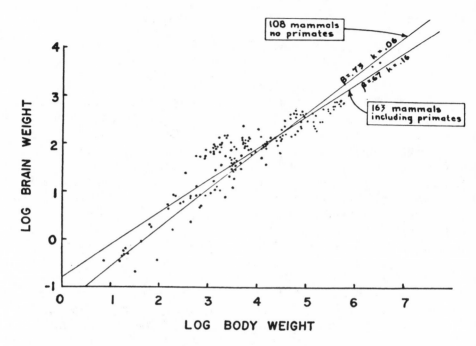

FIG. 4.1.   Log brain weight (grams) as a function of log body weight (grams) for 163 mammals. (from Jerison, 1955, p. 447).

Jerison then developed an "encephalization quotient" (EQ) which showed the ratio of actual brain size (E_i) for a species (i) to expected brain size (E_e) for "average" living mammals taking body size (P_i) into account. Average or "expected" brain size was given by the formula $Ee = 0.12\ P_i^{2/3}$. The EQ_i for a given species i is the ratio of its brain size E_i to the expected brain size E_e of an average mammal of the same body size, i.e., $EQ_i = \dfrac{Ei}{Ee}$. Substituting for Ee, then $EQ = \dfrac{Ei}{0.12P_i^{2/3}}$.

The value of the EQ for Homo Sapiens with $E_i = 1350$g and $P = 70,000$g would be 6.3. The human brain is thus six times as large as we would expect it to be if we were a typical mammal.

A technique developed by Jerison to compare different groups of animals was to make log–log plots of brain weight to body weight and then to draw a "minimum convex polygon" to enclose the plots of a given set of data. Using this technique Jerison revealed clear differences between higher and lower living vertebrates. The convex polygons for these data are shown in Figure 4.2. He has used this method for presenting much of his data derived from fossil forms.

THE ENLARGEMENT OF THE MAMMALIAN BRAIN

Jerison emphasized that selection pressures towards enlargement of the brain beyond the requirements for larger bodies (i.e., in his terms, pressures towards the development of intelligence) were probably rare until birds and mammals diverged from their different reptilian stocks. Even in these higher vertebrate classes, he contended, selection for enlarged brains did not continue to all orders. He later emphasized the point again when he pointed out that the various specializations of the lower vertebrates did not result in sufficiently great increments in brain tissue to raise any of them above the lower vertebrate polygon (Figure 4.2). This, he said, was one sense in which he considered brain size to be a conservative evolutionary character since a single brain:body map covered the entire 500 million years evolutionary span of the lower vertebrates. Using Jerison's technique, Ebbesson and Northcutt (1976) showed that this was not strictly true as the agnathan lamprey has a brain-body ratio considerably lower than any of the gnathostomes. These authors argued for three separate levels rather than two, namely the agnatha, the lower gnathostomata, and the birds and mammals. This, however, does not detract from Jerison's claim that brain size is indeed a conservative characteristic.

What then could lead to this dramatic shift from the submammalian to the larger mammalian brain size as exemplified by Jerison's two polygons? These earliest mammals were small, relatively undifferentiated animals, most being probably ecologically similar to small species of primitive living groups like hedgehogs and opossums. In fact, claimed Jerison, some of the Mesozoic niches invaded by these animals appear to have remained occupied by species that are not much different now than they were when the original invasion occurred. Two endocasts from this Mesozoic collection, that have been preserved relatively intact, are those of a Triconodon and a Paleocene multituberculate Ptilodus. Jerison's analysis of these two specimens yielded EQs of 0.28 and 0.26 respectively (p. 212). This placed them on the lower fringe of the mammalian polygon and clearly well above that of the reptiles.

The initial enlargement of the brain in mammals as they evolved from reptilian ancestors some 150 million years ago was, Jerison believed, related to the development of new sensory capacities for life in nocturnal niches. Mammals began their evolutionary course early in the evolution of reptiles but these premammalian species were not among the dominant reptile groups. On the contrary, they were ones that had, to all intents and purposes, lost the race for ascendancy. They were small relatively unspecialized animals that were able to survive only by adapting to a part of the environment not dominated by the large reptiles.

Jerison noted that one characteristic of these dominant reptiles was that they were poikilothermic (or cold-blooded) and thus dependent on the

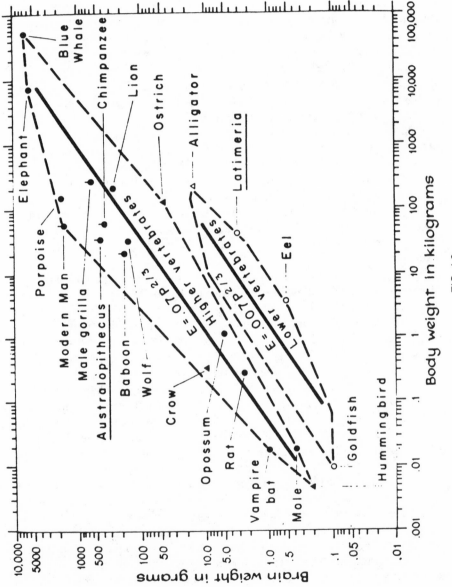

FIG. 4.2.

warmth of the environment to achieve optimum activity. It has been argued, however, that the most highly evolved of them (the flesh-eating dinosaurs) may have evolved a warm-blooded condition. Desmond (1975), in his book "The Hot-Blooded Dinosaurs," brought together evidence and arguments in support of this view. Thus he saw the reptiles giving rise to two endothermal lines. Archosaurs (a group intermediate between crocodiles and the dinosaurs) would, he said, "stand in relation to the Dinosauria as the mammal-like reptiles stand to mammals" (p. 166). This view was further developed by McLoughlin (1979) who argued that "the dinosaurs and their relatives among the progressive Archosauria were indeed warm blooded" and considered that their history "is one of splendid success and high evolutionary style" (p. 8). This would help account for their dominance over the small emerging mammals. It is evident, however, that these animals did not develop a heat preserving cover of hair or feathers and this is likely to have been a significant factor in their evolutionary demise, being unable to survive the rigors of the Cretaceous cold. These dinosaurs were, he believed, clearly a dominant species and there was evidence too of evolution of brain enlargement in some of the later coelurosaurs and dromaeosaurs. These appear to have been agile and fleet footed bird-like animals with large brains and huge eyes to coordinate their sophisticated reflexes. Desmond considered that such dinosaurs, being

> capable of more skilful behavioral feats than any other land animals hitherto, were separated from other dinosaurs by a gulf comparable to that dividing man from cows: the disparity in brain size was staggering. The potential inherent in dromaeosaurs and coelurosaurs for an explosive evolution as the Tertiary dawned cannot be doubted (p. 211).

A lively debate over this question of whether the most advanced of the dinosaurs were indeed endothermic ensued and culminated in a symposium held at the 1978 AAAS National Meeting in Washington. The papers from this symposium were published in 1980 under the title, "*A cold look at the warm blooded dinosaurs*," edited by R. D. K. Thomas and E. C. Olson. At this symposium a broad range of views emerged from those who held that dinosaurs were fully endothermic to the view that no unequivocal evidence of homeothermy had been established. For example Bakker argued that "The empirical data now available which bear in one way or another on vertebrate

---

FIG. 4.2. (*facing page*)   Log brain weight log body weight plots for higher vertebrates (birds and mammals) and lower vertebrates (fish and reptiles). Data on the fossil hominid *Australopithecus* and on the living coelacanth *Latimeria* are added. Minimum convex polygons are shown by dashed lines enclosing visually fitted lines with slopes of two-thirds (from Jerison, 1969, p. 579).

bioenergetics fall into an unambiguous pattern: dinosaurs are statistically in-distinguishable from fossil mammals, while the codonts and therapsids are an intermediate between Good Reptiles and these two groups" (Bakker, 1980, p. 457).

Nicholas Hotton III on the other hand put forward the view that "dino-saur-grade inertial homeothermy mimics the major effects which Bakker (1971, 1972, 1975a, b, this volume) treats as unequivocal evidence of endo-thermy in dinosaurs" (Hotton, 1980, p. 350). Overall the symposium cer-tainly stressed that a dichotomy between ectothermy and endothermy is not a viable way of representing the range of heat-regulatory mechanisms that might be observed in vertebrates.

The dominant reptiles were undoubtedly diurnal visual animals with a very well established visual system. The retina of the eye, and this certainly in-cludes the reptilian eye, has extensive information-processing machinery that enables these animals to respond selectively to many different stimuli. This retina provided for spatial plotting but the backup of a large brain necessary for temporal sequencing was lacking. Thus, said Jerison, it is unlikely that this visual world was a particularly rich one for the reptiles. While this was likely to be true for the stem reptiles from which both the mammals and the archosaurs originated, it may not be the case for the more advanced dino-saurs, the dromaeosaurs and the coelurosaurs. As Desmond has pointed out, these animals may well have had large, well developed and highly evolved brains centered around an advanced visual system. These dominant reptiles gave origin to the second line of modern homeothermic vertebrates, the birds.

To return to our story of the separation of mammals from reptiles, a likely niche or environmental domain that would not be dominated by the major reptiles would be one where activity had to take place in a cool environment, where the diurnal poikilothermic reptiles would become relatively inactive, and in dim light when the main reptilian distance receptor, the eye, would be relatively ineffective. A nocturnal, cave-dwelling existence would meet these demands but critical changes would be needed for these small, unspecialized and generally insignificant reptiles to master such a habitat. The first of these to be effected was probably an increasing capacity to maintain a high and steady internal body temperature, i.e., the warm-blooded condition enabling these animals to remain active in the cooler environment. Jerison proposed that another significant change was in the way these animals perceived the world around them.

In these nocturnal reptiles of the late Triassic period of some 200 million years ago, audition and olfaction would have had to supplement and largely supplant vision. Vision is spatially coded in the retina but auditory and olfac-tory stimuli are essentially temporal in nature. There was therefore need for discrete auditory events to be linked together over time to provide a continuous sequence of events. This "time binding" would give the animals a continuous schema, so that the auditory signals would fit into a spatial representation. Jerison went on to point out that the reptilian daylight vision, essentially a cone system, evolved into the mammalian rod system, a system useful in twilight, particularly for movement detection. In the nocturnal premammals this visual capacity would not be able to provide the distance information that it did for diurnal reptiles. However, it would change patterns of auditory and olfactory information into objects in space that remain constant over time. How the world is perceived is determined by the brain, a construction or representation being developed within the nervous system to account for the sensory and motor information processed by it. In this way, said Jerison, the nervous system develops or processes information into objects in space and time. For the auditory and olfactory systems to provide effective representations of this kind, however, considerable evolutionary enlargement of the brain was needed to provide networks comparable to those of the retina in the visual system.

Ford Ebner (1976) argued along similar lines for the evolution of mammals from small nocturnal reptiles. While the majority of reptiles are diurnal and have nearly pure cone retinas, mammals with primitive brains have nearly pure rod vision and are largely nocturnal. From this it may be deduced that mammal-like reptiles were selected for movement detection at low light intensities. He also pointed to the more highly developed auditory mechanism in mammals. A further important difference, said Ebner, is that, while mammals have an internal system for activating the neocortex through the brainstem reticular formation including the intralaminar thalamic nuclei, reptiles appear to have no such system. Rather, he concluded, the reptiles have a system that is similar to the light-activated geniculostriate system of mammals. For the reptiles then, daylight was likely to be the primary stimulus for cortical arousal. In the mammal and presumably in the evolving nocturnal premammal, on the other hand, the critical arousal stimuli could be determined and set, or reset through the activity of the reticular system depending on the particular circadian rhythm of the species. Thus for the nocturnal mammals the period of maximal arousal was set or tuned to the absence of daylight.

With the extinction of the great reptiles at the end of the Mesozoic era some 70 million years ago there followed a successful mammalian invasion of diurnal niches. Here were animals that were able to utilize time to develop spatial schema. Diurnal vision was now re-evolved to fit into this system. Thus, claimed Jerison, mammalian vision would, in addition to spatial mapping, be time binding. Visual images could be stored in some form of order and could maintain constancy under transformation of time and space. Thus images of objects could be constructed.

Jerison summarized this development as follows:

Just as hearing as a distance sense had been modeled after the natural reptilian sense of vision, so it may be assumed that the newly re-evolved mammalian diurnal vision was modeled after the, by then, natural distance sense of mammals, the auditory sense, which had been evolving for more thañ 100 m.y. of the previous history of the mammals. The assumption that a new system is modeled after a pre-existing system is one of my basic general assumptions (Jerison, 1973, p.21).

The role of temporal relationships is thus seen by Jerison as a key element in the evolution of man's ability to construct a perceptual world; with the classifying of information from one or several sources to give us objects perceived as invariate in time and space. This is congruent with a view advanced earlier by Lashley (1951) in his paper "A problem of serial order on behavior."

The next significant stage in primate evolution was the move into an arboreal habitat. This put strong selective pressure on the development of fine visual sensitivity with redevelopment of cone vision; Jerison considered mammalian cone vision to be analogous and not homologous to cone vision in reptiles. This was accompanied by increasingly well developed central processing of visual information that would lead to increasingly fine definition of constancies of objects against the fast changing mottled background of vegetation and light and shade. Under these conditions, said Jerison, "there would be many advantages to the use of color and a constructed 'real' space with objects and things in it. It would," he said, "be difficult to move about freely in such an environment on the basis of prepotent cues from certain patterns of stimulation that act as effective stimuli for fixed action patterns because the stimulus patterns would be unstable and changing" (Jerison, 1973, p. 413).

This move into a new arboreal niche could thus account for the increase in brain size in the pre-primates and primates. Jerison argued that similar factors were potent in the expansion of the brain in birds. However, in birds, the pressures for the development of central neural representation of vision led to expansion of the midbrain instead of forebrain cortical structures.

Beyond the expansion associated with the move to life in the trees, the great apes and man show a further explosive expansion of the brain and, in particular, the neocortex over and above that demonstrated by tupaiids or tree shrews, and prosimians or primitive primates. Before examining Jerison's view on how this expansion may have occurred, however, let us return to another significant interplay in evolutionary history that led to notable increases in brain size, one described by Pearson as the interaction by predator and prey with continuing change in the characteristics of both (Pearson, 1964). Jerison examined the evolutionary history of this interaction, as revealed by brain endocasts, and concluded that it led to an evolutionary expansion of the brain over and above that correlated with evolution of new sensory capacities.

For this study of tertiary ungulates and carnivores the species were classified as Archaic (extinct orders from mid-Paleocene to late Eocene, i.e., about 60 to 40 m.y. ago), Paleogene (Lower Eocene to the end of the Oligocene, i.e., 55 to 22.5 m.y. ago), Neogene (Miocene and Pliocene, i.e., 22.5 to 2.5 m.y. ago) and Recent (living species more or less matched in niche and body size to fossil samples).

Brain and body sizes and Encephalization Quotients (EQs) were estimated for each animal and the results were plotted and examined statistically in various ways. Perhaps the most significant figure involved the plotting of cumulative frequency distributions for EQ's for each group. This is presented in Figure 4.3.

The analyses showed that, for a given era, carnivores or flesh eaters had relatively larger brains than the ungulates or grazing animals on which they preyed. Another significant feature was the increasing spread of relative brain size with each new era. This is best shown by graphs that plotted these distributions as shown in Figure 4.4.

It should be noted here that Radinsky (1975), in an examination of felid (cat) brain evolution, disputed Jerison's figures for the EQs of the Oligocene carnivores Hoplophoneus (the early sabertooth cat) and Smilodon (the sabertooth tiger). Whereas Jerison's estimates were EQs of 0.32 and 0.53 for Hoplophoneus specimens and 0.38 for Smilodon, Radinsky derived values of 0.73 for Hoplophoneus and 0.59 for Smilodon. As Radinsky pointed out, this would place at least these two Paleocene species within the modern range. The main area of dispute appears to be in the estimates of body weight which Radinsky placed much lower than did Jerison. Radinsky elaborated his claim with an additional analysis, namely that of brain size against Foramen Magnum area; this again placed his fossil felids all within the range of modern felids for relative brain size.

His conclusion was that the possibility of evolutionary increase in relative brain size in felids must be viewed with caution. However, he then pointed out that evolutionary increase in relative brain size has been demonstrated in the Canidae (Radinsky, 1973). Further, as a result of his detailed analysis of felid brain endocasts, he concluded that there was an apparent evolutionary increase in the volume of the neocortex in the neofelids and that this coincided with their major evolutionary radiation. This suggested to him that "perhaps it was improvements in the central nervous system that allowed neofelids to outcompete paleofelids" (Radinsky, 1975, p. 251). In essence then it would seem that Radinsky's evidence is not incompatible with Jerison's position.

Jerison concluded, from these studies, that diversification was the main characteristic of progressive evolution of the brain with increasing diversity

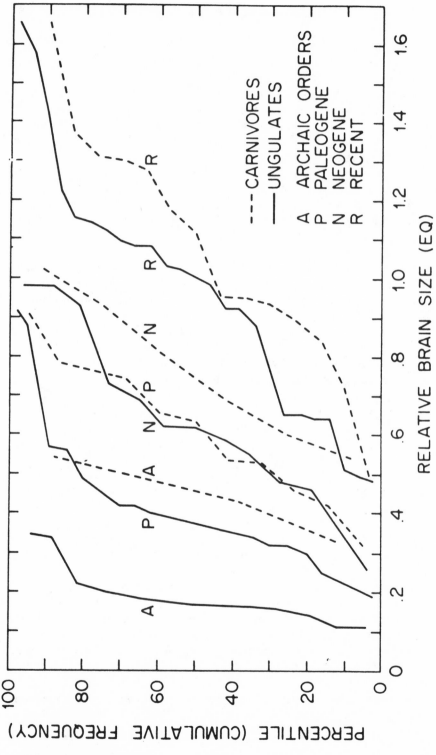

FIG. 4.3. Cumulative frequency distributions of encephalization quotients for tertiary ungulates and carnivores (from Jerison, 1973, p. 311).

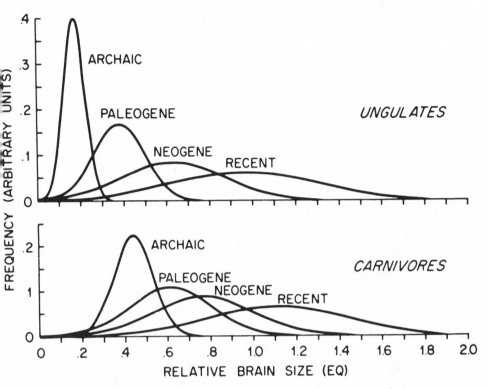

FIG. 4.4.   Frequency distributions for encephalization quotients for the tertiary ungulates and carnivores depicted in Fig. 4.3 (from Jerison, 1973, p. 315).

as more niches were occupied and competition increased, leading to increased average brain size. Another main point was that such evolution was conservative with brain sizes remaining stable over long periods of time. Thus it was only on rare occasions that there were substantial changes in brain size over and above those required for increase in body size. Such changes, said Jerison, are reflected as increases in EQ.

One such change resulted from the carnivore-ungulate interaction and Jerison then referred to what Simpson (1965) has described as "an evolutionary experiment on a grand scale." The South American "Neotropical" ungulates of the Tertiary period were isolated from the selective pressure of competing progressive carnivores. These ungulates were considered as the control group against which the evolution of Holarctic or Northern Hemisphere ungulate brains could be compared. The result appeared to be a striking one and is represented in Figure 4.5.

The South American fossil ungulates formed a compact group in terms of brain/body ratios with neither the spread (diversification) nor the progressive increase in EQ shown by the Holarctic groups. While there was some di-

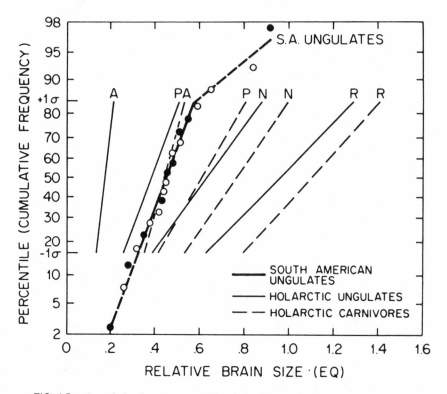

FIG. 4.5. Cumulative frequency curve for the entire sample of Neotropical ungulates compared with the basic data on Holarctic ungulates and carnivores. A, Archaic; P, Paleogene; N, Neogene; R, Recent. For Neotropical ungulates, filled circle for Paleogene; open circle for Neogene (from Jerison, 1973, p. 330).

versification early in the adaptive radiation of these Neotropical Ungulates the South American assemblage did not change from the Paleocene level of brain size or diversity over the 50 m.y. of their tertiary radiation.

An interesting postscript to this area of investigation and to the debate between Jerison and Radinsky has now been added. Radinsky (1981) examined a wider range of extinct South American ungulates covering the same time span and many of the species considered by Jerison. He employed Jerison's (1973) technique for deriving EQs but arrived at a very different conclusion, namely that there were two evolutionary trends, both of which showed increases over time. The first was an increase in size and convolution of the neocortex and the second was an increase in EQ or relative brain size. He concluded that the South American and Holarctic ungulates were comparable in terms of increasing size of brain and in increasing variability.

The differences between Radinsky and Jerison in this area appear to arise from three sources. The first is the continuing disagreement between the two on the issue of estimation of body weight. Jerison made a substantial allowance for species he considered to be heavily built by doubling estimated body weight and thus reducing the EQ. Radinsky made no such allowance. Secondly, Radinsky grouped his animals rather differently and thirdly he was able to employ a wider range of species. Thus this question remains unresolved.

The final step in our evolutionary history was the dramatic increase in brain size or, more precisely, in EQ, seen in the transition from tree dwelling insectivores, prosimians, and primates to man.

5 The Evolution of the Primate Brain

THE FOSSIL RECORD

Our most cogent evidence for establishing the chain of primate evolution must come from the study of fossil remains. Such remains have, however, not been easy to locate for, as Dobzhansky (1955) has pointed out, the very nature of our ancestors' life style, namely arboreal in tropical rain forests, has provided an environment highly unfavorable for fossilization. Even more rare are reasonably well preserved endocasts for the study of brain evolution. What have been recovered, with a few notable exceptions, have been a few bone fragments and a handful of teeth. Szalay & Delson (1979) in their detailed examination of primate taxonomy based on the paleontological record pointed out that "The understanding of the origin and interrelationships of the order is based largely on the fragmentary evidence of the cranium, dentition and aspects of the postcranial skeleton (p. 23). Because of the interest in human evolution, however, such shreds of evidence as there are have been exploited to the utmost with numerous publications resulting. The interested reader may explore such works as Buettner-Janusch's *"The origins of man"* (1966); Colbert's *"The evolution of vertebrates"* (1955); Dobzhansky's *"Mankind evolving"* (1962); R.E. Leakey's *"The making of mankind"* (1981); Le Gros Clark's *"The fossil evidence for human evolution"* (1955); *"The antecedents of man"* (1962), and *"Man, apes or ape men? The stories of discoveries in Africa"* (1967); or R.H. Tuttle's *"Assembly of writings on Paleoanthropology"* (1975). A clear and readable account of *"The early relatives of Man"* is given in Simons' (1964) paper in *Scientific American*. Jelinek's (1975) *Pic-*

torial Encyclopedia of the Evolution of Man gives a graphic view of man's evolution, particularly as evidenced by various artifacts.

I do not attempt to review this material but examine briefly some of the more recent developments that appear relevant to my main theme, namely the increase in size and complexity of the brain.

In his discussion of primate evolution, Jerison (1973) noted what he described as a very early and characteristic feature of the primate brain, a repackaging as it were. This is evidenced, he said, by a "broadened, flattened and significantly spheroid brain" (p. 368). This was associated with the flexioning of the hindbrain and disappearance of the dorsal midbrain exposure. This spheroid packaging was seen as giving a more efficient housing to the enlarging primate brain than the linear, cylindrical organization in the more primitive vertebrates. Jerison claimed that this change was clearly evident in the skull shape of an early Paleocene prosimian specimen (*Plesiadapis tricuspidens*) of some 60 m.y. ago. Thus, he concluded, differentiation of primate from insectivore would have occurred some time before this.

Radinsky (1977) was more cautious than Jerison in his appraisal of the significance of Plesiadapis, pointing out that the skull, while complete, was badly crushed, making estimates of brain size very difficult. He agreed that the brain was probably relatively smaller than in modern prosimians but said evidence was not strong. He also agreed that the proportions of the brain case suggested that the Plesiadapis brain was relatively broad and flat but added that some living rodents and marsupials have skulls of similar proportions. It was not until the second wave of primate evolutionary radiation in the Eocene (some 55 m.y. ago), said Radinsky (1970), that characteristic features of the primate brain became clearly evident. These were the presence of large occipital and temporal lobes and reduction of the olfactory bulbs. It is, he continued, "still not known whether these neurological specializations characterized the earliest members of the order" (p. 220) with evidence for the earlier Paleocene radiation of primates consisting mainly of fragments of jaws and teeth.

Simons (1976) went so far as to suggest multiple origins of primate species in the Paleocene radiation, claiming that Radinsky's so-called second or Eocene radiation could be the result of diversification "from two or more stocks that have separated from other primate lineages at the same time as the middle Paleocene radiation" (p. 385). In fact, as he pointed out, "the time and place of origin of order primates remains shrouded in mystery" (Simons, 1969, p. 319). Simons, in his 1969 paper, claimed that primates are in fact among the oldest of the placental mammals, sharing a common ancestor as far back as possibly 70–80 m.y. ago.

The oldest primate endocast in good shape is that of the small prosimian Tetonius from the early Eocene. While this and other early prosimians show

expansion of visual cortex, the frontal lobes are smaller than in modern prosimians. The more recent representatives of this second radiation, namely
Necrolemur from the late Eocene and Rooneyia from early Oligocene, i.e.,
some 40 and 35 m.y. old respectively, yield brain/body ratios overlapping
modern prosimians, according to Radinsky (1975).

As noted earlier, there is continuing debate between Radinsky and Jerison
on the most appropriate method for estimating ratios for relative brain size.
While Jerison has been able to make direct estimates of brain weights from
endocasts, his major problem has been the absence of any direct method of
estimating body weight and his and Radinsky's estimates of this parameter
have shown substantial variation. Radinsky developed an alternative method
for estimating this ratio by comparing brain volume with the cross sectional
area of the foramen magnum. This is based on a well established relationship
between body weight and cross sectional area of the medulla oblongata.

Foramen magnum measurement has the advantage that, with fossil endocasts, one does not have to make guesses at the likely body weight of the animal, but against its use, Jerison has argued that accurate measurement of the
foramen magnum in imperfect fossils is also very difficult and at times impossible. He also argued, from data on living species presented by Bauchot
and Stephan[1] (1967), that there is a significant brain size factor that relates to
size of the foramen magnum, which is thus not only determined by body size
but absolute brain size. Thus, a large-bodied small-brained animal would
have a relatively large foramen magnum but a small-bodied, large-brained
animal would also have an enlarged foramen magnum. Thus, argued Jerison, if there is either enlargement of the cranium or enlargement of the body
independent of brain enlargement then there is likely to be an enlargement of
the foramen magnum. This is not the case with the cross section of the medulla, which relates much more closely to body size. The confounding observed for foramen magnum size would have the effect of reducing differences among species in Radinsky's analysis.

Radinsky (1977) confirmed that while foramen magnum area is highly correlated with body weight, he had also found it to be correlated with brain
size. Thus, he agreed that "brain weight-foramen magnum area comparison
may underestimate relative brain size differences between groups" (p. 85).
Following re-analysis of his data he agreed that his earlier estimates of brain
size in Necrolemur and Rooneyia were too high. However, his recalculated
estimates of EQs for the early prosimians were still substantially lower than
Jerison's because his estimates of body weight were higher. His final conclu-

---

[1]Bauchot, R. & Stephan, H. Encéphales et moulages endocrâniens de quelques insectivores et
primates actuels. In Problèmes actuèls de paléontologie (Évolution des vertébrés). *Colloq.
Int. Cent. Nat. Rech. Sci.*, 1967, *163*, 575–587 (from Jerison, 1973).

sion was that, at most, his results suggested that "the earliest primates for which we have endocasts had brains that were somewhat relatively smaller than those of modern prosimians, but that by the late Eocene, some prosimians had brains that fell within the relative size range of modern prosimians" (Radinsky, 1977, p. 85). This conclusion is quite consistent with Jerison's findings.

In his examination of the evidence for the broadening and deepening of the primate brain, Jerison drew attention to the widely held view of earlier neurologists and neuroanatomists that expansion of the frontal pole of the neocortex represents the pinnacle of primate brain evolution. We have noted that in the early prosimian endocasts there is an absence of the developing prefrontal area. On the other hand, the temporal lobes and cerebellum both showed substantial expansion. Thus, it now appears that temporal lobe expansion took place in the Paleogene epoch before rapid neocortical expansion became evident. Such early expansion of the occipital pole and temporal neocortex, which is a highly significant processing system for both visual and auditory information, would certainly fit comfortably with Jerison's theory of the causal factors for initial enlargement of the primate brain. These findings are also congruent with the view of such writers as Kluver (1951); Radinsky (1970, 1975, 1976) and Campbell (1976) who argue that expansion of the temporal lobes is at least as significant as that of the frontal lobes in the corticalization of the brain.

Jerison's conclusion from his analysis of prosimian evolution was that prosimians had responded to the earliest selection pressures that led to primate brain enlargement but then had remained static. The Madagascan lemurs for example, isolated from the mainland, occupied a wide variety of niches and became specialized to them. In terms of brain size they remained essentially "average" mammals, the adaptations being accomplished by various skeletal adaptations. The secondary role of the brain in these adaptations supported Jerison's conclusion that the "post paleogene prosimians no longer responded to selection pressures by enlargement of the brain" (Jerison, 1973, p. 386). From this he concluded that different sets of selection pressures were likely to have generated the continuing increase in brain size.

While there are gaps in the prosimian story, the evidence for the evolution of monkeys, apes, and hominids from prosimian origins is scant indeed. The earliest evidence of an anthropoid brain is from the late Oligocene, some 25–30 m.y. ago with partial endocasts of Aegyptopithecus. Radinsky (1975) considered this animal as possibly ancestral to humans as well as apes. Its brain exhibits an expanded primary visual cortex bounded by a lunate sulcus, there is a central sulcus as in modern anthropoids, and the olfactory bulbs are reduced. The frontal lobe appears to be relatively smaller than in modern anthropoids. From about the same era, Radinsky (1975) reported two other specimens, Apidium, a genus perhaps related to the Old World or catarrhine monkeys, and Dolichocebus, a likely ancestor of the New World or platyrrhine monkeys of South America.

For the Old World monkeys or cercopithecoids, two specimens, Mesopithecus and Libypithecus were located in the Miocene and Pliocene followed by what Jerison (1973) described as a rather good assemblage of Pleistocene monkeys and baboons. The endocasts of these two specimens, said Jerison, are so close to living species that they need not be considered separately.

On the basis of the sparse evidence available, Simons (1976) attempted an estimation of the likely times of origin of the three anthropoid superfamilies, cercopithecoids (the Old World or catarrhine monkeys), ceboids (the New World or platyrrhine monkeys), and hominoids (the great apes and man).

He argued that the first division would have been between the platyrrhine and catarrhine monkeys and that this would have taken place well before the appearance of Aegyptopithecus, which had clear catarrhine characteristics. It would also have to have taken place in sufficient time to permit the platyrrhine migration into South America. Simons dismissed the alternative view that these species were transported on branches or other raftlike structures to South America after the continents had separated on the ground that, at that time (40 m.y. ago) the southern continents were much farther apart than was originally believed, with the South Atlantic being some 70% of its present width, and this would have made rafting impossible. The animals would have died of thirst long before they reached South America.

He then pointed out that anatomical and biochemical evidence places the hominoids and cercopithecoids much closer to each other than either is to the South American platyrrhine ceboids. Thus, he said, the divergence of hominoid from catarrhine must have occurred substantially later than the catarrhine-platyrrhine division. He concluded:

> The best conjecture that can be made at present is that the splitting-time which produced Hominoidea and Cercopithecoidea was about 45 ± 5 million years B.P. and that it was in Africa. The split of Catarrhine and Platyrrhini was probably at about 10 million years earlier in the European-North American land mass. In summary, Hominoidea are best thought to have had their origin in Africa in middle Eocene times" (Simons, 1976, p. 390).

The relationship between the hominoids or apes and the hominids is also still far from clear. Jerison (1973) noted that there has been some success in recent years in constructing the fossil history of the hominoids but this is based largely on non-cranial material. Thus brain size could not be assessed. Simons (1976) observed that, in the early Oligocene, a diverse group of anthropoids occurred in Fayum Africa. Four genera were identified, namely Propliopithecus, Oligopithecus, Aeolopithecus, and Aegyptopithecus. According to Prasad (1975) these were followed by Pliopithecus and Dry-opithecus in the mid-Miocene. Aegyptopithecus was considered by Simons to be the ancestor of the Dryopithecids. These were a varied group of anthropoid species that lived some 14–20 m.y. ago in a habitat described by Leakey (1981) as thick, warm forest country. Another genus identified at this time was the massive Gigantopithecus.

The point of emergence of the first hominid is still shrouded in doubt and controversy, as observed, for example, in the current debate between Richard Leakey and Don Johanson on the relationship between Australopithecus africanus and Homo habilis. A specimen identified as Ramapithecus lived at about the same time as Dryopithecus but has been classed by both Simons and Pilbeam as a hominid. However, the specimen is far from complete and Krantz (1975) considered it likely that it was a smaller (female) specimen of the Dryopithecus species called Proconsul Major. Vogel (1975) also argued that the available fragments were not sufficient to permit the classification of Ramapithecus as a hominid. There is then a further gap of some 10 m.y. to the first clearly identifiable hominid, Australopithecus.

The early anthropoid line, including Aegyptopithecus, has generally been identified with that leading to man. However, Pilbeam (1978) considered these early anthropoids to be already too specialized and too committed to their apedom to have produced the hominids. If Ramapithecus is not an early hominid, then origins of the human line may well be buried in the distant past.

The first identifiable hominid, Australopithecus, was described by Raymond Dart in 1925 as an infant man-ape found in a limestone cave in the Transvaal in South Africa (Leakey, 1981). Pilbeam (1978) observed that these hominids were small of stature (some 4'6"), probably bipedal tool users with a brain size of some 500 cm^3.

Simons (1969) pointed out that there is clear evidence of two strains, Australopithecus africanus and A. robustus, evident some 3.5 m.y. ago and this he said implies a long period of developmental history prior to that time. Further light has been shed on this particular aspect in an assessment of early African hominids by Johanson and White (1979) who examined evidence from the Laetolil and Hadar diggings. Laetolil is a little south of the now famous Olduvai Gorge in Northern Tanzania and Hadar is in Ethiopia. The authors pointed to the Hadar findings as "a remarkable collection of hominid specimens representing a minimum of 35 and a maximum of more than 65 individuals" (p. 321). These specimens have been dated at between 2.6 and 3.3 m.y. old. The specimens from Hadar and Laetolil have been characterized by Johanson and White as representing a distinctive early hominid showing "substantial sexual dimorphism and a host of primitive dental and cranial characteristics" (p. 325). The Laetolil specimens are some 0.5 m.y. older than those located at Hadar. They saw the ancestry of these hominids as lying within the Miocene radiation in Africa with Ramapithecus the most likely source. This new species they named Australopithecus afarensis.

Richard Leakey (1981), on the other hand, argued that the size differences observed in the Hadar collection represented not sexual dimorphism but two separate species co-existing. He considered the larger specimens to be representative of a primitive Homo and the small ones Australopithecus.

After considering these discoveries in relation to the rest of the African picture, Johanson and White argued, as had Simons (1969), for the development of at least two separate hominid lines during the African Pleistocene. One line, the robust Australopithicine, was characterized by a large and sturdy masticatory apparatus with heavy chewing musculature. This is characteristic of a herbivore and root eater. This lineage displayed no substantial tendency to expand cranial capacity, said Johanson and White, and this line became extinct. The other line, the gracile Australopithicines, have been referred to as the genus Homo. This group "lacks the specialization related to a heavily masticated diet but exhibits a definite tendency towards expansion of the brain" (p. 326). Ultimately this line, they claimed, culminated in Homo sapiens. Johanson and White place the Laetolil and Hadar Hominids before the separation of the robust and gracile hominid forms and conclude:

> The implications of the new material for understanding the mode and tempo of hominoid evolution are great. The apparent lack of morphological differences between fossils separated by at least 0.5 million years at Laetolil and Hadar suggests relative stasis in the earliest documented portions of hominid evolution. The dramatic morphological changes initiated between 2 and 3 million years ago suggest that this relative stasis was upset. Although the precise reasons for the phyletic divergence that led to A. robustus through the earlier intermediate A. africanus are not well understood, a South African origin for this stock is plausible. Whatever the case, the clear niche divergence between H. erectus and A. robustus about 1.5 million years ago indicated by the eastern African fossil record indicates that an increased evolutionary rate for the period between 2 and 3 million years ago may ultimately be shown by larger fossil samples (p. 329).

Prior to the Hadar and Laetolil discoveries, the Leakeys (Louis and Mary) had discovered remains of another erect primate in their diggings at Olduvai Gorge in Tanzania. This they named Homo habilis, the tool user (Leakey, Clarke, & Leakey, 1971). Their son Richard, in 1972 uncovered an almost complete habilis skull in Northern Kenya (Leakey, 1973). The Leakeys argued that Homo habilis was on the direct Homo line and distinct from Australopithecus africanus. These hominids, like Australopithecus, were small-brained with man-like teeth and skeletons, they were clearly upright bipeds and tool users. In fact Pilbeam (1978) considered them to be simply a geographically separate population of Australopithecus africanus. These species were extant some 1.5–2.5 m.y. ago.

About 500,000 years ago, i.e., in the middle Pleistocene, a more advanced hominid, Homo erectus, was in evidence. These people had larger brains than Australopithecus, rather less than 1000 cm³, but this was still substantially less than Homo sapiens. Homo erectus was apparently an efficient upright walker, used tools, was a capable hunter and used fire.

There is then, said Pilbeam, a gap until some 150,000 years ago with the appearance of the first true man, Homo sapiens, in the form of Neanderthal man. Their brains were as large as in modern man, i.e., some 1300 cm³ but their jaws, teeth, and faces were larger. They were replaced, over the final 50,000 years by Neolithic man.

An evolutionary tree for primates based on those presented by Jerison (1973, p. 366) and Radinsky (1975, p. 660) and taking into account suggestions from Simons is outlined in Figure 5.1.

COMPARATIVE STUDIES OF PRIMATE EVOLUTION

The work of Stephan, Bauchot, and Andy (1970) has provided a set of comparative studies that has added significantly to our understanding of the evolution of the primate brain. These authors carried out comparative volumetric analyses of the brains of living insectivores and primates.

The basis for their work was the view that "A fairly reliable and characteristic feature of directed progressive evolution is the concentration, enlargement and differentiation of the nervous system" (Stephan & Andy, 1969, p. 372). Their approach has been to examine changes in the relative size of discrete regions of the brain in various levels of primate species compared with a level established from what they designate as the "basal" insectivores. These specimens, which were comprised of tenrecs, hedgehogs, and shrews, were classed as basal because all of the so-called "progressive" structures were least developed and uniform. They considered these animals to be similar to the early forerunners of the placental mammals. Thus, they argued, these animals form a good base for evaluating evolutionary progress.

These monumental studies covered 63 different species with 22 insectivores (11 basal and 11 progressive); 20 prosimians, and 20 simians, and Homo sapiens. Separate volume estimates were made for 11 separate divisions of the brain, namely neocortex, paleocortex and amygdaloid complex, hippocampus, septum, striatum, schizocortex (entorhinal cortex and subiculum), olfactory bulbs, diencephalon, mesencephalon, cerebellum, and medulla oblongata. Brain weight/body weight ratios were established and "progression indices" calculated. These express how many times larger a given structure is than that of a basal insectivore of equal body weight.

The neocortex showed the most striking increase in progressiveness with the prosimian neocortex averaging 14.5 times and the simian 45.5 times that

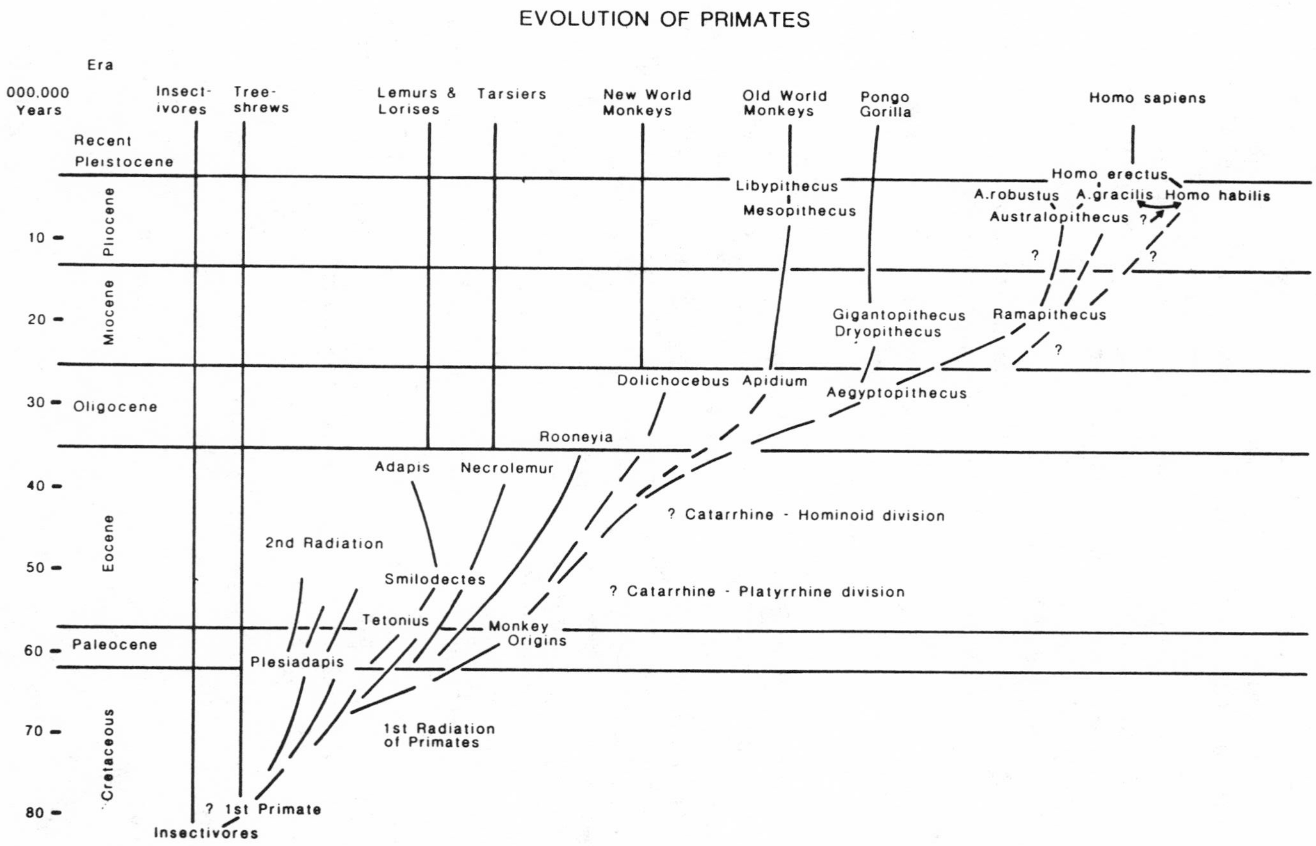

EVOLUTION OF PRIMATES

FIG. 5.1   A possible line of evolutionary development for primates.

80

of basal insectivores of equivalent weight. Homo yielded the immensely great difference of 156 times the neocortex of the basal insectivore equivalent. Stephan and Andy regarded this as representing the morphological substrate for the very high and complex functional capacity of man's central nervous system.

While the progression of other structures is much less than the neocortex, almost all of the other 10 brain systems showed substantial progressive increases. The second largest was the striatum with an average of 5 in prosimian and 9 in simian. Again Homo was substantially the highest with a value in excess of 16 times the expected value from basal insectivores. The only structures to show reduction were the olfactory bulbs with reduction of one-third to one-eighth of expected size for prosimians and simians and a value of less than one-fortieth for humans. Mesencephalon and medulla oblongata were, with few exceptions, larger than in the basal insectivores but did not show a clear trend to gradual enlargement as one ascended the primate scale.

In discussion of their concept of an ascending primate scale Stephan and Andy (1969) pointed out that:

> This scale of increasing neocorticalization represents a quantitatively well founded, so-called ascending primate scale. It does not, of course, represent any direct evolutionary line in which the respective higher forms have passed through the individual lower stages. However, it is very possible, and even likely, that one or other of the lower forms is similar to those stages which the higher forms have run through during phylogenesis (pp. 375–376).

An intriguing analysis of the Stephan et al. (1970) data was undertaken by Douglas and Marcellus (1975). They developed their technique on the argument that brains of closely related species are strikingly similar in overall proportions while those more distantly related are likely to show considerable differences. This, they believed, remains true even when other bodily features show either convergence or divergence. Thus they used brain parameters for taxonomic analysis.

For this analysis they converted the Stephan et al. volumetric data for the various brain structures in the 63 different species to encephalization ratios. This they did by forming a ratio of log volume of the particular structure with log volume of the medulla. These ratios were then analyzed in a multivariate analysis. They employed medulla volume rather than body weight after establishing correlations between these two measures, the lowest of which was .92. They then opted for medulla volume as being the more reliable measure in view of the many factors that can randomly influence body weight in any given specimen.

Having obtained these ratios, Douglas and Marcellus considered the ratios for a given brain region in all species as a set of points along one of the dimen-

sions of multidimensional "brain space." Each species was then seen to occupy a position in this space corresponding to the relative distribution of the
total mass to the various separate brain structures. A computer was employed to calculate the 1953 interspecific differences, which ranged from 050
which indicated a very close relationship to a "distance" of 1068 between the
most primitive and advanced species.

A factor analysis revealed two major factors. One, highly related to total
encephalization, they considered defined evolutionary level or grade; the second, called limbic, they considered to be more related to specialization within
an evolutionary grade. They then constructed family trees within each of the
three major classes, insectivores, prosimians and simians, connections being
based on distance values between species. Their assumption in constructing
such family trees was that, while sideways movement between species was legitimate, evolution never went backwards.

"Depending on the value system of the readers," said the authors,

> the distances and the family trees can be viewed in different ways. If the reader
> refuses to accept the validity of the comparative approach as applied to modern
> species, then the present data can be viewed as showing similarities or differ-
> ences between brains" (p. 180).

Their study of the insectivores revealed the probability of two distinct lineages, one leading in the tenrec-hedgehog direction and the other to the tree
shrew-primate pathway. Their conclusion, that the closest insectivores by far
to the primate line were the tree shrews, is consistent with evidence considered in the next chapter. This is true also of their conclusion that their evidence could not resolve what they called the tree shrew dilemma, i.e.,
whether the tree shrew is an advanced insectivore or an early primate, since
the shrew taxon was located about equidistant between Desmana and the
lower prosimians. The insectivore family tree, together with that for the prosimians and simians, is presented in Figure 5.2.

The prosimian analysis also yielded some very interesting relationships.
There appear to be two main lines. The first, the lemurs and lorises, the authors considered to represent the end result of progressive evolutionary
changes within the prosimian group. This view is consistent with Jerison's
evaluation of the Madagascar prosimian line.

The second group included the browsing prosimians and Tarsius. It is only
among this group that one can find a species even remotely related to Tarsius,
which is unique among prosimians. The output of prosimians, concluded
Douglas and Marcellus, had to be via the browsing prosimians and tarsiers,
first because there are no other candidates and more importantly because
Tarsius has a brain very similar to the marmosets, the most primitive of the
simians.

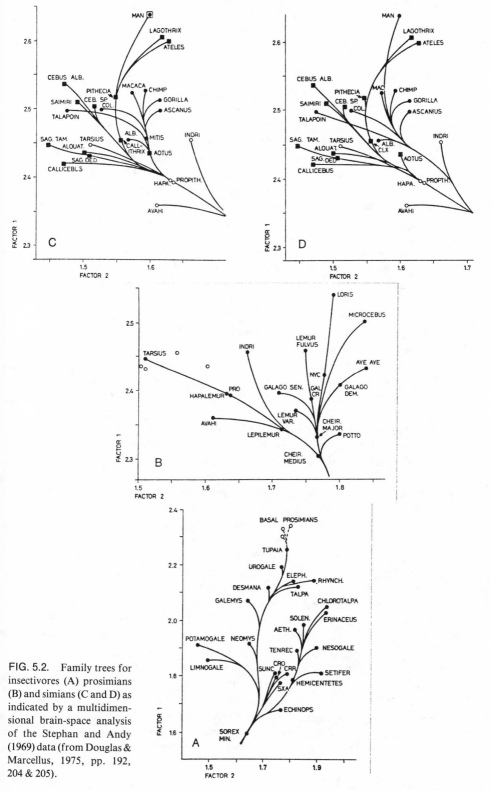

FIG. 5.2. Family trees for insectivores (A) prosimians (B) and simians (C and D) as indicated by a multidimensional brain-space analysis of the Stephan and Andy (1969) data (from Douglas & Marcellus, 1975, pp. 192, 204 & 205).

In their examination of the simians, Douglas and Marcellus argued the possibility that man evolved from a platyrrhine rather than a catarrhine ancestor or that all three lines evolved from some common prosimian ancestor. From their analysis they point out that the marmosets form the most primitive simian cluster, being located close to the tarsioids. Distances between the marmosets and some catarrhines (*Cercocebus albigena* and *Cercopithecus mitis*) are shorter than between marmosets and ceboids. Then follows *Macaca mulatta* and *Cercopithecus ascanius*, with both species having close connections with the "ape" subtaxon including chimpanzee and gorilla. There are, however, three platyrrhines closer to man than the nearest catarrhine (the rhesus monkey). This evidence, they said, suggests that man could well have originated from the platyrrhine line.

The authors then argue that all the earliest simians in the Eastern hemisphere had features characteristic of modern platyrrhines. For example, Simons concluded that both Apidium and Parapithecus had platyrrhine dental and other characteristics. In fact, said Douglas and Marcellus, while these two genera are claimed to be catarrhines, if they were living today and were located in Brazil they would be classed as platyrrhines. They then argued that "it is entirely possible that relatives of modern platyrrhines once had an almost worldwide distribution and that the modern American monkeys represent a conservative remnant of this once catholic group" (p. 207).

Further evidence for the possibility that man evolved from platyrrhine stock comes from Douglas and Marcellus's finding that a platyrrhine, *Aotus trivirgatus*, is clustered very closely with the primitive catarrhines *Cercocebus albigena* and *Cercopithecus mitis* referred to earlier, with Aotus being "truly like the primitive catarrhines in every respect" (p. 201). They then concluded that the catarrhines probably sprang from an animal with an Aotus-like brain. In fact, of the Oligocene monkeys, *Parapithecus* is much like the modern marmoset and Apidium closely resembles Aotus, more so in fact, said Gingerich (1973), than it resembles any modern catarrhine.

Yet a further possibility considered by Douglas and Marcellus is that the major divisions of catarrhine, platyrrhine, and hominoid evolved separately from an animal whose fossil remains would be called prosimian. They suggested Necrolemur and Rooneyia as possible candidates.

Summing up, this particular technique developed by Douglas and Marcellus has provided a method of analysis likely to be of considerable significance in the comparative analysis of the brains of living species. It has also served to underline the size and nature of the gaps that still exist in our attempts to plot the line of man's evolution through the primates.

While Stephan et al. considered the brain of more advanced primates in terms of what would be expected in a basal insectivore of comparable body weight, Passingham (1973, 1975) examined relative brain components of other primates in relation to human brain size. He noted that the volume of neocortex found in man does not differ significantly from that predicted for a nonhuman primate with the same total brain volume as man. However, he did demonstrate, from data derived from Shariff (1953) that, in primates from Tarsius to man, while the proportion of sensory or koneocortex does not change, there is a marked increase in both agranular and eulaminate cortex. Passingham pointed to Hebb's suggestion that the ratio of association cortex to sensory cortex might provide an index of brain development and observed that this indeed appears to have been confirmed.

In the light of Stephan et al.'s work and Passingham's further extension of it, Radinsky (1975) attacked an older notion, expressed particularly by Le Gros Clark (1971), that the most distinctive feature of primates is their tendency towards a brain large in proportion to body weight "and which is particularly characterized by a relatively extensive and often richly convoluted cortex." Radinsky concluded that "only one species of primate, *Homo sapiens* has a brain that exceeds that of all other mammals in relative size" (p. 661). Prosimians have only "average" brain-body ratios for mammals and anthropoids are matched by some carnivores and ungulates and by the cetaceans. The human brain is in fact distinguished only by its great relative size and this increase occurred quite recently. Radinsky concluded, "one of the fascinating unsolved problems in interpreting mammalian evolutionary history is discovering what selective presures were responsible for that recent and unique increase in the relative brain size of our ancestors" (p. 663). I therefore conclude this section with a brief look at Jerison's speculations on why this increase occurred.

ENLARGEMENT OF THE PRIMATE BRAIN

In his analysis of the enlargement of the primate and especially the hominid brain, Jerison pointed out that there are three significant gaps. The first such hiatus is between the prosimians and the monkeys. While temporal lobe expansion was evident in the early paleogene prosimians, evidence on the further course of expansion of both the temporal and frontal poles is lacking as there is a great void between the Paleocene and Eocene prosimians and the cercopithecoids first evident in Miocene. The second gap is occasioned by lack of specimens between monkey and ape while the third relates to the evolution of the hominid brain during the Pleistocene. The Laetolil and Hadar findings may have closed this gap marginally but until the relationship between Australopithecus and Homo habilis is resolved, even this is unclear. There is in fact a fourth major gap, emphasized by Simons, namely that relating to the emergence of the prosimians from the earliest placental mammals.

While most living prosimians are nocturnal, those in Madagascar, where they have been isolated from predators, have occupied both diurnal and noc-turnal niches usually assumed by the more advanced primates. This, Jerison believed, gave a clue to the adaptive zone of the early anthropoids. He saw them as a continuation of the lemuroid line with adaptation to diurnal tree living. The observed increase in brain size, i.e., about two to three times that of the prosimians, he believed reflected changing selection pressures from at least two different elements referred to earlier. These were the need for par-ticular and advanced visual processing to cope efficiently with an active diur-nal life in the trees and the pressures for survival in the presence of large-brained predators. The evidence from Rooneyia, which Jerison regarded as a transition form, showed, he said, that primates responded to selection pres-sures by brain enlargement with behavioral, rather than skeletal, adaptation.

Raczkowski (1975) has pointed out that the arboreal theory of Smith and Le Gros Clark accounts for the emergence of tree shrew-like morphology from the terrestrial insectivore. But, he said, neither of these authors believed that arboreal life in itself would convert an arboreal insectivore into a pri-mate. Raczkowski considered that increasing reliance on vision would pro-vide the key to such understanding. However, Jerison contended that the emergence of the hominid line, while dependent upon the newly developed visual capabilities, probably resulted from a quite different set of pressures.

The move of the prehominids out of the trees into an earthbound niche, probably savanna country like that occupied presently by the baboon, was seen as a key factor. Such animals, with a long history of brachiating, would find bipedal gait a possibility and this would provide a better view of grass-land. It would also free the hands for manipulation. Brachiating animals would already have hands adapted to the use of branches as tools and this could lead to the development of genuine tool using.

Krantz (1975) has in fact proposed a theory that encompasses the "double descent" of man. He began with Aegyptopithecus as a likely common ances-tor of monkeys and of apes including man. This animal had ape dentition but limb and tail configuration of a monkey. The world grassland environment became evident in the early Miocene. The first descent of the apes from the trees to the savanna, said Krantz, occurred at about this time, with the Mio-cene apes, Dryopithecus, Pliopithecus, and Ramapithecus, within the time span of 25 m.y. to 10 m.y. ago. They were, he believed, probably tailed, ter-restrial quadrupeds. These apes showed a number of both brachiating and quadrupedal characteristics in their skeletal remains. The era of these ground apes came to an end when they were dispossessed by a new wave of monkeys, the Cercopithecoids, that took to the ground in the Pliocene. The first identi-fiable ground-living true monkey was Mesopithecus, a member of the Colo-bines. The few apes that survived this invasion did so by taking to the forests on the edges of the savanna, one group in Asia and the other in Africa. This was then followed by parallel evolution in these two ape families. Like the forest monkeys before them, these apes then disappeared from the fossil record because of their forest habitat.

The Colobine descendants of Mesopithecus suffered the same fate as the earlier ground apes when, some 5 m.y. ago, they were overrun by a fresh wave of true monkeys–the Cercopithecines: the baboons and macaques, and these today continue as the dominant nonhuman primate group on the ground.

At about this time, argued Krantz, the African apes, already good brachiators, returned to the ground for the second time, this time with bipedal locomotion. Why this happened is open to dispute but may well have been due to rapid decline in forest areas. This group then gave rise to Australopithecus. Krantz's theory is shown diagrammatically in Figure 5.3.

This theory, he believed, would help to resolve the vast gap that had become evident between the conventional geological time dating of the hominoid-hominid fossil record, including potassium-argon dating, and the biochemical method of Wilson and Sarich (1969). The Wilson and Sarich method led to a man-ape separation of only 5 m.y. compared with a separation of at least 15–25 m.y. using conventional methods. According to Krantz's theory, the final separation, the second descent of the apes that led to man, would have occurred some 5 m.y. ago.

Jerison pointed out that we do not know enough about the transition from monkeys to apes to make valid evolutionary judgments about brain evolution at that stage. We can, however, pick up the story again with the Australopithicines.

Washburn (1951) recognized that different evolutionary characters may evolve at different rates and it is now generally accepted that the relatively small-brained Australopithicines had sufficient characteristics to warrant their definition as hominids. These characteristics, said Jerison, indicated that enlargement of the human brain followed the invasion of the hominid niche, i.e., enlargement of the brain was not necessary for the initial invasion of it. He pictured the early hominids as moderately large primates (20 kg or more) who lived in a niche similar to that occupied by living baboons, i.e., open savanna country, and with a brain that, by human standards, was quite small. Tools, haphazardly collected, would serve primarily for digging, hunting, and defense. A social organization would be essential for survival against predators.

The next event of major significance would appear to be the evolution of the carnivorous primate with the separation of Australopithecus robustus and A. gracilis. This division was referred to previously by Simons (1969) and more recently by Johanson and White (1979). While the fruit and root eating

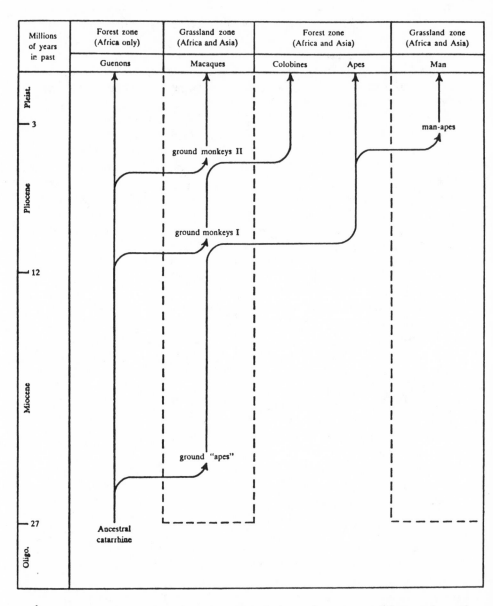

Millions of years in past	Forest zone (Africa only)	Grassland zone (Africa and Asia)	Forest zone (Africa and Asia)		Grassland zone (Africa and Asia)
	Guenons	Macaques	Colobines	Apes	Man

ground monkeys II

ground monkeys I

man-apes

ground "apes"

Ancestral catarrhine

Pleist.

Pliocene

Miocene

Oligo.

3

12

27

A   This evolutionary picture of the higher primates according to the author is drawn in such a way as to emphasize adaptative shifts between forests and grasslands. Only five major types of living primates are shown for the sake of simplicity. Both the forest and the grassland zones are shown twice to avoid lines of evolution crossing one another geographically, which in fact they did. Only in the African forests has there been an unbroken line of arboreal primate occupancy, and this has been the source of repeated invasions of the grasslands. Dates of separations in this scheme are closely comparable to those calculated by Sarich on quite different grounds

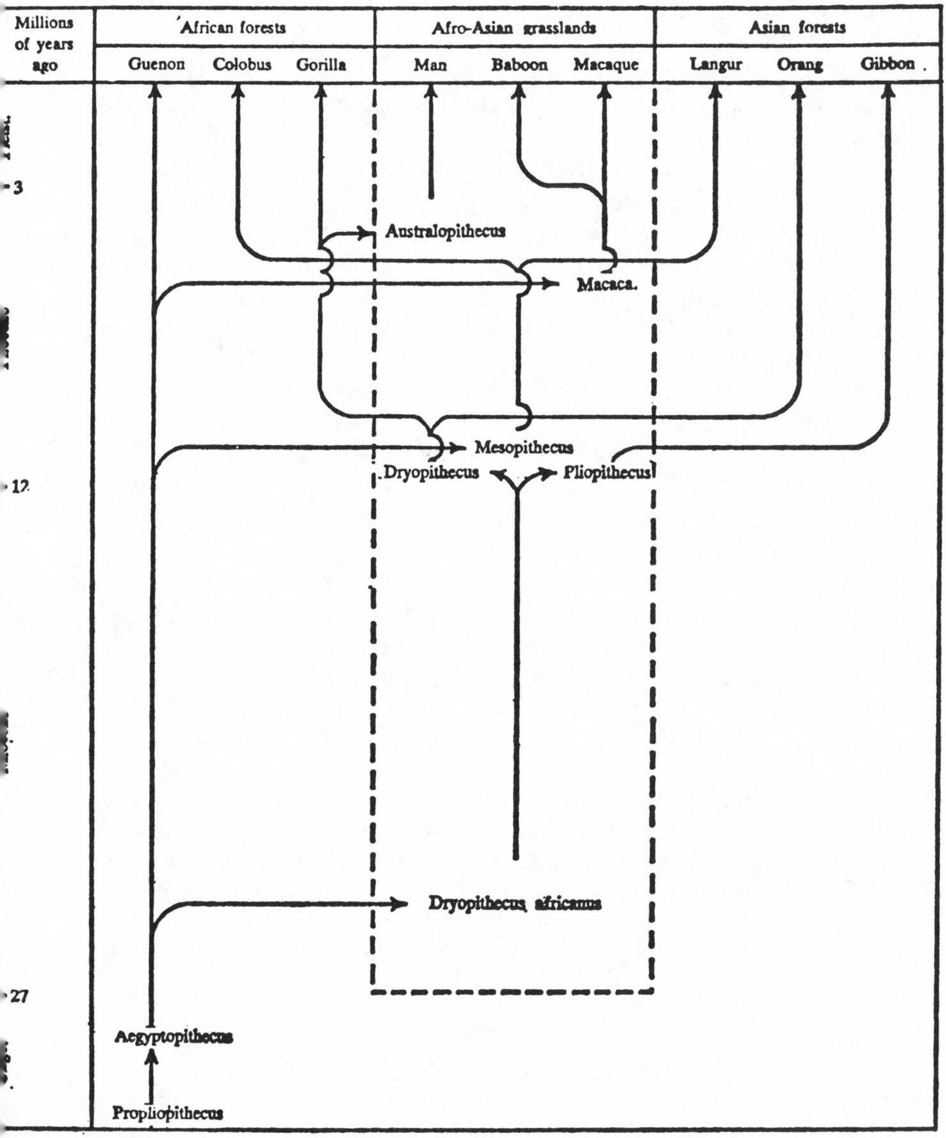

Millions of years ago
African forests
Afro-Asian grasslands
Asian forests
Guenon
Colobus
Gorilla
Man
Baboon
Macaque
Langur
Orang
Gibbon
3
Australopithecus
Macaca.
Mesopithecus
Dryopithecus
Pliopithecus
12
Dryopithecus africanus
27
Aegyptopithecus
Propliopithecus

B Primate evolution according to the author is drawn this time according actual geographical regions and includes more living and fossil types. This art has the drawback of several lines crossing one another on the African forest-assland boundary, but it also shows separations between African and Asian velopments, which were combined on the previous chart. The line of man's cestry can be followed from the African forests to the grasslands, back into the rests, and finally onto the grasslands again with man's second descent

FIG. 5.3. Krantz' theory of the double descent of man. (A) illustrates the theoretical descents from the trees to the grasslands. (B) illustrates this theoretical structure fitted to the fossil record of primate evolution (from Krantz, 1975, pp. 145–146).

A. robustus showed no tendency to expand cranial capacity and became extinct, the gracile hominid exhibited rapid expansion of the brain, and continued to evolve.

The carnivorous and predacious habit would, said Jerison, increase the use of tools. It would also lead to a much wider range and more thinly concentrated population. Social organization would be more for attack than defense. This would also result in a clearer advantage of auditory signaling systems and to visual and neural systems developed in relation to the scanning of broad vistas and retaining information about them.

The Australopithicines survived as a genus for some 4–5 m.y., i.e., it was a moderately long survival period and selection pressures during that time did not lead to the dramatic enlargement of the brain that is associated with true man. What, then, could have led to the final hominization of the brain over a short period of some 0.5–0.25 m.y. ago? Jerison argued that the key factor was rapid climatic change at this time with the onset of an ice age. Thus, during the Pleistocene, tribes on the periphery of geographic ranges faced this challenge. The increasing cold would require restriction of range and new adaptations for hunting and protection from the cold. This was associated with overcrowding. He saw communication as the key to these adaptive measures and associated this with brain enlargement. The potential was there in the broad ranging carnivorous ape-like hominid that had survived from Pliocene to mid-Pleistocene. Jerison then continued:

> The adaptation for social yet carnivorous habits in such a broad-ranging species, challenged by an environment in which there was seasonal narrowing of the range and need for an artificial climate (through fire and clothing) and artificial prey (through domestication or semi-domestication of some animals) were accomplished by brain evolution rather than skeletal evolution and resulted in the broad and flexible behavior repertoire of the human species (p. 424).

This change from Australopithecus to Homo was, said Jerison, probably the last significant organic change in man's brain as it evolved to its present status.

Apart from the comparative volumetric studies of primate brains by Stephan, Bauchot, and Andy, we have been concerned in this chapter with evidence on brain evolution that is provided by the fossil record. In the next chapter I explore evidence of changes in the organization and structure of the evolving brain as revealed by comparative studies of the neural tissue of living species.

6 The Vertebrate Nervous System in Comparative Perspective

While studies early in the century by anatomists such as Elliot-Smith, Herrick, and Johnston and culminating in the classic three-volume work of Ariens-Kappers, Huber, and Crosby in 1936 gave great initial impetus to the comparative analysis of the vertebrate brain, the current picture is still fragmentary with many gaps to be filled. Much detailed work on individual species has been and is progressing as attested by the volume of publications in such journals as the *Journal of Comparative Neurology* and *Brain Research*. What are generally lacking are integrative long term efforts to resolve particular evolutionary problems. As we note in this chapter, there are however some outstanding exceptions that have resulted in substantial advances in our knowledge of comparative neurology.

In the present analysis I consider changes that have been observed in the various brain structures from hindbrain to forebrain as we ascend from one phylum to the next along the path of human evolution, beginning with a brief consideration of hindbrain, midbrain, and diencephalic structures. My main concern, however, is with the changes in the telencephalon and its major divisions of basal ganglia, rhinencephalon, and neopallium.

BASAL STRUCTURES

The Brainstem

Ebbesson and Northcutt (1976) point out that a significant characteristic of the brain of the anamniotes, i.e., all the vertebrates below the reptiles, is the variation in the expansion of specific sensory areas with great expansion in some species and absence in others. They relate these changes to the adaptation of the particular species to its characteristic niche. Two examples they cite relate to the taste systems of teleost fishes. Species that sort food from mud taken into the mouth have an elaborate system of taste buds in mouth, palatal structures, and pharynx, the nerves of which terminate in greatly enlarged vagal lobes. In some of the carp, for example, the recurrent branch of the facial nerve has come to innervate large areas of head, body and fins, with termination in a huge facial lobe. A striking somatotopic organization has been revealed in this lobe. They also draw attention to a very great range of structural variation evident in the forebrain of the anamniotes.

Such wide diversification should not be at all surprising in view of the very long periods of separate evolutionary development. It is worthy of note that, in the mainstream leading to the mammals, i.e., the lampreys, the coelacanths and dipnoi, and the amphibia, the lower brainstem structures were not subject to such highly selective development of sensory receptive regions.

The Midbrain

In the roof of the midbrain or tectum are found centers for correlation of optic and interoceptive impulses. In the biologically older water dwelling vertebrates, tracts from the lateral line systems synapse in this mesencephalic region with other sensory inputs. With the movement to land, as observed in land dwelling amphibians, these lateral line centers have disappeared, being replaced by cochlear structures and the midbrain centers for correlation of auditory with other impulses appear. Various theories of how these changes came about have been proposed and are considered in reviews by Wever (1976) and Stebbins (1976).

In all submammalian vertebrates these tectal and subtectal centers of the mesencephalon form the main terminal centers for the ascending sensory pathways with some projection to thalamic nuclei (Ebbesson & Northcutt, 1976). With the increasing development of the thalamus and cortex, tectothalamic pathways of increasing complexity develop and, in the mammals, the auditory centers become clearly tectal in location forming the inferior colliculi.

In mammals, while the tectal pathways remain, the cortical sensory tracts increase in size and importance. The tectal fibers remain small, a fact which Diamond and Hall (1969) saw as pointing to the earlier phyletic origin of this system. Much larger fibers, allowing for more rapid transmission, are evident in the thalamocortical system. Bishop (1959) noted that small fibers in the visual and auditory systems project to the phylogenetically older midbrain system while the large fiber tracts bypass these centers and go directly to the dorsal thalamus and thence to the neocortex.

Much of the ventral midbrain is occupied by the large ascending and descending fiber tracts. Medially the midbrain reticular system is present in all vertebrates, with scattered groups of cells in the lower phyla becoming more and more organized into compact nuclear masses in the more recently evolved species.

The Diencephalon

In almost all vertebrates the diencephalon is divisible into four major regions, epithalamus, dorsal thalamus, subthalamus, and hypothalamus. These are thus phylogenetically old though Ebbesson and Northcutt (1976) point out that, in most of the anamniotes, the nuclear boundaries are poorly defined.

The epithalamus contains the habenular nuclei, which are olfactory-somatic correlation centers. According to Ariens-Kappers et al. (1960) this is the least variable of the four regions, remaining much the same in structure from cyclostome to man.

On the other hand, the thalamus, which is the major receptor system of the diencephalon, has undergone considerable development, firstly with the evolution of the ascending sensory pathways and the tectum in submammalian forms and, in mammals, with the evolution of the neocortex. The evolution of neocortex is intimately connected with that of the thalamus so changes in the thalamus are considered in more detail when I examine the evolutionary changes in the neocortex.

Underlying the thalamus, at the base of the diencephalon, the hypothalamus exhibits one peak in evolutionary development in the teleosts or bony fish, where it is a major center for visceral integration. In the amphibia it is quite a small structure that then appears to have undergone a period of active evolutionary development through the reptiles and mammals where it has become a key structure in the maintenance of a stable internal environment through regulation of internal bodily processes. It forms the head ganglion for regulation of the autonomic nervous system and, through the hypophysis it regulates hormone activity. The hypothalamus is also a central structure for the mediation of motivational and "reward" and "punishment" responses. The organization and functioning of this region in mammals will receive detailed consideration in a later work.

The Telencephalon

The forebrain structure showing the greatest development through vertebrate and particularly through mammalian evolution is the telencephalon and, in particular, the cerebral hemispheres and the neocortex. In examining the evolutionary development of this region I follow Ariens-Kappers et al.'s (1960) format and first consider the submammalian telencephalon followed by the mammalian telencephalon excluding the neocortex. I then examine the evolution of the neocortex and the related thalamus in mammals in the next chapter.

THE SUBMAMMALIAN TELENCEPHALON

There is great morphological variation in the anamniote telencephalon. Ebbesson and Northcutt (1976) point out, too, that there is now striking evidence that contradicts the older view that the olfactory apparatus completely dominates the telencephalon in these animals. Relatively large regions are involved in visual processing and other senses are almost certainly included as well.

In the most primitive vertebrates the telencephalon consists of a single tube directly continuous with the diencephalon and contains a single ventricular space. This is the telencephalon medium. Evolutionary changes saw the appearance of a paired telencephalon with paired lateral ventricles. This process is first evidenced with the appearance of paired olfactory bulbs in the agnatha. Then, with changes in the lateral wall structure, the paired cerebral hemispheres appear and the central telencephalon or "telencephalon medium" is reduced as seen in the amphibia.

There is a significant difference in the embryonic development of the telencephalon in the actinopterygian or ray fin fish and all other anamniotes. This is referred to by Ariens-Kappers et al. (1960) and is again underlined by Ebbesson and Northcutt (1976). In the actinopterygia the hemispheres develop by a process of eversion. In the remaining anamniotes including the crossopterygia and amphibians they are formed by a process of evagination. This is shown in Figure 6.1.

This further emphasizes the early separation of the ray fin fish and the lobe fin fish. The latter gave rise to the amphibia while the Actinopterygia or ray fin fish diverged and exhibited a distinctive pattern of brain evolution. My interest centers on the main line leading to mammalian evolution, i.e., the lobe fin fish.

Ariens-Kappers et al. (1960) described the basic organization of the primitive forebrain in the following terms. In the lateral wall two major divisions may be differentiated, an upper dorso-lateral region that forms the primitive pallium or roof and a lower ventro-lateral division, the precursor of the striatum. This latter region thickens into a large spheroid structure while the pallial region extends over it.

The pallium, from which the cortex of higher vertebrates evolved, has three major divisions, the primordial paleopallium precursor to the olfactory

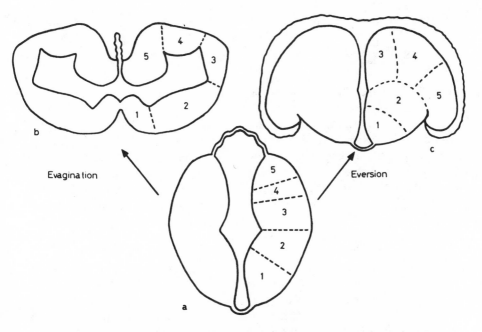

FIG. 6.1.   Hypothetical representation of how the fundamental subdivisions of the embryonic telencephalon (a) might be preserved after evagination (b) as in the amphibian or after eversion (c) as in the teleost. 1, septal region; 2, striatum; 3, pyriform lobe; 4, general cortex; 5, hippocampal region (from Scalia & Ebbesson, 1971, p. 379).

or piriform cortex lying ventrolateral, the primordial neopallium, dorsolateral, and the primordial archipallium, precursor of the hippocampus, located in the dorsomedial sector. A discussion of significant features within each major class follows.

The Chordata encompass all those animals that have a notochord or dorsal column that supports a dorsal nerve cord. In the most primitive of the living chordates, the Urochorda, of which the Ascidians or sea squirts are representative and the Hemichorda, wormlike creatures including Balanoglossus, the notochord is rudimentary or seen only in larval stages. Even the classification of these animals as chordates is not certain.

In the remaining chordates a notochord extending throughout the greater part of the dorsal axis is present throughout life or is transformed into a backbone or vertebral column. There is also a dorsal nerve column with an internal canal. These chordates are divided on the basis of possession of a skull or cranium into Acrania and Craniata.

The Acrania or lancelet fish, of which *Amphioxus lanceolatus* is the best known representative, are a group of small water dwelling animals with a single primary brain vesicle and no distinct head region.

The remaining vertebrates are Craniates, all having a skull and a complex brain. Again these are subdivided into the *Agnatha* or jawless fishes, including the lampreys and hag fish and the *Gnathostomata* or vertebrates with jaws.

The Agnatha (or jawless fish).   In these animals, the Cyclostomes, the basic structure of the vertebrate brain is clearly established with well-defined forebrain, midbrain, and hindbrain. The telencephalon is dominated by the olfactory bulbs and lateral olfactory area. The primordial hippocampus is located in the dorsomedial portion of the undivided telencephalon medium (Ariens-Kappers et al., 1960; Crosby, DeJonge, & Schneider, 1966) with a ventrally placed structure that appears to be homologous with the striatum of higher forms. Ariens-Kappers et al. noted that this is the first appearance of somatic correlation centers within the telencephalon and these centres, throughout subsequent phylogeny, are to exert an enormous influence on forebrain evolution.

The Gnathostomata comprise all the remaining vertebrate groups beginning with the true fish or *Pisces*. Under this heading come:

A. *The Elasmobranchii or Chondrichthyes.* This group includes the sharks, skates, rays, and ratfish. These animals, all water dwelling, have a skeleton of cartilage. It is likely that the sharks and rays diverged very early from the mammalian line of evolution and that they have undergone considerable parallel evolution of the brain (see Chapter 3) so they do not receive further consideration here.

B. *The Osteichthyes or bony fish.* Hotton (1976) noted that from early Devonian, the bony fish were comprised of two subclasses. These were the Actinopterygii or ray fin fish that eventually diversified to dominate the seas and the lobefin fish or Sarcopterygii that were dominant initially but were then largely surpassed by the number and diversity of the ray fins. The ray fin fish demonstrate a specialized structure divergent from the main line of vertebrate evolution and are not considered further. The Sarcopterygii however are believed to be ancestral to the amphibia. Living specimens include Latimeria and the lung fish.

From an examination of the African lungfish, Protopterus, Schnitzlein (1966) concluded that, while living Dipnoi could no longer be regarded as direct ancestors of amphibians, the telencephalon of *Protopterus* has not undergone the extensive changes characteristic of those of most fish. He noted that the large lateral ventricles typical of the higher vertebrates, but lacking in the bony fish may be observed in the African lungfish. He concluded that the homologies between the nuclei and tracts of the telencephalon of the lungfish and comparable regions of the amphibians and the reptiles are more easily established than with similar areas of the teleosts.

The Amphibia.   In these, the earliest of the land dwelling vertebrates, we can observe a generalized structure that would seem to exemplify the fundamental plan of the higher vertebrates. Evagination of the frontal lobes is clearly established with most of the telencephalic structures present in the hemispheres and the telencephalon medium accordingly much reduced.

The primordial hippocampus or archipallium occupies the dorsomedial portion of the wall of the cerebral hemisphere and is characterized by a further spread of cells towards the surface of the mantle. Hoffman (1966) distinguished three distinct cellular configurations in the primordial hippocampus in urodeles or tailless amphibia. The dorsal para-hippocampal area he identified with the subiculum. The central area, readily observed at all levels of the hemisphere, he related to the hippocampus proper or Ammon's horn. This structure merges caudally with the primordial piriform area and anteriorly with the amygdaloid complex. The most ventral of the three regions, an area of densely packed clusters of smaller cells, he identified with the dentate gyrus. These relationships are shown in Figure 6.2. Here then there is already a clear differentiation between the three major divisions of the hippocampal formation, namely subiculum, Ammon's horn, and dentate gyrus.

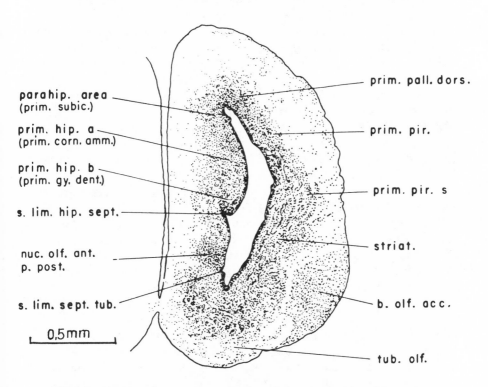

FIG. 6.2.   Drawing of a transverse section through the rostral portion of the accessory olfactory bulb of an anuran. The three cellular groups (parahip. area, prim. hip. a, and prim. hip. b) are apparent in the primordial hippocampal formation (from Hoffman, 1966, p. 64).

The primordial neopallium is located in the dorsal convexity of the hemisphere extending to the caudal pole with the archipallium or hippocampal region above and the piriform lobe, below. The neopallial region is characterized by small neurons with bifurcating axons, one branch of which goes dorsally to the hippocampal area and the other to the more ventral piriform region.

The paleopallium or piriform lobe, while lying below the neopallium still has a dorsolateral location. More ventrally are to be found the striatum and amygdala with the septum in the ventromedial region.

Olfactory pathways dominate the forebrain system in amphibia with primary olfactory tracts to primordial piriform, hippocampal, and dorsal pallial regions and to some amygdaloid structures. Some fibers also reach the septal area. In addition to these primary pathways there are large bundles of secondary and tertiary fibers. Fibers originating largely in the medial olfactory nucleus go primarily to the piriform region and to a lesser extent to the dorsal pallium, septum, and amygdala. Tertiary and higher order connections between the striatum and various forebrain structures are also present. Striato-pallial connections relating the dorsal part of the striatum with the primordial pallium were considered by Ariens-Kappers et al. (1960) to be of particular significance as they furnished pathways important for further pallial development. Another important bundle is that connecting striatum and amygdala. There is also a well developed septal-hippocampal pathway, part of which establishes the beginnings of the alveus or surface layer of fibers of the hippocampus. A pathway from the primordial hippocampus to the medial septal area has also been distinguished.

The stria medullaris, a phylogenetically very old pathway with fibers from the paleopallium and dorsopallium, connects the forebrain system with the habenula. Fibers from the amygdala reach the stria medullaris via the stria terminalis while fibers from hippocampus and septum enter via a separate septo-habenula tract.

The medial forebrain bundle connects the ventrolateral hemisphere structures with the hypothalamus, and lower brainstem. This forms an important link between olfactory, visceral, and gustatory impulses. Part of this bundle is a tract connecting with the striatum. The striatum thus constitutes a major coordination center in this animal.

Ariens-Kappers et al. (1960) summarized the evolutionary development of the amphibian telencephalon in the following terms:

The pallial areas have undergone considerable differentiation as compared with those of cyclostomes and plagiostomes and are completely evaginated into the hemisphere wall. A new pallial area has appeared in amphibians, the primordium palliidorsalis, but no true cortex has differentiated and none of these fields are removed from olfactory influences, although non-olfactory impulses are begining to reach the pallium. The basal olfactory areas have increased in nuclear differentiation and show greater specificity of fiber connections. A more or less clearly differentiated amygdaloid complex (archistriatum) is present with its characteristic fiber connections, and the other striatal areas occur in the capacity both of receptive centers for ascending thalamo-frontal fibers and of efferent cells of origin for fibers of the lateral forebrain bundle (p. 1311).

The Reptiles.   Riss, Halpern, and Scalia (1969) claimed that a thorough understanding of the reptile brain would provide the key to reconstruction of mammalian forebrain evolution. These authors pointed out that, among living reptiles, the Crocodilia are believed to be most closely related to the reptilian stem from which birds evolved and that the fossil record indicates little change in these reptiles since late Triassic times. These animals might therefore give some idea of the characteristic brain structure of both the dinosaurs and birds. An even earlier reptile exists in the form of turtles, with fossil evidence for ancestors of these animals being traced to the Permian period. These ancesteral turtles were relatives of the stem reptiles thought to give rise to mammals. Pritchard (1967) considered that the genus Protocnemas has changed little since the Cretaceous period some 140 million years ago.

On the other hand Hopson (1969) argued that the synapsid reptiles that gave rise to the mammals separated from the main reptilian line very soon after the reptiles themselves evolved as a class. He then traced the course of mammalian emergence from synapsids to therapsids to cynodonts. He commented that "only within recent years have we learned enough about them (the cynodonts) and about the very early mammals to say with confidence that all mammals are indeed descended from a single group of cynodonts" (p. 207). Hopson's conclusion that "many of the features characteristic of living reptiles were never present in the early reptilian ancestors of mammals and therefore that modern reptiles cannot be considered to represent an "evolutionary stage preceding mammals" (p. 200) is of particular significance for my own line of development of this topic.

In reptiles the telencephalon shows greater structural differentiation and marked relative increase in size compared with earlier animals. All orders show an inverted type of telencephalon with a highly developed striatal complex, this development being in the direction observed in avian forms.

A general cortex makes its first appearance in reptiles, the bandlike structure characterizing this new cortex being represented in all three cortical areas, i.e., hippocampal, piriform, and neocortical. This is exemplified in Figure 6.3.

Aves.   In birds there is a further marked deviation from the mainstream of evolutionary development. In most birds the olfactory system is reduced and there is little development of neocortex, this frequently being present only as a thin corticoid band. On the other hand the striatal areas are vastly

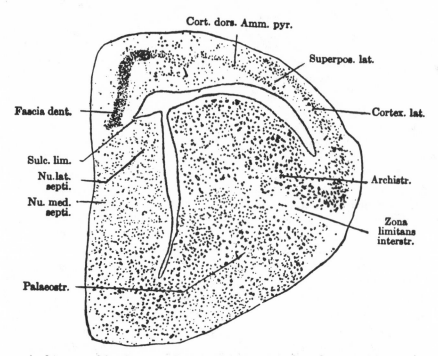

Cort. dors. Amm. pyr.

Superpos. lat.

Fascia dent.

Cortex. lat.

Sulc. lim.
Nu.lat.
septi.
Nu. med.
septi.

Archistr.

Zona
limitans
interstr.

Palaeostr.

Archistr., archistriatum; *Cort.dors.Amm.pyr.*, dorsal cortex (*Ammon's* pyramidal cells); *Cortex lat.*, lateral cortex; *Fascia dent.*, fascia dentata; *Nu.lat.septi*, nucleus lateralis septi; *Nu.med.septi*, nucleus medialis septi; *Palaeostr.*, paleostriatum; *Sulc.lim.*, sulcus limitans; *Superpos.lat.*, superpositio lateralis; *Zona limitans interstr.*, zona limitans interstriata.

FIG. 6.3.　The forebrain of the lizard *Lacerta agilis* showing a generalized cortex (from Ariens-Kappers, Huber & Crosby, 1960, p. 1317).

increased, this going hand in hand with the development of the dorsal thalamus and the collicular systems with dominance of the visual sense.

THE MAMMALIAN TELENCEPHALON

While the avian telencephalon shows marked resemblance to the more specialized reptiles, the mammalian telencephalon may be compared more readily to the lower and more generalized type of reptile represented by the living turtles. However, even in the lowest living mammals, it is clearly distinguishable from that of reptiles through the tremendous development of the neocortex. Evolutionary development in mammals is characterized by the increasing size and differentiation of the neocortex and the development of the corpus callosum.

The neocortex, developing between the paleocortex and the archicortex, exerted pressure on both these regions so that the paleocortex was pushed in a ventral direction while the lateral edge of the archicortex or hippocampus was lifted up and rolled in on the medial side of the hemisphere. This rolling in of the archicortex around the hippocampal fissure produced the typical form which led to its name of Ammon's Formation or Ammon's Horn, i.e., resembling a ram's horns. Along the undersurface, the neocortex bulges out on all sides of the olfactory lobe forming the limiting fissure.

In examining the comparative development of the mammalian telencephalon I first consider the subcortical structures in this chapter with a separate chapter devoted to the mammalian cortex.

Subcortical Structures of the Mammalian Telencephalon

The *septal nuclei* in mammals include the basal grey matter from the region in front of the anterior commissure and back between the overlapping hippocampal areas. With the development of the corpus callosum there is a drawing out of the more caudal septal nuclei forming the septum pellucidum. Johnston, in his famous 1913 paper, saw the hippocampus as an evolutionary extension of the lateral septal area but more recent views favor the concept of separate evolutionary origins of these structures (Ariens-Kappers et al., 1960). Crosby et al. (1966) described quite separate septal and hippocampal structures from cyclostomes to man with broadly similar structural organization. Hoffman (1966) in his examination of the anuran limbic formation noted that the precommissural septum is a prominent feature. He observed a clear separation between septum and primordial hippocampal formation by the hippocamposeptal limiting sulcus and a relatively cell free zone. He pointed out that "The anterior continuation of the hippocampus terminates in a nuclear mass which is the septohippocampal nucleus of the present terminology but which probably falls within the primordium hippocampi of Johnston (1913)" (Hoffman, 1966, p. 67).

As already indicated, a primitive septum was evident early in vertebrate evolution with differentiation of its nuclei at this early stage and the structure has remained essentially the same throughout subsequent phylogeny. Particular interest has attached to the evolution of the septum in primates and much of our knowledge of changes in the structure from insectivores to man comes from the comparative studies of Andy and Stephan.

These authors point out that, while it had been held earlier that the septum atrophied in both structure and function in primates and man, their work has indicated that the septum undergoes progressive increase with its greatest degree of development in the human brain (Andy & Stephan, 1966a, 1976). One of the bases for the view that the septum atrophied in primates was the belief that it was an olfactory structure and that, with the decline in olfactory func-

tion in primates, septal decline would follow. Another factor was the observed change in structure from a plump, round formation in more primitive
forms to a narrow, elongated structure in the higher primates (Andy &
Stephan, 1966a). This is evident in Figure 6.4.

In a series of studies of the septal nuclei of primates, using primitive insectivores as the basal group, Andy and Stephan have shown that, when taken as
a proportion of both whole brain and forebrain weights, there has been a decline in the proportion of the brain occupied by the septum as one moves
through the various species from basal insectivores to advanced insectivores,
through prosimians and simians to apes and humans. There has, however,
still been a dramatic increase in the septal to body weight ratio (Andy &
Stephan, 1976). These comparisons are shown in Figure 6.5.

They further observed that, in prosimians, the total septum is some 2.9
times larger than in the basal insectivores while in man there is a fourfold increase in size. Thus, while the septum has been overshadowed and outpaced
by the very rapid development of the neocortex in primates, in absolute terms
it has continued to enlarge. Furthermore, practically all of the septal nuclei
have exhibited this increase. Only the nucleus septalis triangularis shows re-

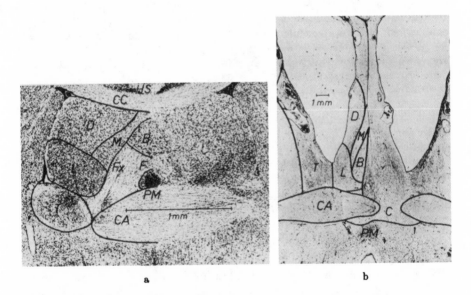

a   b

FIG. 6.4.   Frontal view of the septum in (a) an insectivore: *Sorex araneus* and (b) human. B, diagonal band of BROCA; C, bed nucleus of the anterior commissure; CA,
commissura anterior; CC, corpus callosum; D, nucleus septalis dorsalis; F, nucleus
septalis fimbrialis; Fx, fornix; HS, hippocampus, pars supracommissuralis; L, nucleus
septalis lateralis; M, nucleus septalis medialis; PM, nucleus preopticus medianus; T,
bednucleus of the stria terminalis. (from Andy & Stephan, 1966, p. 391).

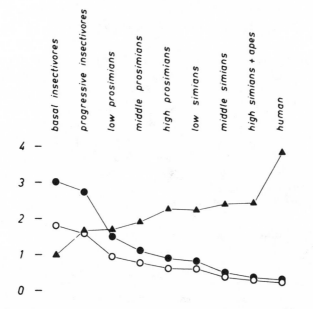

Comparison of the size of the septum at ascending levels of the primate scale by two different methods. The numbers on the left side indicate the percentage proportion of the septum related to the total brain (open circles) and telencephalon (solid circles). The same numbers represent progression indices for the septum in relation to body weight (triangles). These indices determine the enlargement multiple of the septum in the progressive group in comparison to that in basal insectivores (the latter have the index = 1).

FIG. 6.5.   Progressive changes in size of the septum from basal insectivore to human using two different methods of assessment (from Andy & Stephan, 1976, p. 4).

duction while the nucleus of the anterior commissure remains unchanged (Andy & Stephan, 1966b).

Andy and Stephan (1976) showed that the septal nuclei may be divided into four major groups, including not just the medial and lateral septal nuclei of the older subdivisions but also the dorsal and caudal components.

The septal system may, in fact, be regarded as a forward extension of the diencephalic structures of hypothalamus and preoptic nuclei. Thus this system is (1) A basal center concerned in the correlation of olfactory impulses with ascending visceral or hypothalamic impulses and their discharge to hippocampus and habenula. Here the connections from amygdala and piriform cortex are of relevance. (2) An important way-station between the overhanging hippocampal region and the preoptic and hypothalamic nuclei. In this the medial forebrain bundle is a dominant pathway.

The Amygdala. This structure has been identified in all vertebrates including the cyclostomes or agnathans where it is observed as a small, undifferentiated mass of cells (Crosby et al., 1966). In both fish and amphibia basolateral and corticomedial groups of nuclei have been identified. The corticomedial region, consisting of the medial and cortical nuclei and nucleus of the lateral olfactory tract, is linked with olfactory input and is recognized as the older structure phylogenetically. The basolateral group, comprised of basal, lateral and basal accessory nuclei, is considered to be a more recently evolved region separating from the primitive corticomedial amygdaloid structure. The basolateral nuclei may be interconnected with both the hippocampal formation and cortical systems through the hippocampal gyrus (Crosby, Humphrey, & Lauer, 1962). Direct pathways have also been demonstrated between the basal amygdala and anterior cingulate cortex at least in the monkey (Pandya, Van Hoesen, & Domesick, 1973) and between the basolateral, lateral, and anterior cortical nuclei of the amygdala and discrete areas of the cerebral cortex in rat and cat (Krettek & Price, 1977); and dog (Kosmal, 1976). These cortical areas are all outside the primary sensory and motor areas and, according to Krettek and Price, "may represent a stage of cortical development intermediate between that of the more primitive olfactory cortex and that of the neocortex" (p. 717). In the higher mammals the basolateral complex overshadows the corticomedial group. The organization of the amygdaloid nuclei in an Australian marsupial (*Setonix brachyurus*) is shown in Figure 6.6.

In evolutionary development both the position of the amygdala within the temporal lobe region and its orientation have varied systematically with increasing neocortical development and changing size of the component nuclei (Johnston, 1923; Crosby & Humphrey, 1944). As well there has been some increase in the clarity of demarcation between nuclei. These changes have been presented, in some detail, by Stephan and Andy (1977) in their study of the changing amygdala from insectivore, through prosimian and simian species to man.

The changing location of the amygdala and of its parts appears to have involved two separate components. In basal insectivores the external surfaces of the medial and cortical nuclear groups form the ventral surface of the posterior piriform lobe and they are oriented in a horizontal plane.

FIG. 6.6. (*facing page*)   Organization of the amygdaloid nuclei in the quokka (an Australian marsupial *Setonix brachyurus*) seen in coronal section through the line shown in the inset. The identified nuclei are the medial (AM) and cortical (ACo) of the corticomedial group and the basal (AB) and lateral (AL) of the baso-lateral group. (Figure prepared by P. N. Meyer.)

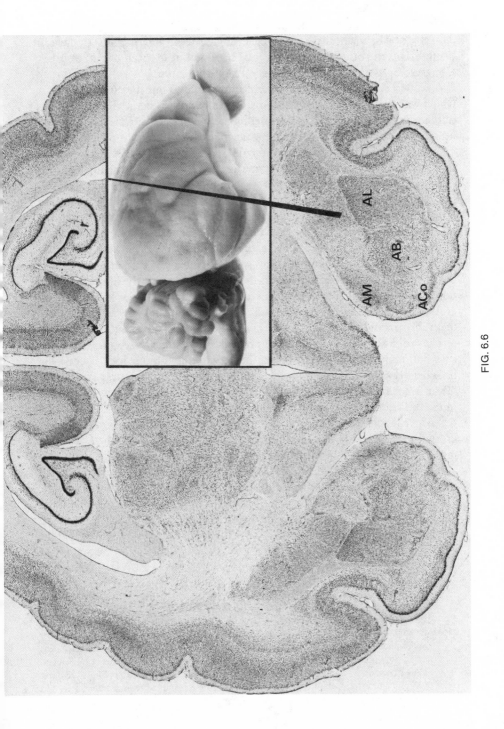

FIG. 6.6

The first component of change is a rotation resulting in a change in the border relations between the main nuclear components. The cortical nucleus is behind the centromedial group in lower forms but is rotated so that it lies alongside or even rostral to the medial nucleus in man.

A second rotation is around a longitudinal axis. Thus the cortical nucleus which was originally on the ventral surface lateral to the medial nucleus, is pushed ventrally and then ventromedial to the medial nucleus. Crosby and Humphrey (1944) recorded a total rotation of 140° from shrew to human.

In terms of relative size of the amygdala, Stephan and Andy (1977) found that the structure undergoes a dramatic reduction in proportion of total brain size from insectivores, where it constitutes some 3.7% of the total, through prosimians (1.4%) and simians (1.0%) to man where it accounts for only 0.25% of the total brain. This type of comparison would, they said, lead one to conclude that the amygdala undergoes reduction during primate evolution, but other comparisons indicate that this is not so. Rather, the changing proportions reflect the tremendous enlargement of other brain parts and particularly of the neocortex. In contrast, by comparing the amygdala with body weight, using an allometric formula similar to that employed by Jerison, they concluded that it in fact undergoes distinct progressive enlargement throughout the phylogenetic range they were examining.

They then set out to consider the progressive changes in separate nuclei as they had for the septum. However, they could only clearly identify borderlines between two groups of nuclei throughout the primate series. These were (1) an anterior, central, and medial nuclear complex and (2) a lateral, basolateral and cortical nuclear group. It was, they said, not feasible to separate the cortical nucleus from the basolateral group. While the centromedial group of nuclei declined in proportion to the total amygdala, the allometric index indicated no change in proportion from insectivore to man. However, the nucleus of the lateral olfactory tract, which was part of this complex, did undergo a sharp reduction from 8.2% of the centromedial group in insectivores to about zero in simians and man. As is evident from the above, the cortico-basolateral group shows progressive enlargement from 56% of the total amygdala in insectivores to 76% in simians to 81% in humans. This study then provides valuable information on size variation in the amygdala throughout the primate series.

FIG. 6.7 (facing page)   The structure of the corpus striatum as seen in sagittal section through the rat brain prepared for the demonstration of AChE. Also displayed is the dorsal hippocampus. Identified nuclei of the corpus striatum are the caudate-putamen (CPu) and globus palidus (GP). Labelled structures of the hippocampus are the CA1, CA2 and CA3 divisions of Ammon's Horn, the dentate gyrus (DG), the subiculum (SuB) and presubiculum (PrS). (Figure prepared by P. N. Meyer, adapted from Paxiovos, G. and Watson, J: The rat brain in stereotaxic coordinates Academic Press, 1982.)

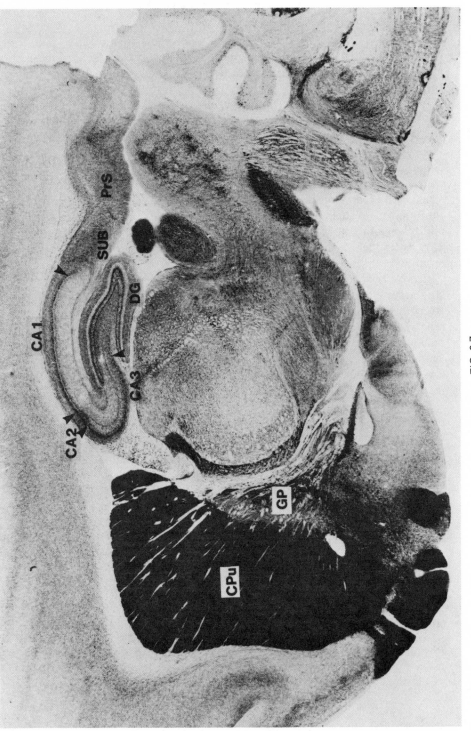

FIG. 6.7

107

The Corpus Striatum.   Deep within the hemisphere are a group of nuclei that are also known as the basal ganglia. They comprise the caudate nucleus and two other structures, the putamen and globus pallidus which, together, form the lentiform nucleus.

As with the hippocampus and amygdala, this structure is clearly represented in the agnatha, and development and differentiation is evident throughout the ascending phyla. Two distinct zones, an older, more primitive paleostriatum linked with the olfactory system and a neostriatum that connects with the dorsal thalamus are clearly discernible in the lungfish and anurans (Crosby et al., 1966). The neostriatum lies dorsal to the paleostriatum. In mammals the main mass of the caudate nucleus, together with the putamen, are believed to be derived from the neostriatum of earlier forms while the globus pallidus and part of the caudate are from the paleostriatum (Ariens-Kappers et al., 1960; Crosby et al., 1966). The structure of the corpus striatum in the rat is shown in Figure 6.7.

Crosby et al. (1962) described primitive forebrain afferent and efferent striatal systems that are evident from cyclostomes to man. Ascending sensory fibers to dorsal thalamus and to hypothalamus relay through the receptive striatal field to the forerunner of the globus pallidus. From the globus pallidus efferent bundles descend through the interpenduncular nuclei of ventral thalamus and midbrain. This system interconnects with the cerebellum for coordination of muscle tonus and movement associated with the maintenance by the animal of its normal resting or active position.

With the evolution of the cortex there has been superimposed over these primitive connections a massive system of cortical pathways. Associated with this has been a corresponding enlargement and differentiation of thalamus, cerebellum, and basal nuclei in the mammals.

Crosby et al. (1962) when considering these phylogenetic relations, speculated that the primitive neuronal circuits are significant for satisfactory function in the young human infant and that

> normal discharge of the thalamus through the striatum to hypothalamic centers appears to be dependent, at these ages, on the reception by the thalamus of such sensations as warmth and pressure resulting from being held by the mother, as well as from the pleasurable sensations resulting from eating (p. 380).

For a more detailed examination of comparative studies of the corpus striatum of species ranging from amphibian to mammal, the reader might consult Divac and Oberg's (1979) work *"The Neostriatum."*

7 The Evolution of the Mammalian Cortex

A cortex or layer of grey matter comprised of cells and fibers on the surface of the cerebral hemispheres first appeared in the reptiles and represented all three cortical divisions, i.e., hippocampal, piriform, and neocortical. It is in the mammals, however, that the cortex, particularly the neocortex, becomes a dominant brain structure. The three regions considered here all fall within the ambit of Rose and Woolsey's (1948) criteria for cortex, namely three layers with the superficial layer constituting a fiber layer and having phylogenetic primacy.

We have noted earlier that three separate cortical anlages were evident in the earliest living vertebrates, the agnathans, and were clearly distinguishable in the amphibia. The ventrolateral pallium has given rise to the olfactory bulb and tubercle and the piriform cortex. The dorsomedial pallium is precursor to the hippocampus or archipallium while, interposed between the two, the dorsolateral pallium has given rise to the neocortex.

THE RHINENCEPHALON OR ALLOCORTEX

The *rhinencephalon* was so called because it was originally believed that the primitive cortical structures that constitute this region were concerned only with the sense of smell. It is now clear that this is not the case. This region has two separate and distinct origins, with the paleopallium giving rise to the piriform complex and the archipallium preceding the hippocampal complex.

The Paleopallium. This term applies to the piriform cortex. This includes the olfactory bulb and stalk which Brodmann classed as primitive cortex as it is without layers, together with the olfactory and vomeronasal nerves, the anterior perforated substance and portion of the hippocampal gyrus. While this structure has developed phylogenetically in conjunction with the developing olfactory system and is of substantial size in the osmic mammals, it has never been entirely olfactory in function. In the primates, culminating in man, there has been a decline in olfactory function and, as shown by Andy and Stephan, the paleocortex is one of the few brain structures that has failed to show increase in size in the phylogenetic sequence from insectivores to man. However, this structure is still evident in primates although nonolfactory functions have probably assumed increasing significance. Even in mammals such as the dolphin, in which the olfactory system is vestigial, this cortex is still evident (Crosby et al., 1962).

The Archipallium. The hippocampal formation in mammals shows the double V formation of interlocked Ammon's Horn and gyrus dentata throughout the marsupials and monotremes. This configuration is clearly revealed in the rat hippocampus as shown in Figure 7.1.

The changes in the hippocampus most evident throughout mammalian evolution are those associated with the increasing size of the neocortex and in particular the development of the corpus callosum. With increase in the mass of the corpus callosum, the hippocampal formation is rolled backward, downward, and outward into the temporal pole so that what was once a mediodorsal structure is, in the primates, located ventrolaterally in the temporal lobe and in close proximity to the piriform cortex. Remnants of the dorsal hippocampus remain over the top of the corpus callosum as the Indusium Grisium.

A very significant study of the ontogeny of the human hippocampus was that reported by Humphrey (1966), in which she identified separate anlages for the dentate gyrus and Ammon's horn from the beginning of hippocampal development at six weeks. By the eleventh week the CA1, CA2, and CA3 divisions of the Cornu Ammonis are evident. While the dentate gyrus is the first part of the hippocampal formation to be identified at six weeks as a cell-free marginal layer adjacent to the lamina terminalis, cell formation is not evident until about the thirteenth week. At this stage a ball-like mass of cells begins to form and from this the granular cell layer is seen to develop. This evidence further supports the view that the hippocampal formation is not a single entity. Of equal significance is Humphrey's observation that, in its develop-

---

FIG. 7.1. (*facing page*)   The configuration of the hippocampus of the rat as seen in horizontal section. The identified structures are CA1, CA2, CA3, and CA4 divisions of Ammon's Horn and the pyramid cell layer of this structure (Pyr), the granular cell layer of the dentate gyrus (Gr) the subiculum (SuB) the presubiculum (PrS) and the entorhinal cortex (ENT). (Figure prepared by P. N. Meyer.)

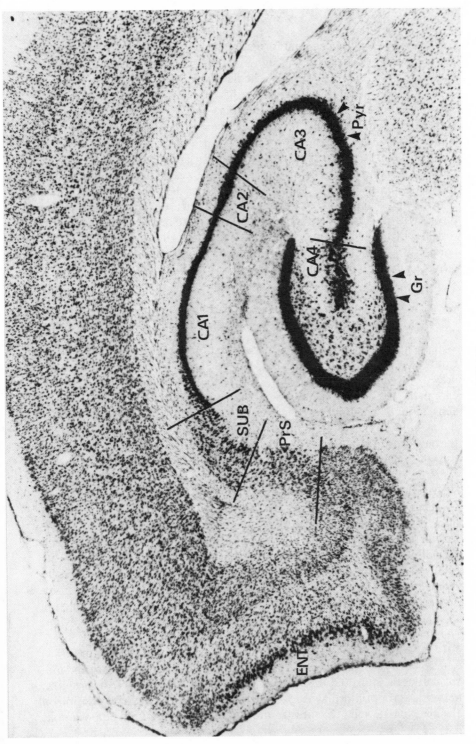

FIG. 7.1.

111

ment, the human hippocampal formation passes through stages that successively resemble the lungfish and anurans (18–22 mm embryo) and reptiles (44
mm embryo). This is followed by the development of a ball-like cluster of
cells in the dentate gyrus, a stage that has not been observed in any living
forms. However, Humphrey reported that such a formation has been observed in the fetal monotreme, Echidna (the spiny anteater). While an adult
monotreme, Ornithorhynchus (the duck-billed platypus), and marsupials
show the characteristic mammalian dentate gyrus, Humphrey (1966) speculated that perhaps some adult vertebrate, not yet studied or now extinct,
might exhibit the ball-like cell mass for the gyrus dentatus.

In mammals major input pathways from all cortical regions may be traced
through the cingulate gyrus and entorhinal cortex to the hippocampus. While
rostral portions of the hippocampus receive olfactogustatory input, the temporal or ventral hippocampus is dominated by amygdaloid-piriform and, in
primates, amygdaloid-temporal relations (Crosby et al., 1966).

THE MAMMALIAN NEOCORTEX

While Livingstone was prepared to state that "emphasis on neocortex as the
epitome of mammalian and particularly human development may be over-
drawn" (Livingstone, 1978, p. 18), there is no doubt that an essential difference in the brains of mammals as compared with all other species is the very
substantial and continuing expansion of this structure. As has been pointed
out at various times (e.g., Livingstone, 1978; Pribram, 1960; Sanides, 1970),
the neocortex is more correctly referred to as the isogenetic or isocortex and I
use this term interchangeably with neocortex but with isocortex as the term of
preference.

Even the most primitive living mammals show a striking advance in development of the isocortex compared with any living reptile or bird. While the
olfactory sense in the more primitive vertebrates has direct access to those
frontal structures primordial to the cortical mantle, the other senses have no
such direct connections. The expansion of the mammalian isocortex appears
to have been due primarily to the invasion of the cortex by afferent fibers
from the other sense modalities. How this may have come about has considerable significance for our understanding of brain organization and function
in mammals and critically in man, and was considered in the previous
chapter.

In the evolution of isocortex, there has been a complex pattern of differentiation of the original cortical mantle to yield (a) separate sensory and motor cortices and (b) the frontal and posterior cortical systems. In primitive
vertebrates the primordial neopallium is located in a dorsolateral position on
the hemisphere wall. Thus it is found between the primordial hippocampus

or archipallium, which is dorsomedial, and the primordial piriform region or paleopallium, which is ventrolateral. In studies of the cortical structures of various South African reptiles, Dart (1934) found, to his surprise, "not one homogenous cyto-architectonic field but two primordial neopallial areas (para-piriform and para-hippocampal respectively of almost equivalent area)" (p. 4). This is demonstrated in Figure 7.2.

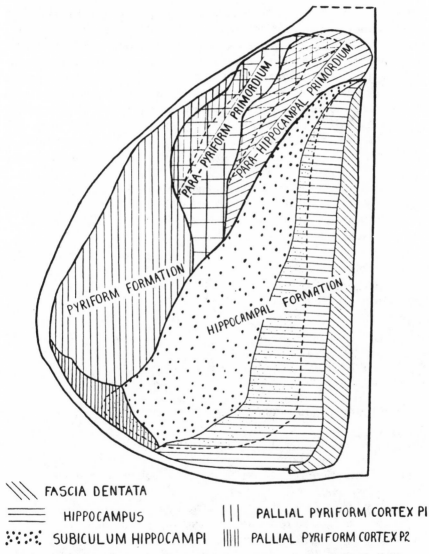

FASCIA DENTATA

HIPPOCAMPUS ||| PALLIAL PYRIFORM CORTEX PI

SUBICULUM HIPPOCAMPI ||||| PALLIAL PYRIFORM CORTEX P2

FIG. 7.2.   The dual origins of the neopallium in the lizard *Agama nigricollis* (from Dart, 1934, p. 4).

Both these structures met the criteria for neocortex; i.e., both lay between hippocampal and piriform formations, stimulation evoked muscle responses in both and both received radiations from the thalamus. Thus each structure has motor and sensory function. Dart demonstrated that the para-piriform region receives thalamic fibers through the lateral forebrain bundle via the neostriatum while the parahippocampal structure receives thalamic fibers by way of the medial forebrain bundle via the medial or paleostriatum.

Dart then argued that Le Gros Clark and Boggon (1933a,b) had, in fact, established the dual structure and function of the mammalian isocortex. They showed that fibers to the cingulate and prefrontal cortices originate from the medial thalamic nuclei (anterior and dorsal nuclei), while the remainder of the isocortex receives its input from the lateral group (ventral and geniculate nuclei). The distinction that Dart was making was thus essentially between frontal and posterior neocortex. He differentiated the medial and lateral regions in that way, he said, because the neopallial tracts projected by the lateral zone of the thalamus reach the cortex through the lateral forebrain bundle while fibers from the medial group traverse the more ancient paleostriatal pathway of the medial forebrain bundle.

In a series of studies with Australian monotremes and marsupials, Abbie (1938, 1940a, b, 1942) developed a notion of the two-fold nature of the neopallium involving separate contributions from the archicortex and the paleocortex. He was able to trace the formation of the isocortex through successive waves of what he described as "circumferential differentiation" away from each of these structures.

Quite independently of Abbie's work and initially through cytoarchitectonic and myeloarchitectonic studies of the human neocortex, Sanides developed an almost identical view of the evolution of the neocortex (Sanides, 1969, 1970).

Over a number of years he extended this concept of "successive waves of circumferential differentiation" to what he described as a broad spectrum of Eutheria, including primates, carnivores, rodents, and insectivores.

Differentiation of Motor and Sensory Isocortex

Using myeloarchitectonic techniques, Sanides extended Bishop's work on the evolutionary significance of myelinization of sensory input systems to cortical organization. Bishop (1959, 1965) had concluded that, in the ascending sensory systems, large fibers with increased myelination and consequent increased conductive speed were characteristic of more recently evolved pathways. The older, more primitive systems, on the other hand, consisted of fine, lightly myelinated fibers, making for much slower conduction. Older midbrain-tectal pathways for vision and hearing are comprised of these smaller fibers while the more recent thalamo-cortical paths have heavily myelinated fibers. From studies of the myelin content of intracortical fibers

Sanides demonstrated a stepwise increase in the degree of myelinization as he progresed away from the cortices of origin, i.e., the hippocampal and piriform cortices (Sanides, 1969).

Using cytoarchitectonic techniques Sanides again demonstrated successive waves of increasing specialization with increasing lamination and increasing cell differentiation. There was thus increase in size of the pyramid cells of layer V as he progressed towards the area gigantopyramidalis of the primary motor cortex and increasing density of layer IV granule cells in the sensory cortex.

In his 1970 paper, Sanides described the evolution of these successive rings in mammals in some detail. The first and most primitive growth ring is the periallocortex made up of two cell layers separated by a more or less cell-free area. Sanides found that this periallocortex appeared not to be differentiated into separate periarchicortex and peripaleocortex. Instead he showed that the outer stratum in the region of the paleocortex is continuous with the dense band of that structure with densely packed multiform cells rather larger than granule cells while the inner stratum is continuous with the cell bank of the archicortex and is characterized by pyramid-like cells. Thus he considered that the ring of periallocortex can best be understood as having evolved as a common derivation of both the other cortical structures with each structure contributing one cell layer. Originally this isocortex would have been present as a core of new cortex built up from both paleocortex and archicortex. In searching for an equivalent cortical organization in reptiles, Sanides observed that a dorsolateral component of the dorsal cortex underlies the lateral paleocortex in both the Squamata (the lizards and snakes) and in the turtles. However, the character of this structure differs between the two groups. In the reptiles other than turtles the dorsolateral component is associative rather than motor. Only in turtles is there a morphological organization that appears to be the equivalent of the mammalian periallocortex involving both sensory and motor functions. This supports the view of Riss, Halpern, and Scalia (1969) referred to earlier, that the turtles are close to the stem reptiles from which the mammals ultimately evolved while the remaining reptiles, including the crocodiles and alligators, are part of the saurapsid line, the dominant reptiles from which birds evolved.

The next stage, consisting of two separate rings of proisocortex, shows as its main feature the appearance of a granular layer IV that fills the gap between the two discrete layers observed in the periallocortex. While the cell and fiber structures of the two separate rings, i.e., that related to the archicortex and that to the paleocortex, are similar, Sanides (1970) observed that each is influenced by what he called the "spring source," as seen in the evolution of specific sensory and motor cortices.

The third neocortex growth ring, again in two segments, is the paralimbic cortex and the lateral parainsular zone. It is these rings that contain the so-called secondary sensory and motor areas.

Within this context Sanides considered the origins of these secondary sensory and motor areas. He argued that this differentiation depended on the specific development of one or other of the two primary layers. The outer layer through granular cell development, particularly in layer IV and decrease in layer V pyramid cells led to the evolution of koneocortex. An increase in the significance of the inner layer pyramid cells in layer V with a decline in layer IV granular cells yielded the motor cortex. The so-called supplementary motor area lies between the proisocortex of the anterior cingulate gyrus and the area gigantocellularis of the motor cortex. This area thus occurs in a phylogenetically older cortical structure than the so-called primary area. The same is true for supplementary sensory cortices which lie in the parainsular zone between insular proisocortex and the primary sensory koneocortex. This intermediate area Sanides designated as the prokoneocortex. Thus the so-called supplementary motor and sensory systems are primary in origin and have finer, less well myelinated fibers with small pyramid cells in the motor cortex and a less concentrated granule cell layer in sensory cortex. This view is consistent with that put forward by Bishop and is congruent with Diamond's analysis of sensory cortical evolution which I develop shortly. It was also put forward earlier by Woolsey and Fairman (1946) who differentiated the somatic and auditory areas I and II by electrophysiological means.

The final rings of differentiation are seen in the area gigantopyramidalis in the motor area and the densely packed granule cells of the koneocortices of the sensory area. Sanides (1970) concluded that this latest step occurred probably in the Eocene some 50 m. y. ago since Erinaceus (the hedgehog), for example, did not reach this stage and is considered to be a survivor of the Paleocene, archaic mammal radiation.

Studies by Lende (1969) on the differentiation of the motor and sensory cortices in monotremes, marsupials, and insectivores give a further comparative perspective on this question. Lende stated that his concern was with the patterns of neocortical representation for both perception and for volitional acts.

He commenced his discussion by outlining the organization of neocortical representations in the more advanced placentals as revealed by the work of Woolsey and others. He chose the pattern of somatic sensory localization as the basis from which to consider other patterns. This primary sensory area has an homuncular representation of bodily sensation in the post central or parietal sensory cortex. This area he called a somatic sensory-motor area I. (SmI). This is mirrored by a primary motor representation within the precentral stimulable or motor cortex. This he designated motor-sensory I. (MsI).

Lende observed that, within the SmI region, which is primarily somatosensory, a motor response function can be observed and is localized to approximate the sensory pattern. Likewise, in the MsI region, which is primarily a motor area of low threshold, a coincident somatic sensory field has been demonstrated.

The second sensory and motor areas SmII and MsII are each adjacent to the primary areas shown in Figure 7.3.

In the hedgehog (*Erinaceus europaeus*) Lende and Sadler (1967) established the outlines of MsI and SmI with auditory and visual areas located as in other placentals. SmII was located inferior to SmI and was largely overlapped by the auditory area.

While they did not establish MsII, they considered that this presumably lay on the medial surface. The interesting feature of this study was the very considerable overlap that each area had with its neighbors with no "silent" areas to be found on the exposed neocortical surface. In the large areas of overlap between MsI and SmI, in the Rolandic region they found, not overlapping fringes, but an area where both "the largest sensory responses and the lowest motor thresholds were usually obtained" (p. 265).

Studies of the neocortical pattern in marsupials were carried out for both the American opossum (*Didelphis virginiana*) and the Australian wallaby

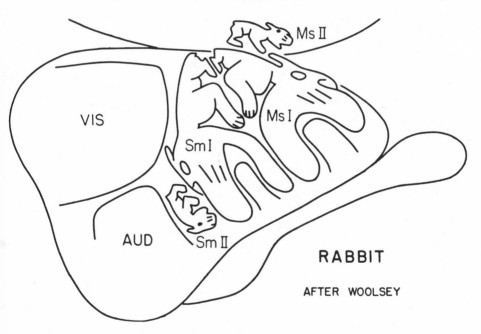

FIG. 7.3.   The primary and secondary motor areas in rabbit neocortex. Homunculus-like figures illustrate the plan of representation in placental animals. VIS, visual sensory cortex; SUD, auditory sensory cortex; Sm I, somatic sensory-motor area I, Sm II, somatic sensory-motor area II; Ms I, somatic motor-sensory area I; Ms II, somatic motor-sensory area II (from Lende, 1969, p. 263).

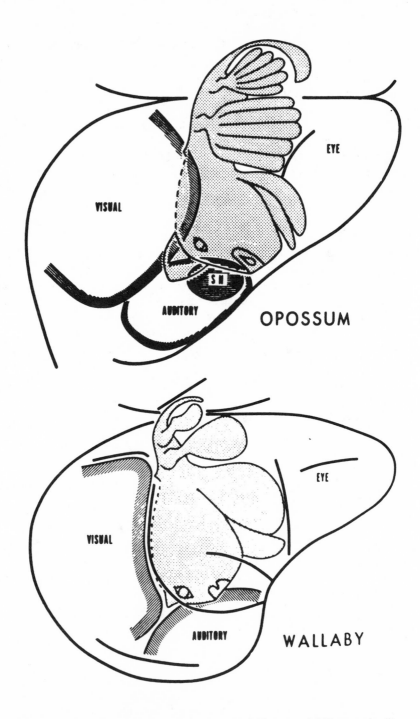

FIG. 7.4.   The overlapping sensory and motor areas in the marsupial. Homunculus-like figures indicate the single sensory-motor area in each marsupial. Note lack of homologue of precentral motor area (from Lende, 1969, p. 267).

(*Thylogale cugeroii*). While the distribution of sensory areas was essentially similar to that found in placental mammals, Lende found a striking difference in the motor studies with no evidence for a separate MsI region in the marsupial. Instead, the motor field completely overlapped the somatic sensory field. This is exemplified in Figure 7.4. The pattern of cortical localization was also plotted in a monotreme, the Australian echidna or spiny anteater (*Tachyglossus aculeatus*).

In the echidna, Lende (1964) found the sensory areas to be concentrated in the posterior pole of the hemisphere with the areas adjacent but clearly separated by dividing sulci. A separate motor area was located immediately in front of the somatic sensory area and again separated by a sulcus. It had no identifiable sensory counterpart. A further motor area was found to exactly overlap the somatic sensory area and to approximate nicely its pattern of localization. While the two motor areas yielded similar thresholds Lende believed the posterior area should be titled SmI and the more anterior, MI. A unique feature of the echidna brain was the great expanse of "silent" cortex rostral to the sensory and motor areas with, as Lende put it, "no broad hints of its function from either neuroanatomical or behavioral observations" (Lende, 1969, p. 272).

While there are thus some basic similarities between the monotremes and the marsupial and placental mammals, there are also some striking differences. These could well express a common origin from basic cynodont therapsid reptilian stock with a very lengthy period of separate evolution since then, as suggested by Hopson (1969).

Lende (1969) concluded that, "We may theorize that the present patterns of cortical localization evolved from a polymodal pallium containing completely superimposed representational areas. With increasing corticalization these areas developed increasing spatial individuality to the point of separation by interfields" (p. 273).

Sanides' study of "waves of differentiation" with increasing specialization of cortical structures suggested another anomaly in the way the neocortex has been viewed in the past. The striking increase in frontal integrative cortex and of parieto-occipito-temporal integrative cortex in the series from prosimians through monkeys and apes to man has led to the commonly accepted view that the so-called association cortex is more recent in origin than the "primary" sensory and motor areas. Sanides (1969) attacked this point of view. He was able to trace the initial existence of both anterior and posterior integrative cortices in the neocortex of the European hedgehog which, he claimed, exhibits the most primitive neocortex of the placental mammals. At the same time he found no evidence of granular koneocortex or of an area gigantopyramidalis in the hedgehog. When dealing with primate evolution, said Sanides, "it has been overlooked that we were dealing with a typical feature of primates, i.e., the most generalized neocortical structure is bound to become the most prevailing one with the widest scope for further differentiation" (p. 406).

Posterior (Sensory) Isocortex

Diamond (1967) expressed the view that "everything known about the origin and development of cortex in vertebrates points to the importance of sensory neocortex in the adaptation of mammals to the external environment" (p. 66). He developed this theory from studies of living species. As we have seen, Jerison has amplified a very similar approach in terms of the evolutionary history of mammals expressed through fossil remains.

In studies of mammalian neocortical structure and function the two most widely used species have been the cat and the rhesus monkey, and attempts have been made to establish general principles about the nature of neocortical organization on the basis of such studies. These two animals represent lines that diverged early in mammalian evolution, have occupied different niches, and have evolved very different life styles. It is not surprising, therefore, to find that there are indeed some very significant differences in cortical organization and function between these two species. An examination of these differences and consideration of species that have retained the basic primitive structure may yield information that will give us a better insight into how the cortical structures have evolved. Irving Diamond and his coworkers earlier at Chicago and then at Duke University have devoted considerable research effort to just such an enquiry over the past quarter century. Their enquiries have related particularly to the posterior or sensory neocortex.

Diamond (1967) pointed out that the "increase in ratio of nonolfactory to olfactory cortex occurred not just once in the ascending mammalian series which culminates in man but independently in several lines." He went on to say: "Whatever benefits are conferred by sensory neocortex, these have been sufficient grounds for providing the chief impetus to further evolution time and time again" (p. 52).

What was the nature of these projections from the sensory system to the cortex in the earliest mammals and how did these projection systems evolve? In both cat and monkey there is evidence for precise localization of projections between thalamus and sensory neocortex with little overlap between the visual, auditory, and somesthesic systems. As well, the receptive cells in the thalamus have restricted receptive fields within a given sensory modality, e.g., a limited range of auditory frequencies, a localized part of the visual field, or some small part of the body surface.

Two primitive species examined by Diamond's group, the marsupial opossum and a primitive insectivore, the hedgehog, yield a very different picture. In the opossum for example, degeneration within the nuclei of the thalamus only became evident following massive cortical lesions which then produced degeneration in all three projecting nuclei, viz., the lateral geniculate, medial geniculate, and ventral posterior nuclei of the thalamus. Diamond concluded that this indicated widespread collateral projections from each of these nuclei to all parts of the neocortex (Diamond, 1967).

As well it has been shown that receptive fields for single cells of the thalamic nuclei in the opossum are very much wider than for the cat and monkey. For example, Diamond pointed to the findings of Erickson, Jane, Waite, & Diamond, (1964) that, within the ventro-posterior nucleus, 29% of 55 cells sampled were responsive to stimuli from wide fields of body surface and 8% were also responsive to auditory stimuli.

In the hedgehog, which Diamond and Hall (1969) saw as a living prototype of the primitive mammal, there is even less differentiation than in the opossum, which has probably undergone some further evolutionary development parallel to that of the primates as a result of the arborial habitat. It is difficult to draw boundaries between the various sensory projection nuclei of the thalamus of hedgehog and there is little differentiation within the cortex. Almost all of the sensory cortex is covered by projections from the lateral and medial geniculate and ventroposterior nucleus with few, if any, "silent" areas between the sensory fields. These findings are consistent with those of Lende, discussed earlier. Diamond and Hall pointed out that the pattern of distribution of sensory inputs from thalamus to cortex in the hedgehog conforms closely to the picture given by Elliot-Smith of the cortical organization in a hypothetical primitive mammal as shown in Figure 7.5.

All of these features, they claimed, "establish the hedgehog as a baseline from which the course of development of neocortex in different mammalian lines can be traced" (p. 254), a view also expressed by Sanides. Even in the hedgehog, visual areas I and II could be clearly distinguished. A finding of considerable significance, said Diamond and Hall, was that instead of one relay nucleus there was evidence of two separate relay systems to the cortex — the first was via the lateral geniculate and the second via the lateroposterior nucleus from the optic tectum. This latter projection they considered likely to be the more primitive relay pathway and, in the hedgehog, there is extensive overlap of the cortical projections from the two systems. They then speculated, on the basis of Herrick's studies of amphibia, that there was a stage in evolution in which visual impulses reached the thalamus only via the tectum and that the thalamus in such a hypothetical reptile-mammalian ancestor was polysensory, projecting diffusely to a general sensory cortex. In support of this view they obtained evidence, already discussed earlier, that the auditory and somatic relay nuclei in the hedgehog are not completely differentiated, neither being modality specific.

Assuming a primitive multi-sensory cortex that then becomes more and more differentiated with mode specific receptor regions Diamond asked

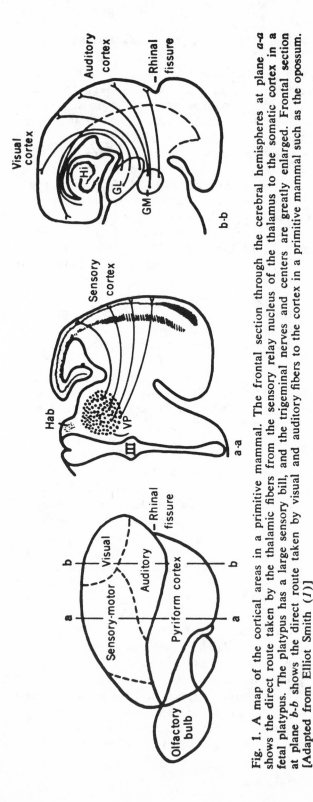

Fig. 1. A map of the cortical areas in a primitive mammal. The frontal section through the cerebral hemispheres at plane *a-a* shows the direct route taken by the thalamic fibers from the sensory relay nucleus of the thalamus to the somatic cortex in a fetal platypus. The platypus has a large sensory bill, and the trigeminal nerves and centers are greatly enlarged. Frontal section at plane *b-b* shows the direct route taken by visual and auditory fibers to the cortex in a primitive mammal such as the opossum. [Adapted from Elliot Smith (*1*)]

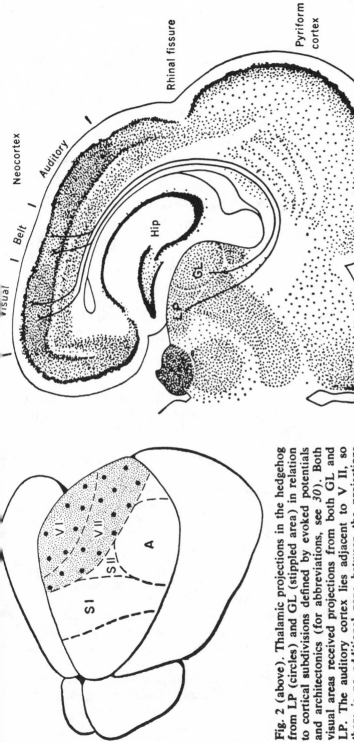

Fig. 2 (above). Thalamic projections in the hedgehog from LP (circles) and GL (stippled area) in relation to cortical subdivisions defined by evoked potentials and architectonics (for abbreviations, see *30*). Both visual areas received projections from both GL and LP. The auditory cortex lies adjacent to V II, so there is no additional zone between the projections from GL and GM. **Fig. 3 (right).** Diagram of pathways from the visual thalamus to the visual cortex in the hedgehog. Axons leaving GL and LP enter the internal capsule and travel through the white matter underlying the cortex. In drawing the cortex an attempt was made to suggest the increased granular layer characteristic of a belt of cortex. In the diagram each thalamic fiber sends one collateral to the belt and one to the visual cortex; in order to produce severe retrograde degeneration, both branches must be severed. Between these two sensory zones is a belt of cortex. In drawing the cortex the visual area and the auditory area.

FIG. 7.5.   Thalamo-cortical connections in the hedgehog compared with those envisaged in a hypothetical primitive mammal (from Diamond & Hall, 1969, p. 253).

whether differentiation followed an even rate for each modality. His major comparisons were between primate and carnivore and for his pursuit of the primate line he began with the tree shrew, *Tupaia glis*. The tree shrews occupy an interesting position taxonomically. While they have been classified as a primitive primate this is still open to dispute and they border nicely between insectivore and primate. While Tupaia exhibits many features in common with hedgehog, the overall expansion of the neocortex has been in the primate direction with the striate cortex in particular showing marked development. With this there has also been a very marked increase in the development of the thalamic visual regions.

As well as the increase in size and differentiation of the striate cortex, a new large temporal area, separating auditory and visual regions, is evident. In the thalamus the lateral geniculate laminae are clearly defined. There is also an increase in the size of the latero-posterior nucleus, the origin of the pulvinar nucleus of the primates. Lateral geniculate projections now correspond precisely with the striate cortex which exactly defines Visual Area I. Visual Area II is part of the target of the pulvinar. As well, the new temporal area between visual and auditory cortex receives pulvinar input (Diamond & Hall, 1969; Hall & Diamond, 1968; Snyder & Diamond, 1968). The tree shrew appears to be at the transition point between arborial insectivore and primate. This evidence fits precisely with that presented earlier from Douglas and Marcellus's (1975) analysis (Chapter 5).

The pulvinar nucleus and its projections are of considerable significance in tracing the primate line of evolution. This structure is well developed in lemurs and, said Diamond (1967),

> It is doubtful whether a true pulvinar can be found in other mammals such as cat, rat, opossum and hedgehog. We conclude that the visual centers have dominated the primate thalamus and cortex from the very beginning — not a surprising conclusion in view of the prepotent role of vision in the cognitive life of primates (p. 63).

Removal of the striate cortex in primates results in severe visual deficit. Diamond and Hall (1969) reported seemingly quite contradictory findings for *Tupaia glis* where complete striate cortex ablation in that animal resulted in virtually no apparent deficit in visual pattern discrimination learning. Deficits were evident when for example, triangles of different orientation were circled or masked by a ring. Even then the deficit could be overcome by further training. Diamond, on the assumption that the bush baby (*Galago senegalensis*) would be intermediate between tree shrew and primate, then explored the effect of ablation of the striate cortex in that animal on visual pattern discrimination. The sensory loss revealed was severe, being equivalent to that observed in monkeys (Atencio, Diamond, & Ward, 1976; Diamond, 1976).

Diamond (1976) examined anatomical relationships to see whether these would offer a solution to this conundrum. In the tree shrew it was shown that the pulvinar, which has been regarded as an intrinsic nucleus (see Pribram, 1960) in fact received ascending projections from the superficial superior colliculus with the whole of the pulvinar being tecto-recipient. The border between areas 17 and 18, the zero vertical meridian, defines the division between projections from the lateral geniculate projecting to the rostral extremity area 17 and pulvinar to the caudal boundary of 18 as shown in Figure 7.6.

Thus area 18, conceived as association cortex, receives visual input from the superior colliculus via the pulvinar. In view of Bishop's work this would be expected to be the more primitive of the two input systems. Clearly, in the light of the effect of striate ablation on visual form discrimination learning in the tree shrew "the tectopulvinar system can mediate the capacity for visual pattern discrimination in the absence of the geniculostriate system" (Diamond, 1976, p. 62). Why then the striking difference between Tupaia and that observed following ablation of the striate cortex in Galago and the primates? The answer appears to be in the nature of tectopulvinar projections in these animals. Firstly, Glendenning, Hall, Diamond, & Hall (1975) showed that the superior pulvinar and rostral inferior pulvinar did not receive input from the superior colliculus, such fibers being directed only to the caudal half of inferior pulvinar in Galago. Secondly, it was shown that the cortical target of this pulvinar region is limited to the medial temporal lobe area. Areas 18 and 19 do not receive fibers for the tecto-recipient zone of pulvinar (Diamond, 1976). Thus, said Diamond, the tectopulvinar system in Galago differs markedly from Tupaia and, in Galago, it does not border the geniculostriate system as it does in Tupaia. Further evidence also suggests, said Dia-

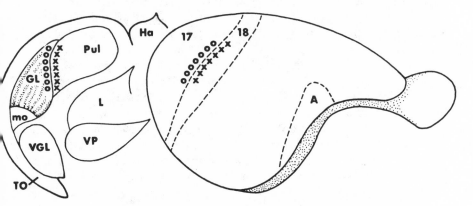

FIG. 7.6.   Diagram of the projection of the lateral geniculate and pulvinar nuclei to cortex in *Tupaia*. The representation of the zero vertical meridian in the lateral geniculate projects to area 17 at its border with area 18. This projection is depicted by small circles. The adjacent region in the pulvinar projects to area 18 — this projection is depicted by triangles (from Glendenning, Hall, Diamond, & Hall, 1975, p. 453).

mond, that the tectopulvinar system of primates resembles that found in Galago. This, Diamond argued, may explain the difference in the effects of area 17 ablation in Tupaia and primates. In Tupaia, areas 18 and 19 are the target of the tectopulvinar system. This is not so in primates. The tectal projection is to caudal pulvinar only and thence to the medial temporal zone. Areas 18 and 19 depend entirely for their input on area 17. Thus, in the primates, area 17 lesions constitute a functional removal of areas 18 and 19 as well.

Further evidence supporting the linkage between the tree shrew and the main line of primate evolution comes from a study by Glendenning, Kofron, and Diamond (1976) in which they compared the organization of striate granular layer IV and the lateral geniculate projections to it in Galago with that of Tupaia. They concluded that:

> Tupaia, Galago and Macaque appear to form a graded series with respect to layer IV. In all three species layer IV proper consists of two tiers. Further, in all three species the lower tier is densely populated but density of cells of the upper tier relative to the lower tier varies. In Tupaia the ratio is approximately 1:1, in macaque the lower tier is much more densely populated than the upper tier; and in Galago, the ratio of density of upper to lower tier is intermediate (p. 545).

Diamond then concluded that the first principle of visual organization, found in both Tupaia and in the squirrel, is a twofold projection to this cortex. The lateral geniculate projects to area 17 or striate cortex. The superior colliculus projects, via the pulvinar or lateral posterior nucleus to the belt area adjacent to area 17, i.e., area 18 and any additional areas lying between area 19 and the auditory cortex. In primates these two pathways can be identified. They are adjacent in the thalamus but have become separated in the cortex with the tectopulvinar path now projecting only to the medial temporal region.

The carnivores show a rather different line of development. Both pathways have been identified in the cat but the cat differs from our prototypical mammal in a number of ways. Diamond (1976, p. 66) has summarized these. Briefly, the lateral geniculate nucleus projects to both areas 17 and 18 with the zero vertical meridian dividing the lateral geniculate into two sub-divisions. The thalamic area receiving superior colliculus projections is separated from the lateral geniculate nucleus whereas they are adjacent in the primate line. As well, the medial intralaminar division projects to area 18 and 19 and to the subsylvian gyrus adjacent to the auditory cortex. The comparison between primate and cat is shown in Figure 7.7.

While there is convincing evidence that vision is the dominant sense modality in primates this is certainly not the case in other classes of mammals. For the other mammal studied in considerable detail, the cat, Diamond (1967)

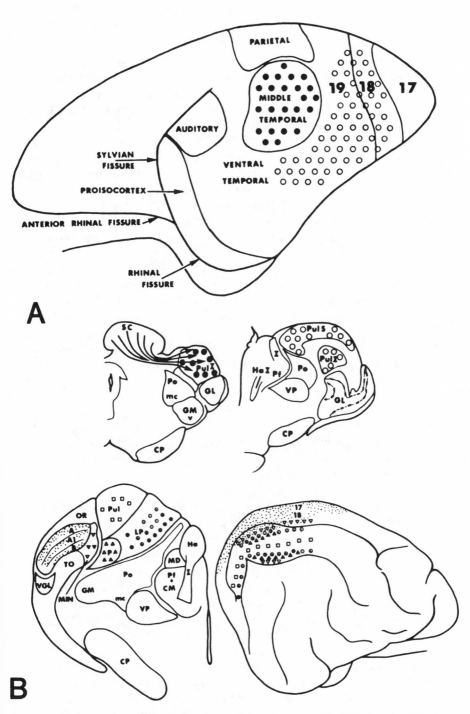

FIG. 7.7. Visual projections from thalamus to cortex compared in (A) primate and (B) cat (from Diamond, 1976, p. 66).

suggested that there is a different story with indications that it was the auditory system that played a significant role in the evolution of the carnivores. As discussed earlier, the carnivores are generally nocturnal predators where visual information is far less valuable than are auditory signals. This is backed up by findings that the ratio of auditory to visual cortex is much higher in the carnivores. Diamond (1967) also outlined behavioral studies which indicate that auditory cues are prepotent to visual cues in the cat. In a detailed analysis of the sub-division of the auditory cortex in the cat, Winer, Diamond, and Raczkowski (1977) compared their findings using retrograde transport of HRP with earlier degenerative and electrophysiological studies. They revealed a complex pattern of interrelationships. While each cytoarchitectonic division appears to have unique connections there also appears to be overlap in connections from thalamic subdivisions to cortex. There is also evidence that the thalamic subdivisions are the targets of different ascending tracts, at least four such tracts beng identified. The authors then asked, "How is the division of the cortex functionally related to these separate pathways?" (p. 412). They answered that, while the cortical subdivisions are likely to be the consequence of parallel ascending pathways, no single cortical subdivision can be identified with a single pathway. They concluded that, "The pattern of projections from the thalamus makes it clear that the subdivisions around A1 constitute a belt related to the core and that all the parts constitute a single system" (p. 412). As well, the cortico-cortical connections between the various subdivisions of the auditory cortex are much richer than those with any other cortical area. The core and belt structure observed in the thalamo-cortical organization of the prototypical mammals (see Figure 7.5) is thus preserved though each is now comprised of an extensive complex of subdivisions. The belt is thus closely wed to the core but is both auditory and somatosensory and may be visual as well.

While the ratio of auditory cortex to visual cortex is much higher in carnivores than primates (Diamond, 1967) studies of the auditory pathways in *Tupaia glis* by Casseday, Diamond, and Harting (1976) revealed a similar basic structure to that observed in the cat. The primary pathways ascend through the lateral lemniscus to relay in the core of inferior colliculus, thence to the ventral division of the lateral geniculate, finally targeting on the primary auditory cortex (the koneocortex or A1 division). As well, these authors produced evidence for the view that there are up to four pathways paralleling the primary pathway, including both the medial geniculate and posterior nuclei of the thalamus. Some appear to bypass the inferior colliculus.

In the comparison of cat and tree shrew the authors concluded that the similarity "in division of auditory cortex into a core and a belt suggest that this division reflects a general mammalian plan or organization of neocortex" (Casseday et al., 1975, p. 337). Further, they pointed out, both species exhibited a number of parallel secondary pathways, some of which did not include the inferior colliculus. This finding in itself, they concluded, might help to resolve some of the apparent anomalies that occur in behavioral studies, e.g., absence of effect of ablations of the inferior colliculus on auditory discrimination but a marked effect if deeper structures are involved.

In more recent work Diamond's group employed anterograde and retrograde axonal transport techniques using HRP and radio active isotopes to further explore these various pathways. The work confirmed earlier findings but revealed in much more detail the nature and specificity of these pathways. Diamond (1982, 1983) noted that these various studies revealed striking similarities in the organization of thalamo-cortical relationships for each of the three sensory systems, visual, auditory and somasthesic. Each system had parallel pathways relaying in different thalamic nuclei. Of these pathways, one in each modality appears to have a limited cortical target, the core or primary sensory cortex while others have extensive targets including many cortical subdivisions. He differentiated between essential projections, where ablation of the target resulted in degeneration of the source neurons, and sustaining projections when ablation did not result in neural degeneration because the neurons had other projections to different regions. In area AI, the auditory core, essential projections were observed for the ventral subdivision of the Medical Geniculate nucleus. Sustaining projections were observed both to the core and to each other subdivision. In each system one pathway has been shown to have extensive cortical targets. For example the pulvinar nucleus in Galago projects to the entire visual field (Raczkowski & Diamond, 1980). Furthermore it has been seen that in the tree shrew all of the pulvinar nucleus is a target from the superior colliculus while, in Galago, substantial parts of the pulvinar receive visual tectal fibers (Diamond, 1979, 1983).

On the basis of this evidence Diamond (1983) argued that the term "association cortex" is misleading implying as it does that such cortex is athalamic. Even if it were considered to be the target of "intrinsic thalamic nuclei" said Diamond this would be misleading in view of evidence of tectal sensory input to such nuclei. He stated that he preferred the more neutral term "belt" for the traditional association areas and would refer to the primary sensory areas as "core areas" (p. 252).

These cortical subdivisions of "core" and "belt" said Diamond, might be considered to form a limited number of cortical fields. He defined such a field as "a constellation of cortical areas constituting one continuous area functionally unified by the reception of sensory projections in a given modality" (Diamond, 1979, p. 29). Furthermore he added, it seems to be the rule that all subdivisions of a field receive diffuse projections, of a sustaining nature from one thalamic nucleus e.g., the magno-cellular division of the Medical Genieulate nucleus for the auditory field, the pulvinar for the visual field. Thus the unity of the field stands revealed by such single diverse projections.

Another set of findings from these more recent studies has indicated that cells of different size in the thalamus receive specific sensory inputs, eg., from different sized retinal ganglion cells in the visual system, and project to different layers in the sensory cortex (Carey, Fitzpatrick, & Diamond, 1979, Fitzpatrick, Itoh, & Diamond, 1983, Itoh, Conley, & Diamond, 1982, Penny, Itoh, & Diamond, 1982). Parallel occipital pathways between cortex and thalamus involving specific cortical layers were also revealed (Casseday, Jones, & Diamond, 1979, Diamond, 1983). Diamond observed that, on the basis of this work, a case could be made for the view that a functional unit in e.g., the visual system could be defined as a pathway of given fibre size and cell size. He noted that in both the somatic and visual systems the small cell, small fiber pathways project to the superficial layers of the sensory cortex (Diamond, 1983, p. 272). Thus in terms of Bishop's hypothesis these would be more primitive pathways.

These studies of sensory cortex by Diamond's group have revealed trends consistent with those hypothesized by Sanides. The most striking evolutionary change is the shift from generalized receptive fields over large areas of cortex as seen in Erinaceus and Didelphis to highly localized receptor fields in primates and carnivores with the development of densely granular koneocortices. Two further trends appear to be closely linked.

Sanides was able to trace the initial existence of integrative or associative cortex in the hedgehog and considered this to be primary cortex. In his studies of prefrontal cortical development (discussed in the next section), he outlined waves of successive differentiation in the prefrontal cortex as a separate development from that observed for sensory and motor cortex.

Diamond observed a primary division of both the visual and auditory systems into two (a core and a belt) with two separate relay systems from the thalamus. In the visual system of the hedgehog, one relay path was via the lateral geniculate and the other via the lateroposterior system from the optic tectum. The belt system was considered to be the more primitive and the belt area would incorporate both associative cortex and visual area II. In the belt area, increasing division and complexity of organization was observed as one moved from hedgehog to tree shrew to monkey. While there are differences in the organizational characteristics of the cat auditory and visual core and belt systems, a highly complex organization comparable to that of primates was observed in the carnivore.

This picture of increasing differentiation of associative cortex in the belt area is complicated by the differentiation between sensory areas I and II, with changes in both organization and function. In the visual system, for example, the more primitive relay pathways are from optic tectum or superior colliculus to lateral posterior nucleus (pulvinar in primates) and thence to part of the belt area. In hedgehogs there is extensive cortical overlap but this is not so in higher forms. In the tree shrew visual area II is part of the target of pulvinar in area 18. In the primates, including Galago, however, areas 18 and 19 have become purely associational with the tectal projection through the caudal pulvinar to the medial temporal zone. As indicated, this picture is quite different in the cat although showing a similar complexity in organization.

Thus, while not yet fully delineated, three trends appear evident in the evolution of the sensory neocortex, namely increasing localization and specialization of the major sensory pathways to koneocortex, differentiation and organization of the more primitive second sensory areas, and increase in complexity and differentiation of the associative cortex of the belt areas.

Further evidence that supports these trends towards increasing specialization in the evolution of the cortical mantle comes from other studies utilizing the H.R.P. technique for tracing the sources of afferent input to the cortex. In a series of studies, Divac and co-workers traced the pattern of axonal distribution to the cortex from neurons in subcortical centers in rat and rhesus monkey (Divac, 1980; Divac, Kosmal, Bjorklund, & Lindvall, 1978; Divac, Lavail, Rakic, & Winston, 1977).

These studies indicated that there were a number of different distribution patterns to the isocortex that were characteristic of different subcortical centers. Based on studies of 51 rat hemispheres Divac (1980) pointed to five different classes of projection. For some centers such as midline nuclei of the thalamus, the lateral hypothalamus, raphe nuclei, and locus caeruleus, axon terminals were dispersed throughout the isocortex, the number of labeled cells being proportional to the size of the cortical area injected regardless of where the injection occurred. This he designated: disperse pattern. For other centers labeled cells were found only after injection in a specific cortical area e.g., the ventral posterior nucleus of the thalamus projects discretely to the somatosensory cortex. He classed this type of pattern as regional. A modification of this was regional-preferential in which labeled cells were evident only from a particular region of the cortex but the density of labeling varied for different subregions. Thus, for the rat, labeled cells were evident in the mediodorsal thalamic nucleus following injections to the anteriomedial cortex and the dorsal bank of the rhinal sulcus. However, a few labeled cells were also found following injections in the polar cortex. Thus the two loci of dense projections were spanned by an area of sparce projection. Other types of projection he classed as preferential, with dispersion of projections over the whole cortex but with dense projections to a particular area. For example the ventromedial nucleus showed labeled cells from projection anywhere in the cortex but a dense patterning from frontal cortical injections. The fifth pattern Divac described was bilocular-preferential with labeled cells evident from two separate cortical locations but many more cells labeled from one location than the other. Thus the lateroposterior nucleus of rat thalamus showed a few labeled cells following injection into the anteriomedial cortex but many such cells after posterior dorsal cortex injection.

Divac drew special attention to several populations of neurons that innervate many widely separated regions of the cortex e.g., the raphe nucleus and locus caeruleus. Here, he said, "the axon of one neuron may innervate formations as widespread as parts of the neocortex, thalamus, brain stem, cerebellum and even spinal cord." (Divac, 1980, p. 307) Such neurons he considered might well mediate certain general functions such as setting the activation level of large brain regions.

This patterning of projections to the whole of the isocortex ranging from highly specific to very diffuse thus mirrors the types of projection described by Diamond for the posterior isocortex.

The Frontal Isocortex

Sanides (1969) considered the central sulcus of the higher primates to have decisive meaning for the understanding of the whole neocortical organization. This sulcus he said, forms "the basic dividing line separating an anterior part, the frontal lobe, rich in pyramid cells from a posterior part, the morphological complex of the parieto-occipito-temporal lobes rich in granular cells" (p. 405).

Luria also appears to have subscribed to such a division. In a theoretical analysis of brain organization Luria (1973) proposed three principal functional units of the brain. The first was involved in regulating tone or waking; the second, the obtaining, processing, and storing of information and the third in programming, regulating, and verifying of mental activity. We are here concerned with Luria's third system, structures of which are located in the anterior regions of the hemispheres, namely the motor and premotor cortices and the prefrontal granular cortex. The main outlet channel Luria considered to be through the great pyramid or Betz cells of the motor cortex. However, he argued, this system could not work in isolation since movements require a tonic background. This he considered to be provided by the motor ganglia and fibers of the extra pyramidal system. These structures of "superimposed secondary areas of the motor cortex" he said prepare the motor programmes and then transport them to the great pyramid cells. However, he went on, superimposed secondary and tertiary zones play a major role in preparation of the motor programmes. He saw, as the most important part of his third functional unit of the brain, the granular frontal cortex. This region, said Luria, "plays a decisive role in the formation of intentions and programmes and in the regulation and verification of the most complex forms of human behaviour." (Luria, 1973, p. 84) This system is characterized by a very rich system of connections with virtually all parts of the brain.

Thus Luria viewed the motor and premotor cortices together with the prefrontal granular cortex as all forming part of a single complex system, the motor analyzer, concerned with programming, regulating and verifying mental activity. The prefrontal cortex, within this context, is viewed as the third motor system (Luria, 1966).

While this division of the isocortex is certainly evident it would seem that, in the light of the evolutionary history of the isocortical system, a more significant differentiation would be between the prefrontal granular cortex and the rest of the isocortex. In fact, as discussed earlier, Sanides considered the process of "circumferential differentiation" to encompass the increasing specialization of both the motor giganto-pyramidal cortex and the sensory koneocortex from the primary undifferentiated sensory-motor isocortex. He considered, as a separate process, the differentiation of the prefrontal cortex from the rest.

Another to consider the origins of the isocortex was Karl Pribram, who examined neocortical organization in terms of thalamocortical relationships (Pribram, 1958a, 1958b, 1960). Pribram, like Dart, differentiated between frontal and posterior isocortical systems. He argued that each system could be further analysed into extrinsic and intrinsic components in terms of input and output channels.

In a brief description of the evolution of the vertebrate forebrain Pribram (1958a) noted that, with the development of the pallium or roof, there has been comparable differentiation in the thalamus. Thus, in cyclostomes, the thalamus and in particular the dorsal thalamus is not well developed. In the elasmobranchs there is telencephalic enlargement of both the basal (i.e., striatalseptal) and the pallial regions. With this a clearly distinguishable dorsal and ventral thalamus becomes evident. In the amphibia the central mantle shows medial growth over the brain core structures of striatum, septum, and amygdala. With increase in paleopallium (or primal hippocampus) together with the beginning of a general cortex in amphibia the dorsal thalamus shows considerable enlargement. Thus, said Pribram, "the major divisions of the vertebrate prosencephalon are clearly discerned in all tetrapods" (Pribram, 1958a, p. 144).

While, in reptiles, the archipallium shows ascendancy over the paleopallium and general cortex, in mammals it is the general, or neocortex, that dominates. In reptiles the dorsal thalamus differentiates into recognizable internal and external portions and the subgrouping is even clearer in mammals. In the internal core Pribram identified the central, medial, and anterior nuclear masses, while, in the external division, he named the geniculate complex and the ventral and posterior nuclei. It is this division into external and core nuclei in the dorsal thalamus described earlier by Le Gros Clark and Boggon (1933a, b) that forms the basis for Pribram's divisions of the neocortex.

The ventral and geniculate nuclei of the external region receive the terminations of the large, topographically discrete, specific afferent tracts. In the central core the anterior nuclei receive inputs from the posterior hypothalamus and the central nuclei from the reticular core. The remaining two nuclear groups, the posterior nucleus in the external portion and the medial nucleus in the internal core, Pribram described as having inputs largely from the cortex and other thalamic nuclei, i.e., inputs that are intrinsic to the system. These systems Pribram called the intrinsic nuclei. There is thus an intrinsic nucleus related to each of the two major divisions of the thalamus.

The external intrinsic nuclei project to the appropriate sensory areas of the posterior neocortex with the posterior nucleus, the intrinsic nucleus for this division, projecting to the so-called secondary sensory or association areas. For these areas Pribram prefers the term sensory-motor cortex (personal communication). The internal extrinsic nuclei project to the anterior limbic structures of cingulate cortex, rhinencephalon, and basal ganglia while the medial, i.e. intrinsic nucleus, projects to the prefrontal cortex. Figure 7.8 sets out Pribram's conceptualization of the system.

Pribram (1960), in a review of theory in physiological psychology, put forward argument and evidence to support his conceptualization of the role of the posterior and frontal intrinsic thalamo-cortical systems. The main thrust of his experimental work since then has been to further explore the reality and significance of the concept.

Deficits from cerebral lesions within the posterior intrinsic system, he said, bear a similarity to those from similar lesions in the primary projection or extrinsic systems and, if sufficiently localized, also relate to one or other of the sense modalities. When the functions of the posterior intrinsic systems are interfered with, essential discrimination remains intact. A monkey with such a lesion in the visual intrinsic system can, said Pribram, still catch a flying gnat in mid-air or pull in a peanut attached to a fine silk thread. However, the animal is now unable to differentiate the complex relationships between cues. In this situation identification goes awry and the situation becomes unintelligible to the animal. It does not know what to do. It suffers from agnosia. Behavior thus ceases to be, or is not modified in the light of stimulus-response relationships when stimulus differences have specific relationships to the effectiveness of the response.

Deficits that result from frontal intrinsic system damage are, he argued, very different. This system, because of its connections, can be conceived as the association cortex for the limbic system and these deal with the dispositions of the organism necessary to maintain homeostasis. The frontal lesion appears to interfere with the monkey's ability to be instructed on how to behave in a subsequent part of a situation. Deficits appear to be due to confusion of intentions, and disruption of planned behavior.

Pribram argued that because of its connections with the external projection system the posterior intrinsic system is sensitive to differences between past and present constancies in receptor stimuli. On the other hand, the frontal intrinsic system, because of its connections with the limbic system, is sensitive to past and present constancies in dispositional state (Pribram, 1960).

The Prefrontal Granular Cortex

There has been a spectacular evolutionary development in the prefrontal cortex in the higher primates and in particular in man. Luria drew attention

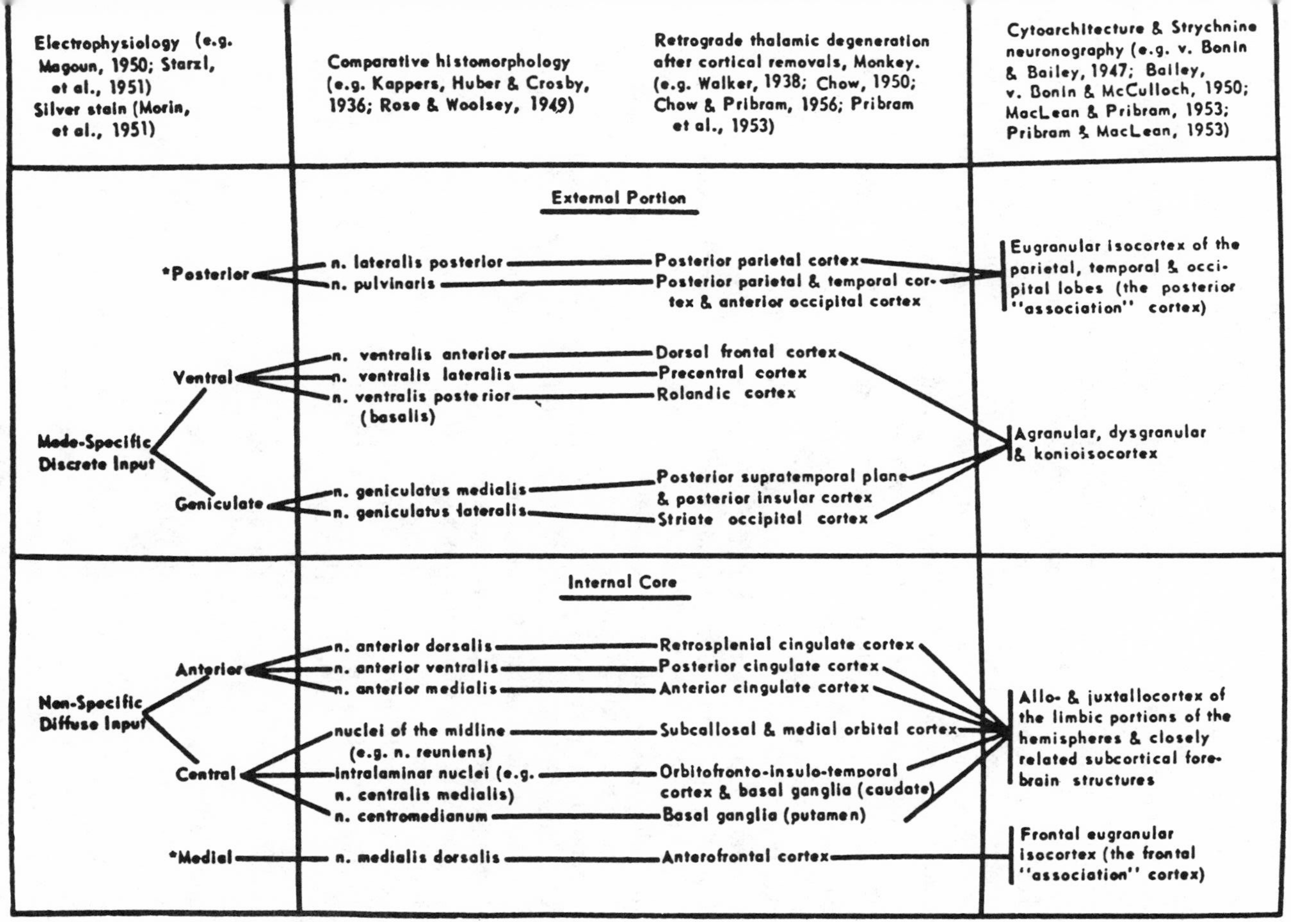

Electrophysiology (e.g. Magoun, 1950; Starzl, et al., 1951) Silver stain (Morin, et al., 1951)

Comparative histomorphology (e.g. Kappers, Huber & Crosby, 1936; Rose & Woolsey, 1949)

Retrograde thalamic degeneration after cortical removals, Monkey. (e.g. Walker, 1938; Chow, 1950; Chow & Pribram, 1956; Pribram et al., 1953)

Cytoarchitecture & Strychnine neuronography (e.g. v. Bonin & Bailey, 1947; Bailey, v. Bonin & McCulloch, 1950; MacLean & Pribram, 1953; Pribram & MacLean, 1953)

External Portion

Mode-Specific Discrete Input

*Posterior
- n. lateralis posterior — Posterior parietal cortex
- n. pulvinaris — Posterior parietal & temporal cortex & anterior occipital cortex

→ Eugranular isocortex of the parietal, temporal & occipital lobes (the posterior "association" cortex)

Ventral
- n. ventralis anterior — Dorsal frontal cortex
- n. ventralis lateralis — Precentral cortex
- n. ventralis posterior (basalis) — Rolandic cortex

Geniculate
- n. geniculatus medialis — Posterior supratemporal plane & posterior insular cortex
- n. geniculatus lateralis — Striate occipital cortex

→ Agranular, dysgranular & konioisocortex

Internal Core

Non-Specific Diffuse Input

Anterior
- n. anterior dorsalis — Retrosplenial cingulate cortex
- n. anterior ventralis — Posterior cingulate cortex
- n. anterior medialis — Anterior cingulate cortex

Central
- nuclei of the midline (e.g. n. reuniens) — Subcallosal & medial orbital cortex
- intralaminar nuclei (e.g. n. centralis medialis) — Orbitofronto-insulo-temporal cortex & basal ganglia (caudate)
- n. centromedianum — Basal ganglia (putamen)

*Medial
- n. medialis dorsalis — Anterofrontal cortex

→ Allo- & juxtallocortex of the limbic portions of the hemispheres & closely related subcortical forebrain structures

→ Frontal eugranular isocortex (the frontal "association" cortex)

FIG. 7.8. The organization of thalamo-cortical relationships as conceptualized by Pribram (from Pribram, 1958a, p. 149).

to the fact that, in man, the frontal division of the cortex accounts for one quarter of the total neocortical mass and that, together with the infero-temporal region, is the most complex and phylogenetically the newest part of the brain. Luria (1973) also noted that, in human anatomy the prefrontal cortex does not mature until late i.e., when the child is between four and seven years.

According to Ariens-Kappers et al., (1960) the frontal granular cortex is scarcely evident in ungulates and only constitutes a small area of the neo-cortex in carnivores. Akert (1964) attacked this widespread view that the pre-frontal cortex is absent in lower mammals and present only in a primitive form in carnivores. He pointed out that, if we take as the criterion for the ex-istence of a prefrontal cortex, the establishment of connections between the cortex and Nucleus Medialis Dorsalis of the thalamus, then it is clearly estab-lished that both rat and marsupial opossum have a well defined prefrontal cortex.

Pribram, Chow, and Semmes (1953) had demonstrated in the rhesus mon-key that, while the agranular motor cortex received afferents from the lateral ventral nucleus of the thalamus, the prefrontal granular cortex received tha-lamic input from the dorsomedial nucleus. Akert (1964) presented evidence on the nature of this thalamocortical relationship in cat, dog, squirrel mon-key, and rhesus monkey, using retrograde degeneration techniques following prefrontal cortical lesions. He demonstrated that in these four species the frontal granular cortex is largely, if not completely, co-extensive with the re-gions receiving the essential projections from the dorsal part of the medial nucleus of the thalamus. In all four species three subdivisions of this nucleus were identified each with a projection system to a discrete portion of the pre-frontal cortex. These three systems were "(1) pars paralamellaris to cortical area 8: (2) pars parvocellularis to the dorso-lateral cortex (area 9), and (3) pars magnocellularis to the orbital cortex" (p. 394). As well, he identified in the rhesus monkey an area of the frontal granular cortex that received no es-sential thalamic connections. He represented this diagrammatically as shown in Figure 7.9.

The discovery of small clearly defined frontal and posterior integration areas in the European hedgehog led Sanides to develop a revised view of dif-ferential trends in the prefrontal cortex. He observed that, while the deriva-tion of the primary sensory and motor cortices from the preceding ring is rel-atively easy to define, it is much more difficult to indicate the evolutionary path of the integration cortices. He therefore proposed (Sanides, 1970) a ten-tative design for the prefrontal cortex. He again arrived at the assumption of an older growth ring and a more recent core. This older prefrontal cortex ex-hibits some granularization in a paralimbic, paramotor, and in a caudo-orbital paralimbic belt with somewhat higher granularization in the orbito-medial and the frontopolar zones. The prefrontal core structures comprise

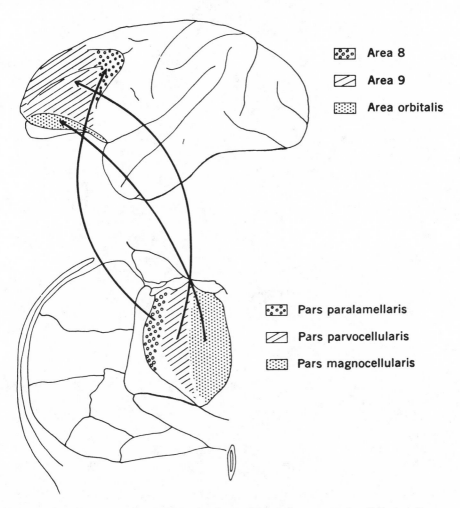

Area 8

Area 9

Area orbitalis

Pars paralamellaris

Pars parvocellularis

Pars magnocellularis

FIG. 7.9.   Cytoarchitectural map showing projections from zones of medialis dorsalis to subregions within frontal granular cortex (from Akert, 1964, p. 393).

"(1) two maxima of frontal differentiation (Max) in the convexity and orbital parts of the inferior frontal gyrus; (2) the middle section of the middle frontal gyrus and (3) the adjacent part of the superior frontal gyrus. This core is highly granularized and possesses large lamina III pyramids and a relatively weak lamina V" (p. 191). This organization is represented diagrammatically in Figure 7.10.

Sanides presented evidence for the view that the prefrontal neocortex is derived from allocortical and paleocortical spring sources. In man the inferior frontal sulcus marked the dividing line between hippocampal and piriform

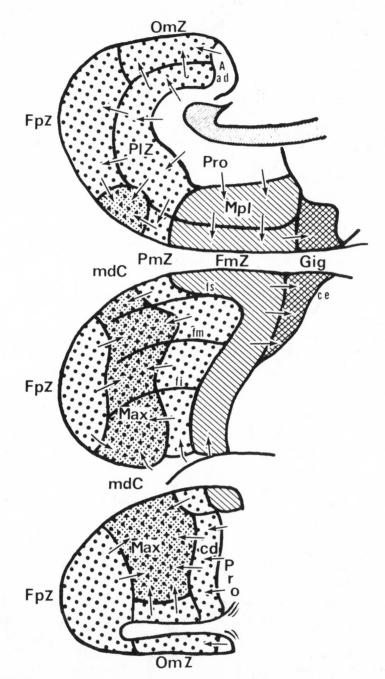

FIG. 7.10. Organization of the frontal lobe in man with precentral motor cortex and prefrontal cortex as conceptualized by Sanides: (a) medial, (b) lateral, (c) orbital aspects; frontomotor zone (FmZ) with highest specialized core, Gig. Prefrontal growth ring (dotted) and highest differentiated midfrontal core (mdC) with two differentiation maxima (Max); Aad, area adolfactoria; ce, sulius centralis; fi, fm, fs, inferior, middle, superior frontal sulci (from Sanides, 1970, p. 189).

regions of influence. In the rhesus monkey Sanides saw the sulcus principalis as fulfilling this role. In support of this he referred to a study by Nauta (1964) in which he had traced prefronto-limbic pathways and noted a dual system. Nauta found the dorsolateral prefrontal cortex projected mainly via the cingulum bundle to cingulate gyrus and from retrosplenial and parahippocampal regions. Thus this prefrontal cortical region has a major input to the hippocampal system. The ventrolateral and orbital prefrontal cortex, on the other hand, project mainly to the rostral temporal lobe and amygdala, i.e., areas in the field of the piriform cortex.

This dual origin of the prefrontal neocortex has also been clearly demonstrated in the rat. Domesick (1972) and Leonard (1969, 1972) have shown, through analysis of pathways from the mediodorsal thalamic nucleus, that two separate regions of the rat frontal cortex comprise the homologue of the monkey prefrontal region. The dorsomedial cortex, anterior to the genu of the corpus callosum in the rat, is comparable with dorsolateral convexity of the prefrontal cortex in monkey while orbital cortex in the rat has comparable thalamic relationships to that exhibited by the orbital cortex of the monkey.

The dual origin of the prefrontal neocortex with close links to two distinct limbic structures, the hippocampus on the one hand and the piriform-amygdala complex on the other, appears clearly established.

Thus, the prefrontal cortex may be seen as the association cortex for two major divisions of the limbic system and, as such, to be involved in processes concerned with the maintenance of the animal's internal environment. As we will see in Volume 2, such maintenance involves coordination of information from external and internal environments and the execution of activities that ensure the satisfaction of needs and the avoidance of harm. The combined prefrontocortical-limbic system may thus be expected to play a significant part in the development and modification of representations relating to organism and environment interactions and thus to the learning processes of the organism.

OVERVIEW: THE EVOLUTION OF THE HUMAN BRAIN

In this review of the evolutionary history of man's brain I have been concerned with the biological improvement of the nervous system. This has involved us with Hobhouse's concept of orthogenic or Aristogenic evolution: with what Hobhouse, Lashley, Jerison, and others have referred to as the evolution of mind.

With this approach it has become evident that the view that the brain has shown a steady and progressive increase in size and complexity needs at least a strong qualification. While the record viewed as a whole reveals progressive improvement, this progress could not be described as steady. It has in fact taken the form of what might be described as a series of quantum leaps with vast periods of time during which the brain has shown little appreciable change. Jerison has considered brain size to be a conservative evolutionary character for this reason. Where survival has depended on the development of fresh information processing capabilities, then the system responsible for such processing, the nervous system, has been the one that has reacted to the particular pressures. Examples that we have explored are the emergence of mammals through adaptation to a nocturnal niche, the battle between predator and prey, adaptation to life in the trees, and the final emergence of man as a social, wide-ranging omnivore.

Another long-standing concept of brain organization, namely that of evolving horizontal levels of control from hindbrain to cerebral cortex, also needs reevaluation in the light of what is now known about our evolutionary history.

This older approach presented a picture of brain evolution in which new structures developed virtually de novo and were grafted onto or were superimposed on older structures, taking over key functions, a concept of encephalization of function. This characterization of brain organization thus envisaged a multilayered, heirarchically organized structure in which each layer exercised its own functions but was subject to overriding control by those at higher levels.

An outstanding proponent of this type of approach, and one who has exercised a strong influence on recent views of brain organization, is Paul MacLean. MacLean first began developing his theory in a paper in 1949 in which he examined Papez' (1937) theory of emotion in the light of his clinical experience. He considered that in primitive forms, the visceral brain would provide the highest correlation center for the directing of the affective behavior of the animal in relation to its basic functions, e.g., eating, drinking, flight, attack, and reproduction. From this he inferred that this region would continue to service such functions in higher animals. He has since elaborated this theory in a number of papers (eg., MacLean, 1967, 1970, 1973) in which he developed the point of view that man's brain is an inherited organization of three basic types — reptilian, old mammalian, and new mammalian, with all three brains intermeshed and functioning together in what he has called the triune brain. This hierarchial representation of the three structures he depicted in the fashion shown in Figure 7.11.

The reptilian brain forms the matrix of the upper brain stem including reticular system, midbrain, and basal ganglia. The old mammalian brain comprises the limbic system and the new mammalian, the neocortex. MacLean saw many of the problems of disturbance of emotion and mood, including the psychoses, as due to a split in or failure to properly integrate the functions of the three systems and, in particular, of the limbic and neo-

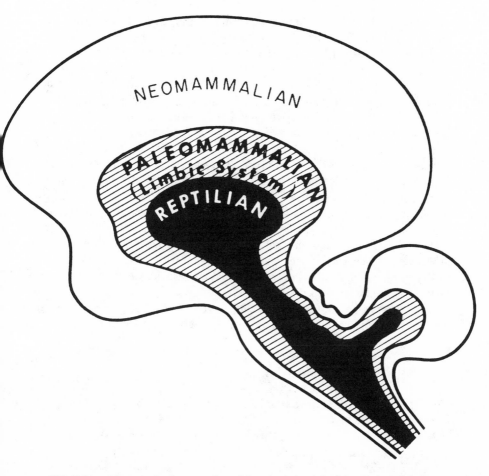

FIG. 7.11.   Diagramatic representation of three brain levels in the evolution of the human brain (from MacLean, 1967).

cortical systems. In this he highlighted the significance of amygdala and hippocampus in the expression of emotion.

While these three regions show great differences in structure and chemistry, all three must intermesh and function together. He went on to say "In popular terms the three basic brains might be regarded as biological computers each with its own special form of subjectivity and intelligence, its own sense of time and space and its own memory, motor and other functions" (MacLean 1970, p. 339).

The subdivision of the brain into unique components functioning at different levels appears contrary to all that we have established about the evolution of brains. Virtually without exception the evolutionary changes that have led to increase in brain size have involved amplification and specialization of already existing brain structure. The basic neural networks have increased in size and complexity rather than new structures being created, as is clearly evident in the evolution of the isocortex with the dual contributions of the limbic cortical regions of archipallium and paleopallium yielding a sensory-motor structure. Jerison in his analysis of brain evolution stated that "the assumption that a new system is modeled after a pre-existing system is one of my basic general assumptions" (Jerison 1973, p. 21). This view was earlier advanced by Weiskrantz (1961), who in an examination of visual encephalization observed "while I would not like to go to the opposite extreme and maintain that the sole consequence of increasing cortical development is a corresponding increase in the complexity of behavior, I do believe that the possibility of progressive *change* in function with advancing phylogenetic status has not received adequate emphasis" (Weiskrantz 1961, p. 38). This position is entirely congruent with the findings of Sanides, Diamond, and others reviewed earlier in this chapter. Pribram too, in an examination of theory in physiological psychology, argued against the view of brain evolution involving horizontal divisions of the brain and progressive encephalization (Pribram 1960). Over succeeding years he developed a very different concept of brain organization that involves a vertical interaction of evolving systems.

Living Animals with "Basal" Brains

One of my objectives was to trace the path of human evolution. Tied to this was a second objective, to establish the most likely animals, among living vertebrates, to represent the neural organization of now extinct "stem" animals along that evolutionary pathway.

During the course of this review of vertebrate evolution we encountered what amounts to a bare handful of animals that might lay claim to have brains representative of the stem species of their class. At base we saw that the central nervous system of the agnathan lamprey retains its primitive characteristics. In fact, in terms of brain/body ratio, it is shown to fall substantially below the second main group comprised of most of the remaining poikilothermic vertebrates. The lobe fin fish, or Sarcopterygii, with Latimeria and Dipnoi as living representatives also exhibit a basic primitive structure. Of the few living amphibia, the frogs, newts, and salamanders all retain the primitive organization of their nervous systems. Among the reptilia, the turtle appears to be the closest to the stem reptiles that provided the mammalian line, with these animals showing little change over a period of some 140 m.y. The rest of the living reptiles appear to be remnants of species that branched away from our main line at an early stage.

The Australian marsupials might also appear to offer several possibilities for study as stem species, but there is recent evidence that, in the process of adaptive radiation, these animals may have undergone an increase in brain size. In a quantitative comparison of the brains of two marsupials, the brush-tailed possum (*Trichosurus vulpecula*) and the quokka wallaby (*Setonix brachyurus*), with brains of a number of eutherian species (rat, rabbit, cat, sheep, and human), Meyer (1981) showed that the marsupial brains fell within the range of eutherian brains when considered relative to body weight. As well, in terms of proportional contribution to whole brain weight, the marsupial brains did not differ in basic composition from that of the eutherian brains. Of the marsupials, the brush-tailed possum might well merit consideration as a stem species although specialized for arboreal life. It has the particular advantage that there are separate representatives in both America and Australia. The two Australian monotremes, the spiny anteater and the duck-billed platypus, on the other hand, appear to have diverged sharply from the mammalian line at a very early stage.

Within the mammalian class, the line would seem to run through the basal insectivores to the arboreal insectivores, the prosimians, and simians. Even within the primate line the resolution of what are likely to be the most representative species is far from clear.

The hedgehog has been selected on occasion as a representative basal insectivore. If we follow Douglas and Marcellus's analysis, the shrews, with *Sorex minutus,* form the most likely base. At the upper end of the insectivore range the tree shrews or tupaiids establish a firm link with the prosimians. The basal prosimians include Potto and Galago. While the lemurs and lorises appear to represent a terminal branch, the line to the simians appears to be through Tarsius to the marmosets. Within the simian taxon the line from marmosets to Macaca to the great apes appears to be fairly well established though, if Douglas and Marcellus are correct, the platyrrhines Aotus, Largothrex, and Ateles warrant close consideration.

This now gives us a reference line in our approach to the study of evolution of the human brain and, in our particular quest, the evolution of learning.

This does not mean that comparative studies of learning, even when our studies are oriented to the better understanding of the origins of human learning, should be limited to these few species. Rather, it should enable us to explore the behaviors of a wide range of species with a particular orientation in view., i.e., the consideration of variations that are evident in these species that diverge from the baseline. The value of studies of stem species for the understanding of the relationships between the evolution of the nervous system and the evolution of behavior has been clearly illustrated in Diamond's work on comparative changes in the posterior neocortex of primates. Diamond examined a seeming incongruity in discrimination learning in the tree shrew in that this animal was able to learn a visual discrimination following loss of the visual cortex. He resolved this incongruity through an examination of the evolutionary development of the visual system from tree shrew to primate.

Studies of the comparative changes in relationships and complexity of organization in the limbic system and neocortex and, in particular, the dual influences on neocortical evolution of hippocampal and piriform structures, or as Sanides called them "spring sources," may also be expected to have a significant impact on our understanding of the relationships between brain organization and learning. I will be examining these relationships in some detail in a subsequent work.

While this approach may give us an orientation for future studies that appears to have been lacking in the past, it will certainly not resolve all the many problems that relate to any attempt at comparative analysis of learning, as will become evident in the chapters that follow. What, then, is the current position in the comparative study of learning and what are these problems? This is the subject of the next three chapters.

III THE COMPARATIVE STUDY OF LEARNING

If we are to consider the evolution of cognitive processes, i.e., the evolution of "mind," we should seek to establish the links between the instrument of mind, the brain, and the product of mind, behavior. My concern here is to seek for such links between the brain and learning.

In the course of my examination of the evolution of the brain and, in particular, the brain of vertebrates, I noted a very substantial increase in the volume of neural tissue, together with increasing complexity of differentiation and organization, within the various brain structures as we moved up the phyletic scale. Arguments have been advanced that such changes were likely to have resulted from survival demands for increased information and information processing capacity together with increased capability to deal effectively with the more complex relationships between stimuli that become evident. This, it was argued, resulted in increased capacity to learn, i.e., to develop and modify neural representations of environmental events.

A question of considerable theoretical interest is whether this increasing mass and complexity of neural tissue resulted in improvement, in quantitative terms, of some single learning process as has been argued by Thorndike, Skinner, and the Pavlovians, among many others, or whether qualitative changes in the process occurred. The view that a single learning process is involved appears to have originated from Darwin who concluded that phylogenetic differences in intelligence were differences in degree and not in kind (Darwin, 1871, p. 105). Thorndike, in 1901, expressed the view that "the only demonstrable intellectual advance of the monkeys over the mammals in general is the change from a few, narrowly confined, practical associations to a multitude of all sorts." Much more recently, Voronin (1962), putting forward the Pavlovian or Russian viewpoint, considered that there has been only quantitative growth or development of higher nervous activity during evolution. Thus he considered that, while learning showed an increasing role in intelligent behavior of animals as they evolved, with increasing precision and delicacy of the process, it did not undergo qualitative change but only showed quantitative augmentation. This view is strikingly similar to Thorndike's concept of neural bonds that form the substrate for his associations.

Harlow (1958) expressed a similar view. He observed that the anatomical record of the evolution of the nervous system displays a continuous and highly organized progress with no evidence that the developmental rate ever suddenly increased. From this he argued that there should be continuity from the simplest to the most complex forms of learning and that "the appearance of a radically new kind of learning at any evolutionary point or period, including that during which man developed, is not in keeping with modern gene theory" (p. 278). Following a review of cross species comparisons on a range of learning tasks Harlow concluded that:

> If one appraises factually and unemotionally the learning data of animals on problems ranging in difficulty from object discrimination to effective measures of human conceptualization capabilities, one cannot help but be struck by the intellectual kinship among the phyletic groups being tested. There is no evidence of an intellectual gulf at any point (p. 282).

Harlow then concluded that all learning and all thinking results from "a single fundamental operation, the inhibition of inappropriate responses or response tendencies" (p. 282).

Lashley (1949), like Harlow, described a continuous stream of quantitative changes in the evolution of the nervous system but, unlike Harlow, saw a contrast between this phenomenon and what he observed as "discrete qualitative changes in integrative behavior." He noted that, of all the body structures, the nervous system was, in some respects the most highly differentiated and exactly determined genetically. In other respects, however, it appeared plastic and adaptable. He argued that nerve nets observed in such regions as the cerebral cortex provided the medium for this plasticity and that this system appeared to be designed to maintain organization of behavior. He observed that even very extensive destruction of brain tissue did not produce disorganization. Rather, behavior became simpler but remained adaptive. Thus, the question, "What is the mental state of the animal?" could, said Lashley, be translated to mean, "What is the level of organization of its activities?" (p. 455). In the case of learning, he considered that the process was likely to involve organization of new schema rather than the formation of limited associations. However, such changes in more complex nervous systems appear to involve discrete qualitative changes in the kinds of integrative behavior involved in performance of particular tasks at different phylogentic levels. As an example he discussed the different types of reaction by different species performing a"matching to sample" discrimination. Some used the matching sample as a pointer, some as a signal and some as a model. He could not see how growth, in quantitative terms, of one mode of responding could transform into another. There appeared to be a clear qualitative difference. The major changes that he saw associated with increased neural capacity were "the development of intelligent foresight and the inhibition of action in anticipation of more remote prospects" (p. 475).

Thus, while Lashley disagreed with Harlow on the match between continuity of evolution of the nervous system and of behavior, both were in accord in their view that inhibition was a key process.

The evidence reviewed in earlier chapters has, however, failed to confirm the view that increase in nervous tissue proceeded at a steady pace and without changes in developmental rate. Rather, the progress has been marked by vast periods of time when little or no change in brain/body ratios was evident, followed by dramatic increases in brain size associated with particular demands for information. These demands usually involved different or more complex information loads. Thus, it is not at all improbable that such changes would produce what Lorenz has described as the "fulguration" of new learning processes. This is not to say that the earlier evolved and "simpler" processes were lost but rather that they would be subject to modification, integration, and control by the more recently evolved "higher" and more complex processes.

The question is one of particular significance for the understanding of human learning and for the construction of theories that attempt to account for this phenomenon. It is therefore one that I examine in the chapters that follow.

In particular, the nature of common learning processes needs to be identified within species if we are to establish the changing pattern of processes between species as we ascend the phylogentic scale. If, as Thorndike and Skinner have predicted, there is a single basic learning process common to all species, then this should be evidenced by consistent relationships between various learning tasks for individuals within a species. I consider the evidence relating to this concept in the latter half of the next chapter.

These analyses pave the way for my review of comparative studies of learning. In Chapter 9, I consider those studies derived from the experimental approach that have been claimed to demonstrate inter-species differences of a systematic kind. I conclude this chapter with a detailed discussion of Bitterman's approach to the study of species differences in learning and a brief note on some findings of my own. In Chapter 10, I examine a very different approach to the study of the evolution of learning processes developed through review of work in the area approached from a particular point of view, namely of an hierarchical organization of learning capacities and behaviors. This involves consideration of the work of such writers as Hobhouse, Thorpe, Lorenz, and Razran. This leads to an assessment of our current understanding of the relationships between brain and learning.

A crucial problem shaping our endeavors to establish an understanding of the evolution of learning is that we can only observe learning in existing species. These species represent the current products of millions of years of independent evolutionary development beyond the point where the ancestors of the particular species diverged from the mainstream of human evolutionary development.

While we cannot observe behavior in extinct species, the geological record does provide considerable evidence on structure or morphology. As Colbert (1958) has pointed out, study of the morphological record may be of considerable value in assessing the likely behaviors of extinct species. One area of morphological change that we have examined in some detail is that of relative brain size, and this may well be of particular significance for us.

It is also evident from the study of morphology that there are living animals that differ very little in structure, including relative brain size or in the very niches they occupy, from their early ancestors. I have referred to these as living representatives of our "stem" ancestors, and Jerison and others have called them "living fossils." For example, certain Mesozoic niches appear to have remained occupied by species that are not much different now than they were at that time. These species include the turtle and the primitive insectivores, of which the hedgehogs and shrews are living representatives. These surviving species should provide a base that will greatly enhance the significance of comparative studies.

Some indication of the extent of the problems associated with the study of the evolution of behavior and divergence of opinion on the effectiveness of the current approaches is brought out by the differing points of view expressed by Razran (1971) and Warren (1965, 1973). In recent years, said Razran, the fundamental equivalence of the main characteristics of simple conditioning in fish and monkey and, for that matter, man, has been clearly demonstrated. This simple conditioning, he continued:

> was already in full bloom on this planet some 500,000,000 years ago in organisms with no cortex, very little forebrain and, indeed, comparatively, not much

brain altogether. What then, one may ask of an unevolutionary neo-behaviorist, is the specific role of cortex and brain in the operation of mind, if mind's governing principle is, as he posits, ultimately nothing but the mechanism of simple conditioning? And is it likely that, in half a billion years, the brain has not evolved for the mind some extra principle of action and change of action? (p. 9).

Razran's underlying hypothesis was that learning may be seen as an evolved and evolving hierarchical organization of learning processes.

Warren (1973), who is perhaps best known for his work on complex discrimination learning in cats and the study of effects of various cortical ablations on such learning, presented a very different point of view. He has argued that laboratory studies of vertebrate learning have failed to yield any convincing support for general learning ability or for the view that such an ability correlates with taxonomic rank.

Both Razran and Warren are in agreement that, in comparative studies of behavior, we are concerned with animals at the end points of divergent lines of evolution that are uniquely adapted to their particular habitats. This, of course, includes specialized behavioral adaptation. With this comes selective responsiveness to simuli that has become inbuilt. For example, a tiger cub's reaction to meat on first contact is to salivate and a hare's respiratory response to rustling grass or similar sounds is evident on the first presentation of such stimuli. Other responses may be learned very quickly as evidenced by the many studies of imprinting. Razran has pointed out that, unlike the tiger cub, puppies do not salivate on first contact with meat but they rapidly learn to do so. Sheep and goats must also learn to react to the sight and odor of grass. Again responses that appear readily in one species may be very difficult to elicit in another, e.g., chicken claw lifting is readily conditioned but not the claw lifting of pigeons. (See, for example, Seligman, 1970; Shettleworth, 1972.) R.A. Hinde (1973) has considered these constraints on learning and the question of "specific preparedness" in some detail. How these various biological constraints may interact with the evolution of more general learning processes is a further area of dispute.

Jerison (1973) considered these types of differences under what he called the "principle of proper mass." This principle states that "the mass of neural tissue controlling a particular function is appropriate to the amount of information processing involved in performing the function" (p. 8). While the relative size or mass of a particular component of the nervous system may be specific to an animal's life style, this does not necessarily relate to evolutionary "progress" or, in Jerison's terms, significant increase in total brain mass. Such changes may, in fact, inhibit such progress. Jerison claimed that, while specific responses and specific skills might be related to the particular habitat and life style of a species, its capacity to utilize information is determined by its total brain mass. This view contrasts strikingly with that presented by

Lockard (1971), who argued in favor of a concept of independent evolution of behavior.

The problems associated with attempts to study the evolution of learning are thus clearly evident but solutions are not so readily apparent. A major consideration for any experimenter in this field is the strategy to be adopted. The amount that any one person can accomplish in terms of tasks used or species examined is distressingly small when measured against all that might be done. This stems from the time-consuming nature of animal studies in general and, in comparative work, from the added necessity to explore various parameters of tests and testing conditions within a species and then to extend this across species. Thus the experimenter must aim to make the most of the limited data he is able to assemble. But how best to proceed?

8 How Should One Proceed?

PROBLEMS AND TECHNIQUES

Widely differing approaches to the study of the evolution of learning have espoused diametrically opposed views. The comparative psychologist, for example, has relied on laboratory studies of behavior while the ethologist has concentrated on observation of the animal's behavior in the field. The approaches to the laboratory study of animal behavior have also differed widely.

Birch (1954) defined comparative psychology as the "study of the evolution of behavior mechanisms" but the fact that this has not been the approach of many psychologists studying animal behavior has been emphasized repeatedly. Beach, in 1950, deplored the fact that the comparative psychologist, in his hunt for animal behavior, found one animal, the white rat, and "thereupon the Comparative Psychologist suddenly and softly vanished away" (Beach, 1950, p. 115). In 1960 he came to question "the logical defensibility of any concept of comparative psychology" and would seek instead "a comparative science of animal behavior" (Beach, 1960). Here Beach appears to have fallen into the common error of confusing the comparative psychologist with those psychologists who study animal behavior as a model for human behavior, a confusion demonstrated by critics who followed him.

That comparative psychology did survive beyond this period was evidenced by the fact that Lockard (1971) mourned its death, again prematurely, in his paper "Reflections on the fall of comparative psychology." In that paper he expressed a view not dissimilar to that of Beach.

151

While Beach in 1960 was demanding, as a requirement for a comparative science of behavior, that the behaviors selected for examination be "natural" to the species and as far as possible species-specific, Bitterman was advocating the use of careful studies of animals from widely separated points in the scale (Bitterman, 1960). At about the same time Bindra (1958) suggested that we concentrate on detailed analysis of a few selected species, perhaps rat, cat, dog, monkey, chimp, and man. These authors agreed that such studies should involve a careful analysis of the behaviors being examined and this was in keeping with Harlow's view that "the primary contribution of the psychologist to behavioral science lies in the fact that he has adapted behavioral analysis to laboratory situations" (Harlow, 1958a, p.4).

As already suggested, perhaps the sharpest difference in approach is between the ethologists on the one hand and the comparative psychologists on the other. Lorenz is reported as having commented that, "While the strategy of psychologists is to assume that the processes of learning in two animals are the same until proved to be different, the strategy of ethologists is to assume that processes are different until they are proved to be the same" (Bitterman, 1975, p. 708).

Lockard, espousing the ethologist's viewpoint, argued that, as each behavior has a genetic basis and, as a result of natural selection, behaviors change to meet the needs of a particular species in a particular niche, then "What we may perceive as a meaningful and natural category is actually a mere collection of unlike phenomena, unlike because they work in different ways at the basic level while appearing similar superficially" (Lockard, 1971, p. 172). He then claimed that "the old view that the same hidden but lawful processes resided in all animals" is untenable (p. 175). However, he said, because of the constraints of the earth's environment and the fact of common descent, there are processes producing similarities. Thus, he argued, those concerned with animal behavior should work towards a theory of similarities and differences. He saw this being achieved by the use of the ethological method. By this he presumably meant analysis of animal-environment interactions within the animal's natural habitat. He saw some limited usefulness for the laboratory method in the exploration of specific questions arising out of the field work.

Like Lockard, Hodos and Campbell (1969) have attacked the notion of a "scala naturae" in the study of comparative animal behavior. Hodos and Campbell made a valid distinction between the "scala naturae" or phylogenetic scale as an hierarchical ordering and the phylogenetic tree as a genealogy. They argued that the hierarchical classification "can provide interesting information about relative performance and relative degrees of structural differentiation" but "it tells us nothing about evolutionary development since it is unrelated to specific evolutionary lineages" (p. 339).

Hodos and Campbell outlined two lines of approach to the study of behavioral evolution. In the first they proposed that animals forming a "quasi-evolutionary series within a common phylum" should be compared. Such animals would be chosen to represent ancestral groups on the grounds that they possess many characteristics that are likely to be unchanged from ancestral forms. But how does one determine which characteristics are primitive? Hodos and Campbell suggested that an animal that is morphologically primitive is likely to be behaviorally primitive and referred to such species as the hedgehog and primitive marsupials. Crocodiles and turtles, they said, also appear to be relatively unchanged.

The second approach they put forward involved analysis of adaptation. Such analysis would be based on

> the study of living animals, selected because they possess differing degrees of specialization (adaptation) with respect to some particular characteristic such as development of sense organs or central nervous system, the amount of postnatal care given to offspring, complexity of courtship patterns, etc. (p. 347).

Such studies they believed would give no direct clues to specific sequential patterns of evolutionary development but would lead to a better understanding of relationships between structure and function. Such an understanding would, of course, facilitate interpretation of comparative findings.

More recently Yarczower and Hazlett (1977) suggested that, while the construction of an evolutionary scale is inappropriate for either of the two alternative approaches suggested by Hodos and Campbell, there is a third approach to the study of behavioral evolution "for which the construction of evolutionary scales is not only legitimate but required" (p. 1088). This third approach is through the study of anagenesis, i.e., of biological improvement. In this sense, the authors claimed the notion of an ascending set of levels with animal groups at each level reflecting improvement of some particular characteristic does not differ markedly from that of evolutionary scale. This view is congruent with Hobhouse's (1926) concept of orthogenic evolution. Yarczower and Hazlett then considered a number of examples, including Bitterman's ordering of fish, turtle, pigeon, rat, and monkey in terms of several classes of learned behaviors, and Von Bekesy's (1960) study of development of the Organ of Corti in bird, alligator, duckbilled platypus, and man as legitimate uses of this approach. In the latter case an orderly reduction in number of hair cells and separation into two groups was revealed.

One of the most noted contributors to comparative psychology was T.C. Schneirla who occupied the scene through the middle years of this century. While Schneirla is probably most widely known for his work on the army ants of Barro Colorado island in Panama, his views on the nature of comparative psychology have exerted a great influence on workers in this field. Schneirla, in 1948,[1] wrote, "Comparative psychology studies similarities and differences in the environmental adjustments and behavioral organization of animals on all phyletic levels as well as individual abilities and behavioral integration within groups" (Schneirla, 1966, p. 283). He considered that the study of the ontogeny of behaviors provided an essential base for examination of the likely evolutionary course of these behaviors. Such studies, he believed, formed "the backbone of comparative psychology" (p. 284). He also argued strongly that no division should be drawn between observational and experimental methods.

In his 1966 paper Schneirla elaborated his view that study of a variety of animals, as such, does not constitute a comparative psychology any more than does the concentration on particular specialized problems. Such a concentration is, he claimed,

> discernible in the records of investigations devoted to Hullian stimulus-response theory, and in the model-making, the Pavlovian, the Lorenz-ethological, and other currently dominant doctrines of behavior. These disciplines tend to be positivistic and deductive, each, in its distinct way, centered on a set of a priori assumptions; according to such interpretations, animals become more and more alike qualitatively in behavior and differ only in degree (p. 284).

Schneirla argued that both the ethologists and the experimental psychologists were equally culpable in this respect. Operationists such as Pavlov and Skinner, he pointed out, have emphasized specific tasks with situations so arranged as to elicit some specific response, e.g., drops of saliva or a bar press. Such contrived tasks greatly restrict what the animal can do, thus excluding or obscuring its potentialities for behavioral organization. The ethologists, for their part, have become largely concerned with "molecular, particularistic considerations which oppose their working out of a molar, holistic view of each type of organism" (p. 285). This involves concentration on innate releasor mechanisms, stimulus releasors, and fixed-action patterns thus minimizing qualitative differences between phyla. Schneirla strongly disputed the use of a concept of instincts that emphasized innate "species-specific" behaviors, arguing for the notion of individual, species-typical behaviors as the developmental product of a particular genetic endowment moulded by a particular evironment.

Both the operationist and the ethological approaches were seen by Schneirla as largely ignoring the animal's potentialities for the organization of behavior and of evading the question of behavioral development, both of

---

[1]Schneirla, T.C.. Psychology, Comparative. *Encyclopaedia Britannica*, 1948, *18*, 690–708 (from Schneirla, 1966).

which he considered to be critical for the evaluation of qualitative differences in behavior between phyla.

Much of Schneirla's work has been brough together in a book of *Selected writings* edited by L.R. Aronson, E. Tobach, J.S. Rosenblatt, and D.S. Lehrman (1972), and in a set of essays edited by the same authors (1970) entitled *Development and evolution of behavior.*

Bitterman has followed the path set by Schneirla in that he has threaded his way between what he has described as two antithetical points of view, namely those of the S-R theorists and the ethologists (the development of Bitterman's work is elaborated in Chapter 9). In the course of this work he has become increasingly concerned with the elucidation of underlying learning processes common across different species. As he pointed out, such processes are not evident directly from observation of learning but are inferred from such observations. He has continued to emphasize the laboratory approach throughout this work. Brookshire (1976) too supported such an approach saying that

> the emphasis of the ethologists on field conditions does not lend itself as easily to the sort of research necessary to determine process laws as does the laboratory although laboratory conditions that more nearly mimic or duplicate natural environments may well be used (p. 193).

In his work Bitterman concentrated on a widely diverse set of species — fish, turtles, pigeons, rats, and monkeys — in his search for consistent underlying processes. Whether such common processes exist, said Bitterman (1976), can only be assessed by systematic study of a wide range of vertebrates, and such studies have not been done.

This approach of Bitterman's is obviously quite different from that of Hodos and Campbell who argue for comparison of animals that comprise a "quasi-evolutionary series"within one phylum and are consequentially related, hopefully, with relationships clearly traced. Bitterman's approach also stands in stark contrast to Lockard's emphasis on species differences and the use of the ethological approach with a limited role ascribed to laboratory studies.

Comparisons over a wide range of species are also valuable in that they are likely to throw up differences that can be explored. Bitterman (1975) argued that, against powerful theories such as those of Thorndike and Skinner that deny divergence in basic learning processes across species, the only sensible approach to the search for commonalities and differences in processes is to begin with markedly divergent animals.

Such comparisons, however, raise a further set of problems. How in fact can we make adquate comparisons across species? If, for example, one attempts to equate background or environmental experience by placing animals in a similar controlled environment, then we must relize that the life spans and natural habitats of different species vary considerably. How does one achieve identical motivation and incentive? If food is used as a reward, then it must be recognized that different species have widely different needs and widely different feeding habits. What consitute identical learning conditions for the particular tasks to be presented, e.g., the preliminary training or period of instruction during which the animal learns the nature of the question that is being asked and the kind of answer that is expected? If we prescribe a given number of preliminary trials then this may mean the achievement of widely different levels of performance. If a given level of performance is used then this will almost certainly mean a variation in number of trials given, not only between species but also within a species.

Bitterman was concerned with these problems. He pointed out that, in comparative studies, we cannot hope to achieve the objective of comparability in sensory mechanisms and in motor capacities of animals to perceive the task or problem or to execute the necessary response behavior. Even more critically, he said, the establishing of equivalence in drive levels and in reward levels across species is impossible. Attempts to compare across species using control by equation of these variables is likely to lead to results that are uninterpretable. He then argued for an alternative approach, namely control by systematic variation. The aim with this approach is to examine a particular learning task in a given species while systematically varying such variables as drive and reward over a wide range and thus establishing optimal conditions for the appearance of a given phenomenon that is not found when we first look for it (Bitterman, 1960, 1975). I examine his use of this technique in the next chapter.

From the foregoing it is evident that there are a variety of approaches to the study of the evolution of learning with, not infrequently, those espousing one approach decrying the work of others. At this stage it seems that any one of these approaches, if pursued with due regard for the findings of others, may yield data of significance for our major question, and there is still a paucity of such data.

My own approach, however, concentrates on studies involving the experimental analysis of learning. This does not mean that I am unaware of the contribution that the ethological approach has made to our overall understanding of the evolution of learning. Ethologists have, however, shown much more interest in fixed action patterns. In this context Thorpe (1961) commented that the most striking and challenging examples of animal behavior for the ethologist are those found to be the most characteristic of the species, i.e., relatively stereotyped, instinctive behaviors. He then went on to say that he found "almost incomprehensible the reluctance of the psychologist both 'human' and 'comparative' to take seriously this stereotyped behavior and to pay due regard to its major theoretical implications" (Thorpe, 1961, p.

87). As already indicated, I believe that an understanding of these inherited or instinctive representational patterns for behavior is basic to the understanding of learning. However, I am concerned with the flexible or modifiable patterns rather than the inbuilt ones here.

Ethologists studying fixed action patterns that have developed to meet the demands of specific environments have tended to argue that these same processes would produce specialized learning abilities again adapted to specific environments. From this position they have then argued that comparisons of learning across different species are largely a wasted effort, a point of view expressed by Lockard and referred to earlier. Phylogenetic generalization, in this context, said Brookshire (1976) can only take the form of rules about the ways in which these special learning abilities emerge through natural selection. As I show in Chapter 10, however, Thorpe and Lorenz have made frequent use of laboratory-based studies in the development of their concepts of a hierachy of learned behaviors (i.e., learning processes).

INDIVIDUAL DIFFERENCES WITHIN SPECIES

As I observed earlier, individual variation within species, as a product of genetic differences, provides the very core of the evolutionary processes that lead to species differentiation. Tryon, who became famous for his development of "maze-dull" and "maze-bright" strains of rats, stressed the need to study individual differences within species. He pointed out that, in order to properly understand the behavior of a species we must consider the variability of behavior among the individuals of that species (Tryon, 1942).

In the early part of this century Lashley was a leader in the attack on the problem of the physiological basis of complex adaptive behavior, of intelligence. This work culminated in his monograph "Brain mechanisms and intelligence" published in 1929. In introducing this work Lashley observed that there is

> little more hope of finding a satisfactory formulation of animal intelligence
> than of human, and we must fall back upon the same method of analysis which
> seems to provide an empirical solution of the human problem, the determina-
> tion of intercorrelations among specific activities (Lashley, 1929, p. 13).

Here Lashley was referring to the scientific studies of individual differences in man that were initiated by Galton with his work on "hereditary genius" published in 1869. This was followed by the massive development of mental tests for the assessment of ability and personality factors. This work relied heavily on the correlation method developed by Pearson. This relatively rapid progress in the study of individual differences in man following

Galton's work was not mirrored in the study of other species. Individual differences in any one type of behavior, e.g., learning a maze, discriminating between two stimuli, fearfulness displayed in an open field situation, have been demonstrated in many studies but these findings have only a limited descriptive value unless such specific differences can be shown to be the resultant of more general characteristics of the animal. The experiments that Lashley undertook were "an attempt to sample the activities of the rat to determine the correlations among them, and to test the influence of certain neurological variables upon them" (Lashley, 1929, p. 14).

Using rats and four different mazes Lashley was not able to establish any significant reliabilities between part and whole test scores, or significant correlations between mazes for unoperated animals. With animals suffering removal of varying amounts of cerebral cortex, however, the correlations were much higher and significant. He concluded that while "the maze methods are inadequate to reveal the slight variations within a normal population, they do form an adequate measure of the enormously greater differences within a group of animals having extensive injuries to the cerebrum" (p. 23).

Lashley then concentrated his efforts on experiments involving the effects of varying size of lesion in the cerebrum of the rat on learning and retention of the mazes. He demonstrated a significant relationship betwen lesion size, maze difficulty, and errors. As a result of this work Lashley formulated his neurological concepts of equipotentiality and of mass action. His now classical pictorial representation of the relationships between size of cortical lesion and errors in maze learning is shown in Figure 8.1.

An examination of various studies involving correlation between measures of ability in the rat was undertaken by Commins, McNemar, and Stone (1932), and this also yielded correlations that were of zero or near zero proportions. These included work by Bagg (1929) on errors made by rats in learning a simple maze and a multiple choice task; by Hunter and Randolph (1924) with rats in a T-maze, a straight-away maze, and a problem box; by Williams (1929) with rats in a discrimination box and a 14″ T-Maze; by Heron (1922) with an inclined plane problem box and a simple maze; and by Lashley with a T-maze and a mirror image of this.

On the other hand, significant positive correlations were recorded in three separate studies. Davis and Tolman (1924), with rats in two different alley mazes recorded correlations of from .40 to .66; Miles (1930) using an alley maze and an elevated maze of the same pattern got correlations of a similar order, and Tryon (1931) with 141 rats in two T-type alley mazes got a correlation of .77.

In their own studies Commins et al., (1932) using a triple platform problem box, a light discrimination box, and a Stone multiple T-maze with rats, obtained near zero correlations. In a second study with 256 rats in a Stone multiple T-maze, a Stone light discrimination box, and two elevated mazes they

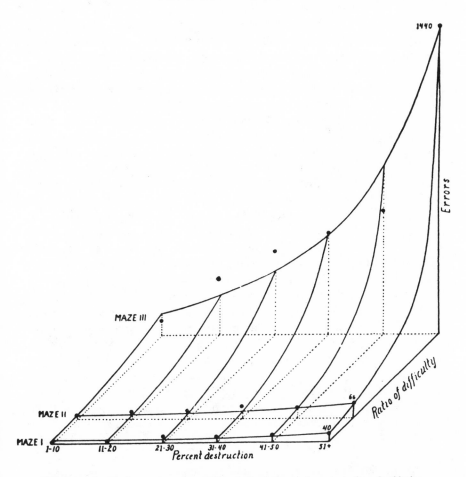

FIG. 8.1.   Lashley's representation of the relation between the extent of cerebral lesion, difficulty of the problem to be learned, and degree of retardation. The separation of the curves represents the relative difficulty of the problems for normal animals; the abscissae of the curves, the percentage destruction; and the ordinates, the number of errors made during training (from Lashley, 1929, Figure 17).

got intercorrelations between the three mazes ranging from .56 to .66. The light discrimination box and problem box showed no correlation with the mazes. This, in conjunction with Tryon's findings indicated some common "maze learning ability" in rats.

Dunlap (1933) gave 10 learning tests to 119 chickens and achieved average correlations of around 0.20, and McCullock (1935) reported testing 85 rats in eight learning tasks, six discrimination tasks, a 27-unit maze, a two pedal problem box, and an "irrelevant" motor task. The resultant correlations were near zero.

One of the most detailed and extensive studies of this period was by R.L. Thorndike, son of E.L. Thorndike. Records were obtained from 64 albino rats on seven tasks, namely an activity wheel, Warden-Warner mazes (two patterns), an elevated T-maze, the Jenkins circular problem box, a latch problem box, the Warner conditioned response test, and the Columbia obstruction apparatus for the measurement of hunger drive.

In introducing the project Thorndike (1953) listed some 30 studies and showed that, for most of them the tests yielded low reliability measures. Some of the more recent studies at the time that were listed did show distinctly higher reliabilities, the outstanding one being a coefficient, after correction, of .988 reported by Tryon (1931) for 141 rats on a 17-unit multiple T-maze. Tryon correlated odd vs. even unit scores. Thorndike observed that these higher reliabilities reflected improved apparatus, with more difficult and more uniform mazes, and better techniques, including objective scoring, gentled or test-broken animals, and carefully controlled situations. In his own study Thorndike extracted 31 different measures from his seven tests. Reliabilities, following application of the Spearman-Brown correction for attentuation, were high (.70 to .95). The intercorrelations, however, were, in the main, low except between mazes. The maze correlations were of the order of .45 to .50. The remaining tests yielded a median value of 0.20. Factor analysis of the data using L.L. Thurstone's center of gravity method yielded three significant factors, namely: (1) docility, maze learning, intelligence, tameness; (2) transfer: distinguishing early from later tests; and (3) a factor specific to the different CR scores. Royce (1950) in his review of factorial analyses of animal behavior noted that Van Steenberg (1939) reanalyzed Thorndike's data and obtained 10 factors of which he could identify five, namely, visual, adaptability to test situations, speed, kinesthetic ability, and visual insight.

Royce (1950) also referred to a study by Vaughn (1937) in which a variety of pieces of apparatus, namely four different mazes, a wildness tunnel, an activity cage, a problem box, a Maier reasoning test, and a perseverance box were employed, again with rats. This study yielded eight factors. Of these Vaughn identified speed, docility, insight learning, and transfer. Royce, from his review of these various studies, concluded, as had Tryon earlier, that any assumption of a unitary learning factor was untenable.

The great majority of studies on generality of traits within individual species has been concerned with learning. Hall (1951) and Royce (1950) both referred to a limited number of studies dealing with other traits. Hall pointed out that, from the work of Anderson and Klein such traits as fearfulness, aggressiveness, activity, exploratory behavior, and sex drive may be characterized as possessing situational generality with some evidence that an animal's rank in a group remains constant over a period of some months.

In the cognitive area, our area of concern, it would seem that the study of individual differences, in terms of generality of traits, was marked by a period of moderate activity and productivity between 1930 and 1940. This has been followed by a prolonged drought. Studies that were carried out were mainly with the white rat and mainly involved simple learning tasks. The learning situations were usually of the trial and error type, e.g., mazes, latch boxes, puzzle boxes, or involved simple discrimination, e.g., the light discrimination box.

Since Hall's review in 1951, contributions in this area have been few. It seems that the largely negative findings and the magnitude of the testing tasks have acted as effective deterrents. As well, the nature of the questions being asked in the study of animal behavior turned away from enquiry into individual differences. Several studies do, however, warrant consideration.

Warren (1961) examined individual differences in discrimination learning in 21 cats, which were trained on four sign differentiated positional (SDP) and four sign differentiated object (SDO) discriminations. These animals had also been trained on a series of discrimination reversals, had been retested on serial reversals of a simple position habit and, immediately following the SDP and SDO discriminations, had learned the Double Alternation Problem. All tasks were given in the Wisconsin General Test Apparatus. Since repeated reference is made to this apparatus, it is represented in Figure 8.2.

Warren found that all correlations between measures of discrimination were positive, ranging from .23 to .81, and 8 of the 10 were statistically significant. None of the five correlations between double alternation learning and discrimination learning was statistically significant.

Using tests of a similar nature to those employed by Warren in a series of comparative studies of learning in the rat, rabbit, and cat, I examined within-species differences in learning of four separate tasks. These were the Hebb-Williams Closed Field Test (Hebb & Williams, 1946; Livesey, 1966), the Hebb-Williams elevated pathway (Hebb & Williams, 1946; Livesey, 1967), a discrimination generalization task (Livesey, 1968) and the Double Alternation Problem (Hunter, 1920; Stewart & Warren, 1957; Livesey, 1965). The numbers were small, with eight rats, 10 rabbits, and eight cats. Nonetheless, some interesting and significant correlations resulted (Livesey, 1970). These are shown in Table 8.1.

For both rats and rabbits, the correlations between three of the tests, the Closed Field, Elevated Pathway, and Discrimination Task were high, while correlations between these tests and the Double Alternation problem were low. For cats the trend was in this direction but the correlations were generally lower. These results were thus similar to those reported by Warren with tasks that would seem to be of the same class. It is interesting to note that, in

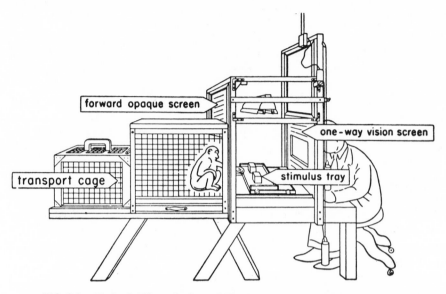

FIG. 8.2.   Harlow's Wisconsin General Test Apparatus (from Harlow, 1958b, p. 15).

both Warren's and my studies, the task which has been specifically associated with the frontal cortical system of the brain, the Double Alternation Task (Leary, Harlow, Settlage, & Greenwood, 1952; Warren, Warren, & Akert, 1961), showed no significant correlation with the remainder.

A further major study to examine the nature of individual differences in animal learning across a number of tests was undertaken by John Davenport's group at the regional Primate Center in Wisconsin. In this study performances of both rats and monkeys were examined using banks of five computer controlled animal testing boxes. In 1972 they reported using the system extensively to test animals for "mental retardation" in projects on hypothyroidism and malnutrition. In their discussion on uses of the system they commented: "In the first three years of this work it became quite apparent that the achievement of final draft intelligence test batteries whose component parts are empirically validated is at least a 10-year proposition (Davenport, Benson, Hagquist, Rankin, & Shelton, 1972).

To date then, studies of individual differences in learning and problem solving ability within species have, in general, failed to yield any clear picture of underlying processes. The earlier work produced largely insignificant correlations between tests with the exception of a common maze learning ability in rats.

It is in fact a noteworthy feature of this earlier work on individual differences in animal learning that the learning activities studied were those that have now been shown not to provide any significant differences between species when viewed in phylogenetic sequence. The available evidence reveals that, for many of these tasks, there are striking similarities in performance between animals in different phyla and characteristically wide individual differences within species. This was one of the main considerations that led E.L. Thorndike to suggest that underlying learning processes might also be the same for all species. Simple discrimination ability, speed of learning of simple tasks, and duration of retention of such learned responses show remarkable similarity between widely different species. Diamond and Chow (1962) pointed out that "in general, simple learning tasks have failed to differentiate higher and lower mammals" (p. 176).

Russian work reviewed by Razran (1961) also supports this view in that no significant difference in rate of simple operant conditioning was observed between fish, chickens, ducks, pigeons, rabbits, dogs, and monkeys. That this is so should come as no great surprise in the light of Razran's observation that such behaviors were likely to have been evident in animals existing more than 500,000,000 years ago (Razran, 1971).

TABLE 8.1
Spearman Rank-Order Correlations between the Four Tests for Rats, Rabbits and Cats

	Closed Field (Error Score)	Elevated Path (Error Score)	Discrimination (Number Correct)	Double Alternation (Sequences to Criterion)
Rats ($n = 8$)				
Closed Field	—	.810*	.613	.143
Elevated Path		—	.768*	.071
Discrimination				−.365
Rabbits ($n = 10$)				
Closed Field	—	.897+	.815+	.273
Elevated Path			.731*	.158
Discrimination				.453
Cats ($n = 8$)				
Closed Field	—	.393	.667*	.298
Elevated Path			.417	.571
Discrimination				−.083

* = $p<0.05$ + = $p<0.01$

The very nature of the tests used, i.e., generally tests of simple learning, makes the absence of evidence for underlying processes not altogether surprising. In fact this work yielded results comparable with those from early work on human individual differences in cognitive processing, where the tests again involved simple sensory and motor tasks. These early measures of human individual differences, developed prior to the beginning of the century by J. McKeen Cattell (Cattell, 1890), were mainly of simple sensory functions that could be scored in precise physical units. Examples include dynamometric pressure, rate of movement, reaction time, bisection of a 50 cm line, memory for letters, to name but a few. Tuddenham (1962) in considering this early work referred to studies by Wissler (1901), who, utilizing the then new Pearson correlation method, examined the consistency of these psychological tests with one another, with anthropometric measures and with college grades. Physical measures showed positive correlations with one another as also did college grades. Correlation between physical measures and college grades were low "and neither category showed much relationship to Cattell's psychological tests." However, it was in relation to these psychological tests that the greatest concern was evident for, in Tuddenham's words, the Cattell tests "failed to even correlate with each other, r's between different pairs ranging from $-.28$ to $+.39$, little more than a mere chance relation" (Tuddenham, 1962, p. 478). In the absence of correlations among them, Wissler could only conclude that each psychological test measured an independent ability. "It followed that such tests had very limited value for predicting the useful capacities of the individual" (Tuddenham, 1962, p. 478).

In the light of these difficulties it is not altogether surprising that progress has been slow. Another daunting feature for the further development of this area is the great amount of work required to produce even modest results. It is evident that, for the resolution of common underlying factors in cognitive processes within subhuman species, we have scarcely scratched the surface. The few more recent studies that I have reviewed in which more complex tasks have been employed have yielded some useful relationships. These findings are again in keeping with the vast body of work from human studies where more complex, problem-oriented tasks have yielded consistent patterns of individual differences in the area of cognitive processing.

These findings have important implications for further work in the study of within-species patterns of learning. From the point of view of our main endeavor however, they serve to strengthen the belief that differences between species will most likely be revealed by tests that tap more complex facets of the learning process involving integration and organization of varied informational input. I consider this proposition in the next two chapters.

9 An Experimental Approach to Comparative Studies of Learning

In 1949 Lashley was constrained to comment that

> there are remarkably few comparative studies which are really significant for the evolution of behavior. A great part are meaningless for the problem, either because the questions were improperly put or because the tests were made with a single species and comparable data are available for no other (p. 456).

A reflection of this dearth of comparative material is seen in the decline in the number of species studied in experiments on animal learning since 1911 as shown by Beach in his 1950 paper "The Snark was a Boojum."

Bitterman (1965) extended by a further decade Beach's graphical presentation of the varying percentage of animal species used between 1911 and 1948. As Figure 9.1 shows, the position remained unaltered from 1948 to 1958.

Much of the work that has been undertaken relates to instinctive and learned behaviors within various individual species, and there are a number of reviews to which the reader may refer. These include the three volume work "Comparative psychology: A comprehensive treatise" by Warden, Jenkins, and Warner (1935), which gives an indication of the number and range of studies undertaken up to that time; Thorpe's (1956) "Learning and instinct in animals"; Razran's (1971) "Mind in evolution" and Corning, Dyal, and Wilton's three volume work on "Invertebrate learning," published over the period 1973–1975. However, my particular concern is with comparative or cross species studies.

In this chapter I examine work involving one or more discrete tasks that has been claimed to demonstrate interspecies similarities and differences of a systematic kind. I also look at some of the controversies that relate to these

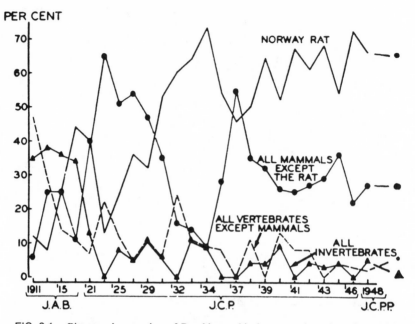

FIG. 9.1.   Bitterman's extension of Beach's graphical presentation of species used in studies of comparative behavior. Figure shows percentage of papers dealing with animals in each of four categories which appeared between 1917 and 1948 in *Journal of Animal Behavior*, the *Journal of Comparative Psychology*, and the *Journal of Comparative and Physiological Psychology* as presented by Beach (1950) with Bitterman's extension of these points to 1958. (from Bitterman, 1965, p. 397).

data. My analysis is confined almost exclusively to laboratory based studies, as I consider such studies to be the most likely to reveal underlying processes of learning.

In the course of this examination I look particularly for evidence pointing to increasing capacity to deal with complex stimulus relationships and to organize information in order to produce appropriate responses. As well I consider the evidence in terms of likely qualitative as well as quantitative changes in capacity to deal with such information. A qualitative change would be evidenced if some new way of organizing and integrating information emerged that had not been evident in other more primitive species. The appearance of such a change would point to the likelihood that new learning processes have evolved rather than there being a single all embracing unitary factor that would account for all learning.

Harlow (1958a), in outlining his position with respect to the evolution of learning, observed that:

The existing psychological-biological data make it quite clear that evolution has resulted in the development of animals of progressively greater potentialities for learning and for solving problems of increasing complexity [After commenting briefly on some of the data obtained from various species he concluded:] It is interesting to look at the evolution of learning from the anatomical point of view. We make the assumption that learning is primarily a function of the nervous system, or at least that complexity of learning is intimately related to the developing complexity of the nervous system (Harlow, 1958a, pp. 269, 271).

This general concept is compatible with the views of Lashley and Pribram, referred to earlier, that size and complexity of the nervous system are associated with increased ability to process and integrate more diverse information. Jerison too considered that the capacity to organize perceptual information within a temporal framework was a significant product of the evolution of larger and thus more proficient nervous systems. When temporal relationships became a critical element in the analysis of distance information, argued Jerison (1973), the threshold was reached for the organization of perceptual worlds, i.e., worlds in which objects were perceived as constant over time under changing conditions. This he considered to be a dimension of intelligence which he defined as a behavioral variable involved in the richness of the perceptual world of a given species. The number of neurons and the density of their interconnections, Jerison considered, should reflect the degree to which sensory systems became elaborated and interconnected and hence the capacity of the animal to perceive events in a real world. He concluded that the integrative functions of the brain, i.e., those functions which will define intelligence for us, are determined by the amount of brain that is typical for an animal of a particular species.

Considering this capacity to organize and utilize information, Pribram (1958a) for example, drew attention to early studies by Yerkes on the response to auditory stimulation in the frog. Yerkes (1904, 1905) showed that some sounds, e.g., splashing of water, led to a more rapid response to a shortly following visual stimulus. The animal was, as it were, alerted or tensed by the earlier stimulus but was able to withhold or delay any response to this stimulus until it received more information, e.g., on where to jump — or more particularly, where not to jump. This, of course, makes good sense biologically as the ability to delay a response in this way has high survival value. Pribram contrasted this increased flexibility in response to particular stimuli by the frog with the inflexible immediate response to stimulation found in the fish.

Lashley, in a study of the behavior of terns, found that the two most striking features in the colonial life and behavior of these birds were the enormous number of habits which they exhibited and the disconnected, impulsive character of their activities. In its reaction to any new situation, the behavior of the bird was characterized by immediate, impulsive responsiveness. It appeared as if one group of stimuli would gain control and determine the bird's reaction in spite of contradictory elements in the situation as a whole. The bird's reaction was largely stimulus controlled (Lashley, 1915). Lashley drew attention to the bird's lack of ability to organize incoming information in order to achieve a coordinated response to the varied and complex information available to it.

It is within this context that I now examine a number of studies involving specific tasks used largely in the study of vertebrate and particularly mammalian learning.

SOME SPECIFIC LEARNING TASKS AND THEIR IMPLICATIONS

1. Delay of Response.   Hunter (1917) showed that tasks calling for delay of response differentiated between animals in different classes. He demonstrated that rats could delay a response for only a few seconds and then only if body orientation was maintained. Raccoons could delay for 30–35 seconds, a dog for five minutes, and children up to eight years of age succeeded in delays of up to 25 minutes. In this task the stimulus is absent at the time of choice so that the animal must be reacting to a substitute for that factor, some representation or trace or some symbolic process. More recent studies by Miles (1957a) and Meyers, McQuiston, and Miles (1962) provided further support for phylogenetic ordering on this task as suggested by Hunter, with rhesus monkeys proving superior to marmosets and marmosets being superior to cats.

Fletcher (1965) concluded that "recent experimenters have verified the general correlation between phylogenetic status and performance on the delayed-response problem without primary regard to absolute limits of delay" (Fletcher, 1965, p. 132). He observed that wide variations in delay could be obtained with different techniques.

2. The Double Alternation Task.   A task closely associated with delayed response is the double alternation problem. In this problem the animal is required to make a choice between two alternatives, e.g., a right or left turn at the end of a runway or between two identically marked locations. In a double alternation sequence the animal is required to give the same response twice in succession to one side and then two successive responses to the alternative side to achieve a successful sequence. There is no change in the spatial arrangement facing the animal so it must make use in some way of stored information about the temporal sequence.

Hunter, in 1920, developed the Double Alternation Temporal maze to study kinesthetic processes in the white rat. In this maze the rat had a common starting point and initial runway path for each response in a sequence. At the end of the runway it could turn right or left. Following choice it returned to its original start point. The apparatus is represented in Figure 9.2.

A correct sequence might be: turn right, back to start point, turn right, back to start, turn left, back to start, and then turn left again. Hunter found, to his great surprise, that "this apparently simple problem was never mastered by any one of nineteen rats who were tested on it under various conditions" (Hunter, 1920, p. 3). He concluded that rats could not learn double alternation in the temporal maze.

Hunter later demonstrated that, if the rat learned the double alternation as a spatial sequence, using four boxes, and if the boxes were then reduced to two and finally to one, thus converting the problem from a spatial to a temporal one, some rats could then successfully execute the sequence. These animals were, however, not able to extend the sequence from LLRR to LLRRLL (Hunter & Nagge, 1931).

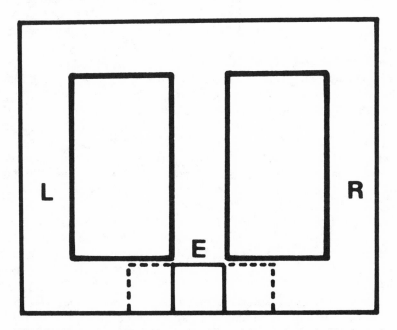

FIG. 9.2.   Floor plan of Hunter's apparatus for training rats in the double-alternation temporal-maze task.

After establishing that raccoons could master a simple RRLL response pattern, Hunter (1928) pointed out that the double alternation problem showed the same phylogenetic relationship as the delayed response task and considered that it involved the same neural or symbolical processes. He observed that: "It is impossible for one and the same stimulus to cause first one response then another unless it is supplemented by some other factor either inside or outside the organism" (p. 377). He considered that this effect must be due to either (1) cumulative piling up in the nervous system of retained effects of responses already made until the response was performed automatically or (2) a symbolic process that provided the cues to change direction.

Gellermann (1931) also pointed to a significant phylogenetic sequence from rat to human in the ability to master the double alternation problem. He demonstrated that the monkey could master the task more quickly and adequately than rat or raccoon and could extend the sequence, and that human subjects mastered it more quickly than monkeys. (Gellermann, 1931a, 1931b, 1931c).

Further significance has attached to this particular learning task as a result of a demonstrated relationship between prefrontal cortical lesion and reduction in learning capacity of both monkeys (Leary, Harlow, Settlage, & Greenwood, 1952) and cats (Warren, Warren, & Akert, 1962). A similar relationship has been demonstrated between prefrontal lesion and delayed response learning (Pribram, Mishkin, Rosvold, & Kaplan, 1952; Orbach & Fischer, 1959; Miles & Blomquist, 1960).

The original temporal maze was used in all these earlier studies but in 1931 Gellermann developed an alternative procedure whereby the animal made a selection from two identical boxes on each choice occasion. More recently this principle has been adapted in the Wisconsin General Test Apparatus (WGTA).

A number of species has been tested for double alternation learning in the WGTA using a technique developed by Stewart and Warren in 1959. In this apparatus the animal is faced with two food wells covered by identical blocks and must make the correct choice of block in order to get a reward. Several species, including cats (Stewart & Warren, 1957), and raccoons (Johnson, 1961) were tested using this apparatus with results comparable to those recorded in the temporal maze. Using a similar technique (see Figure 9.3), I added rats and rabbits to the species examined and I also tested a further group of cats.

By and large the results confirmed those found in earlier studies and I concluded at that time that, for the double alternation problem, the phylogenetic differences already noted had been confirmed and extended. The rat was shown to be able to master the problem but required many more trials than the rabbit or cat. Cats learned the task somewhat more quickly than rabbits but the difference was not statistically significant (Livesey, 1965).

Things are, however, not necessarily as simple as they seem. In a study with rhesus monkeys in 1959, Warren and Sinha had found that their animals took many more trials to learn the task than was the case with Gellermann's animals and, in fact, they took much longer than raccoons, cats, or rabbits. At the time they attributed this difference to specific learning sets that had already been established in their animals over a number of discrimination tasks.

Gellermann, in his work, had also shown that monkeys, having learned a four response sequence, e.g., LLRR were able to extend it, e.g., to LLRRLLRR. Yamaguchi and Warren (1961) compared the ability of cats to learn single or double alternation sequences and sequences of extended length, i.e., beyond the basic four responses. They found that cats learned double alternation more rapidly than single alternation. On the extension of

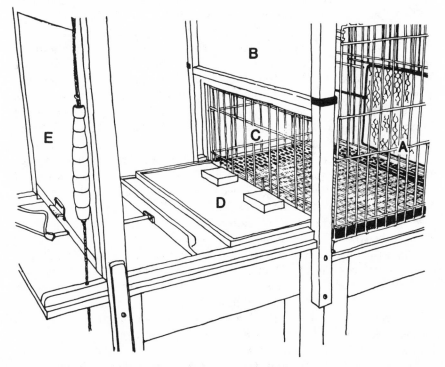

FIG. 9.3.   WGTA configuration used in double alternation testing of rats, rabbits and cats. A, animal holding cage; B, sliding screen; C, grille through which response is made; D, movable tray holding response objects with food wells under; E, one way screen separating experimenter and responding animal.

the double alternation sequence, however, cats failed to reach criterion on an eight-response sequence in 60 days of testing, confirming a previous finding by Stewart and Warren (1957). Johnson (1961), working with raccoons, concluded that neither cats nor raccoons were able to master the eight-response sequence, nor did either species show evidence of improvement as practice progressed. Yamaguchi and Warren found that the single alternation sequence, on the other hand, once mastered was readily extended to six, eight, and even longer response sequences.

While I was with Harry Harlow at the Regional Primate Laboratory in 1966, I took the opportunity to explore further the extension and transfer phenomena. In a study of double and single alternation learning in rhesus monkeys, I confirmed Warren and Sinha's (1959) finding that, in the WGTA, these animals do take a long while to master the four-response double alternation problem (Livesey, 1969). I also established that, once they had learned this sequence, the monkeys were able to extend it to eight and 12 responses. In this respect then the double alternation task was successful in differentiating the performance of primates from that of other species.

On my return to Perth in 1967, Audrey Little and I decided to explore further this problem of sequential learning by running a similar study to the monkey study, using four-year-old kindergarten children. In this study (Livesey & Little, 1971) we found that, like monkeys, children took a relatively long time, i.e., about as long as raccoons, to master the four-response double alternation sequence. The comparisons between the different species examined over these various studies, i.e., rats, rabbits, cats, raccoons, monkeys, and human children, are shown in Figure 9.4.

The children were, however, able to extend the sequences even more readily than the monkeys, once they had mastered the initial sequence. Unlike cats and monkeys, the children learned the single alternation task more readily than the double alternation task and, as with cats and monkeys, learning one of the sequences (e.g., double alternation) appeared to facilitate learning of the other (i.e., single alternation).

Warren claimed, and to me there seems little doubt, that in the case of rats, rabbits, and cats, the double alternation sequence is learned as four distinct responses through cumulative piling up of those response relations in the nervous system. This would seem to apply equally to raccoons. There appears little doubt, either, in the light of both performance and spontaneous verbalization, that the children established a symbolic representation of the sequence and, in consequence, could readily extend it.

The children's verbalizations were recorded during the experiment. These were quite spontaneous but provided valuable clues to their learning processes. For example, they appeared to establish the correct starting side for the sequence by viewing it with reference to the room, e.g., the wall side, the window side, thus relating the task to the specific context. As well, all chil-

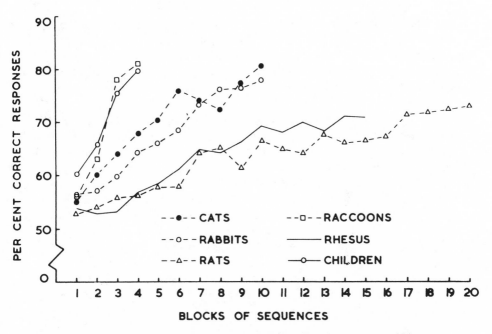

FIG. 9.4. Comparisons of double alternation performance for cats, rats, rabbits, raccoons, monkeys and children. The data for rats, rabbits, and cats are from Livesey (1965), for monkeys, from Livesey (1969), for raccoons, from Johnson (1961) and for children from Livesey and Little (1971).

dren who verbalized about the task gave the solution spontaneously some trials before they actually performed it at criterion level. Three children, for example, made consistent errors while verbalizing "two on the wall side, two on the window side." The best results were obtained when the children verbalized the actual sensorimotor pattern, e.g., "this one now, this one again. Now this one's turn, now this one's turn again."

Monkeys would appear to be at a transition point in the development of concept formation in relation to sequential learning. There was a slow and tentative building up of the sequence relationship but when, at last, this relationship was learned the monkey, unlike the cat or raccoon, was able to do something more than just repeat it, i.e., it was able to use the concept to extend the sequence.

Warren (1965) concluded that the double alternation task is "no more successful than simple discrimination problems in differentiating the performance of primates from other mammals" (p. 268). In fact it would seem that task performance shows a dramatic shift from one class of solution to another in transition from sub-primates to primates. In sub-primates a differentiation in rate of learning was observed between rats, rabbits, cats, and raccoons in terms of Hunter's concept of "cumulative piling up in the nervous system of retained effects of responses already made." In the rhesus monkeys and four-year-old children, we see a shift to the development of concept formation and the use of symbolic representation with the ability to extend the sequence beyond the four response patterns. This shift could constitute a qualitative difference between subprimates and primates.

3. *Visual Discrimination Learning with Increasing Number of Cue Dimensions.* From a series of studies emanating largely from his laboratory at the Primate Research Center in Wisconsin, Harlow noted the phylogenetic significance of increasing the number of alternative possible solutions involved in a visual discrimination task.

Harlow (1958a) pointed out that simple object or cue discrimination can be achieved by a wide range of animals, including fish, mice, rats, pigeons, cats, and dogs as well as monkeys, apes, and man. This task, he said, involves one condition of ambiguity, i.e., the animal has to decide whether to respond to place or object. In this case the correct solution is to respond to object irrespective of place. The oddity problem involves a single additional dimension of ambiguity or choice. Three objects are presented, two the same and one different. The animal is required to respond to the odd object irrespective of place.

While no pigeon, rat, cat, or dog has been observed to solve this problem, pigeons, rats (Wodinsky & Bitterman, 1953), and cats (Boyd & Warren, 1957) are reported to have solved simplified versions of the oddity problem, i.e., when the correct cue is always located on the outside. This task, said Harlow, is also beyond the intellectual capacity of the young child. Five-year-old children can solve the standard oddity problem and children as young as 3 years 6 months may also be successful with decreased salience of irrelevant cues and increased salience of the odd cue (Gollin & Schadler, 1972).

By adding a third choice dimension, with either odd or non-odd objects being correct, dependent upon the color of the test tray, the problem becomes so difficult that no subprimate can learn it. It can be mastered by monkeys and apes but, said Harlow, many human beings cannot solve problems of this difficulty. One chimpanzee was successful in mastering a discrimination with five-condition ambiguity (Nissen, 1951), and, said Harlow, the capacity to categorize color exhibited by a rhesus monkey (Weinstein, 1955) was "disarmingly humanoid." He went on to point out that such tasks had been used to measure human conceptual abilities, i.e., they had been developed for use with man and had then been adapted for the study of other primates. Thus, he continued, if there is any improper comparison between the species, then

it must be unfair to the subhuman, not the human, animal. Be this as it may, the tests clearly demonstrate that defining man as a possessor of mental abilities which occur in other animals only in most rudimentary forms, if at all (Dobzhansky, 1955), must necessarily disenfranchise many millions of United States citizens from the society of Homo sapiens (Harlow, 1958a, p. 282).

It was this evidence, in particular, that led Harlow to argue that all learning forms a single continuum based on one fundamental operation, namely, the capacity to inhibit inappropriate responses.

In these particular studies we can observe quite dramatic shifts in the capabilities of species to solve these discrimination tasks with increasing capacity to use more complex information.

However, the changes involved would seem to be quantitative in nature, as Harlow indeed suggested, rather than there being any qualitative shift in the kind of capacities involved.

4. *Learning Sets.* Learning sets have been described as "a sensitive behavioral index of intellectual capacity" (Miles & Blomquist, 1960, p. 477). The term "learning set" denotes learning about the nature of a particular class of problem, e.g., object discrimination, which results in progressive improvement in the learning of each new problem as the animal is trained on an increasing number of problems of that class. If the ability to develop a learning set is indeed an indication of phylogenetic improvement in the capacity to organize and utilize complex information, then it would be expected that the speed and efficiency with which this class of learning could be mastered would be indicative of the level of neural organization.

Harlow, in his original study in 1949 using simultaneous visual discrimination and discrimination reversal learning demonstrated that rhesus macaque monkeys rapidly learn how to master such tasks to the level of one trial learning. He showed that human 3-to-5-year-olds were superior to the monkeys in forming discrimination reversal learning sets. He considered such sets to be of major importance in the development of intellectual organization and personality structure (Harlow, 1949).

A number of studies on the development of learning sets in different species followed. In a study with rats, Koronakos and Arnold (1957) showed that these animals could form learning sets, though at a lower level of efficiency than had been demonstrated for cats (Warren & Baron, 1956), or raccoons (Shell & Riopelle, 1957). This latter study showed raccoons to be inferior to monkeys on this task but their performance was comparable to that of Warren and Baron's cats.

Miles (1957b) demonstrated that there were clear differences in ability to form learning sets between various primate species with the macaque proving superior to the squirrel monkey, which was, in turn, superior to the primitive marmoset. Meyers, McQuiston, and Miles (1962) further demonstrated that three cats were able to form learning sets but at a level inferior to that of the marmoset, thus confirming the earlier work of Warren and Baron (1956). The picture that best represents the established view of learning set differentiation between species is from Hodos (1970) and is given in Figure 9.5.

Warren (1965) drew attention to the finding that, when rats were tested in the WGTA with three dimensional objects (Tyrrell, 1963),[1] thus using a situation comparable to that experienced by monkeys, their performance was similar to that of cats tested under similar conditions. Warren concluded, at that time, that

> the available data suggested that the phylogenetic development of capacity for learning set formation in mammals is best described as a continuous function with no sharp discontinuation between adjacent taxa but with marked quantitative differences between the extremes of the distribution (p. 263).

While, said Warren, mammals and birds differ from fish and reptiles in that they learn repeated discrimination reversals in successively fewer trials, primates are not markedly more proficient than other mammals or birds.

More recently, however, Warren changed his view on this class of learning and in 1973 stated that his conclusions on learning set could no longer be defended. The curves in those earlier studies were based on small samples (three to six animals) and failed to provide a realistic indication of species variations. More recent studies have shown that such within-species variation is wide indeed.

This, in itself, would certainly not invalidate Warren's earlier claims, since wide individual differences within species are evident with almost any learning task. The essential requirement, to establish at least a quantitative difference, is to demonstrate an increase in mean performance from species to species. As well as the wide individual differences within species, Warren claimed that "group differences have been reported recently which cannot be reconciled with the idea that quantitative indices of learning set formation are related to phylogenetic status or cortical complexity" (Warren, 1973, p. 486). He gave as examples a study by Doty, Jones, and Doty (1967), which showed performance of mink and ferrets to be superior to marmosets and platyrrhine monkeys; and by Plotnik and Tallarico (1966), in which four white Plymouth chicks did as well as rats, raccoons, and marmosets. As well, he said, dolphins perform less adequately than chickens and most mammals (Herman et al, 1969); and further, that galagos, lorises, and lemurs have only a marginal capacity for solving learning set problems (Jolley, 1964).

Warren then went on to argue that the quantitative learning scores failed to yield uncontaminated measures of learning capacity. One of the contaminating influences is the effectiveness of multiple cues over single cues in dis-

---

[1]Tyrrell, D. J. *The formation of object discrimination learning sets by rats*. Paper read at the Eastern Psychological Association, New York, 1963 (from Warren, 1965).

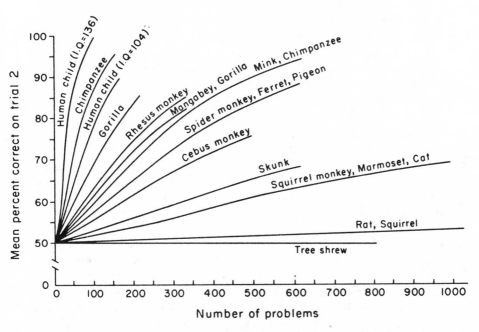

FIG. 9.5. A family of "ideal" curves representing the development of learning sets in various animals. The curves were obtained by the fitting of smooth curves to empirical data points. The data of the human children and chimpanzees were from Hayes et al (1953); those of the gorillas, from Fischer (1962); those of the rhesus monkeys, from Harlow (1959); those of the mangabeys, from Behar (1962); those of the squirrel monkeys, from Miles (1957); those of the marmosets, from Miles and Meyer (1956); those of the cebus monkeys and spider monkeys, from Shell and Riopelle (1958); those of the squirrels and rats, from Rollin, cited in Warren (1965); those of the ferrets, minks, skunks, and cats, from Doty et al. (1967); those of the pigeons, from Ziegler (1961). As there were data for only two subjects for each of the human, gorilla, and chimpanzee in the development of learning sets, the curves of each subject are shown separately (from Hodos, 1970, p. 35).

crimination learning with species differing in terms of which cues are effective. For example, he said, primates respond more to color than form (Meyer et al., 1965; Zimmerman & Torrey, 1965). Cats, unlike monkeys do not respond strongly to color cues. The junk objects often used in visual discrimination learning-set formation provide differences in color that would aid primates rather than cats. Again, as Warren pointed out, some species respond more successfully to visual and others to nonvisual cues. Primates, for example, are highly visual animals, while rats and cats are not.

While Warren's arguments do not necessarily rule out learning set formation as a valid measure for cross-species comparisons, it is evident that a fresh approach to species comparisons in this area will have to be developed, probably along the lines advocated by Bitterman.

5. Successive Discrimination Reversal Learning.   One particular class of learning set problem, namely discrimination reversal, has received special attention from several groups of workers. The findings are of particular relevance to the problem of between-species comparisons and in particular to the question of whether qualitative as well as quantitative differences in learning can be observed between vertebrate species.

In essence, in this paradigm the animal learns a simultaneous discrimination task to a set criterion and then, at this selected point the significance of the cues is reversed. The animal is then trained to criterion with the new contingency when the cues are again reversed, and so on. Gossette (1969a) described this methodology as "one of the few developed to date that can yield systematic interspecies performance differences that are phyletically and taxonomically meaningful" (p. 283).

Gossette carried out extensive studies of discrimination reversal learning in reptiles, birds, and mammals. He worked mainly with a successive spatial discrimination reversal series. Animals were given 20 non-correction trials each day and training continued until 18 or more correct responses were given in a daily 20-trial session. The reinforcement contingencies were then reversed on the following day. Training continued until criterion was again achieved when a futher reversal was effected and so on with the completion of the original acquisition and 19 reversals (Gossette, Gossette, & Inman, 1966). The nature of this particular task and the cues employed go a long way towards meeting Warren's objection of effect of contaminated cues on measures of learning ability on learning set tasks.

In studies of spatial reversal across 14 different avian and mammalian species, Gossette reported that "error scores significantly separated remotely and closely related species in a way consistent with taxonomic rank (Gossette, 1966, p. 175). Among birds, Passeriforme species displayed fewest errors; Psittacine and Columbiforme species were next with the Galliforme producing the most errors (Gossette, Gossette, & Riddell, 1966). Among mammals the task distinguished between two species of the new world monkeys with the Squirrel monkeys making consistently more errors than the Capuchins. The squirrel monkeys also made more errors on the first reversal than on the initial discrimination, as did the avian species, but maximum errors for the Capuchins occurred on the original discrimination problem (Gossette & Inman, 1966). Three species of Procyonidae and one species of Mustelidae yielded performance that overlapped with that of the primates (Gossette, 1966). As can be seen from Table 9.1, the number of animals in each group was generally small, i.e., between three and six.

Both the alligator (*Alligator mississippiensus*) and the crocodile (*Crocodilus americanus*) showed reduction in errors on spatial discrimination reversal with crocodiles achieving significantly fewer errors than the alligators (Gossette & Hombach, 1969).

TABLE 9.1
Reversal Indices and Mean Error for Original Discrimination and First Reversal of a Spatial Habit for Six Mammalian and Nine Avian Species

Species	N	Original Discrimination		First Reversal		Reversal Index	
		M	Range	M	Range	M	Range
Mammal							
Capuchin Monkey	5	14.8	5–26	7.2	6–10	0.65	0.27– 1.40
Squirrel Monkey	3	17.3	10–31	38.7	26–50	2.83	1.33– 5.00
Coati-mundi	4	20.25	14–26	24.7	13–38	1.25	0.54– 1.89
Cacomistle	3	12.7	5–20	6.33	5–8	0.66	0.39– 1.20
Skunk	4	15.5	8–24	30.00	19–30	1.94	1.35– 2.16
M		16.1		21.4		1.46	
Bird							
Common Crow	4	12.5	2–17	40.5	15–60	6.25	1.41– 4.25
Red-billed Blue Magpie	3	14.0	7–25	11.0	10–13	1.04	0.40– 1.43
Greater Hill Myna	10	28.7	1–62	52.4	13–98	2.12	0.73–34.00
Pigeon	5	14.8	7–27	20.0	4–37	1.78	0.36– 3.90
Ringneck Dove	4	38.5	2–95	38.0	10–88	2.68	0.37– 5.00
Trumpeter	4	53.3	18–87	97.0	45–148	3.08	1.13– 8.11
Chukar	6	12.0	8–26	31.5	8–62	3.32	0.67– 6.43
Bob-white Quail	3	14.7	2–22	56.7	1–112	2.75	0.50– 6.91
White Leghorn Chicken	5	18.2	6–47	54.6	20–49	4.16	1.82– 7.00
M		21.0		45.5		4.06	

Source: From Gossette & Gossette (1967).

In other studies Gossette examined brightness discrimination reversal (i.e., a visual cue discrimination) in some groups of birds and mammals that had previously been tested on the spatial task. For the birds he found a similar ordering on brightness discrimination reversal as for spatial reversal. From this study he concluded that the brightness discrimination was a more difficult task for the birds and that this had the effect of magnifying the differences between the four species (Gossette, 1967). Four mammalian species, namely squirrel monkeys, cacomistles, skunks, and kikajous, were also tested on this brightness discrimination reversal task. The ordering of species was again similar across the two tasks. From these results Gossette and Kraus (1968) concluded that the SDR method rather than the specific task yielded differences in interspecies performance.

Gossette then examined the effects of varying motivation and incentive levels on spatial discrimination reversal with a variety of birds and mammals. Using two drive levels (5–10% reduction or 25–30% reduction of ad-lib feeding weight) with pigeons, doves, Guinea fowl, chickens, partridges, and squirrel monkeys, Gossette found consistent differences in performance under low drive compared with high drive with more errors under high drive. These differences were sufficient to yield different ordering of species if drive conditions were ignored (Gossette, 1969a). He also showed a consistent difference in performance in pigeons with different incentive levels (1 seed or 4 seeds per reinforcement) with the low incentive condition yielding more errors (Gossette & Hood, 1968). He concluded that both drive and incentive levels influence the magnitude of negative transfer and consequent rate of improvement in SDR problems. Whether these factors could control asymptotic error level or only the rate of achieving such a level was not clear said Gossette, but he added, these effects made the calibration of interspecies differences more difficult, as it would be necessary to calibrate D and K variables. He considered that it would, however, be worth the effort (Gossette, 1969a).

While Gossette considered that successive discrimination reversal was effective for differentiation between species, he agreed that it was a very time consuming procedure. Some years earlier Jeeves et al. had developed the Reversal Index (RI) as a measure of phylogenetic level. This consisted of the ratio of trials to criterion on the initial discrimination to trials on the first reversal (Rajalakshami & Jeeves, 1965). Rumbaugh and Jeeves (1966) compared this index with a reversal/acquisition ratio (R/A) conceived by Rumbaugh and Pournelli (1966). This required the administering of a long series of problems so that reversal/acquisition ratios could be plotted as a function of A% (initial acquisition) correct values. This was an even lengthier procedure than that employed by Gossette. As a result of the Rumbaugh and Jeeves (1966) study they concluded that the RI ratio was more useful with animals low on the phylogenetic scale but that the R/A index was likely to be more valuable for primates. However, Jeeves and Winefield (1967), in a study with squirrel monkeys concluded that the RI might be useful with primates as well as subprimates. To test the effectiveness of the reversal index, Gossette examined scores for a range of 15 different avian and mammalian species. The RI values for these species are shown in Table 9.1.

The overall difference between birds and mammals was highly significant, with birds displaying the larger ratios. There was, however, considerable overlap of RI scores across both birds and mammals (Gossette & Gossette, 1967). These authors pointed out that initial discrimination testing is particularly sensitive to pretest variables including ease of habituation, other pretest training and level of emotionality. As well, the first reversal usually results in more errors than does the initial discrimination. They suggested that location of the error peak might, in fact, be more useful for ranking species than the RI score. However, in another study with pigeons, Gossette did show that the RI is much less affected by variation of drive and incentive levels than the raw error scores. This, he considered, lent support to the use of RI for cross species comparisons (Gossette & Hood, 1967).

Whether these findings indicate a qualitative difference between species or support the argument for quantitative changes has been the subject of considerable debate. Gossette, for example, has argued that the differences between birds and mammals, which do show error reduction, and fish, which do not, may be methodological in origin. I leave further exploration of this particular question until my survey of Bitterman's work in the next section, as Bitterman has undertaken extensive studies of cross-species performance on discrimination reversal learning and his studies have led him to suggest that the differences may indeed be qualitative in nature.

THE WORK OF M. E. BITTERMAN

Without doubt Bitterman's work constitutes the outstanding contribution of recent times to the experimental analysis of comparative or cross-species similarities and differences in learning. Bitterman has been actively engaged in this work for some 25 years and over this period has addressed himself to the question of whether there has been any evolutionary divergence in learning processes. In his approach to this question he has threaded his way between what he described as two antithetical points of view. On the one hand there was a very influential group of learning theorists, including Thorndike, Pavlov, and Skinner, who argued for a common learning process underlying all vertebrate learning. The contrary view is that learning processes are species specific. Lockard, for example, argued that so-called learning processes are "a mere collection of unlike phenomena" (Lockard, 1971, p. 172). Thus, in the most extreme statement of the ethologist's position there is, said

Bitterman, "the implication that each instance of learning must be treated as a specialized capability" (Bitterman, 1975, p. 700).

Bitterman, in 1960, laid out his strategy. This was to be based on the various relationships in learning established during more than a half century of work with the rat. "I am interested," he said, "in the extent to which similar relationships can be found in the fish with a view to determining whether a single theory will fit both fish and rat." He concluded:

> When I ask about the effects of partial reinforcement or resistance to extinction in the fish or about the course of habit reversal in the crab I have not the slightest notion what the answer will be. I can only wait eagerly for the outcome of my experiments (Bitterman, 1960, p. 712).

In pursuit of his objective Bitterman became increasingly concerned with the elucidation of underlying learning processes that might be common across different species. As he pointed out (Bitterman, 1965), such processes are not evident directly from observation of learning but are inferred from such observations. He has continued to emphasize the laboratory approach throughout this work. He concluded in 1976 that "whether there are common processes and, if so, what they are, can only be known from the systematic study of a wide range of vertebrates; but there has been no such study" (Bitterman & Woodward, 1976, p. 169). Bitterman, himself, is one who had persisted with such a systematic approach (Bitterman, 1960, 1965, 1969, 1975).

In 1975 Bitterman reviewed his progress to that time. While there are, he considered, undoubted qualitative similarities in learning performance by taxonomically disparate animals, the question of whether there are qualitative differences remained open to enquiry. He defined qualitative differences as differences "in the sense that phenomena of learning characteristic of some animals fail entirely to occur in others" (Bitterman, 1975, p. 700).

In this review he began by drawing attention to an experiment by Elliott (1928)[2] who was then working in Tolman's laboratory. In that experiment rats learned to run a maze for bran mash or sunflower seeds. They consistently made more errors when running for the less desired sunflower seeds. When, having worked for bran mash, the rats were switched to sunflower seeds, their performances deteriorated to a point below that achieved by animals running for sunflower seeds alone.

This is the negative contrast or "Crespi Effect" (Crespi, 1942), and has been widely demonstrated for rats in such situations as a straight runway with speed of running related to magnitude of reward, and in the Skinner Box with number of bar presses the dependent variable. Both negative and positive

---

[2]Elliott, M. H. The effect of change of reward on the maze performance of rats. *University of California Publications in Psychology*, 1928, *4*, 19–30 (from Bitterman, 1969).

contrast effects have also been demonstrated for the rat working for sucrose solution with lick rate the dependent measure (e.g., Flaherty & Largen, 1975).

Bitterman pointed out that the Crespi Effect posed problems for theorists who espouse the S–R reinforcement principle that large rewards produce stronger connections than small rewards and that these stronger bonds are more stable. An alternative assumption is that the animal learns something about the reward itself and this comes to be "anticipated" or expected. Large rewards therefore produce "not better learning but different learning with level of performance determined by the hedonic value of anticipated consequences" (Bitterman, 1975, pp. 700–701).

In this context it could be argued that, if the expectation fails to be realized, then the animal experiences disappointment or frustration and decrement in performance results.

While this effect is clearly evident in mammals, what happens with fish? Using a specifically designed apparatus (see Figure 9.6) Bitterman, (1966), set goldfish the task of swimming down a tank to press a target key for tubifex worms.

They were given one trial per day and latency of response was recorded. Small rewards (four worms) produced poorer performances than large rewards (40 worms). In this then, goldfish performed like rats. However, after 30 days, the reward levels were shifted. The downward shift from 40 worms to four produced no decrement in performance over a further 36 days of training, as seen in Figure 9.7.

Other analogous studies, including the use of a "runway for fish," confirmed this finding (Bitterman, 1969). Thus, he said, goldfish do have some respect for the S–R reinforcement principle. This was also observed in studies of resistance to extinction.

In the rat (Gonzalez & Bitterman, 1962), there is an inverse relationship between magnitude of reward and resistance to extinction. A larger reward produces more rapid learning and, on cessation of reinforcement, more rapid extinction. According to S–R theory a large reward should produce stronger bonds and consequently should be more resistant to extinction. In fact, said Bitterman, this is what happens with both goldfish (Bitterman, 1969) and turtles. In pigeons (Brownlee & Bitterman, 1968), on the other hand, the effect appears to be similar to that found in the rat. It is also well established that in rats and other mammals partial reinforcement during acquisition leads to greater resistance to extinction, the so-called partial reinforcement effect (PRE). This effect is observed whether massed or spaced trials are used and this is also true for pigeons. Fish (African mouthbreeders) and turtles, on the other hand, show this effect only if they are given massed practice on acquisition but do not show it if practice is spaced (Bitterman, 1975).

Bitterman concluded that, if the Law of Effect operates in the fish, then we ought to consider the possibility that it operates in the rat but that "its opera-

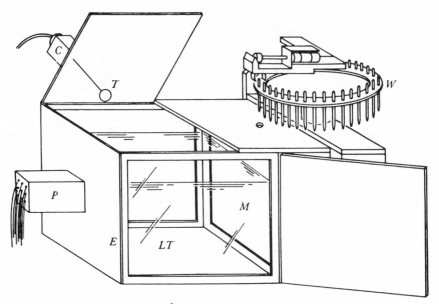

1 INCH

An automated unitary Thorndikian situation for the fish. The animal is brought in *LT*, its individual living tank, to *E*, a black Plexiglas enclosure; *P*, colored-light and pattern projector; *T*, Plexiglas target upon which the discriminanda are projected when the lid of the enclosure is lowered; *C*, phonograph cartridge; *W*, worm dispenser, with solenoid-operated jaws that squeeze the bulb of a dropper and so discharge a worm into the water; *M*, diffusing Plexiglas panel illuminated by a magazine light for several seconds following the discharge worm. (Scale only approximate.)

FIG. 9.6.   An automated lever pressing apparatus for fish developed by Bitterman (from Bitterman, 1966, p. 466)

tion in the rat is masked by anticipatory processes" (Bitterman, 1969, p. 452). In support of this he pointed to an experiment by Rosen, Glass, and Ison (1967) in which rats, in a Crespi experiment, were dosed with a barbiturate and then gave results like fish. Bitterman elaborated on this view in his 1975 paper saying that: "To explain the results for goldfish it may be assumed that their performance is not governed by anticipation of reward—that they are Thorndikian animals in which larger rewards simply produce stronger connections." With regard to rat behavior he went on to say: "It is possible also, however, that the difference between goldfish and rat is emotional," (Bitterman, 1975, p. 706) with the rat getting upset by discrepancy between anticipated and actual rewards while the goldfish did not.

The aspects of Bitterman's work that appear to have aroused the greatest controversy relate to his early studies of successive reversal and probability learning. He noted that in the rat a typical learning set pattern could be observed. On the initial reversal there is some increase in errors compared with acquisition. This is then followed by a gradual decline in errors with each successive reversal. In some way or another the animal is learning the nature of the task. This is true whether spatial or position discrimination (in which the rat learns to go to one side consistently for reward) or visual (cue) discrimination is used. In the latter task the animal might be required to differentiate between two different colors or between two different shapes presented simultaneously. The rewarded or positive cue is then presented randomly to left or right on successive trials.

In the case of fish (African mouthbreeders), however, Bitterman found a different picture, with absence of any progressive improvement with successive reversals. His findings are summarized in Figure 9.8.

Bitterman made the point that he was not comparing the two species, rat and fish, in terms of numerical scores but on the basis of functional relation-

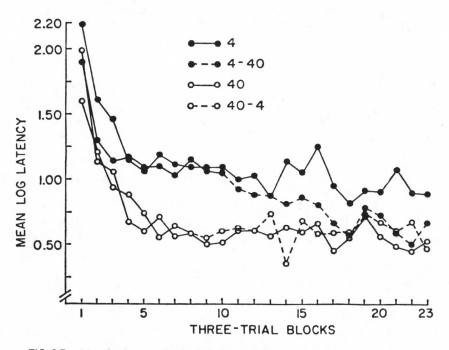

FIG. 9.7.   Mean log latency of a simple instrumental response in the goldfish as a function of amount of reward. One group was rewarded throughout with 4 worms; a second with 40 worms; a third was shifted from 4 to 40 worms; and a fourth from 40 to 4 worms. Postshift performance is shown by broken lines (from Lowes & Bitterman, 1977, p. 456).

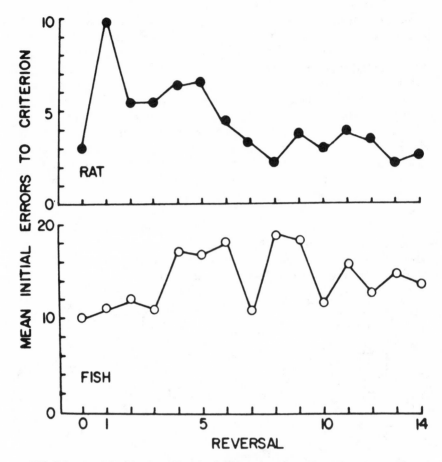

FIG. 9.8.   Spatial habit reversal learning in fish and rat (from Bitterman, 1965, p. 399).

ships. Is the observed difference, he asked, merely quantitative? Is it that fish learn more slowly or learn better with different levels of motivation? Using his technique of control by systematic variation he explored a variety of experimental conditions with fish, including variation in motivation and reward and a variety of different forms of cue presentation. Reliable evidence of improvement in reversal learning by fish failed to appear under many different conditions (Bitterman, 1965).

The pigeon, like the rat, exhibits progressive improvement in successive discrimination reversal with both spatial and visual cues but in another species, the turtle, a somewhat different pattern emerged. Using a specially developed discrimination chamber (shown in Figure 9.9) Bitterman (1964) examined discrimination reversal learning in the painted turtle (*Chrysemys picta picta*). One group of turtles was trained on a spatial problem with both targets the same color and another group on a visual (*cue*) discrimination task (red vs. green). Progressive improvement with successive reversals was observed in the spatial task but there was none in the visual task. These results are shown in Figure 9.10.

In experiments employing probability learning Bitterman also demonstrated differences between fish and rat. In the usual choice discrimination situation animals are rewarded 100% of the time for one choice and zero for the other. What would happen if the reinforcement contingency were

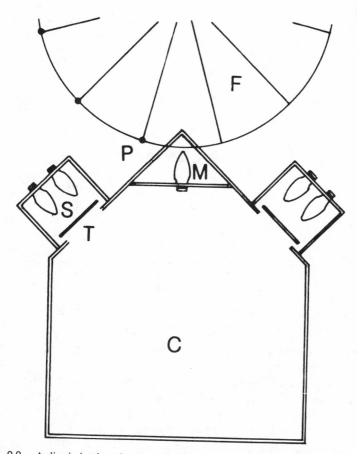

FIG. 9.9. A discrimination chamber for use with the turtle developed by Bitterman showing floor-plan of a choice-situation with two targets, one of which may be covered for experiments of simple instrumental behaviour; C, animal's compartment; T, target of translucent Plexiglas nosed by the animal; S, Christmas-tree lamps for projecting colored light on the target; M, magazine-lamp turned on during the reinforcement-cycle; F, feeder; P, pellet of hamburger rotated into the compartment at the beginning of the reinforcement-cycle and out again at the end (from Bitterman, 1964, p. 189).

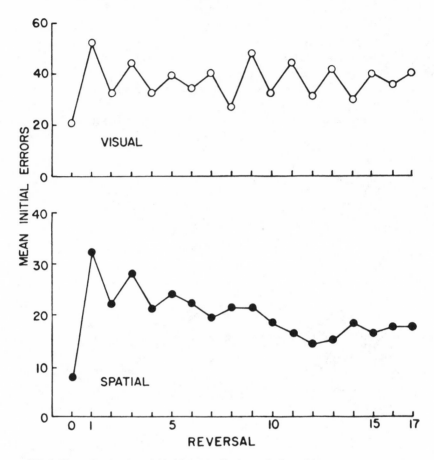

FIG. 9.10.   Visual and spatial habit reversal in the turtle (from Bitterman, 1965, p. 405).

changed so that responses to one of the two alternatives is rewarded 70% of the time and responses to the other 30% of the time?

In this situation fish responded with random probability matching, i.e., they responded, in a random fashion, 70% of responses being to the location that was reward 70% of the time and 30% to the other. Rats, on the other hand, eventually tended to maximize their chances of reward by responding, all, or almost all, of the time to the alternative that offered the higher probability of reward (Bitterman, 1965).

Bitterman (1965) next asked the question: What would happen to rat performance in these tasks if its neural tissue were reduced by extensive cortical resection? In this event, Bitterman found that, in reversal learning, the cortically damaged rat behaved like a normal rat in spatial reversal, i.e., reversal from one side being correct to the other being correct, with progressive improvement with increasing number of reversals. With object discrimination reversal, on the other hand, there was no such improvement. The rats' performance resembled that of the fish. Again, with probability learning, the performance of the lesioned animal was indistinguishable from the normal in position learning. In form or object discrimination the operated animals showed random matching like the fish.

Bitterman in 1965 argued that these studies of successive discrimination reversal and probability learning indicated qualitative differences between vertebrate species. This view, however, attracted considerable dissension. Gossette, for example, considered that the differences between birds and mammals, which do show error reduction, and fish, which do not, might be methodological in origin. Mackintosh too claimed that differences between fish, birds, and rats in both successive discrimination and probability learning are quantitative and not qualitative, with fish, birds, and rats forming an orderly sequence.

A debate of considerable interest ensued between Bitterman and Mackintosh on this issue. This was recorded in Gilbert and Sutherland's (1969) "*Animal Discrimination Learning*" and the main points made by these two authors at that time are worth recalling. The argument revolved around a number of issues with reply and counter response, and I touch briefly on some of these.

In discussion of reversal learning, Mackintosh (1969) drew on data from three separate studies with fish data from Behrend, Domesick, and Bitterman (1965), pigeon data from Sterns and Bitterman (1965) and rat data from Gonzales, Roberts, and Bitterman (1964). The results of these studies are presented by Mackintosh as shown graphically in Figure 9.11.

The initial learning scores are similar and thus, said Mackintosh, it is reasonable to compare the three performances. He considered that each class of animal differed quantitatively from the others with the implication that all three species showed improvement over successive reversals. In terms of quantitative differences he argued that results from a wide range of studies, including those of Gossette referred to earlier, suggested that birds were reliably better than fish but, with the possible exception of magpies and mynahs, were not as proficient as rats.

Bitterman disputed the validity of Mackintosh's comparisons of the absolute performance values of the three different species across the series of reversals on the basis of his argument (referred to in Chapter 8) that such cross-species comparisons cannot be justified or, at the very best, should be viewed with considerable caution. He also pointed out that the learning curve that Mackintosh had selected for fish was one of 13 groups of goldfish and African mouthbreeders trained under a variety of conditions and that not one, including the one selected by Mackintosh, had yielded a statistically reliable improvement over reversals. He noted that, in his analysis, Mackintosh had

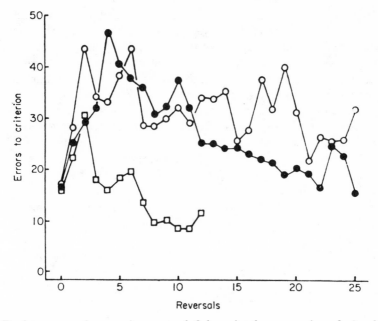

Performance of rats, pigeons and fish trained on a series of visual reversals. O—O Fish: ●—● Pigeons: □—□ Rats.

FIG. 9.11.   Visual reversal learning in rats, pigeons and fish (from Mackintosh, 1969, p. 143).

arbitrarily selected portions of the data (first six and last six reversals) and had not taken account of individual variance.

Mackintosh also referred to a study by Setterington and Bishop (1967) in which a group of African mouthbreeders, given 20 trials per day with a reversal every day for 80 days, showed significant reduction in error scores over the course of the experiment. Bitterman compared this result with those of Behrend and Bitterman (1967) in which they showed no improvement. The two studies, said Bitterman, differed in one important respect. The intertrial interval was two seconds in the Setterington and Bishop study and 10 seconds in the replication. Bitterman then concluded that "the improvement found by Setterington and Bishop is due to the development of a simple win-stay discrimination based on carryover from trial to trial of the sensory consequences of response" (Bitterman & Mackintosh, 1969, p. 164). Mackintosh pointed out that it was reasonable to attribute this effect to proactive interference and argued that if length of intertrial interval affects reversal learning in both fish and rat then this points to a quantitative rather than a qualitative difference.

In probability learning Mackintosh disputed that there was anything intrinsically special about a matching asymptote that makes an animal selecting the majority stimulus of a 70:30 problem on 70% of trials significantly different from one that selects this majority stimulus on 80% or 90% of trials. The second is performing more accurately than the first and that is all. Again, he argued that the three classes of fish, bird, and rat form a continuum of performance with quantitative but not qualitative differences.

Bitterman, on the contrary, argued that rats perform differently to fish and do not simply do more of the same thing that fish do. In fish the matching is on an individual basis and is not an artifact of grouping. He cited as an example the 50–50 ratio for a visual discrimination problem. For fish and pigeons this is just another ratio with individual scores clustering about the 50% level. Properly motivated rats, on the other hand, exhibit strong position habits. Turtles, like pigeons, match randomly on visual problems but not spatial problems. Here Mackintosh replied that this would be expected from the typical behaviors of these animals, i.e., rats respond spatially with a fixed position response and fish respond to color and alternate between them. Even if this were so in the case of 50–50 ratios, it seems not to answer the question of why differences are evident with the 70–30 schedule.

Mackintosh's third line of attack related to underlying processes. He argued that, while reversal learning would be maximal on a win-stay, lose-shift strategy, probability learning would require a different approach, namely staying with the stimulus that offered the greater number of rewards. This would be antagonistic to the win-stay, lose-shift approach. If different strategies were employed in the two situations, then learning one type of task would be likely to handicap the animal on learning the other. He showed that if rats were trained on serial reversal of a brightness discrimination this did not interfere with subsequent learning of a 75–25 brightness probability problem (Mackintosh et al., 1968).

He then argued that differences between rat, bird, and fish are due to differences in the extent to which they can learn to attend to a given cue when this is not consistently correlated with reinforcement. Thus, he said: "A straightforward difference in stability of attention in the face of changing reward conditions seems sufficient to explain the data so far presented" (Mackintosh, 1969, p. 149).

Bitterman argued against Mackintosh's assertion that attentional processes were the key to the two tasks and advanced the view that poorer performance by fish might be due, not to a deficiency in attention, but to a deficiency in forgetting, an inability to inhibit or "forget" information that is no longer needed. In support of this view he cited an experiment by Gonzalez, Behrend, and Bitterman (1967) that examined reversal learning to red and green cues by a pigeon. This study, claimed Bitterman, showed that when one examined retention measures from day 1 to day 2 within each reversal (i.e., with the same cue positive on both days) compared with day 2 of one condition and day 1 of its reversal (i.e., with positive cue changed) it was clear that there was an increase in forgetting from day-to-day in each instance. He considered that this increased forgetting was responsible for much of the improvement in reversal learning. This he contrasted with similar curves for goldfish learning, which showed no decrement in retention and no improvement in reversal learning. Thus, he argued, the difference between fish and pigeon arises because of the differences in the learning-retention mechanism.

While further argument was advanced by each party in support of his particular point of view, it became evident that the issues were to remain unresolved with each protagonist convinced that he was right; Bitterman arguing for qualitative differences between fish and rat, with reptile showing an intermediate stage, while Mackintosh presented the view that the differences are quantitative only, with one of the major factors being a graduated increase in the ability of the animals to direct attention to relevant cues.

Yet another critic of Bitterman's approach is Warren, who has claimed that there are substantial grounds for doubting whether mammals and birds do differ fundamentally from reptiles and fish in reversal and probability learning. He pointed out that, using a rather different test situation that provided more information (redundant relevant cues of shape and color and strict contiguity of the stimulus-response-reinforcement sequence), Squier (1969), for example, was able to demonstrate that two fish of the species *Astronotus ascellatus* (Oscars) could dramatically improve their rate of learning. Again, Mackintosh (1969) was able to show that young chickens could maximize in a visual probability learning task as quickly as rats when chickens were presented with the problem in a Grice discrimination box.

Warren also observed that rats frequently fail to maximize their rewards when tested in automated operant chambers. In fact it has been demonstrated that rats generally have more difficulty in mastering discrimination tasks when working in an automated apparatus (Livesey, Han, Lowe, & Feakes, 1972). Warren concluded that differences between fish, reptiles, and mammals might depend not on basic phylogenetic differences but might reflect differences in apparatus (Warren, 1973).

From an examination of the varying effects achieved it seems more likely that differences observed were not so much due to differences in apparatus per se, but the information that the apparatus offered. With the information more precisely organized, fish and the birds are able to attain, as it were, another level of organization. Thus Warren's evidence would seem not to negate Bitterman's position. Bitterman, in fact, argued along similar lines. He pointed out that, in progressive reversal learning for example, turtles, pigeons, rats, and many other species generally show improvement under a wide variety of conditions. With fish, on the other hand, improvement occurs only rarely, though it can occur. For example, fish trained with a "center key" — a white target to start each trial — and fish exposed to the positive color during presentation of the reward show improvement. He went on to say: "The fact that such stratagems are quite unnecessary to produce substantial improvement in choice experiments with other vertebrates leads to the suspicion of difference in process, a suspicion which is strengthened by analysis of the course of improvement" (Bitterman, 1975, p. 706).

Bitterman, in his 1975 paper, restated his position. He observed that experiments on probability learning have distinguished goldfish, painted turtles, and pigeons from rats and monkeys. In progressive improvement in reversal, painted turtles, pigeons, rats, and other vertebrates show such improvements under a wide variety of conditions. In fish, on the other hand, such improvements occurred rarely. In a personal communication (1983) Bitterman pointed out that as early as 1966 he and Holmes reported both visual and spatial reversal improvement in turtles (Holmes & Bitterman, 1966). In this study they employed a 2-day reversal, or reversal on reaching criterion, rather than the original 4-day reversal, which had shown improvement on spatial but not visual reversal. His group then continued to look for improvement in fish, and this was eventually found under several conditions (Woodward, Schoel, & Bitterman, 1971; Englehardt, Woodward & Bitterman, 1973). In the first of these papers progressive improvement was shown, not in terms of choice, but in readiness to respond to a single stimulus. In the latter study, already referred to, special conditions were established in which the fish responded first to a center key to bring on the two stimulus lights. Results of this experiment are shown in Figure 9.12.

At the time Engelhardt et al. (1973) argued that

> There is good reason to suspect that progressive improvement in reversal as we know it in rats and pigeons is also multiply determined (Bitterman, 1972) and the possibility should be considered (in view of the relatively restricted range of conditions under which it is found in goldfish) that the determinants are not entirely the same in goldfish as in more advanced animals (p. 149).

One determinant that they argued for was the inability of the fish to inhibit or "forget" the previously learned response.

Mackintosh, in the debate already referred to, indicated that he considered this to be a possible factor. On the other hand, Gossette (1968, 1969b) has argued against this retention deficit or proactive inhibition explanation for the reversal learning effect. He claimed that the evidence for a proactive inhibition explanation occurred only under the special training procedure used by Bitterman, namely, a modified correction procedure with guidance. This procedure, said Gossette, ensures that every trial is terminated by a reinforced response to the positive stimulus. This he considered should "facilitate

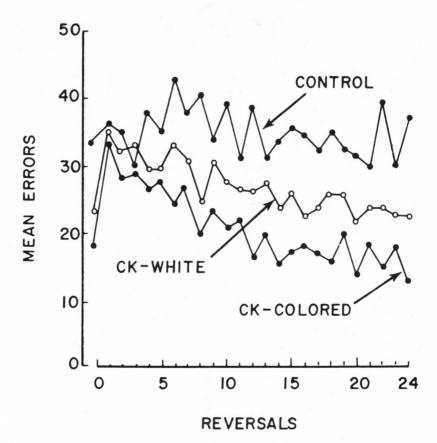

FIG. 9.12.   Two day reversal performance by goldfish with a center-key to activate the stimulus lights (from Englehardt, Woodward, & Bitterman, 1973, p. 147).

growth of a new preference, especially in the early stages of reversal training when incorrect (non-reinforceable) responses predominate" (Gossette, 1969b, p. 176). It is of interest, said Gossette, that the one clear case of SDR improvement in fish involved an unlimited correction procedure employed by Setterington and Bishop (1967). Note however that Bitterman had argued that this result was due to massed practice effects that produced a simple win-stay strategy (Bitterman & Mackintosh, 1969, p. 164).

Using a non-correction procedure, Gossette found no evidence of pro-active inhibition on nonreversal days for two reptilian, 11 avian, and six mammalian species. He considered that two major phenomena would ac-count for the reversal learning effect. The first was a negative transfer effect that typically appears in the early stages of reversal learning and that, he be-lieved, constituted a major source of interspecies differences. The other was the decline in error over successive reversals, i.e., the "reversal habit," which, he argued, was controlled by sensory components of reinforcement and nonreinforcement.

This does not resolve the nature of the "reversal habit," however. In this regard it is worth noting that both attention and proactive inhibition form integral parts of a system that functions to detect error or change and to modify behavior in the light of such detection. The core of the error detection process is the building up of patterns of relationships so that the animal develops expectancies in the light of information provided. The ability of the animal to build up appropriate representations and the speed with which it is able to detect changes, i.e., events contrary to expectations, and to react to them provides a key to both reversal and probability learning. As I argue in a subsequent chapter, the development of such expectancies may be related to the evolution of emotional reactivity. If, as Bitterman has suggested (Bitterman, 1975), fish lack the capacity for such emotional responses while rats do not, this would seem to form the basis for a real qualitative difference between fish and rat.

Another, quite different line of attack on Bitterman's approach came from Hodos and Campbell (1969). They stated that "since no rat was ever an ancestor of any monkey, it is not clear whether the rat and the monkey independently evolved the rat-like pattern or whether it is inherited from a common reptilian ancestor" (p. 345), i.e., that since goldfish, turtles, pigeons, rats, and monkeys do not constitute a direct evolutionary series, comparisons between them can tell us nothing about the evolution of behavior.

Bitterman had, in his 1965 paper, been careful to note that "the uncontaminated linear order which now appears in the table, while undeniably esthetic, is rather embarrassing from the standpoint of the far-from-linear evolutionary relationships among the species studied" (p. 409). He also noted that

> clearly, I should like to be able to write bird rather than pigeon and I should like by fish to mean more than mouthbreeder, and so forth. It will be interesting to discover how representative of these classes are the particular species studied — whose choice was dictated largely by practical considerations (p. 409).

He then elaborated on his argument in favor of using diverse, widely separated, species. His statement, which appears to encapsulate the philosophy of his approach went as follows:

> As to the evolution of behavior, I see no reason why the behavioral properties of extinct animals cannot, like their morphological properties, be inferred from those of living descendants on the principle that (barring convergence) properties common to a set of animals are attributable to their common ancestor. The more distinctly related the animals compared, the more remote the common ancestor about whose functional properties we are informed, and the more likely we are to come upon any functional divergences that may have occurred.

The discovery of different learning processes in any two species whatever would permit at least the conclusion that there has been divergence, which is by no means so trivial as it might appear to one unacquainted with the history of thought on the subject. Comparisons of more closely related animals certainly are not without interest; as I have noted before, unique results obtained with goldfish or pigeons immediately suggest the question of generality over order or class (49). It should be evident, however, that comparisons of distantly related animals, although not much more costly than comparisons of closely related animals, provide a much broader picture of the evolution of behavior (Bitterman, 1975, p. 704).

To the argument that comparisons of such diverse animals as goldfish, turtles, pigeons, rats, and monkeys do not constitute an evolutionary series and that there is no meaningful way of ordering living species relative to lines of descent, Bitterman suggested that "one simplifying dimensional principle is recency of common ancestry to man" (Bitterman, 1975, p. 704). In this sense, then, Bitterman's approach has an element in common with those advocating the study of the anagenesis of learning. In this sense, too, it may be related directly to my own point of view. However, Bitterman has stated clearly (personal communication, 1983) that he is not an anagenicist but an evolutionist. This is perhaps most clearly emphasized by his recent studies of learning in the bee. Some of these studies (Bitterman, 1976; Couvillon & Bitterman, 1980, 1982) were referred to in Chapter 3. In recent work (Bitterman, Menzel, Fietz & Schafer, 1983; Couvillon, Klosterhalfen & Bitterman, 1983; Menzel & Bitterman, 1983) Bitterman's group continued their studies of associative learning in the honey bee including the development of a conditioning technique using restrained animals as in many vertebrate studies. Menzel and Bitterman (1983) found that results obtained with restrained subjects in conditioning of proboscis extension in the bee were closely similar to those observed in free-flying subjects. The results indicated that the restraint technique yielded a valid picture of associative learning in these subjects and further, and more significantly, that both techniques "are validated as windows on reality." They continued:

What may be said about comparisons of different techniques applied to the same animal may be said also about comparative studies of different animals with techniques that are of necessity very different. The more divergent the animals in which function similarities are found, the more confidence can be placed in the power of the techniques and in the biological importance of the findings (Menzel & Bitterman, 1983, p. 214).

Increasingly, with the passage of time, Bitterman directed his approach to the study of underlying learning processes. He argued that, while similarities and differences between animals may be interesting in their own right, what is of principal importance is what these behaviors tell us about the nature of the underlying processes that govern behavior. In his consideration of under- lying learning processes in his 1975 paper, Bitterman observed that different phenomena may be produced by the same process and conversely that iden- tical phenomena may result from different processes. One example that he gave was the Elliott-Crespi depression effect and the inverse relationship be- tween magnitude of reward and resistance to extinction observed in rats and other mammals. He argued that those two phenomena might well be due to a common process that is evident in rats but is absent in goldfish and turtles since the first species shows both effects and the latter two neither. However, he continued, if "an animal can be found that shows one phenomenon but not the other, we may suspect that the processes are different" (p. 704).

As an example of a similar phenomenon in different animals being due to different processes, Bitterman examined the partial reinforcement effect. Rats show the effect for both massed and spaced trials as do pigeons, but fish and turtles show it only in massed trials. This, said Bitterman, suggests the operation of different processes. One is probably sensory carry-over, effec- tive only in massed trials. Another process, operating only in animals show- ing the PRE in spaced trials, might be the same as that which produces both the depression effect and the inverse relationship between reward and resist- ance to extinction.

With Woodward, Bitterman in 1976 examined the occurrence of common processes in the areas of classical conditioning, reward and punishment in operant conditioning, extinction of learned responses and avoidance and omission learning. They considered in particular, the concepts of S–R conti- guity, S–S contiguity, S–R reward, and anticipation of reward and punish- ment strength, and concluded that there was a reasonable case for thinking of some such phenomena as being general to vertebrate learning. They pointed out that the broad functional ideas they had considered made no real contact with the neural substrate but were consistent with what we know about brains. While they agreed that much yet remains to be done in this area they concluded that:

> Systematic comparative work is expected to yield a patterned array of func- tional similarities and differences that, together with neurophysiological, bio- chemical, and even paleontological data, can help lay bare the mechanisms of learning (Bitterman & Woodward, 1976, p. 187).

I will return to these issues in subsequent work.

One further issue that Bitterman has raised in relation to common pro- cesses deserves mention at this stage. Bitterman has attacked the concept of species-specific or species-typical learning abilities, i.e., learning specially adapted and often unique to a particular species. He has argued, again on the

basis of common underlying processes, that "Even if associative predispositions are assumed, there is no reason to believe that unique processes are required for their realization" (Bitterman, 1975, p. 708). He developed this argument in 1976, pointing out that species-specific avoidance responses of the
type discussed by Bolles and the phenomenon of autoshaping suggest com-
munality rather than divergence in the learning process. His argument revolved round the point that learning involves strengthening of existing or
inbuilt tendencies rather than their establishment de novo (Bitterman, 1976).
This argument appears to be congruent with Jerison's concept of "the principle of proper mass" referred to in Chapter 8.

SOME TESTS OF "INTELLIGENT" BEHAVIOR

Finally, in this chapter, I consider briefly a set of comparisons I completed
some years ago in a study of "intelligent" behavior across several species.

This effort is perhaps most noteworthy for the fact that it underlines some
of the problems we have been examining. For the purposes of this study three
species, the white rat, the white rabbit, and the common domestic cat were selected. To each representative of each of these species, four tests, selected as
tests of "intelligent" behavior, were given. These were the Hebb-Williams
Closed Field and Elevated Pathway (Hebb & Williams, 1946), a discrimination task developed for the project, and the Double Alternation problem.

The reasons for choice of species and tasks are relevant to our argument.
The choice of species was governed by the following considerations, namely:

1. The time factor limited the number of species to be studied.
2. The test problems and test apparatus should present comparable situations for the different species chosen. This would limit the size and range of
species. If the apparatus were to be duplicated in varying dimensions for animals showing major size variation or if animals relied on different media for
locomotion, e.g., fish, birds, reptiles, then this would increase very substantially the problem of comparability of results.
3. Since all the tests used were to involve, primarily, the sense of vision, all
animals used should have sufficient visual acuity and capacity for visual discrimination to cope with the material presented.

The rabbit and cat were selected as two species of about equal size but, in the
light of Von Bonin's (1937) evidence, widely separated on brain-body ratio.
The rat was chosen as the third species because it was substantially smaller
than the rabbit but with a comparable brain-body ratio. Von Bonin gave as
the k factor for rodents, in which class the rabbit was included at that time,
values ranging from 0.06 to 0.16, while for the cat the value was 0.64. In this

regard Von Bonin himself observed that "the order (of species) differs some-what from that of Dubois. The greatest change has occurred in the case of the cat which has moved up considerably" (p. 388).

The tests used were chosen for a laboratory setting and with a view to ex-emplifying particular apects of behavior. A wide range of materials and tech-niques have been used in testing animal perception and animal learning (Munn, 1950; Stone, 1951; Woodworth & Schlosberg, 1955; Thorpe, 1956; Dethier & Stellar, 1961). Types of experiments traditionally regarded as pro-viding evidence for intelligent or insightful behavior included tool using, with the use of sticks, boxes, etc., string pulling problems, and detour problems. Included here, too, would be Maier's studies of reasoning ability, in which the animal's ability to manipulate the effects of previous experience to pro-vide a new solution is tested (Thorpe, 1956; Viaud, 1960).

Much, if not all, of this material was, however, inappropriate for my pur-pose. Difficulties that would arise in the use of such material in the compara-tive study of intelligent behavior include the effects of past experience, the different manipulative abilities and experience of various species in tool using situations, and the problem of scoring or quantification of such data for both individual and species comparisons. In the selection of the particular tests for this study, a major objective was to take account of these various species constraints. These constraints also limited choice of species.

Of the four tests selected, two, the Hebb-Williams Closed Field Test and the Hunter Double Alternation Temporal Problem as adapted to WGTA, had been extensively developed and refined and much was known about them. Of the other two tests, one, the Elevated Pathway, was proposed by Hebb and Williams at the same time as the Closed Field, but had not been futher developed, and the other, a discrimination task, was developed for this study (Livesey, 1968).

Of the tasks chosen, two, the Closed Field and the Elevated Pathway, were seen as providing closely related tests of perceptual organization involving re-lationships between the field and problems set up in the field. These tests in-volve path finding and detour-type behaviors set in a standardized form. The setting itself might be conceived as a miniature and formalized representation of problems encountered in the natural habitats of the species being studied.

The third task, also involving perceptual organization, was a visual dis-crimination task carried out in an apparatus based on Munn's (1931, 1950) multiple discrimination apparatus. Initially the animal learned to differenti-ate an X from four Os. When criterion was reached the test consisted of 10 trials on each of 10 different generalization tasks and concluded with reversal of cues.

The fourth task, the Double Alternation Problem, differed from the other three in several major aspects. The first three tasks involved the learning of a relatively simple task or relationship, followed by testing on a series of new but related situations of increasing difficulty. In the Double Alternation Problem the animal is required to learn a complex task to a given criterion of proficiency. The first three tasks are more concerned with the perception of relationships between elements of present experience in the light of past experience but involving new situations. The Double Alternation Task involves the relationship between past and present experiences in a temporal sequence.

My expectations about species differences were framed in terms of what was known about relative brain-body ratios. From Von Bonin's analysis it was anticipated that cats would show a substantially greater capacity to handle these tasks than either the rabbit, an animal of about the same body size but with a smaller brain, or the rat. Differences between rabbit and rat were expected to be less but, in view of Rensch's (1956) findings relating to body size in related species, to favor the rabbit. Because of the closeness of the species in terms of neural organization, the pattern of intercorrelations found for any one of the species was expected to be observed for the other two.

The intercorrelations between tests within species have already been examined in the previous chapter, and details of these various studies are available in the literature (Livesey, 1965, 1966, 1967, 1968, 1969). The performance of each species on each test is summarized in Table 9.2.

The significance of the differences between species was assessed using the Mann-Whitney U test. The cats were significantly more proficient than the rats on all four tests. They were also superior to the rabbits with significant differences on the Closed Field and Elevated Pathway tests. The rats produced equivalent scores to the rabbits on the Closed Field and Elevated Pathway tests and on the Discrimination task but the rabbits were significantly more effective on Double Alternation.

A factor that contributed to the choice of the cat as a suitable animal for this study was Von Bonin's cephalization index, relating brain weight to body

TABLE 9.2
Mean Performance for Rats, Rabbits and Cats in the Closed Field, Elevated Pathway, Discrimination and Double Alternation Tasks

	Rat (8)	Rabbit (10)	Cat (8)
Closed Field (errors)	66.25	73.20	29.50
Elevated Pathway (errors)	45.50	49.00	22.375
Discrimination (correct responses)	43.00	47.40	51.375
Double Alternation (sequences to criterion)	613.75	271.00	238.75

weight. In the case of the cat, he reported this as 0.64, a figure that was substantially higher than those of .34 and .40 for cynomorph and platyrrhine monkeys, .20 for the lemuroids, and .18 for the carnivora as a whole.

On this basis the cat appeared to be an ideal choice as an animal that differed substantially in brain-body ratio from the other two species but was, at the same time, not substantially bigger than the rabbit. However, an examination of Von Bonin's data revealed an error in computation with the average body weight for 12 cats being given as 370.5 grams, i.e., less than one pound weight. It seemed obvious that the average weight should have been 3705 grams.

Reworking Von Bonin's figures with an average body weight for cats of 3705 grams and using Jerison's figure of ⅔ as the mammalian index (see section 1.5) rather than Von Bonin's .655, a cephalization index of .13 was obtained for cats.

How does this compare with the rabbits? Of the 10 rabbits used in this study, six were still working in an experiment when this material was being examined. The brains of the remaining four had been weighed and preserved and the average weight of the rabbits was known. The average brain weight was 10.5 grams and the average body weight approximated closely to 2000 grams. This yielded a cephalization index of 0.07.

The rats used in this study had been disposed of by the time this issue arose so for rats a comparable cephalization index was derived, using the brain weight-body weight data given in Craigie's Neuroanatomy of the Rat (Zeman & Innes, 1963) for male rats with body weights ranging from 230 grams to 380 grams. This gave an index figure approximating 0.04. Thus for the three species concerned we now had a cephalization gradient of rat 0.04, rabbit 0.07, cat 0.13.

The findings with respect to the three species fitted more comfortably with this reduced value for cats as also did those relating to cats and raccoons in the Double Alternation Problem and to cats, raccoons, and marmosets on learning set tasks. This finding is also in keeping with Warren and Warren's (1959) note on their failure to find differences in learning ability between cats and raccoons.

While these results were thus compatible with the brain index hypothesis it is evident that only the most tentative conclusions could be drawn from the data. For example, the subjects were not selected as being in any way representative samples of their species. They were simply those available. As well, the number of subjects representing each species was very small. In addition, with interspecies comparisons, the problem of "identical conditions" across species in such areas as maturation rates, experience, sensory and motor capabilities, and motivation remains crucial. In this study an attempt was made to meet these problems by trying to set up optimal conditions for each species as a special case of Bitterman's "control by systematic variation."

Finally, the very nature of the problems may have been a significant factor. For example, in the Hebb-Williams Closed Field test a division of the problems of this test into at least two categories was demonstrated, i.e., those that could be solved by direct visualization of the pathway and those for which direct visual solution was not possible, and where some trial and error is required for their solution. It has been shown that these two classes of problems differentiate between species, as cats finding the "visual" problems much easier to solve than the "nonvisual" ones, whereas rats do not (Pollard, 1961, 1963; Livesey, 1966). This finding supports Warren's argument that species differences in cue discrimination may be contaminated by differences in responsiveness to cues, e.g., color vs. form.

This study serves to highlight the difficulties that are inherent in comparative analyses of learning. For cross-species differentiation, only direct comparisons of performance in terms of correct responses or errors were made.

However, a glimpse of possible underlying processes, or rather mechanisms, was given by the within-species correlations between tests referred to in Chapter 8. It was noted that in both my study and in that of Warren's (1961) with cats, significant correlations were observed between a number of tests. However, in both studies the Double Alternation Task yielded no significant correlation with the other tests. Double alternation learning, together with delayed response learning, is disrupted by prefrontal cortical lesion but not posterior cortical lesion, while visual discrimination tasks are affected by posterior cortical lesion but not prefrontal lesion, a classic double dissociation. This points to differentiation of learning function in terms of brain organization, a proposition that will be examined in more detail in later work.

I next examine a very different approach to the comparative studies of learning in which various authors, through a synthesis of many different studies with a wide range of species, argue for an hierarchical structuring of learning processes.

10 Three Approaches to an Hierarchical Organization of Learning Processes

In "Mind in Evolution" first published in 1901, Hobhouse observed that there was nothing to prove that individuals that prevail over others in the struggle for existence are in any way "higher," i.e., in any sense "morally better, intellectually more developed, physically more beautiful or in any way more desirable" (Hobhouse, 1926, p. 2). Moreover, he said, evolution is not normally upwards; rather the plan is like a tree. Furthermore, once a species has moved some distance along a branch, there is little or no chance of it returning to the mainstem. The tendency, in fact, is not to produce any "higher" type but rather to produce as many types as possible.

Is there then, he asked, any progressive evolution towards some "higher" type? He argued that "the highest thing that man knows is mind" (p. 5). Evolution upwards would thus be the evolution of mind or orthogenic evolution. Hobhouse presented the view that mind is the bringing together of elements so that they have a bearing on one another. Thus, in the processes of mind, there is "order and system, correlation and proportion" (p. 6). Actions are seen to be arranged to a certain plan. The correlative processes may involve adapting means to ends, using past experience to interpret a perception, and so on. He thus saw the essence of mind as organization and correlation.

Hobhouse then examined what might be classed as an hierarchical ordering of these correlative processes of mind, which was based on empirical evidence available to him at the time, including both experimental and observational data. Hobhouse himself contributed substantially to this data base. Each stage in the classification reflected increasing capacity for intelligent behavior or "integration of mind." Stage 1 involved correlation by heredity: "an indirect correlation of experience, reaction and welfare, before intelligence, that is, the capacity of the individual to learn from experience, comes into play" (Hobhouse, 1926, p. 396). At this level responses to stimuli are the outcomes of inherited structure; i.e., they are instinctive or reflexive.

Hobhouse next outlined various levels advancing to what he regarded as the highest non-human stage involving concrete experience and practical judgment; the manipulation of practical ideas through "original" application of experience and "complex adjustment of one consideration to another" (Hobhouse, 1926, p. 294). This class of behavior had been demonstrated in experiments in tool handling by monkeys. As Razran observed, Hobhouse antedated Kohler in the employment of tool-using techniques to test learning in monkeys but, unlike Kohler, he claimed that such learning was a primitive type of learning involving "assimilation and readjustment." The final stages in the evolution of mind, the development of concepts and conceptual thought, Hobhouse attributed to humans alone through the evolution of language.

He then elaborated his principle of organization, putting forward the view that the growth of mind, of intelligence, and social life, rest on a "high development of physical organization," which he saw as involving organic unity, but a unity in which there is an individuality of distinguishable parts. Thus, he said,

> from first to last the essence of orthogenic evolution is a progress in organization. Such a progress takes two forms. There is a development in organic unity or "organicity" as parts and wholes come to be more and more completely interdependent and there is increase of scope, as life or purpose of the organization becomes more and more comprehensive. The lower phases of this movement are worked out by biological forces, the higher are the work of mind (Hobhouse, 1926, p. 418).

Hobhouse outlined a very different approach to the nature of learning than that developed by learning theorists such as Thorndike or Skinner. In his approach, Hobhouse focused on increasing complexity in learning processes, arguing that these are organized in an hierarchical fashion. He saw, as the essence of this increasing complexity, an increasing organization both of physical components and of mental processes. The organization of mental processes involves an increasing capacity to correlate past events, stored in the nervous system, with present information to enable adaptations of means to ends with the achievement of particular ends being effected through planned behavior.

This emphasis on organization and the close relationships between neural organization and learning is very similar to Lashley's analysis of the functioning of the nervous system in the mediaton of behavior. This approach is evident too in the writings of both Thorpe and Lorenz and was taken up explicitly by Razran.

W. H. THORPE

Thorpe, an outstanding biologist and ethologist, has been a dominant figure in the Cambridge group of British ethologists for some 30 years. In his book, *Learning and Instinct in Animals,* published in 1956, he anticipated significant developments in the conceptualization of learning that were to emerge over the following 25 years.

Thorpe argued that expectancy was a significant factor in the effectiveness of reinforcement and this constituted a major principle in learning. His views were congruent with the much earlier conceptualization of Tolman who, in 1932, based his account of learning on what he designated as "sign-gestalt-expectancy" with an expectation being an "imminent cognitive determinant aroused by actually presented stimuli" (Tolman, 1932, p. 44).

Thorpe also disputed the notion that learning is the expression of a single fundamental process and argued for a hierarchy of levels of learning. The nature of perception itself formed the base of Thorpe's theory. He considered that:

> perception is not simply an automatic response to simple sense-data or, in human terms, not merely cognition, but is, on the contrary, an active organizing process, itself possibly including an element of purpose, tending all the time to build up the primary perceptions into more and more complete and unitary systems. (Thorpe, 1956, p. 3)

If this is so, he argued, then perception occurs over time, i.e., it is not an instantaneous event, and involves conative, memory, and anticipatory components. He continued:

> a living organism is essentially something that perceives. Therefore some element of anticipation and memory, in other words, *some essential ability to deal with events in time as in space is, by definition, to be expected throughout the world of living things* (p. 4).

This point of view is closely in accord with that expressed by Lashley and later by Jerison.

Thorpe stated that his objective in his book was to relate two modes of the development of behavior, i.e., instinct and learning, and I have already outlined his views on this relationship in Chapter 1. He considered that much animal learning could be seen as "a process of adjusting more or less fixed automatisms or patterns of behavior and more or less rigid releasing mechanisms to changes and chances of life in the world" (p. 49). As we will see, this view is not dissimilar to that put forward by Lorenz.

He then pointed out that, while learning might be viewed as a smooth course of development from unicellular animals to man, closer examination

reveals discontinuities. It is, he concluded, probably physiologically errone-
ous to consider that all learning is the expression of some single fundamental
process. Thorpe then described an hierarchical classification of learning under the headings of habituation, conditioning and trial and error (or instrumental) learning, latent learning, and insight learning. More than half his
book is devoted to a review of learning within each class of animal from protozoa to mammal under each of the above headings.

His exposition of latent learning and insight learning is particularly relevant. Thorpe regarded latent learning as a form of insight learning which involved three separate elements not necessarily found in the simpler types of
learning. These are (1) learning without specific motivation; (2) transfer of
learning whereby the animal is able to use previously learned behavior in response to changed motivation (e.g., discovery of food when it is not hungry
but is looking for water may facilitate later location of that food when it is
hungry); and (3) a faculty enabling the animal to select or attend to certain
parts of a previously learned whole.

Thorpe associated latent learning with exploratory behavior and an exploratory drive. By describing a piece of behavior as exploratory, he said,
one places the organism displaying that behavior on a relatively high behavioral level. Since latent learning involves simultaneous integration and reorganization of previous experience based on its exploratory activity it necessarily involves insight learning.

Insight was considered by Thorpe to be essentially the apprehension of relations while insight learning, including the appropriate organization of ef-
fector responses he defined as *"the sudden production of a new adaptive response not arrived at by trial behavior* or *the solution of a problem by the
sudden adaptive reorganization of experience"* (Thorpe, 1956, p. 100).

In examining the relationships between trial-and-error and insight learning, Thorpe then turned to consider the nature of reinforcement. He pointed
out that, while Pavlov assumed an innate physiological construction whereby
food assuaged the particular need, some behaviorists evoked the Principle of
Effect for trial and error learning. Thorpe examined the difficulties encountered in attempting to utilize this principle to account for all learning and, in
particular, difficulties associated with avoidance learning, secondary-reward
learning, and latent learning. He pointed out that the concept of need raised
problems in that an established need is the absence of something and that absence cannot, in itself, excite the sensory reception. "The preciseness with
which 'need' has been defined is illusory," he said. "It is a biological statement
that does not coincide with the psychological conception Hull had in mind"
(p. 103).

Thorpe then advanced what is now a widely accepted concept in the reinforcement of behavior, namely his "Principle of Expectancy," which "in its
essence assumes that a reinforcement must be such as to confirm an expect-

ancy." The expectancy, which may be innate, is generated by the changing need state and a particular environmental setting. Thus, said Thorpe, "for reinforcement to be effective we have to assume some kind of anticipation during the appetitive behavior to account for the retroaction of the reward" (p. 104). How then does this relate to trial-and-error learning? Thorpe argued that, while initially the animal obviously does not "know" what its activity should lead to, its behavior is such as to suggest that it is expecting "something." Then, he continued:

> By trial-and-error it acquires, perhaps extremely slowly, perhaps very imperfectly, an insight into, a perception of, temporal relationships; to quote Tolman's vivid but awkward phrase — "a what-leads-to-what" expectancy. And this *"understanding"* is the essential basis of reinforcement in a trial-and-error learning situation.
>
> Another important conclusion follows from the expectancy principle. Not only may the appetitive behavior which constitutes the "trial" part of trial-and-error be largely non-random in the sense of being innately restricted, it is or becomes non-random in at least some degree as a result of being expectant. Thus trials are in a great many cases real trials, and may be based upon real hypotheses however elementary and feeble. They are often part of "cognized behavior routes leading to the satisfaction of expectancies" (p. 105).

Tolman had earlier argued that, when a hungry rat was, for example, running in a maze it would initially have a "sign-gestalt-expectation," which might be largely inbuilt, that food may be reached through this particular alley, plus a complementary expectancy that food may not be located there. Learning would then change the balance of these two expectancies so that one would dominate through the process of "mnemonization," i.e., the attachment of a memorial significance to the stimuli present for the sign-object, i.e., the food.

KONRAD LORENZ

One of the most influential of the European ethologists over the past 50 years, Konrad Lorenz's primary interest has been centered on built-in behaviors and fixed-action patterns. Over the years he has espoused what may be considered to be an extreme position in the ethological viewpoint with his emphasis on genetic mechanisms to the exclusion of environmental influences. I have touched on some of his views in this area earlier. However, this approach has been tempered in more recent years by his growing acknowledgment of the adaptive significance of learning and it is this aspect of his work that I examine now.

In his approach to learning Lorenz has continued to emphasize a very strong genetic base. Of particular interest to me has been his conceptualization of the innate teaching mechanism. In this he appears to have followed a similar time course to my own formulation of a concept relating the evolution of affect and emotion to the evolution of learning. In this I argue that affects evolved as a mechanism that informs the animal of its success or failure in its interactions with the environment. My formulation of this concept began in the mid 1960s, following which its history was marked by a series of papers that failed to achieve publication. The first printed reference to this concept appears in the proceedings of the CIBA Foundation on Hippocampal Function, published in 1975 (Livesey, 1975). I examine this idea in some detail in the next chapter.

Three publications by Lorenz over the past 20 years have been of particular significance for the present analysis. These are his *Evolution and Modification of Behavior* published in 1965, an essay on the "Innate basis of learning" in Karl Pribram's *On the Biology of Learning* published in 1969, and his *The Foundations of Ethology* published in 1981.

The key to understanding Lorenz's approach is in his definition of adaptation which he saw as the process that molds the organism to its environment to achieve survival. This process is, he believed, one which forms within the organic structure an image of the environment. This "learning process," in terms of my argument in Chapter 1, may be the product of innate mechanisms or may be produced through plastic neural organizations during the lifetime of the animal.

For adaptation to occur, Lorenz considered that the property of negative feedback is essential. In fact, he believed this property to be essential for the development of life itself. He expressed the view that "One of the events that must have happened at the origin of life is the 'fulguration' of a feedback cycle containing, in its chain of causation, one link whose effect on the next one bore a negative sign" (Lorenz, 1969, p. 17). He adopted the term "fulguration" from theistic philosophers who had used the word *fulgaratio* or lightning to describe the act of creating something entirely new.

Lorenz then went on to point out that permanent equilibrium would not be possible with an open system in a variable environment without this negative or dampening feedback. He considered that homeostasis or self regulation involving negative feedback must have occurred concurrently with the molecular structure that enabled duplication. In all adaptive behavior, said Lorenz, it is the molecular structure of the machinery on which the organism's way of responding is based that is altered by the individual's experience. However, he argued, many of the processes by which the organism acquires information involve the functions of mechanisms that can repeat their performance any number of times without undergoing adaptive change. These include the mechanisms involved in kinesis or orienting mechanisms, phobic responses as seen for example in protozoa avoiding noxious stimuli, and taxes or directional determinants. As discussed earlier, the mechanisms for modifying these classes of adaptive behavior reside in the genetic structure of the animal with changes brought about by the various processes of combination, reconstruction, and mutation that occur with the formation of each new generation. In fact, as Lorenz pointed out, one of the chief functions of sexual reproduction is to disseminate new information quickly through a population.

While such machinery can only be changed through the genome, it is, said Lorenz, a fundamental error to regard such unlearned or phylogenetically programmed behavior as "stereotyped." Such programming can result in complex behavior systems with hierarchically organized appetences, releasing mechanisms and fixed motor patterns that are guided by built-in orienting mechanisms. Such a structure "commands a wealth of cognitive processes that gather information and enable the organism to act on it instantaneously" (Lorenz, 1969, p. 33).

In striking contrast to these "inbuilt" mechanisms, said Lorenz, is one where changes or modifications are effected in the animal's structure during its lifetime. These changes, which result from the interaction between the animal and its environment, are effected in the nervous system and lead to modifications of behavior. This process is called learning.

Lorenz then went on to argue that in no sense could modifications through learning be random. Indeed, he said, the chance that any random modification in behavior would be adaptive would be no greater than a random gene mutation or recombination and the chance in that case is extremely small. He therefore concluded that, if a regularly occurring modification is adaptive then "we are safe in assuming that this modifiability is 'selected for' — in other words, that it is the function of a built-in mechanism." He then added that such an open program "has for its prerequisite, not less, but much more genetically acquired information" (Lorenz, 1969, p. 34).

All such adaptive modifications are dependent on alterations to the machinery by which the organism's way of responding is controlled. Such modifications involve both the short-term gathering of information and the long-term storing and retrieval of such information. Lorenz's conceptualization of the nature of such gathering and storing mechanisms, i.e., of the nature of learning itself, is epitomized in his statement that:

> The more complicated a biological system, the less likely it is that a random modification will effect anything but disintegration. In the whole world there is hardly a system more complicated than the central nervous organization underlying the behavior of a higher animal. One of the greatest achievements of phylogeny is to have constructed systems of this sort in such a way that they are still adaptively modifiable by an input occurring during the individual's life. There never was a greater error in the history of science than the empiricist philo-

sophers' belief that the human mind, before any experience, was a *tabula rasa*, a blank, unless it is the reciprocal, but intrinsically identical, assumption of nonbiological psychologists that "learning" must, as a matter of course, "enter into" any physiological behavior processes whatever. The worst aspect of both these reciprocal errors is that they obscure the central problem of learning – the question: how does learning come to be adaptive? (Lorenz, 1969, p. 36).

In elaboration of his claim that learning is not a diffuse and all pervasive process entering into all physiological processes, Lorenz argued that, when modification of such a process does occur, it is the result of built-in mechanisms that are phylogenetically programmed for modification and that occur at preformed places in the program. Such open parts of a phylogenetically developed program for an animal will concern variable unpredictable parts of the environment. Other parts programmed in invariable form contain the information that tells an individual what to do and what not to do. As an example, Lorenz cited the honey bee. This insect can learn to use irregular forms as landmarks by which to steer a course to the hive but cannot be taught to use such forms as positive or negative signals for food. Food signals, he claimed, have to be geometrically regular and preferably radially symmetrical (Lorenz, 1965). He thus argued for interrelated systems of phylogenetically adapted and individually modifiable behaviors.

The apparatus that generates the modification of behavior, Lorenz labeled as an innate teaching mechanism, which he argued, in providing reinforcement or the opposite, must contain sufficient innate information to feed back clear signals on biological success or failure. The existence of such mechanisms must be postulated to explain the adaptive function of learning. Such an innate mechanism, he said, must be there to make learning possible and, in order to achieve its modifying effect, it must be resistant to modification.

Refinement and elaboration of Lorenz's conceptualization of both the teaching mechanism and of learning is evident over the period covered by his three major works referred to here, i.e., between 1965 and 1981.

In 1981 Lorenz observed that his formulation of the concept of the "innate school marm" started out as a reductio ad absurdum and it was not until some 10 years later, in the 1960s that he came to recognize the basic strength of the idea. The critical question for the concept was: How was it possible that, whenever an animal modified its behavior through learning, the right process was learned in terms of the animal's survival? Lorenz observed that, so far as he could see, Anokhin (1961) was the first among the theorists of learning to identify the conditional reflex as "a feedback circuit" in which it was "not only the stimulus configuration arriving from the outside, but more especially the *return notification* reporting on the completion and the consequences of the conditioned behavior that provided an audit of its adaptiveness" (Lorenz, 1981, p. 9). Lorenz concluded that this "innate school marm," which informs the organism whether its behavior is useful or detrimental by reinforcing one and extinguishing the other, "must be located in a feedback apparatus that reports success or failure to the mechanisms of the first phases of antecedent behavior" (p. 9). As discussed in Chapter 11, this concept, though formulated somewhat differently to that of Anokhin and Lorenz, has been in the literature for a long time.

What then is the nature of this teaching mechanism as conceived by Lorenz? In his earlier discussion of the process, Lorenz (1969) argued that in many appetitive behaviors from simple kinesis to learned motor skills the behavior is continued until the organism reaches a "specific" stimulus situation in which it comes to rest. Such a system might, for example, guide an animal in selecting conditions favorable for survival with respect to humidity, temperature, and so forth. In such situations, innate confirmation would reside in the receptor organization which "knows" the right conditions and reinforces the precedent behavior that achieved that condition. He considered the immediate reinforcement to be "relief of tension," which he described as "a classic case of Hullian conditioning."

In elaborating further on the evolution of this teaching mechanism, Lorenz (1981) claimed that "Without any known exception, animals that have evolved a central nervous system are able to learn from the consequences produced by their own actions" (p. 289); success acts as a "reward" and failure as a "punishment." Such a system he considered to be highly teleonomic and in consequence was, he believed, invented many times in metazoan evolution. Lorenz (1969) had argued that:

> With the "fulguration" of this new feedback cycle, a new information acquiring system has come into being, which conveys specific information about what to do and what not to do, not to the species' store of genetic information but directly to the physiological machinery that determines the individual's behavior and retains the message (Lorenz, 1969, p. 46).

Once this evolutionary "fulguration" of positive feedback was achieved, argued Lorenz, a number of physiological mechanisms previously operating separately, came to be integrated into a new functional whole. In this way a new selection pressure was brought to bear on these older independent mechanisms. One example given by Lorenz was in the evolution of releasing mechanisms. Prior to the development of learning, this mechanism contained all the necessary information on what to do and when to do it, stored in genetic form. With the advent of learning much of this information could be assured by the learning method through trial and error. The rigid genetic program then became unnecessary and might, in fact, be a handicap.

For this forward step in adaptive evolution to appear, however, the nervous system had to first achieve a sufficiently high level of development. Lorenz argued that, while the advantages of the cognitive mechanisms of conditioning are obvious, a sufficiently complicated and integrated central nervous system was essential for its appearance. A system able to feed back information about success or failure into another system when activity has preceded that of the "teaching" system in time and to thus influence the future activity of that system must, he said, have a certain minimum number as well as a considerable complexity of the neural subsystems that make up the system. These older systems that are tied into the new one, e.g., a releasing mechanism that gains in selectivity, appetitive behavior that is modified, and motor patterns constructed on the basis of the reports of success or failure, all contribute, said Lorenz, to the making of an adaptively modifiable system, but they are not modified themselves. Thus this behavior system involves a rather elaborate genetic program.

In his 1981 volume, Lorenz made a very sharp distinction between various classes of associative learning in terms of the functioning of the innate teaching mechanism. One type, he considered, involved learning without feedback reporting success. Another major class involved learning effected through feedback of the consequences of behavior.

Associative learning without feedback he considered, resulted from a connection or association between a stimulus that initially had no releasing effect (a CS) and a key releasing stimulus (an IRM, the US), which released a particular behavior pattern. With the CS preceding the US on a number of occasions the two stimuli became linked so that, on experiencing the first stimulus, the animal came to expect the second and to prepare for it. Lorenz pointed out that, in the normal environment, such repeated contiguity would almost invariably have teleonomic significance. He gave as an example the association between thunder and rain and hence the effect of thunder on mountain goats causing them to seek shelter. He put forward the view that loci within the central nervous system would be sensitive to such temporal sequences as stimuli arriving along different pathways and would be capable of building a lasting representation of the new signal complex. In fact, there is strong evidence for the existence of such loci within the CNS as I will detail in a later work.

This learning process is therefore one of stimulus selection enabling the animal to prepare to perform, or not to perform action relevant to survival upon registering what had previously been an irrelevant stimulus. The animal, in this situation, learns by having something happen to it. Lorenz did not make clear the nature of the innate teaching mechanism or even if there was one, as he labeled such learning association without feedback. However, the key feature in such an association is the relationship between the previously neutral stimulus and an IRM, the US.

Lorenz then distinguished another class of associative learning characterized by feedback of the consequences of the animal's actions in terms of "reward" signaling success and "punishment" signaling failure. For such a process to be effected, an "open" system with a much more complicated neural structure would be necessary. He pointed out that such a system, teaching the animal to behave effectively by performing the appropriate action to achieve consummatory behavior, was highly teleonomic. This system, he said, must be capable of transmitting a reliable report of success or failure as far back as the mechanisms of precedent appetitive behavior. He then went on to point out that Pavlovian conditioning relating salivation to food did not fall into the category of conditioning by association without feedback. In the Pavlovian situation the dog salivated to the CS only when hungry. What Pavlov had demonstrated was not a true conditioned reflex (as in the eye-blink response to an air puff) but instead a rather complex system of appetitive behavior, disguised by the fact that the animal was restrained. In the conditioned reflex, said Lorenz, the CS releases the one response previously elicited by the US. In conditioned appetitive behavior the CS releases a sequence of behavior preparatory to the consummatory act. Even if the CS is received at the same time as the releasing of the consummatory act, the animal associates the CS with the preceding appetitive behavior. For example, said Lorenz, if a bee is presented with a food tray on yellow paper and, in a few seconds between alighting and sucking the food, the yellow sheet is changed for a blue one, then the bee learns to fly to the yellow background despite receiving food on a tray with a blue background. Lorenz then argued that mechanisms of adaptive behavior provide the site in which modification is most likely to be effective with the built-in teaching mechanism being "situated in the fixed motor pattern of the consummatory action itself; its immodifiable form furnishes rewarding reafferences only in the teleonomically correct environmental situation; in any other it acts as a punishment by being 'disappointing' " (p. 313). The exact nature of the teaching mechanism was not specified, though its "rewarding" or "punishing" effects were emphasized.

Another class of associative learning with feedback, very different from that just described, was next identified by Lorenz. In this type of learning, not a stimulus but a particular behavior pattern is selected. This involves trying out a repertoire of behaviors to find which will achieve success, e.g., Thorndike's cat in the puzzle box. Lorenz considered this to be an advanced form of learning closely linked with exploratory behavior. He further differentiated this "operant" behavior from the situation in which the animal tries one particular behavior in a variety of situations until it finds the appropriate environment or stimulus configuration. Using the example of a dog learning to bury a bone, Lorenz pointed out that the dog uses the same digging and scratching behavior but in different situations, e.g., on a parquetry floor, until it finds the right soil conditions for digging and burying. In these circumstances, argued Lorenz, it is the stimulus that is selected and not the behavior. In fact, he considered this type of stimulus learning to be far more common than operant learning: that quite highly developed animals (such as greylag geese) rely on this "stimulus substitution." He considered that over-assessment of the importance of operant conditioning and underestimating that of other classes of learning by psychologists stemmed from generalization of properties observed in the studies of learning in rats and man — "both extraordinarily exploratory creatures." (Lorenz, 1981, p. 336)

Lorenz considered that operant conditioning by reinforcement occurs, in the natural setting, "almost exclusively within the context of exploratory behavior" (p. 336), i.e., a highly advanced class of learning found only in animals with well-developed nervous systems. In fact, while he regarded the activities of the cat in the puzzle box as operant learning, he considered that a pigeon pecking a key or a rat pressing a lever falls outside this class of behavior, noting that this behavior had been pre-selected by the experimenter as also had the stimulus, with the apparatus offering very few alternative behaviors to choose from. He would almost wish, he said, to call this operant conditioning.

Lorenz considered various alternative possibilities for the location of the "innate teacher" in various classes of learning in various species. He argued that nest building in birds and rats might well be contained in the motor pattern itself. His conclusion was that there was a multiplicity of learning mechanisms that had evolved independently of each other in the various phyla and that "each of these programs is based on vast quantities of information that have been phylogenetically acquired and that are genetically coded" (p. 337).

In conjunction with the development of his conceptualization of the innate teaching mechanism, Lorenz developed and elaborated his views on the evolution of various classes of learning. He postulated a number of distinct levels related to the complexity of the nervous system.

In *Evolution and Modification of Behavior* (1965), Lorenz defined learning as any adaptive modification of behavior and emphasized those classes of learning that did not involve associative processes. In particular he considered such learning functions as habituation, the increase in selectivity in unlearned stimulus-specific responses, the calibration or improvement in aiming mechanisms, e.g., pecking behavior, the setting of internal clocks, the functional integration of motor patterns, and motor learning. More recently, in *The Innate Bases of Learning*, he touched briefly on such processes, and, with them, also considered imprinting. He then examined conditioning, which he considered to involve an entirely new process, i.e., "one that derived information from the success as well as the failure of a behavioral pattern *just performed*" (Lorenz, 1969, p. 46).

Views on the nature of conditioning and associative learning underwent considerable refinement and development over the next two decades and this is clearly evident in Lorenz's 1981 volume in which he differentiated clearly between classical conditioning, conditioned appetitive behaviors, and operant conditioning. This differentiation hinged on his conceptualization of the innate teacher, as was detailed in the preceding section.

Lorenz then went on to consider insight learning and exploratory behavior. He considered insight to be a perceptual process evolved through the necessity for more and more information about the spatial nature of the animal's environment. Thus, he regarded insight as the functioning of a complex system that has been phylogenetically programmed for instant information. While insight and learning are separate processes, Lorenz considered that there is an element of learning in all insightful behavior and that, even in the most primitive kind of trial and error learning, the animal does not react entirely indiscriminately but, by virtue of inbuilt taxes and so forth, possesses some measure of direction or "insight" in its behavior that considerably improves its chances of success. His views on insight learning thus come into close coincidence with those of Thorpe.

Lorenz (1981) noted that only in species with highly differentiated nervous systems and only in situations of great stress does an animal try a variety of behaviors to find one that affords relief (e.g., the cat in the puzzle box); i.e., engages in operant behavior. However, he said, only in the context of exploratory behavior do we find learning processes agreeing with the behaviorist's concept of "operational conditioning."

Exploratory behavior was considered by Lorenz to be characterized by "strong and autonomous appetitive motivation directed at stimulus situations *new* to the individual" (Lorenz, 1969, pp. 55-56). Furthermore, such behavior only became evident under situations free from other motivational tension. Such behavior is, he considered, closely akin to play, with curiosity supplying motivation as strong as any other appetitive behavior. In a novel situation the animal directs at the object arousing curiosity a whole range of behavioral patterns. He described the actions of a young raven confronted with an entirely new object. It first treated the object as a dangerous predator, approaching cautiously, delivering a strong peck and then making off. If the object responded it tried to get behind and attack it. If not then the raven tried to tear it to pieces and taste it. If the object was not edible it gradually lost its attractiveness and may be used to perch on. Thus, the object's characteristics are explored and it is "made familiar."

Exploratory behavior, argued Lorenz, is an excellent example of how a new and efficient cognitive function can come into being through "rewiring" of a number of already extant subsystems. This new invention, he said, involves a strongly motivated appetitive behavior, namely curiosity, utilized in a conditionable system to acquire maximum new information. While the physiological mechanisms involved are not new, argued Lorenz, "the new systematic properties coming into existence with this new fulguration make a tremendous difference. In fact *most of the differences between man and all other organisms is founded on the new possibilities of cognition that are opened by exploratory behavior"* (Lorenz, 1969, p. 57).

Like Thorpe, Lorenz linked exploratory behavior and latent learning, arguing that latent learning was a product of exploratory behavior.

In terms of my particular point of view, the major contributions from Lorenz to our understanding of learning in man are his emphasis on the "fulguration" or creation of new learning processes that he related directly to increased complexity and organizational capacity of the brain, and his concept of the "innate teaching mechanism." Like Lashley and Harlow, Lorenz emphasized the relationships between the evolution of the nervous system and the evolution of learning. He developed a very clear conceptualization of the "fulguration" of new learning processes at critical stages in evolution. These "creations" he linked directly to the increasing capacity of the nervous system in terms of size, complexity and organization. A major factor in these changes was seen as increases in the capacity of the "innate teacher" to instruct the animal about the significance of its behaviors and hence to direct new learning.

Lorenz's writings also revealed clearly his view that many different kinds of learning mechanisms had evolved independently of each other, with different mechanisms characterizing different phyla and with the independent evolution of similar mechanisms in different phyla. His emphasis on the significance of genetic mechanisms even in learning processes is also strongly in evidence.

As already indicated, my particular concern is with that line of evolution that led to the human condition and this approach is dominant in the work of the next writer.

GREGORY RAZRAN

Against this background I examine Razran's highly organized hierarchical structure of learning, and we may note in the course of this analysis some strong similarities to that advanced by Thorpe many years earlier.

In his *Mind in Evolution* Razran presented a most detailed and extensive analysis of studies involving cross-species comparisons in the area of learning and cognition. Razran's underlying hypothesis was that learning may be seen as an evolved and evolving hierarchical system with more primitive lower levels persisting but with higher levels being more efficient and more flexible for the needs of the organism and normally controlling lower levels. He saw habituation and sensitization as basic learning processes, followed by associative or conditioning learning. He considered configured learning, learning of patterned or compound stimuli, and symbolic learning to be more recent evolutionary developments. Razran developed his view of the evolution of learning on the basis of laboratory studies of living species. These studies covered what Razran estimated to be some 90% of the Russian publications in the area together with a very extensive sampling of American, English, and German work. The animals considered ranged from protozoa to man.

Razran himself described his book as "a ramified outgrowth of my long interest in what is termed in Pavlovian tradition 'evolution of higher nervous activity' " (Razran, 1971, p. vii). He took his title from Hobhouse's *Mind in Evolution* published in 1901 and his theory clearly has its roots in Hobhouse's work, as Razran himself made quite explicit.

Razran developed the proposition that there are some 11 levels of learning, hierarchically organized in terms of evolutionary appearance. These ranged from habituation or, as he described it, "the decrement or disappearnace of reactions through reacting," which is evident in all animals from protozoa to man, to symbolic learning evident only in the highest primates. He listed seven major levels. These, in ascending order, were as follows: (1) Habituation; (2) Sensitization, or increment of response through acting. These were followed by three types of simple associative or conditioned learning, namely: (3) Inhibitory conditioning, or decrement and disappearance of a reaction through associated antagonistic reaction, i.e., punishment; (4) Classical conditioning or evocation of a reaction by a stimulus of associated reactions; (5) Reinforcement conditioning or strengthening of a reaction through associated reaction, i.e., operant or reward conditioning. Finally, he listed two classes of "higher learning," namely: (6) Learning to perceive, i.e., configured learning of different types, and (7) Learning to think: the various types of symbolic learning.

Razran next set out the formal properties of relationships between higher and lower levels of learning in five propositions. These were:

1. Higher levels of learning should bring into being some new forms and laws of learning manifestations.
2. Lower levels should continue as subsystems within higher systems. Thus higher level learning is normally a resultant of higher and lower learning.
3. Higher level learning should be more efficient in organism-environment interaction but lower level learning may be more universal and less disruptable.
4. Normally higher level learning should control lower level learning but under some conditions lower level learning may predominate as a result of its greater universality and lesser disruptability.
5. Interaction between higher and lower levels may be synergic or antagonistic (Razran, 1971, pp 23–24).

Razran then presented experimental evidence from the Russian, Western European, and American laboratories to effect a synthesis of evidence in support of this theory and, in so doing, demonstrated his great talent for such an endeavor. He dealt separately with each class of learning, chapter by chapter, but I only touch on a few critical issues here.

Habituation. Razran defined habituation as the process whereby responding is reduced with repetition of a stimulus that has no apparent effect on any of the life processes of the animal. He demonstrated that this process is evident throughout the animal kingdom from protozoa to man. Habituation, he claimed involves only *non-associative* means of learning and involves only innate reactions. He concluded that, despite the evolutionary fixity of the habituatory mechanism, the extent and role of uncomplicated habituation has shown a continuing decline in evolution from nereids to man with the process being superceded, subordinated, specialized, and transformed in the service of more advanced adaptive mechanisms.

Sensitization. This second level of learning was defined by Razran as increased reactivity with repeated non-associative stimulation. He saw this process manifested in two behavioral modes, with (a) the innate reaction increased in incidence and magnitude and with decreased latency and lowered threshold of reaction and (b) pseudo-conditioning with new reactions added to the organism's repertoire. This, said Razran, "may be the first crucial rung on the evolutionary ladder of positive learning . . . yet this rung is one that has been largely passed over" (p. 59). While, he said, behavioral sensitization does not seem to be present at the dawning of organic life, there is evidence for its widespread and prevalent operation in annelids, prevertebrate chordates, and possibly spinal mammals.

Associative Learning

Aversive Conditioning. Of the three classes of associative learning, Razran regarded aversive, inhibitory, or punishment learning as quite distinct from, and more primitive than, classical and operant conditioning. In typical punishment, he claimed, the punished reaction or response does not acquire any characteristics of the punishing stimulus, nor is the punishing stimulus likely to be strengthened by the punished reaction. The chief parameters of punishment learning, he stated, are the absolute and relative intensity of the punishing stimulus, its subsequence to the punished reaction and the degree of interactive antagonism. Finally, he found punishment learning to be highly effective throughout the metazoan kingdom with effectiveness increasing in early evolution and reaching an asymptote relatively early. A plausible corollary, he said, is that punishment is the form of associative learning least affected by concomitant cognition.

Classical Conditioning.   This was held by Razran to be the very core of the associative process. Only for classical conditioning, he said, is "double stimulation" a sine qua non. He pointed to some 7000 experiments in this area, published in 29 different languages. Razran examined a number of studies of classical conditioning in early phylogeny. He noted that conditioning had been demonstrated in the earthworm (Ratner & Miller, 1959) with a bright light as US and vibration as the CS, and in snails (Sokolov, 1950)[1] with a 0.2% methyl blue solution injected into the water as US and a change of illumination as CS. On the other hand, Ross (1965) had been unable to demonstrate classical conditioning in coelenterates though they had readily shown aversive inhibitory conditioning. In the light of this and other similar evidence Razran concluded that none of the experiments "disproves the view that classical conditioning is a higher evolutionary level of learning than is aversive inhibitory conditioning and, of course, sensitization and habituation" (p. 135).

Operant Conditioning.   On the third class of associative learning, i.e., reinforcement or operant conditioning, Razran observed that, while this was certainly a development of Thorndike's Law of Effect learning, the two most widely current techniques, the straight runway and the Skinner Box, had specific Russian antecedents. Zeliony (1913)[2] used a runway technique in which he measured speed of running and length of step as rats learned to run to a food tray in response to a tone, recording the footsteps on the pathway with smoked paper. The Skinner Box technique was mirrored in Ivanov-Smolensky's bulb-pressing method to study reinforcement conditioning in children and patients in mental hospitals. The subject pressed a bulb to obtain a piece of chocolate or the exposure of changing pictures or objects (Ivanov-Smolensky,[3] 1927).

The Learning of Perceptions

The classes of learning dealt with to date all fall within the category of learned behaviors considered by Razran to be "already in full bloom on this planet 500,000,000 years ago" (p. 9). In the remaining chapters he considered several classes of higher order learning, including what he called the learning

---

[1]Sokolov, V. A. Conditioned reflexes in snails *Physa acuta*. Vestnik Leningrad University, 1959, No. 9, 82–86 (from Razran, 1971).

[2]Zeliony, G. P. Procede technique pour l'etude des reflexes musculaires conditionnels. *Compte Rendu des Seances de la Societe de Biologie, Paris,* 1913, *75,* 659–660 (from Razran, 1971).

[3]Ivanov-Smolensky, A. G. Studying the grasping reflex in children. *Mediko-Biologichesky Zhurnal,* 1927, No. 2, 33–41 (from Razran, 1971).

of perceptions and symbolizing, or the learning of thinking, planning, and willing. The learning of perceptions he discussed under the headings of sensory preconditioning and configuring.

Sensory Preconditioning. This involves the prior association of two neutral stimuli before one of the two is paired with a US. Following the establishment of a conditional response between the CS and US, it has been shown that the other neutral stimulus, not paired with the US, is also able to produce a CR.

Razran noted that sensory preconditioning was first described by the Russian Panferov[4] in 1926 in salivatory conditioning of children, and later by Narbutovich and Podkopayev[5] in 1936, using salivatory and shock conditioning of dogs. The Narbutovich and Podkopayev study exemplifies the process as clearly as any and was described by Razran as follows: For 2 dogs the experimenters sounded a noise for 5 seconds and then this was joined, for a further 5 seconds, by the sight of a whirligig. In a third dog the sound of a tuning fork preceded the presentation of the flash of an electric light. The number of these pre-conditioned pairings ranged from 21–30. Then the whirligig was paired with electric shock to the hind leg of the first two animals and the sound of the tuning fork was paired with food in the third. Following establishment of the appropriate CR the experimenters then demonstrated that "The noise, paired with the whirligig but not the shock evoked leg flexion, and the lamp paired with the tuning fork but not with the food came to evoke salivation" (Razran, 1971, p. 186).

Razran then described a number of studies, mostly Russian, that examined the phenomenon over a range of species and under varying conditions. In discussing the American work in this area he made a number of points of which I would note particularly the following: (1) no American study mentioned Soviet counterparts although some four times as many studies had been carried out with greatly increased range of problems investigated; (2) The American methodology was superior to the Russian; (3) nonetheless, said Razran, "American findings are strikingly similar to the Russians', reported as a rule a number of years earlier" (Razran, 1971, p. 201).

On the basis of his analysis of the work in this area, Razran claimed that Russian workers have demonstrated clear sensory preconditioning in dogs and cats, as also have the Americans. Russian researchers have also demonstrated some signs of such sensory preconditioning in turtles and clearly demonstrated sensory preconditioning in canaries, starlings, white mice, hedge-

---

[4]Panferov, Yu. K. Chained conditioned reflexes in children. In *Theses, 2nd All-Union Congress of Physiology.* Lenigrad: 1926. Pp. 153–156 (from Razran, 1971).

[5]Narbutovich, I. I. & Podkopayev, N. A. The conditioned reflex as an association. *Trudy Fiziologicheskikh Laboratorii I.P. Pavlova,* 1936, *6* (2), 5–25 (from Razran, 1971).

hogs, bats, polecats, and chimpanzees. They were unable to establish such sensory preconditioning in fish, frogs, salamander, axylotls, amblystoma, or in puppies less than six months old. As well, they examined maximum retention times for reaction to the associated stimulus in different animals. These were found to range from 14 days for birds, 15 for rodents, 19 for insectivores, 29 for bats, and several months for carnivores. One baboon retained the association for a year (Razran, 1971, pp. 198–200).

Configuring.   In this class of experiment the animal learns to respond for food reward to a compound stimulus but not its components, e.g., a compound of a tone, a light, and a different sound. The two main variations used are (a) simultaneous presentation, called complexes by the Russians; (b) successive presentations called chains; and (c) dynamic stereotypes which are special successive compounds of four to eight CSs of which all but one are paired separately with US and one is left unpaired.

Razran observed that Soviet experments had shown that configuring is not pre-existent in the compound CS but develops in the course of conditioning. Three stages have been observed. In the initial stage, when components are tested alone, they are not affected by being in the compound and produce the conditioned reaction. In the intermediate stage weaker components lose their effectiveness when presented on their own and finally only the compound is effective.

These Russian experiments have explored in some detail the notion that achievement of full configural conditioning divides learning of higher and lower vertebrates. For example, a three-component successive sound was given to fish, turtles, birds, rabbits, dogs, and baboons. All animals learned to respond to the compound stimuli but there were marked differences in the ability of the animals to configure the stimulus sequence. Goldfish and turtles could only perform the task if there was specific extinction of responses to each individual component. Even then only 2 of 6 fish and 3 of 5 turtles succeeded. Twelve of the 15 birds succeeded without differential conditioning as did 2 of 8 rabbits. Of the rabbits, four more were successful following differential conditioning. Both of 2 dogs and both of 2 baboons succeeded without differential conditioning (Baru, Malinovsky, Ovchinnikova, Prazdnikova, & Chernomordikov,[6] 1959).

In a study of simultaneous configuring, total inactivation of components without differential conditioning of the three components was achieved by the various species involved as shown in Table 10.1 (from Razran, 1971, p. 210).

---

[6]Baru, A. V., Malinovsky, O. V., Ovchinnikova, N. P., Prazdnikova, N. V., & Chernomordikov, V. V. Conditioned motor food reflexes to chains of stimuli in some vertebrates. *Trudy Instituta Fiziologii imeni I.P. Pavlova,* 1959, *8,* 107–113 (from Razran, 1971).

TABLE 10.1
Simultaneous Configuring in Several Classes and Orders of Vertebrates.
Total Inactivation of Components without Differential Conditioning in
Three-Component Compounds. (After Sergeyev, 1967)*

Kind of Animal	Number of Animals	Number of Compound Trials Producing a Configure Through Overtraining
Fish, frogs, and turtles	"Large number"	"Failure after 700 to 1,000 trials"
Titmice	5	95–220
Starlings	4	76–92
Guinea pigs	4	89–126
Hedgehogs	6	78–104
Bats	3	65–90
Dogs	5	56–80

*Sergeyev, B. F. *Evolution of associative temporary connections.* Moscow, Akademiya Nauk SSSR, 1967 (from Razran, 1971).

Razran concluded that configuring is within the capacity of birds and mammals but not fish and turtles. That is not to say, said Razran, that some fish genius could not master the task on occasional trials or that all birds and mammals could perform it.

Following this review of the work on sensory preconditioning and configuring Razran argued that these two phenomena of "superconditioning" have much in common. They both represent sensory-sensory learning, and both have been shown to be evident in higher animals, birds, and mammals, but not in species earlier in phylogeny. He also concluded that the brain centers involved were higher in evolution than those involved in simple conditioning.

Razran further concluded that there are significant differences between the two processes. In particular, sensory preconditioning could be regarded as a higher form of an old kind of associative learning but configuring was a process that brought out new end results. Thus neurobehavioral (a + b + c)'s are different from independent a's, b's, c's. There is, he claimed, learned *emergence* or *inference*, which is directly evident in configuring, but not sensory preconditioning. Furthermore, while sensory preconditioning may enhance the organism's "acquired reaction repertories," this effect is rather limited. On the other hand, configuring leads to a very significant gain in adaptive economy. Thus, said Razran,

Organisms that do not configure can respond to N stimuli in only N different ways. Those that do configure may learn to do it in $N!$ ways. And they are able, furthermore, to respond unitarily to larger portions of their environment (Razran, 1971, p. 223).

Both phenomena are, concluded Razran, ascending levels of cognitive perceptual learning. He saw sensory preconditioning as "sign" learning and configuring as "gestalt" learning.

Symbolizing. Razran concluded that learning to perceive bridged a major span in the evolution of learning processes with perceptual learning forming an hierarchy involving (1) the uncovering of existing relationships; (2) the discovery of new and unobvious relationships and (3) the apprehension of objects and complex events, with sensory preconditioning and configuring forming "the behavioral schemata of the trial."

Perceiving, however, did not constitute the highest order of integrative capacity. Above this Razran placed conceiving or concept formation or "the capacity to integrate aspects of different portions of the environment and not just one particular portion" (p. 270). Under the heading of concept formation Razran examined oddity problems and learning-set studies and also considered the ability of animals to form such concepts as triangularity or color, e.g., the color "blue." He pointed out that, while it is relatively easy to demonstrate that an animal can perceive a particular shape and distinguish it from others, it becomes a very laborious task to establish whether that animal is able to form a concept of a particular shape, e.g., triangularity. It has to be shown that the subject will respond to triangularity irrespective of size, color, dimensions, etc., and also that it is responding to the positive and not to some fixed negative cue. He speculated that it was this sheer magnitude of the task of ascertaining whether the animal was simply "perceiving shapes" or "conceiving forms" that resulted in the main research in this area being concerned with shape although it is frequently called form.

Razran concluded that we still know very little about the underlying mechanisms of conceptual learning in animals. While some primates and even subprimates might learn to react differentially to concepts, thus evidencing some abstractive capacity, he believed that this did not warrant the view that such animals are thereby able to think. He continued: "Since they lack replicative behavioral symbols, they obviously cannot communicate what they learn, and since thereby they *ipso facto* lack their meanings, they may well be devoid also of intraorganismic units of thinking" (Razran, 1971, p. 307).

These units of thinking are the symbols that constitute Pavlov's second-signal system or language. Pavlov, in contradiction to his earlier views on the unity of learning, considered that the advent of language introduced a new principle of neural action (Razran, 1971, p. 276).

The process of symbolization Razran defined as *"associative formation of communicable referential replicates of concepts and percepts"* (p. 276). The crux of the meaning of symbols is the context in which they occur. Razran argued that, in the absence of language, animals other than man have not demonstrated symbol learning. He then concentrated his attention during the rest of the chapter on the development of language in human children. This goes beyond the purpose of the present volume.

It is worth noting here that Karl Pribram has given considerable attention to the question of use of symbols by primates other than man. On the basis of his work with rhesus monkeys, Pribram distinguished between signs and symbols. Context free communicative acts he labeled as "signs," these remaining invariant in their meaning over a variety of situations. Thus, he said, a rose is a rose is a rose regardless of where it appears, in the garden, on the dinner table, or in a garbage can. Symbols, on the other hand, are abstract elements, the meaning of which changes with the context in which they appear. The elements of language are the clearest example of this. Pribram cited as an example of a symbol the then current raising of two fingers to signify peace. This, he said, has in other contexts meant victory or acted as a greeting. It has a different meaning again in present society. Pribram (1971) argued that different parts of the brain are involved in constructing signs than those responsible for manipulating symbols. I will be examining this concept in some detail in Volume 2.

In his discussion of signs Pribram pointed out that he originally used shelled peanuts as rewards for his monkeys. He then realized that the monkeys could shell their own peanuts thus saving him this chore. Thus the monkey learned that the peanut shell was the "sign" for the enclosed nut. Discrimination learning, concluded Pribram, is an exploration of the animal's ability to handle signs. In this situation, however, the exchange is one way, the experimenter making the sign and the animal responding to it. But could the monkey use signs to elicit responses either from humans or other monkeys?

The answer was provided by the Gardners (1969) and their chimpanzee, Washoe, who was trained to use the American Sign Language, devised for communication with the deaf. Thus the ape could use her hands instead of her vocal cords. The result was that Washoe not only used the signs to communicate but invented several new ones of her own.

While signs are invariate, having the same meaning over a variety of contexts, symbols derive their meaning from the context. As discussed earlier, the delayed-response and double alternation tasks may involve the holding of symbolic representations for their adequate solution. Symbols, said Pribram, are tokens. He then referred to another study in communication in the chimpanzee; this time the work of David Premack (1970, 1971) with Sarah. Premack employed operant conditioning methods using tokens. The crux of the situation was that these tokens did not call forth a uniform response. Depending on the situation they could be taken to another location, traded for a reward, inserted into a machine or would form part of a communication chain, and so on. The meaning of the token depended on the context in which it appeared, thus it met the criteria for a symbol.

While Pribram thus argued that sub-human primates were capable of using symbols he is in accord with Razran in suggesting that chimpanzees do not make propositional utterances, ie., engage in language per se (Pribram, personal communication 1984). He also agrees with Razran that cognitive learning is considerably different from associative learning (Pribram 1980, 1984).

The work on language learning in the higher sub-human primates has also come under very critical consideration from other sources. For example, in a paper in *Science* (1979) entitled "Can an ape create a sentence?", Terrace, Petitto, Sanders, and Bever argued that, while these various projects have shown that apes can learn a vocabulary of visual signs, there has been no clear evidence that they can combine these signs to create new meanings. With three symbol combinations executed by their own subject Nim (Nim Chimpsky) over the final 19 months of the 3 year study period they found "no evidence of lexical regularities, nor did they (Nim's three symbol combinations) elaborate or qualify what he signed when he produced a two-sign combination" (Terrace et al., 1979, p. 900). This, they claimed, was in keeping with their analysis of the findings of other studies. They concluded that:

> In sum, evidence that apes can create sentences can, in each case, be explained by reference to simpler non-linguistic processes. Sequences of signs produced by Nim and other apes may resemble superficially the first multiword sequences produced by children. But, unless alternative explanations of an ape's combinations of signs are eliminated, in particular the habit of partially imitating teachers' recent utterances, there is no reason to regard an ape's multisign utterance as a sentence (Terrace et al., 1979, p. 901).

Thompson and Church (1980) have also argued, from an analysis of Rumbaugh's (1977) data on language behavior of the chimpanzee Lana, that the abilities displayed by Lana, like those of Nim, "have emphasized paired-associate learning and the goal-oriented nature of the apes' behavior" (p. 314). Both Terrace et al. (1979) and Thompson and Church (1980) are therefore arguing against the notion that current evidence supports the view that apes combine signs to create new meanings, i.e., that they "think." This then, is a further issue that remains unresolved.

A REVIEW OF COMPARATIVE STUDIES AND THEIR IMPLICATIONS

In chapter 8, I argued that a logical relationship existed between brain evolution and the evolution of learning, such that increased neural capacity would be closely associated with increased learning abilities. This relationship could, however, only be established in terms of living species, animals that were the end products of long lines of divergent evolution. In such species, however, the expectation would still persist that animals with larger and more complex brains would reveal increased capacity to organize, store, and utilize information, thereby enhancing their prospects of survival through learning processes.

In pursuit of an answer to this question I set out to establish whether the literature revealed any body of learning tasks that would reliably differentiate between species when such species were ordered in terms of brain evolution. This analysis was not intended to generalize across all species but was directed to animals along the evolutionary track that led to the human condition.

This seemingly straightforward question has, however, been complicated by intense debate over the nature of learning differences between species. Learning theorists such as Thorndike and Skinner and also the Pavlovian school, have argued for one common learning process spanning the full range of animals with an organized central nervous system. The other extreme has been the view advanced by ethologists such as Lorenz and Lockard that each separate evolutionary line and even each separate species have evolved separate learning processes that are adapted to the particular niche occupied by that species. Bitterman, during two and a half decades of experimental analysis of this question, set out to thread his way between these antithetical points of view in an endeavor to resolve this complex question.

Thus, in Chapter 9, I examined a number of tasks that have been claimed to differentiate between species in terms of their phylogenetic position. I then made a more detailed review of Bitterman's contribution in this field. While the tasks chosen by no means exhausted the range of those available, they do serve to exemplify the findings achieved and the problems encountered in this type of approach. Each of these tasks offered early promise of providing clear differentiation between species on a phylogenetic basis, but further research and critical analysis indicated that effects were far less clear cut than appeared to be the case initially. Warren, after a similar review to this concluded that:

> Comparisons of vertebrate species in terms of their performances on standard laboratory tests of learning yield no convincing support for the notion that animals can be characterized in terms of a general ability to learn and that the distribution of this trait is correlated with taxonomic rank (Warren, 1973, p. 500).

In the light of the material presented in Chapter 9, this appears to be an extreme point of view but certainly serves to underline the difficulties evident in this line of research.

Bitterman's work over a period of some 25 years also emphasizes the nature of the problems in comparative research and, in particular, the difficulties that arise in trying to draw firm conclusions from cross-species comparisons. Bitterman emphasized that, in view of species differences in such processes as perception, motivation and motor effectiveness, it would be extremely difficult, if not impossible, to control these variables in such a way as to enable legitimate conclusions to be drawn from cross-species comparisons in terms of direct quantitative analysis. He developed an alternative approach which he designated "control by systematic variation," which I outlined in Chapter 6. This involves the experimental definition of optimal conditions for the learning of each particular task for each species under consideration. The control procedure, he argued, would permit the detection of qualitative differences, if they existed.

In his 1975 paper Bitterman discussed experimental findings that, he considered, indicated certain tasks that appeared to differentiate clearly between different vertebrate species. For example, while the "Crespi" effect was clearly evident in such animals as the rat, it was not observed in goldfish. Fish, he suggested, have respect for S–R reinforcement principles. He further noted that experiments on discrimination learning also appeared to reveal qualitative differences between vertebrates in different classes. Examples of these differences were drawn from studies of probability and reversal learning. Thus, he observed, probability learning results distinguished such animals as goldfish, painted turtles, and pigeons from rats and monkeys. On the other hand, studies of relationships between magnitude of reward and resistance to extinction separated goldfish and painted turtles from pigeons and rats. He concluded this paper with the following observation:

> Are the laws of learning the same in all animals? Certainly it is safe to assume that there are important communalities at least in the learning of vertebrates. Whether there are important differences as well remains to be determined (Bitterman, 1975, p. 709).

A very different approach to the question of phylogenetic differences in learning was outlined in this chapter. This view, based on extensive examination of the literature, also argued for a common basis for learning in the evolving complexity of the nervous system. All four authors whose work was reviewed did, however, stress the view that dramatic changes of a qualitative nature were observable in learning processes that were related to quantitative increases in the nervous system. This view was first advanced by Hobhouse and was elaborated in considerable detail by Razran. It was also evident in the writings of both Thorpe and Lorenz.

Following on the much earlier work of Hobhouse, and, in a sense, paralleling the work of Thorpe, Razran's synthesis of the massive volume of work on learning carried out in both Eastern and Western countries represents a major achievement. In a summary of his position, Razran concluded that all evolutionary levels of learning share some characteristics that are not reducible to, or deducible from, preceding ones. "Inherent in this view," said Razran,

> is the tenet that lower evolutionary levels of learning coexist with and interact with higher ones; that while the higher, mediated by more recent neural acquisitions, are more efficient, the lower are more universal and less disruptable by untoward influences; and that the interaction is paralleled by that of the evolution of the brain (Razran, 1971, p. 311).

On their own, most of the studies reviewed by Razran suffer from at least some of the defects in control procedures that have been highlighted by such writers as Bitterman, Warren, and others, namely small subject numbers, problems of equating across species for motivation, sensory and motor capacities, and so on. Together, however, they form a body of evidence that must lead to a reorientation of our thinking in this area and that demands further empirical examination aimed directly to Razran's theoretical structure.

Thorpe's study of learning did not involve the same formalization of an hierarchy of learning processes as was evident in Razran's approach. However, he did describe a very similar sequence of processes from habituation to insight learning.

As well as his support for this view of the comparative organization of learning and its relationship to neural organization and structure, Thorpe's development of Tolman's concept of expectancy is of considerable theoretical interest for my approach. I will be elaborating on this aspect in chapters to follow.

Lorenz, too, argued for a series of learning processes based on the increasing mass and complexity of the brain so, in this sense, his view of the evolution of learning could be described as an hierarchical one. He advanced the notion of the "fulguration" or "creation" of new learning processes related to the increasing capacity of the nervous system to receive and process information. His conceptualization of the "innate teaching mechanism" formed the cornerstone for his views on how learning might be of survival value for the organism.

While Lorenz has argued for increasing capacity for organisms to learn, related to increasing size and organization of the nervous system, he has disputed strongly the view that there has been any one learning process or set of hierarchically organized processes common to much or all of the animal kingdom. As recently as 1981 he again stressed that: "Very different kinds of learning mechanisms, so-called open programs, have evolved independently of each other in various phyla and . . . therefore, very different explanations have to be found for every case" (Lorenz, 1981, p. 337).

In summary, my objective has been to explore the relationships between increasing brain complexity and adaptive behavior along that evolutionary path leading to man. A body of evidence is emerging that supports the view that increasing mass and complexity of the brain is associated with increased capacity to organize and utilize information in more complex and varied ways. Much of the evidence is still tenuous and subject to disputation. For example, the significance of relationships between specially adapted behaviors involved in learning processes that are unique to particular species adapted to specific environments and the more general learning processes associated with increased brain mass is still far from final resolution.

The conceptualization of the learning process is also undergoing change. A significant aspect of this change relates to an increasing awareness that development and diversification of learning is a major factor in the increasing capacity of animals to react to their environments as we move from phylum to phylum and species to species through the evolutionary hierarchy. An increasing body of evidence supports the view that these changes are, in a sense, qualitative in nature as well as quantitative, with an hierarchical organization of learning processes of the kind conceptualized by Razran. These changes are likely to have evolved in response to strong evolutionary pressures for higher levels of information control, by the creative or "fulgurative" processes discussed by Lorenz. Within the evolutionary stream leading to mankind it is at least quite plausible to postulate that a thread of continuity may be traced in the nature of the learning processes, from the simple origins to man.

Another aspect of perhaps equal significance is the changing views on how representations are established and modified by learning. Thorpe's concept of "expectancy" is one of major significance in this context. Lorenz's emphasis on genetic mechanisms adopts an extreme position, but his view is one that must be weighed carefully; his concept of the "innate teaching mechanism" is a major contribution.

In the next part I turn my attention directly to some of these issues. In particular I examine the question: How does an animal "know" about the effectiveness of its interactions with the environment and how is such knowledge utilized? In approaching this problem I expand the view that the evolution of "emotion" was an essential component of the evolution of an animal's capacity to lay down and to modify its representations of the environment during its own lifespan.

IV THE CONTRIBUTION OF AFFECT TO THE EVOLUTION OF LEARNING

In this part I develop the view, presented in Chapter 1, that affects or feelings provided a mechanism for the evolution of associative learning. My argument developed in chapter 11 is that these affects are products (percepts) of sensations generated within the "reward" and "punishment" systems of the brain, and that these systems constitute a "teaching mechanism of the type postulated by Lorenz. This mechanism registers feedback from events relevant to the survival of the animal and this determines what information will be incorporated into the neural store of representations that direct future action. In my examination of this concept, particular emphasis is given to differentiation between affects or feelings that are associated with emotion and those relating to need.

I argue that it is the interaction between two sets of affective experiences that determines the level of motivation in higher animals, thus governing the direction and strength of the animal's behavior. This argument hinges on the view that emotion is a reactive state evolving from the confluence of the affects of reward and punishment and of expectancies generated through associative learning. Thus, while the primary issue addressed is the evolution of the "reinforcement" component of affect, I need to consider, also, how this encompasses the evolution of emotion.

In chapter 12 I consider the likely course of the evolution of affect and of emotion.

11 Affect and Emotion

THE NATURE OF EMOTION

The study of emotion has attracted considerable attention over the years and there is a wide body of literature to which the reader may refer, including works of Arnold (1960), Black (1970), Candland et al. (1977), Cofer and Appley (1964), Glass (1967), and Young (1961, 1966, 1973) and, more recently, Plutchik and Kellerman (1980). This attention is likely to have resulted both from the intransigence of the problems associated with the study of this topic and the recognition that, in some way, emotion plays a major role in human behavior.

In these various studies the energizing and arousing aspects of emotion have often been stressed (Duffy, 1957, 1962; Lindsley, 1951; Malmo, 1959). The expression of emotion, i.e., the response patterns that accompany emotional arousal such as snarling, spitting, growling, purring, erection of hair, and so forth in animals, and the facial expressions and body movements in man have also been examined in considerable detail. Darwin contributed substantially to this area with his book, *"The Expression of the Emotions in Man and Animals,"* published in 1872. Other aspects to attract attention have been the nature of sex differences in emotion and the problem of the recognition of particular emotions. The physiological changes that accompany emotion have also been the subject of considerable enquiry.

In humans, the subjective aspects of emotion, i.e., the feelings of emotion such as pleasure, rage, grief, delight, to name but a few, have been explored through introspective report. The nature of these "feelings" and their significance for learning is the major concern of this part.

An intriguing feature of the treatment of emotion in the literature is the concentration on the aversive emotions. This is understandable in the studies of animal behavior on the grounds of experimental ease. Emotions such as rage and fear are much more readily identifiable from the animal's overt behavior than are the expressions of pleasurable feelings. Neal Miller for example, devoted considerable effort to the study of fear as a learnable drive (Miller, 1951, 1971).

This bias is, however, harder to understand in the studies of human behavior. Averill, who examined the phenomenon in some detail, referred to Carlson's (1966) study in which, in a content analysis of psychological textbooks, he found twice the space devoted to negative than to positive emotions. In a factor analysis of emotional concepts in the English language Averill (1980a) isolated four factors, the major one being an evaluative dimension (positive versus negative). The distribution of the ratings of the 558 emotional concepts derived for this study on the evaluative dimension was bimodal with a ratio of two negative to each positive emotional concept.

An explanation for this stress on the negative emotions by psychologists may rest on the greater impact of such emotions on others, through the social implications of such emotions as anger, rage, grief, compared with the more internal, personal nature of the positive emotions such as pleasure. These positive emotions may, however, have greater significance for individual learning than the negative ones, as will become evident later.

Another aspect of the study of emotion that may have links with the concentration in the literature on aversive or negative feelings is the belief expressed by many that emotion is a damaging or disruptive experience. Hebb (1949) for example, put forward this view.

Despite our long continuing curiosity about, and enquiry into the nature of our emotions, there is still considerable confusion and uncertainty over what emotion is, with problems of both definition and conceptualization. Pribram (1980), commenting on a symposium on "emotion" that he had attended, noted that:

> the participants discussed factor analysis, limbic neuroanatomy and operant conditioning. Somewhere in the Agenda emotions were hidden from view, lurking in the dark alleys of our ignorance. No one even dared to use the term, and certainly no one discussed emotion as would the man in the street" (p. 246).

Again, in a recent textbook of physiological psychology, we find Cusatis and Levitt (1981) introducing the chapter on emotion with the observation that no satisfactory single definition of emotion had yet been generated, while Polivy (1980) noted that there is still lack of agreement on the nature of emotion or even the number of emotions to be observed. Ursin (1980) also noted that, "There is no generally accepted nomenclature for emotions for man or for animals" (p. 121). He observed that this is a serious handicap and suggested four main classes of emotion; namely fear, aggression, delight, and distress.

The various characteristics of emotion viewed above all constitute changes in the organism from its state before the emotion was initiated to the condition of emotion. The generation of these changes would seem to involve a number of significant processes that constitute a sequence of events characterizing the expression of emotion in man and other animals.

Firstly, there is the perception of some cue or signal, e.g., the sound of a dinner bell, the hiss of a snake, a whiff of perfume, a flash of light, a rustle of grass. In man, at least, this may also include the internal perception or realization of a relationship between previously experienced events that had not been apparent at the time of that initial experience. These percepts involve cognitive processes that link the particular sensations with past experience, either innate or learned.

Secondly, as a result of this perception a particular feeling or affective state is generated, e.g., fear, anger, delight, joy (Arnold, 1960; Bindra, 1970). This affective state is comprised of those various feelings that we experience with the arousal of emotion. The generation of this affective state is, I believe, a crucial element in the evolution of emotion and of the relationship between emotion and learning.

Thirdly, where perceptions generate an emotional state, bodily and behavioral changes follow. These include changes in arousal level involving activation of the organism.

Fourthly, consequent upon the patterns or representations built into the neural structure and the modifications of these patterns through experience, an overt response may be initiated. This response is aimed at resolving the generated expectancy and accompanying arousal state.

Fifthly, this action will lead to a further affective state dependent on the outcome, e.g., satisfaction, frustration, etc. These feelings will then influence the registration of the events linking the initial stimulus, the following affect and the consequent response and will thus influence future behavior.

Magda Arnold (1960) considered that, while most theories of emotion have examined the connection between emotional experience and bodily changes, "few have tackled the problem of how cold perception can cause either the felt emotion or the bodily upset" (Vol. 1, p. 93). Fewer still, it would seem, have considered the significance of the felt emotion, and, in particular, its significance for the survival of the animal.

A substantial array of theories has been generated to explain emotion, with many of these being framed specifically in terms of human function. Theories that are of particular relevance to the present theme are those concerned with comparative aspects or biological origins of emotion, including those that attempt to explain emotion in terms of brain function. A number of reviews from this point of view are available (e.g., Arnold, 1960; Candland et al., 1967; Grossman, 1967; Goldstein, 1968).

In these theories a variety of attempts to conceptualize emotion in terms of its biological correlates is evident. Close links have been drawn between emotion, arousal, and the functioning of the autonomic nervous system. The thalamus and the limbic system and, in particular, the amygdala, hippocampus, and the cingulate cortex have been implicated as sources of emotional experience. The theories of Papez (1937), MacLean (1949, 1970, 1973), Arnold (1945, 1960, 1970) and Pribram (1960, 1967a, 1967b, 1969, 1977, 1980, 1981) have, for example, all linked the limbic system and, in particular, the amygdala and hippocampus with the mediation of emotion.

Arnold (1970) emphasized the relationship between perception and appraisal and a "felt tendency to action." This tendency to action she believed to be mediated by the frontal cortex: She saw the Olds "reward system" as the core of the appraisal system.

Pribram, in what is by far the most detailed and probably the most controversial theory to date, differentiated between the feelings associated with need and those associated with motivation and with emotion. In elaborating on this distinction he stated that it was a mistake of considerable significance to equate all subjective feelings with emotions; he distinguished, for example, feelings of hunger and thirst, love and pleasure, discomfort and perturbation. These feelings he designated as "monitor-feelings," or images that monitor the world within (Pribram, 1977, p. 171). Pribram viewed emotion as the response of an overloaded organism that was withdrawing from the processing of external information so as to engage in internal organization and re-equilibration. Originally he saw this as part of the planning processes of the animal, evident in the face of what he designated as a severe mismatch situation. In 1970 he changed this view somewhat and saw emotions not as plans but as images on which plans are based. Moods, he concluded, are difficult to conceive as plans for action. He went on:

> Feelings as Monitors are well equipped to handle the problem of equilibration and disequilibration resulting from successes or failures of motivated action. . . . . In each instance the salience of the outcome of the action, the reinforcement, is appraised and the process of appraisal monitored, i.e., felt . . . . Feelings as Monitors are therefore Images rather than Plans. As such they form the matrix within which Plans are formed; the "go" Plans making up the motivations of the organism and the "no-go" Plans of which emotions are constituted (Pribram, 1970, p. 52).

Pribram thus categorized the feelings resulting from appraisal as either motivational or emotional, the emotional response taking the animal out of action. It is at this point that Pribram differs from Arnold who considered that the feelings resulting from appraisal constitute the emotional affect which then determines the nature of the action to follow. Thus emotion might either take the animal into action or withdraw it from action.

This distinction of Pribram's is also clearly evident in his analysis of the central mechanisms controlling sensory input. Pribram has argued that a series of experiments that he carried out with Spinelli provide strong neurological support for his position (Spinelli & Pribram, 1966, 1967; Pribram, 1967a, 1967b, 1969). These experiments demonstrated neural systems within the temporal and prefrontal cortex and in limbic system structures of the monkey that can exert control over sensory input. Pribram argued that these findings pointed to two separate mechanisms, one that opens the system to sensory input through the processes of lateral inhibition and the other which closes the system through self-inhibition. He then identified these two systems with separate motivational and emotive processes. Thus, he claimed, when the animal is motivated the system is opened to sensory input with orienting, seeking, and active exploring of the environment. When the organism becomes emotional the system is closed, with internal processing of information. This would include those processes related to registration of relevant events.

Pribram's clear subdivision of affect or feelings into several categories is, I believe, a significant contribution, though he credits James with the basic idea quoting James as saying, "Emotional reaction usually terminates in the subject's own body" while motivation "is apt to go further and enter into practical relations with the exciting object" (James, 1890, p. 442). Pribram observed that while emotional expression terminates in the subject's own body, it acts in a communicative setting enabling animals to read each other's emotional expressions and be influenced by them. Thus, he argued, emotional expression does have a practical influence beyond the animal itself but essentially in a communicative setting.

Like Arnold, Pribram saw feelings as monitors, mediating the appraisal of outcomes of action. Unlike Arnold, he saw emotion as a process that takes the organism out of action with feelings that "do not go beyond the skin" and which are associated with "no–go plans." Both theories are cognitively based, arguing that emotion depends on a process of appraisal of incoming stimuli. A number of other theories, based solely or primarily on the analysis of emotions in man, have also emphasized the cognitive aspects of emotion (e.g., Averill, 1980a, 1980b; Mandler, 1975, 1980; Plutchik, 1980a, 1980b, 1980c; Schachter & Singer, 1962; Tomkins, 1962, 1970, 1980). It is not my intention to review such theories, but I refer briefly to some aspects of the theories advanced by Plutchik and Averill because of their relevance to my general position.

Plutchik has been developing his psychoevolutionary theory of emotion since the 1950s with the publication of his "Outlines of a new theory of emotion" in 1958. The most recent expression of this theory is given in his book *Emotion: A Psychoevolutionary Synthesis"* (Plutchik, 1980a), and in his chapters "A general psychoevolutionary theory of emotion" (1980b), and "Measurement implications of a psychoevolutionary theory of emotion" (1980c). He argued that emotion should be considered in a broad evolutionary perspective and we should seek to identify how emotion functions adaptively in the lives of animals. He developed these ideas to establish an evolutionary theory of emotion. The 10 postulates of his theory are stated in several of the above publications. Of these the first four are of particular relevance and are given in full here.

Postulate 1. *The concept of emotion is applicable to all evolutionary levels and applies to animals as well as humans.*

Postulate 2. *Emotions have an evolutionary history and have evolved various forms of expression in different species.*

Postulate 3. *Emotions serve an adaptive role in helping organisms deal with key survival issues posed by the environment.*

Postulate 4. *Despite different forms of expression of emotion in different species, there are certain common elements, or prototype patterns, that can be identified* (Plutchik, 1980b, p. 8).

The central theme of his theory is that, for an animal to recognize beneficial or harmful effects of its environment it must evaluate that environment. This evaluation process is, he claimed, the cognitive aspect of emotion with the evaluation influencing the type of response pattern that results.

Plutchik considered that there was a particular sequence of events in the development of emotion. He exemplified this sequence in relation to recognition of an aggressor, outlining the following steps: (1) A stimulus event: a threat by an enemy; (2) the cognition of this event: danger; (3) the arousal of an associated feeling: fear; (4) a consequent behavior: running and (5) an effect: protection of the animal. This sequence has much in common with that advanced by Arnold and to the schema I outlined earlier in the chapter. However, it does not take into account the final instrumental relationship between action and outcome (my stage five). As I noted earlier, the outcome of action generates a further affective state that feeds back to the generating event and acts to stamp in or register the relationship between that event and the outcome of the particular behavioral response. Plutchik went on to argue that "cognitive" capacities have evolved along with the evolution of the brain, and that "cognitions have largely evolved in the service of emotions" (Plutchik, 1980b, p. 12).

Averill, on the other hand, has worked exclusively on human emotion and has described emotions as passions, derived from the Latin *pate*, to suffer, thus giving an indication of his approach. These "passions," he said, include those behaviors that seem to happen to a person and over which he has no control. Like Pribram, Averill distinguished between passion and action, action being motivated behavior or something a person does. Emotions were seen by Averill as "passions of the soul" as products of the self (Averill, 1980a). He defined emotion in social, i.e., relational terms, rather than biological terms, seeing emotions as socially constituted responses (Averill, 1980a, 1980b).

Averill (1980a) outlined six connotations of emotional concepts, which he claimed further justified the classification of emotions as passions rather than actions. These were (1) that the behavior in question is uncharacteristic of the individual; (2) that the concept implies irrationality or alternatively (3) that the behavior is nondeliberative or intuitive. Further characteristics listed were (4) the impulsive nature of the emotional response; (5) the implication that the response is intense and that (6) closely related to the notion of intensity is that of persistence.

This view of emotion leaves the impression that the emotional response in man is unusual and perhaps more harmful than beneficial to the behaving individual. This view of emotion as something harmful in man and associated with loss of cognitive control is by no means uncommon in the literature. Hebb (1949) saw emotion as a disruptive process and Young (1973) considered that "when an individual is affectively disturbed by the environmental situation to the extent that his cortical control is weakened or lost and subcortical patterns and visceral changes appear, that individual is emotional" (p. 34). These approaches support the view that emotion in man is either a harmful by-product of essential activities or an evolutionary remnant of once useful adjustments.

In this context then, emotion is seen as disorganizing an individual's behavior, as taking the person out of or away from planned, purposive activity. This view concentrates on highly arousing or disruptive emotional states or hyperemotions, but other emotions such as pleasure, joy, sadness, may not be described in this fashion. Again, certain emotions may result in very directed and purposeful, though aggressive, behavior that clearly takes the individual into action.

That emotion should be seen by some as having little or no biological utility for man is difficult to comprehend when taken in evolutionary context. While emotional reponsiveness is evident in animals other than man, it reaches its highest level of expression in man in terms of the range of responses and in the subtleties and nuances of such responses. This would seem to point strongly to an increasing evolutionary utility for man rather than a decreasing one.

In attempting to give meaning to emotion Averill argued against the view that emotional responses accrue meaning through biological evolution, on the ground that emotional responses, as such, lack inherent meaning, that they cannot be reduced directly to any form of genetically determined "instinct." He then advanced his view that emotions are social in origin and function as transitory social roles. This, he said, did not imply that emotions are counterfeit. They are indeed part of reality. He considered that these realities are expressed in the socialization of the child, enabling it to conceptualize events in terms of e.g., anger, fear, and in the monitoring of behavior. For such monitoring to be effective, afferent feedback from behavior is "given meaning by the cognitive schemata that represent the individual's understanding of the emotional role" (Averill, 1980a, p. 39). This understanding he considered to be intimately related to the meaning of emotional concepts with the experience of emotion being, in this sense, "reflective."

Averill's is a complex cognitive model that emphasizes the social role of emotion and in a number of aspects is opposed to that of Plutchik. Plutchik emphasized the direct evolutionary basis of emotion while Averill denied this. Plutchik argued that the concept of emotion is applicable to all evolutionary levels while Averill has, by implication if not directly, indicated a view that emotion emerged as a characteristic of behavior late in evolution with development taking place in the higher primates and man. Both, however, emphasize the cognitive base of emotional expression.

REWARD AND PUNISHMENT SYSTEMS OF THE BRAIN

Emotion has presented a very peculiar problem to psychologists because one of its most obvious and significant aspects, i.e., the affective tone or feeling of emotion can be observed clearly in oneself but only by inference and introspective analysis in others. It thus appears to be inaccessible to us in animals other than man.

Goldstein (1968) was at some pains to point out that any theory based on emotion must incorporate criteria for emotion that are verifiable and have significance. He contended that, because of this, theories that consider emotional experience in their major postulates cannot be tested by animal experimentation. If this, indeed, is the case, then it is a sad loss for both the theory and practice of psychology, as the study of emotion in animals is essential if we are to gain insight into its evolutionary significance. The problem is a major one but perhaps not insurmountable if we can ask our questions in such a way that the animal can give a clear answer in behavioral terms of how it feels about a particular stimulus or situation.

Darwin, and many that followed him, have stressed the significance of emotional expression in animals and man. The expressive signs and gestures evident in various animals do seem to indicate, with varying degrees of clarity in different species, whether the animal is experiencing pain, fear, rage, or pleasure. The use of such expresive behaviors has, in the past, provided a partial solution, but has still involved anthropomorphic projection from man to other animals. In this regard Konorski (1967) commented:

> If in man the psychic experience of perception of a given stimulus object is manifested by a definite behavioral act and/or a definite evoked potential in the brain and if, in a given animal (monkey or cat), that stimulus object produces exactly the same set of responses, we are justified in assuming that the animal experiences perception of the object in much the same way (p. 4).

Work on the reward (pleasure) and punishment (aversion) centers of the brain provides us with such a comparative physiological and behavioral instrument (Olds & Milner, 1954; Olds, 1956, 1958; Olds & Olds, 1964; Olds, 1969).

These systems have now been explored in a wide range of species, e.g., goldfish (Boyd & Gardner, 1962); pigeon (Goodman & Brown, 1966); chicken (Andrew, 1967); rat (Olds, 1956); rabbit (Bruner, 1967); cat (Wilkinson & Peele, 1963); dog (Stark & Boyd, 1963); dolphin (Lilly & Miller, 1962); monkey (Bursten & Delgado, 1958; Lilly, 1958); and man (Bishop, Elder, & Heath, 1963), with striking similarity in the pattern of anatomical distribution of these effects. As well, in man, we have subjective or affective statements about the effects of stimulation of some of these areas. Heath (1964), for example, has recorded a variety of responses to brain stimulation in humans. Here the sensations from stimulation are translated into the feelings of the reporter. On stimulation of the right posterior septal region comments such as "feels wonderful," sexual thoughts, elimination of "bad" thoughts were elicited. With left caudate stimulation responses included "cool taste," "feels OK," "pleasant feeling," while with stimulation of the mesencephalic tegmentum, one patient called it the "happy button." On the other hand, stimulation of the right hippocampus in one subject produced a feeling of intense aversion and "a sick feeling all over" (p. 288). Thus, in the study of reward and punishment systems, Konorski's (1967) criterion for relating human psychic experience of a particular perception to animal experience of that perception appears to have been met. Similar effects have been observed over a wide range of species including man and, in man, we have been able to record subjective experiences of affect or feeling that accompany the stimulation of the system.

In all of the discussion to date, Lorenz's question, "What for?" with respect to the evolutionary development of the affects of emotion appears to be largely unanswered. The view I am advancing is that emotions emerged as a significant aspect of behavior with the evolution of complex nervous systems and that they evolved in the service of cognition. In particular I am arguing that emotions had their origins in the evolution of systems that enable the animal to perceive outcomes of actions as affects or feelings, pleasurable or painful, i.e., the "reward" and "punishment" effects. These percepts provided a mechanism for the evolution of associative learning and were also the precursors of emotion which emerged as a later evolutionary development.

This approach is not new. For the Greek philosopher Epicurus, pleasure was the ultimate determinant of behavior. Aristotle went so far as to suggest that "cold perception" is transformed into emotion because the person perceives something as being good or bad for him, something that will give him pleasure or pain. But it was Spencer (1870) who, following Darwin's work on evolution of species, made the first systematic attempt to give a scientifically plausible explanation of the role of pleasure and pain in the learning process. His central argument was that: "Natural selection works to produce a correlation between feelings of pleasure and actions beneficial to survival on one hand, and feelings of pain and actions which are injurious on the other" (Wilcoxon, 1969, p. 5). Thorndike's original Law of Effect, in which he argued that the nervous system is so constructed as to lead to survival and strengthening of those connections that were active just prior to a satisfying event and the weakening and eventual disappearance of those connections that were active prior to annoying events, follows this tradition. These theories ran aground because of the subjective nature of affect in the hard-headed behaviorist environment that was current at that time, though both Thorndike and Hull aimed for objectivity in their experiments.

P. T. Young also developed a theory of emotion that is based on affective state or hedonic responsiveness, and he supported this with many years of work on food preference and selectivity in the rat and other species (Young, 1961, 1966, 1968, 1973). Here, too, a basic theoretical difficulty was seen in the identification of the affective process in the rat.

Another who considered emotion to play a key role in learning is Mowrer, who, in the development of his two-factor learning theory, emphasized the role of such emotions as hope and fear, relief and disappointment (Mowrer, 1960).

While I am arguing that affects or feelings form the base from which emotions evolved, as Pribram has so clearly indicated, not all affects are associated with emotion. Another major set of affects are those associated with need.

THE FEELINGS OF NEED

While much as been written about the nature of need as established through so called "drive" centers of the brain, there has been little on the sensations or feelings of need, i.e., the affects of need.

Through the processes of evolution, centers responsive to the changing needs of the animal became established within the nervous system. These centers were keyed to releasor signals that would then initiate appropriate response patterns. The classic Dethier and Bodenstein (1958) study of hunger in the blowfly exemplifies this. This work revealed the purely reflex quality of feeding in that animal. The "hungry" fly is responsive to sugar stimulation of the chemoreceptors. Such stimulation leads to the pumping of sugar solution into the stomach. The rising sugar level there inhibits the chemoreceptors, inhibition of the oral receptors continuing while there is sugar in the foregut. With the emptying of the foregut the fly becomes increasingly active and is again responsive to sugar. The fly can, however, be metabolicallly deprived but behaviorally "satisfied" or inhibited on a non-metabolizable sugar and can starve to death in the presence of glucose because of this. "It is of considerable interest," the authors remarked, "that the consummation of feeding is brought about neither by the fulfilment of a metabolic need nor by the fulfilment of any motor pattern" (p. 17). More recently, Dethier (1976) elaborated on these findings, outlining among other things the beautiful and precise techniques employed in this work. This reflexive stimulus chaining of response patterns is exemplified in many other behavior patterns in animals with limited neural equipment, e.g., in egg laying and copulatory behavior in the mantis (Vowles, 1961).

With the evolution of larger and more complex nervous systems, animals gained increasing control over the development and modification of their neural representations of the environment and hence over their patterns of response to particular stimuli. For effective utilization of this increased potential, the animal requires information about its needs and about the effectiveness of its interactions with the environment in its endeavors to meet those needs. Thus, the organism must be informed of those needs through one set of sensations or feelings and must "learn" how to satisfy them through another set, namely appropriate reinforcements provided by the reward and punishment systems.

Pribram was the first to consider in any detail the affective components of motivational states, including the components that enable the animal to perceive its needs; to "feel" hunger or thirst or drowsiness, and so on. The difficulties associated with attempting to quantify these feelings of need have led animal experimenters to rely on arbitrary indicators of need such as hours of deprivation. However, feelings as such are essential for the animal that has to learn how to satisfy its needs and these must be taken into account for an adequate assessment of behavior. There has been, so far as I am aware, little success in quantifying the feelings associated with changing need, but these relationships may well become established, again through the study of human introspective reports following lesion or stimulation in relevant areas.

Dissociation between the feelings of a need (hunger) and the rewards of eating were observed in a case described by Pribram (1980), in which he examined dietary problems of patients who had suffered bilateral resection of the medial temporal lobe, including the amygdala. Such patients typically ate more than normal with weight gains of up to 100 lbs. When he asked one such patient just before lunch if she was hungry, she said no, i.e., she had no feelings or experience of hunger. The loss of the amygdala appeared to block the perception of the sensations of hunger. A few minutes later, when confronted with the sight of food, however, she rushed to the table and began cramming food into her mouth as fast as she could. Thus, she had come under the control of the food stimuli that activated her food reward system but suffered a disrupted motivational system that failed to inform her when to either start or stop.

There is an accumulating body of evidence that the reward and punishment systems are separate from the need systems but very closely linked with them. This evidence, which is largely physiological in nature, will be subject to detailed consideration in Volume 2.

The evolution of these affect systems for "need" and for "reward" and "punishment" are intimately associated with the evolution of cognitive processes in higher vertebrates. How these evolutionary changes may have come about is my next consideration.

12 The Evolution of Affect

THE ROLE OF AFFECT IN LEARNING

So far we have considered affects or feelings in relation to such psychological constructs as need, motivation, and emotion. In examining the evolution of affect, those related behavioral constructs should be viewed, not as unique entities, but as products of an organized set of neural structures involving particular sensations, perceptions, and responses. These neural structures have been shaped and integrated within an evolving nervous system in response to selection pressures that favor increased capacity for the animal to develop and modify the representations of its interactions with the environment during its own life span.

In this context it is relevant to emphasize that feelings, or affects such as pleasure or fear, are the organism's perceptions of stimuli that generate particular neural activities within specific brain regions. William James (1890), when considering his theory of emotion, wrote:

> And yet it is even now certain that of two things concerning the emotions, one must be true. Either separate and special centers, affected to them alone, are their brain seat, or else they correspond to processes occurring in the motor and sensory centers already assigned, or others like them, not yet known. If the former be the case, we must deny the view that is current and hold the cortex to be something more than the surface of "projection" for every sensitive spot and every muscle in the body. If the latter be the case we must ask whether the emotional process in the sensory or motor center be an altogether peculiar one, or whether it resembles the ordinary perception processes of which those centers are already recognized to be the seat (p. 472).

James opted for the latter point of view. In fact, these brain systems mediating affect can be clearly seen to constitute the "separate and special centers" that James had rejected, namely the "reward" and "punishment" systems. However these too are "sensitive spots" involving perceptive processes and with projections to the cortex both old and new, i.e., limbic, cingulate, and prefrontal cortices. Thus, each of James' alternatives may be seen to contain an element of the truth.

In examining the evolution of the nervous system, emphasis was placed on the increasing complexity of this system. In particular it was noted that more complex systems have the capacity to build, store, and utilize representations of the relevant elements of the environment and of organism-environment relationships and to change or modify these representations with change in the environment. In those animals with more primitive systems, modification of representations is done genetically. Thus, those animals that have been endowed with response systems that give appropriate reactions to critical stimuli survive and multiply, passing the mechanism on to the next generation. Those that cannot give the appropriate response die and the inadequate neural mechanism vanishes with them.

If, however, the animal is to build and modify representations of its environment during its own lifetime then it must be able to differentiate relevant from irrelevant and to establish the relevant information in its nervous system. I am here arguing that the "reward" and "punishment" systems, found within the brains of all the more advanced vertebrates along the evolutionary path to man, provide the mechanisms for establishing such relevance.

The beginnings of such systems would be expected to become evident at the time when larger, longer living animals were evolving and are likely to date back to the early evolution of vertebrates. There would likely be rapid development of such systems with the evolution of mammals and again with the evolution of primates.

In the course of such evolutionary changes, ties between changing need states and the fixed-action or response patterns, developed to satisfy those needs, would become loosened. Complex neural systems would be evolved that would facilitate modification during the animal's life span of neural representations of these response patterns and more particularly of the environmental stimuli that initiate them. For this to take place, systems sensitive to successes or failures of the animal's interactions with the environment would have to evolve. This major evolutionary step would constitute the "fulguration" of the teaching mechanism referred to by Lorenz. These "reward" and "punishment" receptors signal to the animal the nature and effectiveness of its interaction with the environment, reward signals (pleasurable affect) indicating, for example, that a functional chain has been formed between internal state, perception, action and the satisfaction of a particular need.

The capacity for the animal to perceive its needs, i.e., to translate the sensations of need into affects, and to experience the outcomes of its interactions with the environment as feelings, positive or negative, would appear to be of major significance for the evolution of associative learning. These perceptions would then provide the basic prerequisites for the evolution of emotion.

All animals repond to harmful stimuli by withdrawal: This has been demonstrated, for example, in Amoeba. There is thus some registration of the stimulus. Razran has noted that aversive conditioning occurs early in Metazoan history and, while he agreed that this was a learning process, he argued that it was incomplete, with the response (withdrawal or inhibition) produced by the association but with no new association being formed. Similarly, Skinner (1935) argued that punishment acts only to temporarily suppress behavior because of emotional disruption. Razran further claimed that true associative learning or classical conditioning became evident somewhat later in evolutionary history.

In his examination of the evolution of learning, Lorenz supported this view. He claimed that associative learning was an entirely new evolutionary process "that derived information from success as well as from failure of a behavioral pattern just performed" (Lorenz, 1969, p. 46). This evolution of positive feedback, argued Lorenz, could, however, only occur when a relatively complex nervous system had evolved and in conjunction with the evolution a "teaching mechanism" that informed the animal of success or failure with respect to its interaction with the environment.

Lorenz (1969) emphasized the significance of such a system for cognitive processing in the following terms:

> With the fulguration of this new feedback cycle, a new information acquiring system has come into being which conveys information about what to do and what not to do, not to the species' store of genetic information but directly to the physiological machinery that determines the individual's behavior and retains the message, if not with the pertinacity of the genome, nevertheless in the form of an adaptive modification that may last an individual's life span. One single performance of a sequence of behavior patterns can thus bring, within minutes or even seconds, an adaptive change of behavior equal to that which the genome's primal method would need at least the time lapse of a generation to achieve. In fact the gain is twice greater because the genome gains information by its successes only while the individual learns by its failures as well. These advantages are so obvious that it is easy to understand why the cognitive mechanism of conditioning has evolved in practically all metazoans possessing a sufficiently complicated and integrated central nervous system (p. 46).

Once such a system became established it would, as Lorenz has pointed out, come to incorporate the more primitive systems. In this regard, Glickman and Schiff (1967) noted that the evolution of the mammalian brain involved at every stage the development of pathways enabling the newer parts of the system upon which the modern mammal depends for its greater plasticity of action, to interact with the primitive routes of motor control (p. 85).

This view was also developed by both Jerison and Razran.

The affect system would thus shape and direct cognitive behavior. A rising need-state would activate the associated feelings of need, which would generate action to mitigate that need. Consummatory behavior, e.g., ingestion of food, would activate the appropriate reward receptors. As ingestion continued, this would then lead to satiation with decline in the sensations of need. Satiation also leads to the damping of the reward effect and even the triggering of a reverse state — aversion to further food. The neural mechanisms that mediate these functions are to be examined in detail in subsequent work.

The Evolution of Emotion

The feelings associated with successful action to ameliorate needs are produced by reinforcements and constitute rewards. These become linked with the external signals and with the activities of the animal that led to the reward, or the punishment if inappropriate behavior is engaged in. Thus, an instrumental relationship is established. This information is stored so that under similar conditions in the future, e.g., the reactivation of the need state, the external signal comes to generate a preparatory anticipation of the reward. These anticipatory feelings form the essence of emotion. They inform the animal what to expect and indicate likely outcomes. The outcomes themselves also generate feelings and these are significant components of emotion. These various affects lead to the development of new representations or to the modification of existing representations. This effect is particularly strong when due, for example, to changed environmental conditions, expected outcomes fail to be realized; a situation which results in a strong emotional reaction.

Emotion, as I have described it, would thus play a very significant part in the cognitive processing of the animal. Mowrer (1960) argued strongly for such a point of view. Emotions, he said,

play a central indeed an indispensable, role in those changes in behavior or performance which are said to represent "learning." The emotions are involved, first of all, in that they are, strictly speaking, *what* is learned. Fear, hope, relief and disappointment — these we assume are reactions which are most readily and importantly conditionable, and once conditioned, to independent and/or response dependent stimuli, they then guide and control performance in a generally sensible, adaptive manner (Mowrer, 1960, p. 307).

Thus, the first stage in the evolution of emotion would be the "fulguration" of the learning mechanism, the reward and punishment systems. These are likely to have been in evidence early in vertebrate evolution. We know that such a system exists in fish (Boyd & Gardner, 1962). We might thus expect to find it in amphibia and reptiles unless present day fish are demonstrating convergent evolution.

Lorenz advanced the view that the evolution of "teaching mechanisms" was likely to have occurred time and time again in different phyletic streams. It would therefore be of considerable interest to examine the nature of such "reinforcement systems" in, for example, the cephalopod moluscs (the octopus and squid) and in Hymenoptera such as the honeybee.

The second stage in the evolution of affect in vertebrates would constitute the first emergence of true emotion. This would occur when the animal is able to anticipate outcomes and to match expectancy with outcome. These processes would lead to expectancy in the form of feelings of pleasure, excitement, fear, and so on. The occurrence of an expected outcome, depending on its nature, would result in such feelings as satisfaction, fulfilment, relaxation or, alternatively, anger, pain and increased fear, grief, and despair. Failure to achieve an expected outcome, if desired, would become evident as frustration, disappointment or anger or, if feared, as relief. This level appears evident in all mammals and particularly in higher primates and has been discussed at some length by Mowrer (1960).

The third stage involves the use of emotion as a social tool and a communication system. This use of the emotive system has been a major evolutionary feature in the higher mammals and in particular the primates.

With the development of affect, the signaling of the affective state of the animal through the expression of emotion in certain more or less stereotyped forms would have significant survival value and must, as Pribram (1980) has pointed out, form an important aspect of social communication. These expressions signal to the group how the individual feels about a situation enabling others to respond accordingly. While Pribram has drawn attention to this extension of emotion beyond the organism's own body, for Averill the social expression constitutes the major thrust of emotion.

Pribram's interpretation of emotion has revealed a highly complex and sophisticated system. However, his analysis has been based largely on work with primates, including human subjects and Averill's approach has been through the study of human behavior. Both these workers are therefore viewing emotion in the most advanced stages of its evolution. Plutchik, on the other hand, has claimed that emotion is expressed at all evolutionary levels.

The view that I am advancing is that emotion emerged as an evolutionary process much later than Plutchik has indicated, becoming evident in animals with relatively complex nervous systems through the development of systems capable of the perception of reward. Plutchik also argued that cognition evolved in the service of emotion. My argument is the reverse of this, namely that the evolution of emotion followed the demands for increased cognitive processing and served to enhance cognitive processes through the facilitation of associative and higher learning. It is my view that affect evolved because of the demands for cognitive control that were placed on the particular evolutionary line leading to man and that emotion emerged as a further refinement of the relationships between affect and associative learning that resulted in the generation of expectancies. These expectancies lead to instrumental behaviors that are aimed at resolving the anticipated relationships. The success or failure of such actions is registered through the generation of further affects. These expectancies are what we call emotions. Such affects are the "teaching mechanisms" that lead to the neural registration of the effectiveness of behavior. Thus I am arguing that affect serves cognition and that emotion, in its essence, is cognitively determined.

An ongoing debate of considerable interest for my theoretical position is between those who claim that emotion is primary in its occurrence and those who argue that cognitive precursors are essential for emotional expression. Much of this debate has sprung from consideration of emotional expression in man where the characteristics of emotion are the most varied and intricate in the animal kingdom. In the absence of due regard to evolutionary origins it is not surprising that relationships between cognition and emotion become blurred.

If my reconstruction of the evolution of emotion is a valid approximation, then it provides a resolution for these apparently discrepant viewpoints. I examine two recent papers, one by Zajonc (1980) and the other by Lazarus (1982), with such resolution in view.

Zajonc argued that "affective reactions to stimuli are often the very first reactions of the organism, and for lower organisms they are the dominant reaction" (Zajonc, 1980, p. 151). Lazarus, on the other hand, claimed that "thought is a necessary condition of emotion" (Lazarus, 1982, p. 1019). He therefore believed that his view opposed that of Zajonc. This is not necessarily so. Zajonc was talking about affects while Lazarus described emotion. As I have already indicated, while the two are related they are not necessarily the same.

I have argued that the sensations of pleasure or pain arising from the "reward" and "punishment" systems of the brain constitute one major class of affect that evolved as a mechanism that signals to the animal the effectiveness of its interactions with the environment and enables registration of such interactions. These affects are immediate, inbuilt percepts of the sensations that trigger the system, e.g., food, drink, sex, and so on. Many danger signals, e.g., the rustle of grass for the hare, have also been "wired in" by genetic mechanisms.

These affects, then, are primary responses to such stimuli. Zajonc observed that, along with Wundt and Cummings, he considered that "to arouse affect, objects need to be cognized very little—in fact minimally" (p. 154). This would be quite in keeping with the view that an associative representation of a stimulus or object, and the affect that led to its storage, would be likely to be represented within the nervous system as a closely knit unit. The perception of the object would then lead to rapid restoration of the associated affect. In evolutionary terms rapid retrieval of this sort would, in many instances, be essential for survival, e.g., the monkey's response to a snake. Thus, it is not surprising that, to give Zajonc's example, if we see a house then it is likely to have certain affective associations such as a "handsome" house or an "ugly" house. Neither is it the least bit surprising that affect dominates social interaction since the very nature of such interactions would promote associations initiated by affect or feeling.

However, I have argued that these associations form the very core of higher learning and cognitive processing. Affects, and the instrumental feedback of affects in terms of outcomes of behaviors, generate appropriate emotions and ensure the neural registration of events and changes in events. Thus, for the generation of emotion an appraisal process is essential. In Lazarus' terms "cognitive appraisal means that the way one interprets one's plight at any given moment is crucial to the emotional response" (Lazarus, 1982, p. 1019).

The arguments advanced by these two authors thus appear to relate to different aspects of the expression of affect that may be related to separate stages in the evolution of emotion, as follows.

Stage 1. Appearance of primary affects generated by the "teaching mechanisms" of reward and punishment. These sensations are the products of genetically established neural systems and accompany such stimuli as the taste and smell of food and drink, the tactual sensations of sexual intercourse, the pain of a burn and so on. These feelings are immediate perceptual correlates of the particular stimuli and constitute affects without cognitive interaction, though they are vital for the establishment of cognitive associations.

Stage 2. The emergence of associations that link external cues with these affects of reward and punishment as evidenced in classical conditioning. Subsequent appearance of the CS would then lead to the generation of the associated affect with "minimal cognitive participation" as proposed by Zajonc. Even when such associations are built into the nervous system through genetic response patterning, some cognitive awareness of the "releasing stimulus" would be necessary. As Lazarus pointed out, the rabbit, for example, would have built into its system through neural inheritance, "cognitive schemata that signify danger instantly at the sound of a slight rustle in the grass or the sign of a dimly perceived shape" (p. 1022).

Stage 3. The evolution of the full emotional response generated by expectancies and the outcome of action to meet those expectancies. At this stage there is a clear evidence of cognitive interaction at the perceptual, associational, and instrumental levels. This is essentially the emotional expression considered by Lazarus. As he pointed out, cognitive appraisal does not necessarily imply cognitive awareness of the factors on which such appraisal rests, but that unconscious "primitive-processes" may be involved. Such processes would include the classical association of a cue (the CS) and the affect generated by the onset of the US. Emotion, he argued, results from an evaluative perception of a relationship between organism and environment. He went on to observe that "If, as I do, one regards emotion as a result of an anticipated, experienced or imagined outcome of an adaptationally relevant transaction between organism and environment, cognitive processes are always crucial in the elicitation of an emotion" (p. 1024). This view sits comfortably with my own interpretation of the evolution of emotion. I would, however, go further and argue that emotion is, in fact, the product of evolutionary processes for improved cognitive processing.

The intense arousal states and the activity that forms part of emotional expression can then be seen as an essential part of the organism's response to the signal or information content of cues that inform the animal about outcomes in terms of rewards and punishments. As these relationships become learned, with environmental stimuli becoming associated with the emotive signals, so will these stimuli generate the appropriate arousal state. In this context, then, emotion does not result from arousal, it generates it, thus preparing the animal for the activities necessary to cope with the emotion generating signals.

Lacey and Lacey (1970) observed that: "Whether the investigator adopts the concepts of Cannon, Hess, Selye, Lindsley, Duffy or Malmo, the implicit assumption he is likely to make is that these automatic responses can be viewed as meter readings or indices of a complex called emotion or affect or arousal or activation" (Lacey & Lacey, 1970, p. 205).

MOTIVATION AND EMOTION

Grossman (1979) was constrained to remark that "there is little agreement among contemporary psychologists as to how one should define the elusive theoretical construct motivation" (Grossman, 1979, p. 209). This may well be because psychologists are still concerned with a construct developed from the study of complex, highly evolved organisms — usually human — rather than from an examination of the evolution of the underlying biological mechanisms for that process.

In animals in which affect systems have evolved, the feelings of need, e.g., hunger, thirst, appear to be distinct from those of reward and punishment. As well, reward can be separated quite clearly from punishment, yielding separate systems and with the punishment systems likely to have evolved much earlier. Rewards are linked to those systems that signal need. Pain as involved in punishment appears to be mediated by a number of separate systems. An intrinsic system is associated with intense need (Olds, 1969) and also with satiation. A further intrinsic system generates feelings associated with failure to achieve an expected outcome, e.g., feelings of frustration. For example, Grossman (1978) has reported that "inhibitory effects of punishment do not appear to be processed by the same central pathways that mediate the effects of non-reward" (p. 252). A further pain system is related to internal maladaptive processes, including internal lesion, infection and the effects of toxins. Another relates to certain external events, those that are harmful to the animal, such as heat, chemicals, electric shock, cutting or crushing pain, and so on.

Thus the evolution of a number of affect signaling systems has become evident. The learning processes of the animal are tuned to all these systems through the complex processes of emotion.

Motivation is the process of directing and energizing activity. In relation to the needs of the animal we may note that, as feelings of need increase, activities to satisfy those needs are generated. This may be achieved through reflex or instinctive mechanisms as exemplified in the feeding mechanism of the blowfly. In those animals that have complex nervous systems with built in teaching mechanisms of reward and punishment, relationships established between cues or events and the affects of pleasure or pain result in the generation of expectancies consistent with these relationships or associations. When a need state is activated, e.g., for food, it is accompanied by feelings of hunger. With the rising feelings of need, specific expectancies are revived and behaviors guided by these expectancies are then initiated. These behaviors are goal directed and the animal is said to be motivated. Spinelli and Pribram's (1966, 1967) findings fit comfortably within this scenario. For example, a rising need state with related feelings and expectancies would result in the opening of the system with activity, orienting and search. Satisfaction of the need with associated feelings could result in closure in Pribram's sense with registration of a successful association. Mismatch would lead to a more intense neural response with stronger closure to effect readjustment of existing representations. Such a mismatch would thus be likely to lead to an increased arousal state.

Animals are also strongly motivated to avoid pain and punishment. As has been discussed, this is likely to be a more primitive process and one that relies less on associative learning than do reward processes. This motivational state, acting through emotional expectancy, namely fear and its equivalents is, however, linked with learning in a complex way.

If this account of motivation is correct then we need not seek separate motivational systems as such, the process being the product of the feelings of need and the expectancies generated by experience of rewards and punishments. I am therefore arguing that emotion is the product of feelings associated with anticipations and outcomes of actions and that these feelings direct the motivational state of the animal.

These motivational states generate their own affects or feelings, e.g., those associated with effort. Pribram, for example, has associated the hippocampus with will or effort as the driving force of motivated behavior (Pribram & McGuinness, 1975; Pribram, 1976). These appear to be separate sensations quite distinct from those of need and emotion.

Silvan Tomkins (1970) supported this view of motivation quite forcefully. He observed that, while biological drives to breathe, to eat, to drink, to engage in sex, have been and, still are believed by many to be the primary sources of motivation in animals, this is a radical error. He continued,

> The intensity, the urgency, the imperiousness, the "umph" of drives is an illusion. The illusion is created by the misidentification of the drive "signal" with its "amplifier." Its amplifier is the affective response which is ordinarily recruited to "boost the gain" of the drive signal (p. 101).

He considered that the primary motivational system is the affective system with biological drives gaining motivational strength through amplification by affects.

Pribram was the first to develop the view that we must consider the division of affects into those associated with need and those of emotion and motivation. He has, however, separated emotion and motivation in terms of the strength of the affect and the ability of the animal to cope with what these feelings may signify. Thus, he argued, if the events generating the feelings can be acted upon then the animal is said to be motivated. If, however, they are too devastating for coordinated action the animal withdraws from the situation to regroup its responses. This he classed as emotional behavior. Thus Pribram sees motivation and emotion as separate response categories along a continuum of a feeling-coping dynamism. On the other hand, my line of reasoning dictates that, whereas emotions are the products of expectancies generated by and generating feelings in terms of previous experiences and present outcomes, motivation is the product of needs and the "emotional" judgment of outcomes in terms of experience. Thus I argue for an hierarchically organized set of relationships between need, emotion, and motivation rather than a continuum.

Konorski, too, has related drive and emotion. He postulated drives and anti-drives with both preservative and protective drives. Drives, said Konorski, are controlled by the part of the brain which we shall call the emotive system (in contradistinction to the cognitive system). Its centers are situated at two levels in the hypothalamus and in the limbic system; the latter is thought to be involved in the conditioning of drives. When a given drive is satisfied by the corresponding consummatory response or the avoidance of a noxious stimulus, the state antagonistic to it arises, which corresponds to Thorndike's "satisfying state of affairs." We have called this state the "anti-drive" and its psychological counterpart the "mood." Accordingly we have the following anti-drives: alimentary anti-drive (satiation); sexual anti-drive (sexual satisfaction); curiosity anti-drive (indifference); fear anti-drive (relief) and anger anti-drive (placidity) (Konorski, 1967, p. 5).

Konorski identified drive and satiation centers but failed to make the distinction which Pribram did between feelings of need and those associated with motivational states and feelings of emotion. He also failed to develop the significance of the reward and punishment systems in the generation of emotive feelings.

In summary, I have examined the evolution of affect and have related the affect systems to constructs that have been called need, reinforcement, emotion and motivation. Emotion is seen as a complex system evolved to enhance the animal's command over its environment. The major function of this system is to cope with a changing environment through the development of adequate neural representations of that environment and of outcomes of organism-environment interactions. The core of this system is a "teaching mechanism" comprised of the "reward" reinforcement system located in the brainstem core and in limbic structures.

Learned associations between events and rewards or punishments lead to expectancies of future outcomes, these expectancies generating the associated feelings. These expectancies are matched against outcomes with another set of feelings depending on the success or failure of the outcome. These various relationships may then modify existing representations of expectancies through match-mismatch processes.

In the higher mammals in particular, feelings have become externalized as a form of social communication which indicates the emotional state of the signaling animal.

Motivation has been presented as an interaction between the feelings of need and expectancies of reward or punishment that determine the duration and strength of action by the animal. A corollary to this approach is that the evolution of cognitive processes, heavily dependent as it has been on "emotional" affects for determination of events to be incorporated into its neural representations, must, at the same time, influence the evolution of that affective system. Thus, with the evolution of increasing neural complexity, animals become increasingly sensitive to events that are significant to them. Affective responsiveness becomes more and more subtly tuned to the increasing cognitive capacities of the organism. In man, the range and sensitivity of emotional feeling and expression appears to be greater than for any other creature so far evolved. This in itself would argue strongly against the notion that emotion has become a harmful by-product of essential activities or an evolutionary remnant. Rather, it would seem that there has been increasing evolutionary emphasis on emotion and its expression as a key component in the evolution of man.

A more detailed study of the particular systems within the brain that mediate these processes, those structures known collectively as the limbic system, should yield further evidence relating to this point of view. This will be undertaken in Volume 2.

13 Concluding Remarks: Where Do We Stand, Where Do We Go?

What links can we establish between what we know about the evolution of the brain and what we have gleaned from comparative studies of learning to form a consistent scenario for the evolution of learning? My attempt to achieve an answer to this question must of necessity incorporate much that is largely hypothetical, using such strands of evidence as are available.

To gain a more comprehensive view of the nature of learning processes in man, three major lines of enquiry have been pursued.

1. A paleontological and comparative analysis of the evolution of the nervous system, considered as the mechanism for the laying down, modification, and utilization of representations of the environment.

2. A review of comparative studies of the behavioral manifestations of learning.

3. An examination of the hypothesis that the evolution of an innate "teaching mechanism" in the form of "reward" systems of the brain eventuated as a requirement for the evolution of associative learning and that step by step processes in the evolution of this system saw the emergence of emotion, motivation and higher levels of associative learning.

My approach has had the specific objective of gaining a better understanding of learning processes in the line that led to the evolution of the human condition. This approach is in the tradition of Hobhouse's concept of orthogenic evolution or the evolution of mind as exemplified in the work of Razran in the study of behavior, and of Jerison in the study of the evolution of the brain.

Using this approach I have considered processes by which living tissue or protoplasm has adapted in structure and function to accommodate the vicissitudes of a changing and generally hostile environment. As one end result of such evolutionary changes we observe *Homo sapiens;* an animal with a relatively very large brain; a thinking animal capable of accumulating and storing vast quantities of information and of utilizing this information to adapt to an increasingly complex environment, much of that complexity being of its own making.

The human animal is not only able to adapt to its environment but is also able to substantially modify and adapt that environment to its own needs. It is not only able to cope with present events in terms of past experience but can project forward to the future with plans to deal with events that are yet to occur. This end result of one particular evolutionary chain is consistent with Koestler's view of evolution expressed in his observation that, "the main causative factor of evolutionary progress is not the selective pressure of the environment but the initiative of the organism, the restless exploring, perceiving animal" (Koestler, 1967, p. 154). This he labeled "progress by initiative." I do not see this view as in any sense denying the genetic basis of evolution, e.g., I am not suggesting that such activities, in themselves, influence the germ plasm. Rather, it is these activities arising as the product of particular genetic structures, that help to ensure the survival of those animals that are equipped to pursue such restless, exploring activities.

THE EVOLUTION OF NEURAL MECHANISMS

In tracing the history of the evolution of the brain I have argued, as my basic hypothesis, that larger brains have evolved as a very special case, i.e., one where it became essential for the survival of certain species that they be able to receive and process information in a particular fashion. A major part of this processing involves the construction of representations or images of relevant aspects of the environment and of significant organism-environment interactions and outcomes. Not only can these representations be stored and utilized for subsequent behavior, they can be modified in the light of experience.

The older view that the brain has shown a steady increase in size and complexity throughout man's evolutionary history does not fit with the evidence reviewed in this volume. For the vast majority of surviving species the brain appears to have undergone very little increase in size other than an appropriate increase in bulk that is directly related to increase in total body mass. As Jerison (1973) has pointed out, brain size, in fact, appears to have been a very conservative characteristic in evolutionary history. This has proved the case for most invertebrates with the notable exceptions of the cephalopod moluscs and the hymenoptra among the arthropods. For most of the vertebrates, including fish, amphibia and reptiles, this has again proved true once the basic vertebrate brain pattern was established. Among the mammals apart from the primates, a notable exception has been the evolution of the Cetacea. However, our knowledge of the significance of the very large brain observed in e.g., the whales and dolphins is, at this stage, rudimentary.

At certain periods in our evolutionary history there have been quantum leaps in brain mass that appear to correspond to very particular or peculiar demands in terms of survival requirements. This progressive increase in brain size, observed along the path from protozoa to man was by no means the universal path of evolution nor a necessary characteristic of survival for all animals. It is, in fact, a rare and, in many respects, a very expensive creation in terms of the many biological constraints that it imposes on those organisms that possess it. This is particularly exemplified in the heavy energy demands that are necessary to create and maintain a large brain (see, for example, Armstrong, 1983; Lewin, 1982), and in the time required for each individual so endowed to develop the necessary representations to enable it to utilize this large brain effectively in the struggle for survival.

Early evolutionary patterns of neural structure and organization that were laid down millions of years before the appearance of the first vertebrates, have persisted throughout all later evolutionary developments. These include the nature of nerve cells, axons and dendrites, synaptic connections and the direction of impulse flow. There is scanty evidence on which to determine the changes that took place in the nervous system during the emergence of vertebrates from their invertebrate ancestors. What is evident is that the basic neural organization was established early and has persisted throughout the whole of vertebrate evolution as the core structure of the evolving nervous system. The basic ratio between brain weight and body mass that was being established in the early chordates and Agnatha persisted through the evolution of elasmobranchs, pisces, amphibia and reptiles. As Jerison has revealed, this ratio has remained relatively constant for most phyla from the point of their separate emergence to the present day. Possible exceptions, discussed earlier, include the "warm blooded dinosaurs," the dromeosaurs and the coelurosaurs (Desmond, 1975), the living elasmobranchs (Ebbeson & Northcutt, 1976), and the Australian marsupials (Meyer, 1981).

A major expansion of brain size relative to body size in vertebrates became evident with the emergence of the mammals. Factors likely to have led to this and later increases in brain size have been discussed in Chapters 4 and 5.

In Chapter 1 I outlined two theoretical concepts advanced to account for such enlargements of the vertebrate brain. One line of argument developed the view that increases in neural tissue resulted from evolutionary pressures for increased storage and processing of information. This information augmented the neural representations or patterns laid down genetically for the purpose of guiding behavior and permitted the modification of such representations in terms of the organism's life experiences. This view was evident in the writings of such authors as Lashley and Thorpe with increase in brain size being reflected in the transition from behavior that is largely under reflexive or instinctive control to that directed by learning.

A second approach was that expressed succinctly by Harlow when he argued that the development of receptor systems was likely to give animals so endowed a selective advantage and that "as long as increasingly complex receptor systems provide the organism with slight survival advantages one can be assured that increasingly complex nervous systems will develop" (Harlow, 1958a, p. 275). This view was further developed by Jerison (1973).

That these two approaches represent different but closely related and complementary facets of a common stream of evolutionary development is suggested by Harlow's observation that learning capacities of animals in laboratory situations expressed capabilities that had evolved as a correlate of increased resolving power of receptors. Thorpe too, argued that what we were observing was increasing plasticity in perception and response. Lorenz stated the case more generally, saying that differentiation between "lower" and "higher" organisms might be defined in terms of the amount of relevant teleonomically organized information that they might possess. That we are in fact dealing with several distinct facets of a complex process becomes evident too when we consider the periods over which significant brain enlargement of the vertebrate brain occurred and the hypothesized reasons for such enlargement.

A major expansion of the brain relative to body size first became evident some 150 m.y. ago with the emergence of the mammals. This has been related to the struggle for survival of a group of small non-specialized animals, the therapsid reptiles, in the face of intense competition from the large dominant diurnal reptiles. These small animals, in a desperate battle for survival, are believed to have adapted to cool nocturnal niches. The ability to survive in this environment resulted from the evolving of a number of characteristics, including a warm blooded condition and a hirsute covering that were to become the hallmarks of the mammalian class. A highly significant change was adaptation of the sensory systems for the processing of information in a dark environment. This involved increased dependence on hearing and smell and diffuse night vision to locate objects in space and over time. This "time binding" of stimulus input, said Jerison (1973), would provide the animal with continuous schema. These schema would be provided by the development and storage of neural representations of the information coming in through the improved and adapted sensory systems.

The evolution of effective sensory systems to cope with such an environment would, as Harlow (1958), Jerison (1973) and Ford Ebner (1976) have pointed out, be dependent on the rapid expansion of neural structures to process this complex information and this would lead to a marked expansion of the brain and, in particular, the rich neural network of the neocortex. This increasing neural capacity also set the stage for a rapid advance in the development of learning capabilities.

As a result of these evolutionary changes, the small transformed reptiles were able to survive the circumstances that resulted in the extermination of much of the earth's flora and fauna at the end of the late Cretaceous period. These newly evolved mammals were then able to emerge from their nocturnal habitat to occupy the major niches previously dominated by the large diurnal reptiles.

A further expansion of the brain then took place. This appears to have been due to the return of emphasis on vision as a major sense, but now feeding information into an already transformed brain. A further factor was a continuing struggle between predator and prey involved increasing utilization of complex information.

The next major brain expansion, and one that concerns us directly, was that which accompanied adaptation by one group of animals, the primates, to an arborial habitat. Again it seems likely that a major incentive for this expansion was the complexity of the information that had to be coped with for life in the trees. Here there was a necessity to identify objects against an ever changing background of color, light and shade.

As Jerison has pointed out, "it would be difficult to move about freely in such an environment on the basis of prepotent cues from certain patterns of stimulation that act as effective stimuli for fixed action patterns because the stimulus patterns would be unstable and changing" (Jerison, 1973, p. 413). Thus the ability to develop and modify complex representations would be a considerable asset.

Evidence already discussed points to initial brain enlargement occurring in the temporal neocortex, followed by rapid expansion of the frontal cortex. This fits well with the view that the initial expansion was related to improved sensory processing of the varied visual and auditory inputs. This was followed by increased requirements for complex organization of behavior. Jerison has argued that the further expansion of the primate brain from prosimian to simian and anthropoid, could be accounted for in terms of selective pressure to cope with an active diurnal life in the trees and pressure for survival in the presence of large brained predators.

The final stages in the evolution of man from his ape-like predecessors have been outlined in some detail. This involved a further set of selective pressures that resulted in, for living man, a final enlargement of the brain. These pressures are believed to be related to the emergence of a bipedal omnivorous savannah dwelling primate. This animal had to cope firstly with a harsh, arid climate and then with successive ice ages and in the process evolved social, communicative and toolmaking behaviors that resulted in the appearance of *Homo sapiens*. It was argued in Chapter 5 that enlargement of the human brain followed invasion of the hominid niche, the brain at that stage being relatively small. This view is given further support by Lovejoy (1981).

In the course of this examination I have been able to identify a number of living species that appear to have deviated little from their "stem" species in terms of structure, brain size and, presumably, behaviors. This concept of "living fossils" recently received elaboration in a book edited by Eldredge and Stanley (1984). The authors presented detailed case studies of a wide range of species including a number that I had referred to, among them the coelacanth, the crocodile, the elephant shrew, the tree squirrel, the tree shrew, and the tarsier. In this work, living fossils were defined as fulfilling three criteria: "(1) They are living members of a group of marked longevity in the geologic record; (2) they demonstrate very little morphologic divergence from earlier occurring members of the same cladode; and (3) they belong to a cladode that shows very low taxonomic diversity through most, or all, of its known history" (Novacek, 1984, p. 12). In Chapter 7 I pointed to the likely benefits that intensive study of the behavioral capabilities of these animals might bring.

The evolution of larger brains thus appears to be directly associated with increased capacity for the accumulation and processing of information. There has been also an increasing specificity in brain systems for the detailed analysis and processing of information as evidenced by comparative studies of forebrain and especially neocortical evolution. This reveals a series of changes from primitive generalized receptor and motor fields covering large areas of the cortex to more highly specific and localized receptor and motor fields seen in, for example, primates and carnivores. Changes in the analytical and integrative capacity of the system is evidenced by the evolution of secondary or associative cortical fields and the expansion of such structures as the hippocampus, septum and amygdala. Thus, the enlarged brain has the capacity to handle more information in more specialized ways and of organizing and integrating this information more adequately.

THE EVOLUTION OF LEARNING

The comparative psychology of learning is not, as Lockard and others would have us believe, dead, but is making steady and, on occasions, quite spectacular progress in spite of problems about direction and emphasis.

In reviewing the current state of our understanding of the evolution of learning, many and varied approaches to the study of this area were noted and it would be fair to say that the very diversity of this attack has been a significant factor in our present progress.

Dewsbury (1973) for example, has pointed out that while man thinks very highly of his own place in the universe it is forgotten that rats and mice appear to be the dominant mammals of our time and that this may even be regarded as an "age of insects." Dewsbury's approach accords with the viewpoint of the ethologists in that he is considering the full sweep of animal evolution. The objective in this approach is to gain an understanding of the various forms of behavior that have become evident in living species in response to many and varied evolutionary pressures and the accent has usually been on species-specific behaviors. The limit of this approach is exemplified in Lockard's (1971) statement that "what we may perceive as a meaningful and natural category is actually a mere collection of unlike phenomena" (Lockard, 1971, p. 172). However, it should be noted that Bitterman, using very different techniques, laboratory based and experimental, also sought to examine behavior across the full spectrum of living species. His search has been for common processes and phyletic differences in animal learning.

My own appraisal has been from a narrower perspective, with emphasis on the mainstream of the evolution of man. My objective has been to gain a better understanding of how man's cognitive capabilities, and more specifically his learning abilities, evolved. With this emphasis I have ignored the vast array of multilateral branching of the evolutionary tree to trace through one particular path. This notion of orthogenic evolution, the improvement of mind, formed the core of Hobhouse's systematization of cognitive processes and Razran is the most recent exponent of this approach. Jerison, too, developed his examination of the evolution of the brain within this conceptual framework.

While considerable heat has at times developed between the protagonists of each of these approaches to the evolution of learning, both are valid and, in a sense, complementary for our more adequate understanding of evolutionary processes.

The range of species that should be considered in any attempt to unravel the evolution of behavior has also been a hotly contested issue. Hodos and Campbell (1969) for example, have argued for the detailed examination of closely related species in which the evolutionary links have been clearly established. Bitterman on the other hand, would consider the widest possible range of animals in order to draw conclusions about similarities and differences in learning processes. He would then test hypotheses about the presence or absence of particular characteristics in some species intermediate in phylogenetic origins between the original species studied.

Methodological problems in the study of cross species learning also loom large. The question of field studies, the ethological approach, versus controlled laboratory experiments has been a controversial issue. Lockard for example, while conceding that there is some place for laboratory studies claimed that the strong evidence will come from observation of behavior in its natural setting. Lorenz in his writings, already discussed, endeavored to exemplify his arguments exclusively by reference to behaviors observed in their natural settings. However, the main virtue of laboratory studies is that of control and the capability to elucidate underlying processes. Bitterman's approach, for example, demands precise laboratory manipulation and control. Harlow's (1958) statement that "study of animals under laboratory conditions reveals many learning capabilities whose existence is hard to understand in terms of survival value" (p. 273) helps to emphasize the role of such studies. The evolution of more complex nervous systems facilitated the utilization and integration of more complex information patterns. Within its own environment the animal will use this capacity to cope with other situations that it does not normally have to deal with. These capacities are tapped or manipulated in the laboratory. Schneirla, whose work formed the basis of Bitterman's approach, was likewise concerned with the mechanisms underlying adaptive behavior and emphasized the contributions that laboratory studies can make to such an approach (Schneirla, 1950, 1959). However, Schneirla's view was that no division should be drawn between observational and experimental techniques (Schneirla, 1966). Brookshire, in his discussion of these differing techniques agreed that "the laboratory has provided information about learning that is far less likely to have been obtained in field research." (Brookshire, 1976, p. 193).

I argued in Chapter 8 that, while both approaches are likely to provide significant material, the detailed resolution of learning processes may be more profitably pursued through the use of laboratory techniques. However, this approach is also beset with problems. The most fruitful technique advanced so far appears to be Bitterman's analysis by systematic variation. Though the method is very time consuming, valid solutions to questions relating to cross species comparisons are more likely to be forthcoming. Furthermore, with an accumulating body of empirical data from a wide range of experiments using this and related approaches, this line of attack will become less time consuming and more likely to demonstrate significant relationships between species.

The debate over the question of diversity of learning processes is still unresolved. Opinions have ranged from those expressed by ethologists such as Lorenz and Lockard that learning processes may be as diverse as the species that produce them to the clasic view of the learning theorists such as Thorndike, Pavlov and Skinner, that there is a single basic process. The question of qualitative versus quantitative differences in learning has been debated at length as was evident in Chapters 9 and 10. However, there is another line of argument that needs to be considered in any such debate.

I made the point earlier that learning is, in fact, an abstract concept developed to encompass the realities of storage and retrieval processes that enable animals to lay down and to utilize representations of the world around them. With changing neural organization, with respect to both quantity and structural relationships, the ways in which representations are developed and utilized may well undergo significant changes. With increasing specificity of organization in various brain regions, and in particular the telencephalon, separate processing functions are likely to become evident which will change the nature and quality of the "total" learning process. I will develop this concept further when I consider the relationships between the brain and learning. We can however, now bring together the broad strands of evidence that come from our examination of brain evolution and of comparative studies of learning.

The material presented in Chapters 9 and 10 would generally support the view that there have been rather clearly defined qualitative shifts at certain critical stages of evolution. These qualitative shifts are likely to have been associated with periods of rapid increase in brain size. Razran's conceptualization of various hierarchical levels of learning may be considered in relation to such an hypothesis.

Learning associated with the simplest nervous systems or even no nervous system at all, i.e., virtually universal learning in living tissue, is seen in the processes of habituation and sensitization. The next level of learning, the simplest form of associative learning, namely, aversive conditioning or punishment learning, Razran found to be effective throughout the metazoa. This effectiveness increased in early evolution and then rapidly reached an asymptote. This was followed by the appearance of true associative learning, i.e., classical and instrumental conditioning, in animals with increasingly complex nervous systems. Lorenz has argued that, for such learning to become manifest the "fulguration" of a new "teaching mechanism" that involved positive feedback of outcomes was essential as was a sufficiently complex nervous system. I have proposed that the "reward" systems of the brain would constitute this teaching mechanism in the human stream. Lorenz (1981) also described what would constitute a further category of associative learning that would become evident before a nervous system complex enough to cope with positive feedback had evolved. This is learning by contiguity which he considered to constitute true classical conditioning.

Razran next identified a number of classes of higher order learning including learning of perceptions (sensory pre-conditioning and configuring), concept formation and symbolizing. He argued that "learning to perceive" bridged a major span in the evolution of learning processes from associative learning to concept formation. Sensory preconditioning and configuring could be demonstrated in a simple or primitive form in reptiles (turtles) and clearly in birds and mammals but not in fish or amphibia. Symbolization, on the other hand, concluded Razran, was only clearly present where language was evident. Animals other than man, he claimed, have not demonstrated symbol learning.

This classification fits well with Bitterman's distinction between fish on the one hand and mammals on the other, with reptiles occupying an intermediate position. For example, Bitterman argued that fish paid due regard to learning by contiguity and S-R theory in that large rewards produced stronger and more stable connections than small rewards. However, mammals and birds displayed different characteristics such as negative and positive contrast effects, more rapid extinction with large rewards and the partial reinforcement effect. As well, in such tasks as serial reversal learning and probability learning, Bitterman pointed to the likelihood of qualitative differences between fish, reptiles and animals. In serial reversal, birds and mammals showed increasing ability to utilize information gained from previous experience while, in probability learning, they used probability information to maximize reinforcements, while fish failed to do this.

These differences between fish and amphibia, reptiles and mammals, observed by both Razran and Bitterman, may be related to the first major expansion in the vertebrate brain associated with the transition from reptile to mammal. In terms of Jerison's theory this would be associated particularly with enlargement of the cortex servicing auditory and olfactory systems and would accompany a rapid development of perceptual learning, with the ability to differentiate objects, stable over space and time, from a dark, obscure background.

The next development in learning capabilities may well have taken the form of quantitative rather than qualitative changes evident throughout the differentiation of the primate line. These changes are seen in increasing capacity for learning set formation and in the ability to utilize an increasing number of cue dimensions (conditions of ambiguity) in visual discrimination learning. Harlow demonstrated that the higher non-human primates have attained levels of ability in this area of learning that are comparable with that of *Homo sapiens*.

The final advance appears to have been associated with the development of language for communication, i.e., Pavlov's second signal system. This system Razran associated with concept formation and symbolization, claiming that sub-humans are not able to symbolize in the absence of language. However, it appears likely that the basis for concept formation and symbolization is evident in the learning capacity of the higher primates, e.g., in the mastery, albeit slowly and painfully, of the extension of the double alternation problem demonstrated by rhesus monkeys and in the capacity to utilize sign language, at least in an elementary fashion by chimpanzees.

THE EVOLUTION OF EMOTION

I have argued that in larger, longer living animals the capacity to develop and modify neural representations of their environment during their lifetimes would have high survival value and, in fact, proved essential for mammalian evolution. For the effective development of more complex representations of animal-environment interactions a "teaching mechanism" that would inform the animal of the effectiveness of these interactions was an evolutionary necessity. A mechanism that fulfilled this requirement, the "reward" systems of the brain, became evident early in the vertebrate evolution. Such a system has been demonstrated in the goldfish and would seem to be a prerequisite for the emergence of true associative learning.

Closely linked with the appearance of reward and punishment receptors would be another set of affective sensors, those that indicated rising need levels and satisfaction of need. There is no evidence to indicate the exact relationship between the evolution of the two systems but one might speculate that the reward systems would have appeared first. Then, as these systems become refined, there would be an increasing selection pressure for awareness, in affective terms, of particular needs thus focussing for the animal where the most effective rewards would be available.

The next major development would then be the transformation of the affects of reward and punishment into those of emotion through the evolution of expectancy. There is little evidence of when this would have occurred in evolutionary terms. The clearest indication comes from Bitterman's work. In his studies of differences between fish and reptiles on the one hand and mammals on the other, Bitterman concluded that, if the Law of Effect operates in fish, we ought to consider the possibility that it operates in the rat. He concluded that, "its operation in the rat is marked by anticipatory processes" (Bitterman, 1969, p. 47).

He noted that Rosen, Glass, and Ison (1967) had dosed rats with barbiturates after which they gave results like fish. In 1975 Bitterman argued that the difference between rat and fish is emotional, the rat being upset by differences between anticipated and actual rewards while the fish is not (Bitterman, 1957). This would point to the evolution of mammals as a likely point of emergence of emotion, coinciding with the first major expansion of the vertebrate forebrain and the emergence of perceptual learning.

Emotion as an instrument for socialization followed as a further significant evolutionary development. This characteristic is evident in many mammals but assumes major prominence in the evolution of primates and, in particular, in the final emergence of man as a socially organized hunting animal. It is, in fact, the rapid evolution of the social aspects of emotion in these final stages which has led to the highly complex picture evident from the studies of emotion in man. Such writers as Averill and Tomkins have stressed the importance of emotion as an amplifier and pointed to the significance of facial expressions of emotion in man. These views have been presented in Plutchik and Kellerman's (1980) work on *"Theories of Emotion."*

Coupled with this emergence of emotion as a major determinant in the evolution of learning I have argued that there was a shift in the motivation of behavior from determination by inbuilt reflexive and instinctive patterns responsive to changing need states to a system involving interaction between expectancies and needs. Thus motivation and emotion in the higher vertebrates have a common basis in expectancy. Izard and Buechler (1980) concurred with this point of view, stating that, "after basic survival and comfort needs are met, drives generally only assume psychological importance in their interaction with emotions" (p. 167).

In this examination of the evolution of learning I have outlined a continuum of processes. This extends from the largely built-in or instinctive patterns evident in animals with more simple nervous systems, with limited neural capacity, to those more complex systems largely dependent on flexible changes that can be effected by the animal during its own life span.

Increments in learning capacity have been observed to occur in the main, through processes of gradual quantitative accumulation linked with increased neural capacity. However, substantial qualitative changes have also been described, those changes contributing major advances in the ability of animals to profit from experience and to anticipate outcomes. These changes I have associated with periods of rapid increase in brain size.

A significant development is likely to have occurred early in the evolution of vertebrates with the "fulguration" of the reward systems constituting a feedback teaching mechanism. The next qualitative leap appears to have been associated with the rapid expansion of the brain with the emergence of the mammals. This explosion in brain capacity I have linked with the emergence of emotion and the development of perceptual learning. Continuing brain expansion during the evolution of mammals appears to have been mirrored by quantitative improvement in learning capacity and this is probably true for the expansion occurring in the brains of the evolving primates.

However, with the emergence of the higher primates the beginnings of a new class of learning became evident, i.e., the ability to form concepts. Razran (1971) concluded, however, that we still know very little about the underlying mechanisms of conceptual learning in animals and that, while some primates and possibly some sub-primates evidenced some abstractive ability he considered that this did not warrant the view that such animals are thereby able to think.

Associated with this evolutionary stage of the brain and learning was a rapid expansion of emotion as a tool for social communication. This appears to have been a significant factor in the final brain expansion leading to man. A major concomitant of this expansion was the development of language which resulted in a further qualitative leap in learning processes through the capacity to symbolize.

If this is indeed the path that the evolution of human learning has followed, then links between the nervous system and learning that I have postulated should be evident in the neural organization for learning in mammals. This would include systems for the signaling of need and for the reward and punishment of behavior.

We should also be able to establish relationships between information input and the transformation of this information into representations that enable the animal to behave purposefully and anticipate future events to its benefit. In particular, comparative studies of the forebrain and neocortex have demonstrated a shift from generalized receptor and motor areas to highly specialized and localized fields. Together with this is the evidence for dual origins of isocortical organization. The two spring sources in the primitive prosencephalon i.e. the paleopallium and archipallium have given rise to the piriform and hippocampal cortices, one basically sensory and the other motor in function. Consideration of how these two sources were modeled and developed into the complex sensory, motor and limbic structures in man should lead to a better understanding of the neural mediation of learning including the systems for signaling need and the reward and punishment of behavior. An examination of some of the insights that we have gained from studies of the mediation of such neural systems in learning behaviors will be my objective in Volume 2.

A further area of study of particular relevance for our understanding of the evolution of learning, an area that Schneirla regarded as all important, is the ontogeny of learning. I will be considering the impact of studies of the development of the nervous system and the development of learning at a later stage.

While a tremendous volume of work has been completed in the study of learning and in the development of theories of learning, much of this has been undertaken from a purely behavioral point of view. However, the information we now have of man's evolutionary history, together with our knowledge of how the nervous system is organized and functions, must set bounds to the form that modern learning theory can take. More significantly, with such knowledge, we should be able to establish a clear set of principles that will facilitate further research and theory development and hence enhance our understanding of the learning process. An examination of such relationships will be my final goal.

References

Abbie, A. A. (1938). The excitable cortex in the monotremata. *Australian Journal of Experimental Biology and Medical Science, 16,* 143–152.

Abbie, A. A. (1940a). Cortical lamination in the montremata. *Journal of Comparative Neurology, 72,* 428–468.

Abbie, A. A. (1940b). The excitable cortex in *Perameles sarcophilus, Dasyurus trichosurus and Wallabia (Macropus). Journal of Comparative Neurology, 72,* 469–487.

Abbie, A. A. (1942). Cortical lamination in a poliprodont marsupial *Perameles natusa. Journal of Comparative Neurology, 76,* 509–536.

Akert, K. (1964). Comparative anatomy of frontal cortex and thalomofrontal connections. In J. M. Warren & K. Akert (Eds.) *The frontal granular cortex and behavior* (pp. 372–409). New York: McGraw-Hill.

Alvarez, L. W., Alvarez, W., Asaro, F., & Michel, H. V. (1980). Extra terrestrial cause for the cretaceous-tertiary extinction. *Science, 208,* 1095–1108.

Armstrong, E. (1983). Relative brain size and metabolism in mammals. *Science, 220,* 1302–1304.

Andrew, R. J. (1967). Intracranial self-stimulation in the chick. *Nature, 213,* 847–848.

Andy, D. J., & Stephan, H. (1966a). Phylogeny of the primate septum telencephali. In R. Hassler & H. Stephan (Eds.), *Evolution of the forebrain: Phylogenesis and ontogenesis of the forebrain* (pp. 389–399). Stuttgart: Georg Thieme Verlag.

Andy, D. J., & Stephan, H. (1966b). Septal nuclei in primate phylogeny. *The Journal of Comparative Neurology, 126,* 157–170.

Andy, D. J., & Stephan, H. (1976). Septum development in primates. In J. F. DeFrance (Ed.), *The septal nuclei* (pp. 3–36). New York: Plenum.

Anokhin, P. K. (1961). A new conception of the physiological architecture of conditioned reflex. In J. F. Delafresnaye (Ed.), *Brain mechanisms and learning* (pp. 189–229). Oxford: Blackwell.

Ariens-Kappers, C. U., Huber, G. C., & Crosby, E. C. (1960). *The comparative anatomy of the nervous systems of vertebrates, including man.* New York: Hafner. (Originally published 1936)

Arnold, M. B. (1945). Physiological differentiation of emotional states. *Psychological Review, 52,* 35–48.

Arnold, M. B. (1960). *Emotion and personality*. New York: Columbia University Press.

Arnold, M. B. (1970). Brain function and emotion: A phenomenological analysis. In P. Black (Ed.), *Physiological Correlates of Emotion* (pp. 261–286). New York: Academic Press.

Aronson, L. R., Tobach, E., Lehrman, D. S., & Rosenblatt, J. S. (1970). *Development and evolution of behaviour. Essays in memory of T. C. Schneirla*. San Francisco: W. H. Freeman.

Aronson, L. R., Tolbach, E., Rosenblatt, J. S., & Lehrman, D. S. (1972). *Selected writings of T. C. Schneirla*. San Francisco: W. H. Freeman.

Atencio, F. W., Diamond, I. T., & Ward, J. P. (1975). Behavioral study of the visual cortex of *Galago senegalensis*. *Journal of Comparative and Physiological Psychology, 89*, 1109–1135.

Averill, J. R. (1980a). On the paucity of positive emotions. In K. R. Blankstein, P. Pliner, & J. Polivy (Eds.), *Assessment and modification of emotional behavior* (pp. 7–46). New York: Plenum.

Averill, J. R. (1980b). A constructivist view of emotion. In R. Plutchik & H. Kellerman (Eds.), *Emotion: Theory, research and experience* (pp. 305–340). New York: Academic Press.

Bagg, H. J. (1920). Individual differences and family resemblances in animal behavior. *Archives of Psychology, 43*, 58.

Bakker, R. T. (1980). Dinosaur heresy — Dinosaur renaissance: Why we need endothermic archosaurs for a comprehensive theory of bioenergetic evolution. In R. D. K. Thomas & E. C. Olson (Eds.), *A cold look at the warm-blooded Dinosaurs* (pp. 351–462). Boulder: Westview Press.

Bandy, O. L. (1972). A review of the calibration of deep-sea cores based upon species variation productivity and $^{16}O/^{18}O$ ratios of planktonic foraminifera including sedimentation rates and climatic inferences. In W. W. Bishop & J. A. Miller (Eds.), *Calibration of hominoid evolution* (pp. 37–62). University of Toronto Press.

Beach, F. A. (1950). The snark was a boojum. *American Psychologist, 5*, 115–124.

Beach, F. A. (1960). Experimental investigations of species-specific behavior. *American Psychologist, 15*, 1–18.

Behrend, E. R., & Bitterman, M. E. (1967). Further experiments on habit reversal in the fish. *Psychonomic Science, 8*, 363–364.

Behrend, E. R., Domesick, V. B., & Bitterman, M. E. (1965). Habit reversal in the fish. *Journal of Comparative and Physiological Psychology, 60*, 407–411.

Bindra, D. (1958). Comparative psychology. *Annual Review of Psychology, 9*, 399–414.

Bindra, D. (1970). Emotion and behavior theory: Current research in historical perspective. In P. Black (Ed.), *Physiological correlates of emotion* (pp. 3–20). New York: Academic Press.

Birch, H. G. (1954). Comparative psychology. In F. Marcuse (Ed.), *Areas of psychology* (pp. 446–477). New York: Harper and Brothers.

Bishop, G. H. (1959). The relation between nerve fiber size and sensory modality: Phylogenetic implications of the afferent innervation of cortex. *Journal of Nervous and Mental Disease, 128*, 89–114.

Bishop, G. H. (1965). My life among the axons. *Annual Review of Physiology, 27*, 1–18.

Bishop, M. P., Elder, S. T., & Heath, R. G. (1963). Intracranial self stimulation in man. *Science, 140*, 394–396.

Bishop, W. W., & Miller, J. A. (Eds.). (1972). *Calibration of hominoid evolution. Recent advances in isotopic and other dating methods applicable to the origin of man*. University of Toronto Press.

Bitterman, M. E. (1960). Toward a comparative psychology of learning. *American Psychologist, 15*, 704–712.

Bitterman, M. E. (1964). An instrumental technique for the turtle. *Journal of the Experimental Analysis of Behavior, 7*, 189–190.

Bitterman, M. E. (1965). Phyletic differences in learning. *American Psychologist, 20*, 396–410.

Bitterman, M. E. (1966). Animal learning. In J. B. Sidowski, *Experimental methods and instru-*

mentation in psychology (pp. 451–484). New York: McGraw Hill.

Bitterman, M. E. (1969). Thorndike and the problem of animal intelligence. *American Psychologist, 24,* 444–453.

Bitterman, M. E. (1975). The comparative analysis of learning: Are the laws of learning the same in all animals? *Science, 188,* 699–709.

Bitterman, M. E. (1976a). Incentive contrast in honey bees. *Science, 192,* 380–382.

Bitterman, M. E. (1976b). Issues in the comparative psychology of learning. In R. B. Masterton, M. E. Bitterman, C. B. G. Campbell, & N. Hotton (Eds.), *Evolution of brain and behavior in vertebrates* (pp. 217–225). Hillsdale, NJ: Lawrence Erlbaum Associates.

Bitterman, M. E., & Mackintosh, H. J. (1969). Habit reversal and probability learning: Rats, birds and fish. In R. M. Gilbert & N. S. Sutherland (Eds.), *Animal discrimination learning* (pp. 163–185). New York: Academic Press.

Bitterman, M. E., Menzel, R., Fietz, A., & Schafer, S. (1983). Classical conditioning of proboscis extension in honeybees (*Apis mellifera*). *Journal of Comparative Psychology, 97,* 107–119.

Bitterman, M. E., & Woodward, W. T. (1976). Vertebrate learning. Common processes. In R. B. Masterton, M. E. Bitterman, C. B. G. Campbell, & N. Hotton (Eds.), *Evolution of brain and behavior in vertebrates* (pp. 169–190). Hillsdale, NJ: Lawrence Erlbaum Associates.

Black, P. (1970). *Physiological correlates of emotion.* New York: Academic Press.

Bolles, R. C. (1964). Species-specific defense reactions and avoidance learning. *Psychological Review, 71,* 32–48.

Boyd, E. S., & Gardner, L. C. (1962). Positive and negative reinforcement from intracranial self stimulation in teleosts. *Science, 136,* 648.

Boyd, B. O., & Warren, J. M. (1957). Solution of oddity problems by cats. *Journal of Comparative and Physiological Psychology, 50,* 258.

Brookshire, K. H. (1976). Vertebrate learning and evolutionary divergences. In R. B. Masterton, M. E. Bitterman, C. B. G. Campbell, & N. Hotton (Eds.), *Evolution of brain and behavior in vertebrates* (pp. 191–216). Hillsdale, NJ: Lawrence Erlbaum Associates.

Brownlee, A., & Bitterman, M. E. (1968). Differential reward conditioning in the pigeon. *Psychonomic Science, 12,* 345–346.

Bruner, A. (1967). Self stimulation in the rabbit and an anatomical map of stimulation effects. *Journal of Comparative Neurology, 131,* 615–629.

Buettner-Janusch, J. (1966). *Origins of man: Physical anthropology.* New York: Wiley.

Bullock, T. H., & Horridge, G. A. (1965). *Structure and function in the nervous systems of invertebrates.* San Francisco: W. H. Freeman.

Burnsten, B., & Delgado, J. M. R. (1958). Positive reinforcement induced by intracranial stimulation in the monkey. *Journal of Comparative and Physiological Psychology, 51,* 6–10.

Burt, C. (1955). Evidence for the concept of intelligence. *British Journal of Educational Psychology, 25,* 158–177.

Butler, R. A. (1953). Discrimination learning by rhesus monkeys to visual exploration motivation. *Journal of Comparative and Physiological Psychology, 46,* 95–98.

Butler, R. A. (1965). Investigative behavior. In A. M. Schrier, H. F. Harlow, & F. Stollnitz (Eds.), *Behaviour in non-human primates* (Vol. 2, pp. 463–493). New York: Academic Press.

Calvin, M. (1967). Chemical evolution of life and sensibility. In G. C. Quarton, T. Melnechuk, & F. D. Schmitt (Eds.), *The neurosciences: A study program* (pp. 780–800). New York: Rockefeller University Press.

Campbell, C. B. G. (1976). Brain evolution in the order primates. In R. B. Masterton, M. E. Bitterman, C. B. G. Campbell, & N. Hotton (Eds.), *Evolution of brain and behavior in vertebrates* (pp. 393–406) Hillsdale, NJ: Lawrence Erlbaum Associates.

Candland, D. K., Fell, J. P., Keene, E., Leshner, A. I., Tarpy, R. M., & Plutchik, R. (1977). *Emotion.* Monterey: Brooks/Cole.

Carey, R. G., Fitzpatrick, D., & Diamond, I. T. (1979). Thalamic projections to layer 1 of Striate Cortex shown by retrograde transport of horseradish peroxidase. *Science, 203*, 556–559.

Carlson, E. R. (1966). The affective tone of psychology. *Journal of General Psychology, 75*, 67–78.

Casseday, J. H., Diamond, I. T., & Harting, J. K. (1976). Auditory pathways to the cortex in *Tupaia glis. The Journal of Comparative Neurology, 166*, 303–340.

Casseday, J. H., Jones, C. R., & Diamond, I. T. (1979). Projections from cortex to tectum with tree shrew *Tupaia glis. Journal of Comparative Neurology, 185*, 253–291.

Cattell, J. McK. (1890). Mental tests and measurements. *Mind, 15*, 373–381.

Cofer, C. N., & Appley, M. H. (1967). *Motivation: Theory and research.* New York: Wiley.

Colbert, E. H. (1955). *Evolution of the vertebrates: A history of the backboned animals through time.* New York: Wiley.

Colbert, E. H. (1958). Morphology and behaviour. In A. Roe & G. G. Simpson (Eds.), *Behaviour and evolution* (pp. 27–47). New Haven: Yale University Press.

Commins, E. F., McNemar, Q., & Stone, C. P. (1932). Intercorrelations of measures of ability in the rat. *Journal of Comparative Psychology, 14*, 225–235.

Corning, W. C., Dyal, J. A., & Willows, A. O. D. (1973–1975). *Invertebrate learning* (Vols. 1–3), New York: Plenum Press.

Couvillon, P. A., & Bitterman, M. E. (1980). Some phenomena of associative learning in honey bees. *Journal of Comparative and Physiological Psychology, 94*, 878–885.

Couvillon, P. A., & Bitterman, M. E. (1982). Compound conditioning in honey bees. *Journal of Comparative and Physiological Psychology, 96*, 192–199.

Couvillon, P. A., Klosterhalfen, S., & Bitterman, M. E. (1983). Analysis of overshadowing in honeybees. *Journal of Comparative Psychology, 97*, 154–166.

Crespi, L. P. (1942). Quantitative variations in incentive and performance in the white rat. *American Journal of Psychology, 55*, 467–517.

Crosby, E. C., DeJonge, B. R., & Schneider, R. C. (1966). Evidence for some trends in the phylogenetic development of the vertebrate telencephalon. In R. Hassler & H. Stephan (Eds.), *Evolution of the forebrain: Phylogenesis and ontogenesis of the forebrain* (pp. 117–135). Stuttgart: Georg Thieme Verlag.

Crosby, E. C., & Humphrey, T. (1944). Studies of the vertebrate telencephalon III. The amygdaloid complex in the shrew (*Blarina brevicauda*). *Journal of Comparative Neurology, 81*, 285–305.

Crosby, E. C., Humphrey, T., & Lauer, E. W. (1962). *Correlative anatomy of the nervous system.* New York: Macmillan.

Cusatis, M. A., & Levitt, R. A. (1981). Emotions. In R. A. Levitt (Ed.), *Physiological psychology* (pp. 405–442). New York: Holt, Rinehart and Winston.

Dart, R. A. (1925). *Australopithecus africanus*: The man-ape of South Africa. *Nature (London), 115*, 195–199.

Dart, R. A. (1934). The dual structure of the neopallium. Its history and significance. *Journal of Anatomy, 69*, 3–19.

Darwin, C. (1871). *The descent of man.* New York: Appleton.

Darwin, C. (1965). *The expression of the emotions in man and animals.* Chicago: University of Chicago Press. (Originally published 1872).

Davenport, J. W., Benson, R. W., Hagquist, W. W., Rankin, G. R., & Shelton, S. E. (1972). Computerized animal intelligence testing. *Behavioral Research Methods and Instrumentation, 4*, 67–70.

Davis, F. C., & Tolman, E. C. (1924). A note on the correlation between two mazes. *Journal of Comparative Psychology, 4*, 125–135.

Desmond, A. J. (1975). *The hot-blooded dinosaurs. A revolution in palaentology.* London: Blond and Briggs.

Dethier, V. G. (1976). *The hungry fly.* Cambridge, MA: Harvard University Press.

Dethier, V. G., & Bodenstein, D. (1958). Hunger in the blowfly. *Zeitschrift fur Tierpsychologie, 15,* 129–140. Reprinted in C. G. Gross & H. R. Zeigler (1969) (Eds.), *Readings in physiological psychology: Motivation* (pp. 8–21). New York: Harper & Row.

Dethier, V. G., & Stellar, E. (1961). *Animal behavior: Its evolutionary and neurological basis.* New York: Prentice-Hall.

Diamond, I. T. (1967). The sensory neocortex. In W. D. Neff (Ed.), *Contributions to sensory physiology* (Vol. 2, pp. 51–100). New York: Academic Press.

Diamond, I. T. (1976). Organization of the visual cortex: Comparative, anatomical and behavioral studies. *Federation Proceedings, 35,* 60–67.

Diamond, I. T. (1979). The subdivisions of neocortex: A proposal to revise the traditional view of sensory, motor and association areas. In J. M. Sprague & A. Epstein (Eds.), *Progress in Psychobiology and Physiological Psychology* (Vol. 8, pp. 1–43). New York: Academic Press.

Diamond, I. T. (1982). Changing views of the organization and evolution of the visual pathways. In *Changing concepts of the nervous system*, (pp. 201–233). New York: Academic Press.

Diamond, I. T. (1983). Parallel pathways in the auditory visual and somatic systems. In G. Macchi, A. Rustioni, & R. Spreafico (Eds.) *Somatosensory integration in the thalamus* (pp. 251–272). Amsterdam: Elsevier.

Diamond, I. T., & Chow, K. L. (1962). Biological psychology. In S. Koch (Ed.), *Psychology: A study of science, Study II. Empirical substructure and relations with other sciences. Vol. 4 Biologically oriented fields: their place in psychology and in biological science* (pp. 158–241). New York: McGraw-Hill.

Diamond, I. T., & Hall, W. C. (1969). Evolution of neocortex. *Science, 164,* 251–262.

Diamond, S., Balvin, R. S., & Diamond, F. R. (1963). *Inhibition and choice.* New York: Harper & Row.

Divac, I., & Oberg, R. G. E. (1979). *The neostriatum.* New York: Pergamon.

Divac, I. (1980). Patterns of subcortico-cortical projections as revealed by somatopetal Horse-Radish Peroxidase tracing. In A. D. Smith, R. Llinas, & P. G. Kostyuk (Eds.), *Commentaries in the neurosciences* (pp. 303–310). New York: Pergamon.

Divac, I., Kosmal, A., Bjorklund, A., & Lindvall, O. (1978). Subcortical projections to the prefrontal cortex in the rat as revealed by the Horse-Radish Peroxidase Technique. *Neuroscience, 3,* 785–796.

Divac, I., Lavail, J. H., Rakic, P., & Winston, K. R. (1977). Heterogeneous afferents to the inferior parietal lobule of the rhesus monkey revealed by the retrograde transport method. *Brain Research, 123,* 197–207.

Dobzhansky, T. (1955). *Evolution, genetics and man.* New York: Wiley.

Dobzhansky, T. (1962). *Mankind evolving: The evolution of the human species.* New Haven: Yale University Press.

Domesick, V. B. (1972). Thalamic relationships of the medial cortex in the rat. *Brain, Behavior and Evolution, 6,* 457–483.

Douglas, R. J., & Marcellus, D. (1975). The ascent of man. Deductions based on a multivariate analysis of the brain. *Brain, Behavior and Evolution, 11,* 179–213.

Duffy, E. (1957). The psychological significance of the concept of "arousal" or "activation." *Psychological Review, 64,* 265–275.

Duffy, E. (1962). *Activation and behavior.* New York: Wiley.

Dunlap, J. W. (1933). The organization of learning and other traits in chickens. *Comparative Psychology Monographs, 9,* No. 4.

Durham, J. W. (1950). Cenozoic marine climates of the Pacific coast. *Bulletin of the Geological Society of America, 61,* 1243–1264.

Ebbesson, S. E. E., & Northcutt, R. G. (1976). Neurology of anamniotic vertebrates. In R. B. Masterton, M. E. Bitterman, C. B. G. Campbell, & N. Hotton (Eds.), *Evolution of brain and behaviour in vertebrates* (pp. 115–146). Hillsdale, NJ: Lawrence Erlbaum Associates.

Ebner, F. F. (1976). The forebrain of reptiles and mammals. In R. B. Masterton, M. E. Bitterman, C. B. G. Campbell, & N. Hotton (Eds.), *Evolution of brain and behaviour in vertebrates* (pp. 147–168). Hillsdale, NJ: Lawrence Erlbaum Associates.

Edwards, J. S. (1977). One organism, several brains: Evolution and development of the insect central nervous system. In S. J. Dimond & D. A. Blizard (Eds.), Evolution and lateralisation of the brain. *Annals of the New York Academy of Sciences, 299,* 59–71.

Eldridge, N., & Stanley, S. M. (Eds.). (1984). *Living fossils.* New York: Springer-Verlag.

Emilliani, C. (1961). Cenozoic climate changes as indicated by the stratigraphy and chronology of deep sea cores of Globigerina ooze facies. *Annals of the New York Academy of Science, 95,* 521–536.

Engelhardt, F., Woodward, W. T., & Bitterman, M. E. (1973). Discrimination reversal in the goldfish as a function of training conditions. *Journal of Comparative and Physiological Psychology, 85,* 144–150.

Erickson, R. P., Jane, J. A., Waite, R., & Diamond, I. T. (1964). Single neuron investigation of sensory thalamus of the opossum. *Journal of Neurophysiology, 27,* 1026–1047.

Ewert, J. P., Capranica, R. P., & Ingle, D. J. (Eds.). (1983). *Advances in vertebrate neurethology.* New York: Plenum Press.

Fitzpatrick, D., Itoh, K., & Diamond, I. T. (1983). The laminar organization of the lateral geniculate body and the striate cortex in the squirrel monkey (*Saimiri sciureus*). *The Journal of Neuroscience, 3,* 673–702.

Flaherty, C. F., & Largen, J. (1975). Within-subjects positive and negative contrast effects in rats. *Journal of Comparative and Physiological Psychology, 58,* 653–664.

Fletcher, H. J. (1965). The delayed response problem. In A. M. Schrier, H. F. Harlow, & F. Stollnitz (Eds.), *Behavior of non human primates* (Vol. 1, pp. 129–165). New York: Academic Press.

Franz, S. I., & Gordon, K. (1933). *Psychology.* New York: McGraw-Hill.

Frisch, K. Von. (1950). *Bees, their vision, chemical senses and language.* New York: Ithaca.

Frisch, K. Von. (1967). Honeybees: Do they use direction and distance information provided by their dancers? *Science, 158,* 1072–1076.

Galton, F. (1869). *Hereditary genius: An inquiry into its laws and consequences.* London: Macmillan.

Gardner, R. A., & Gardner, B. T. (1969). Teaching sign language to chimpanzee. *Science, 165,* 664–672.

Gartner, S., & McGuirk, J. P. (1979). Terminal cretaceous extinction. Scenario for a catastrophe. *Science, 206,* 1272–1276.

Gellermann, L. W. (1931a). The double alternation problem. I. The behavior of monkeys in a double alternation temporal maze. *Journal of Genetic Psychology, 39,* 50–72.

Gellermann, L. W. (1931b). The double alternation problem. II. The behavior of children and human adults in a double alternation temporal maze. *Journal of Genetic Psychology, 39,* 197–226.

Gellermann, L. W. (1931c). The double alternation problem. III. The behavior of monkeys in a double alternation box apparatus. *Journal of Genetic Psychology, 39,* 359–392.

Gilbert, R. M., & Sutherland, N. S. (Eds.). (1969). *Animal discrimination learning.* New York: Academic Press.

Gingerich, P. D. (1973). Anatomy of the temporal bone in the Oligocene anthropoid, *Apidium* and the origin of Anthropodia. *Folia primatologia, 19,* 329–337.

Glass, D. C. (Ed.). (1967). *Neurophysiology and emotion.* New York: Rockefeller University Press.

Glendenning, K. K., Hall, J. A., Diamond, I. T., & Hall, W. C. (1975). The pulvinar nucleus of *Galago senegalensis. Journal of Comparative Neurology, 161,* 419–458.

Glendenning, K. K., Kofron, E. A., & Diamond, I. T. (1976). Laminar organization of projections of the lateral geniculate nucleus to the striate cortex in Galago. *Brain Research, 105,* 538–546.

Glickman, S. E., & Schiff, B. B. (1967). A biological theory of reinforcement. *Psychological Review, 74,* 81–109.

Goldstein, M. L. (1968). Physiological theories of emotion. A critical review from the standpoint of behavior theory. *Psychological Bulletin, 69,* 23–40.

Gollin, E. S., & Schadler, M. (1972). Relational learning and transfer in children. *Journal of Experimental Child Psychology, 14,* 219–232.

Gonzalez, R. C., Behrend, E. R., & Bitterman, M. E. (1967). Reversal learning and forgetting in bird and fish. *Science, 158,* 519–521.

Gonzalez, R. C., Roberts, W. A., & Bitternman, M. E. (1964). Learning in adult rats with extensive cortical lesions made in infancy. *American Journal of Psychology, 77,* 547–562.

Goodman, I. J., & Brown, J. L. (1966). Stimulation of positively and negatively reinforcing sites in the avian brain. *Life Sciences, 5,* 693–704.

Gossette, R. L. (1966). Comparison of successive discrimination reversal performances across 14 different avian and mammalian species. *American Zoologist, 6,* 175.

Gossette, R. L. (1967). Successive discrimination reversal (SDR) performances of four avian species on a brightness discrimination task. *Psychonomic Science, 8,* 17–18.

Gossette, R. L. (1968). Examination of retention decrement explanation of comparative successive discrimination reversal learning by birds and mammals. *Perceptual and Motor Skills, 27,* 1147–1152.

Gossette, R. L. (1969a). Roles of motivational and incentive levels in the control of successive discrimination reversal (SDR) performance in comparative analysis. *Perceptual and Motor Skills, 28,* 283–292.

Gossette, R. L. (1969b). Analysis of reversal and non-reversal training: Further examination of the retention decrement hypothesis. *Perceptual and Motor Skills, 29,* 171–178.

Gossette, R. L., Gossette, M., & Inman, N. (1966). Successive discrimination reversal performance by the Greater Hill Myna. *Animal Behavior, 14,* 50–53.

Gossette, R. L., & Gossette, M. F. (1967). Examination of the Reversal Index (RI) across fifteen mammalian and avian species. *Perceptual and Motor Skills, 24,* 987–990.

Gossette, R. L., Gossette, M. F., & Riddell, W. (1966). Comparisons of successive discrimination reversal performances among closely and remotely related avian species. *Animal Behavior, 14,* 560–564.

Gossette, R. L., & Hombach, A. (1969). Successive discrimination reversal (SDR) performances of American alligators and American crocodiles on a spatial task. *Perceptual and Motor Skills, 28,* 63–67.

Gossette, R. L., & Hood, P. (1967a). Successive discrimination reversal (SDR) performances of chickens, ringneck doves and Greater Hill Mynas as a function of correction as opposed to non-correction procedures. *Psychonomic Science, 8,* 361–362.

Gossette, R. L., & Hood, P. (1967b). The reversal index (RI) as a joint function of drive and incentive level. *Psychonomic Science, 8,* 217–218.

Gossette, R. L., & Hood, P. (1968). Successive discrimination reversal measures as a function of variation of motivational and incentive levels. *Perceptual and Motor Skills, 26,* 47–52.

Gossette, R. L., & Inman, N. (1966). Comparison of spatial successive discrimination reversal performances of two groups of new world monkeys. *Perceptual and Motor Skills, 23,* 169–170.

Gossette, R. L., & Kraus, G. (1968). Successive discrimination reversal performance of mammalian species on a brightness task. *Perceptual and Motor Skills, 27,* 675–678.

Grossman, S. P. (1967). *A textbook of physiological psychology.* New York: Wiley.

Grossman, S. P. (1979). The biology of motivation. *Annual Review of Psychology, 30,* 209–242.

Hall, C. S. (1951). Individual differences. In C. P. Stone (Ed.), *Comparative psychology* (pp.

363–387). New York: Prentice-Hall.

Hall, W. C., & Diamond, I. T. (1968). Organization and function of the visual cortex in hedgehog. I. Cortical cytoarchitecture and thalamic retrograde degeneration. *Brain, Behavior and Evolution, 1,* 181–214.

Harlow, H. F. (1949). The formation of learning sets. *Psychological Review, 56,* 51–65.

Harlow, H. F. (1958a). The evolution of learning. In A. Roe & G. G. Simpson (Eds.), *Behavior and evolution* (pp. 269–290). New Haven: Yale University Press.

Harlow, H. F. (1958b). Behavioral contributions to interdisciplinary research. In H. F. Harlow & C. N. Woolsey (Eds.), *Biological and biochemical bases of behavior* (pp. 3–23). Madison: University of Wisconsin Press.

Harlow, H. F., Harlow, M. K., & Meyer, D. R. (1950). Learning motivated by a manipulative drive. *Journal of Experimental Psychology, 40,* 228–234.

Harlow, H. F., & McClearn, G. E. (1954). Object discrimination learned by monkeys on the basis of manipulation motives. *Journal of Comparative and Physiological Psychology, 47,* 73–76.

Heath, R. G. (1964). Pleasure response of human subjects to direct stimulation of the brain: Physiologic and psychodynamic considerations. In R. G. Heath (Ed.), *The role of pleasure in behavior* (pp. 219–243). New York: Harper and Row.

Hebb, D. O. (1949). *The organization of behavior: A neuropsychological theory.* New York: Wiley.

Hebb, D. O., & Williams, K. (1946). A method of rating animal intelligence. *Journal of General Psychology, 34,* 59–65.

Herman, L. M., Beach, F. A., Pepper, R. L., & Stalling, R. B. (1969). Learning set formation in the bottlenose dolphin. *Psychonomic Science, 14,* 98–99.

Heron, W. T. (1927). The reliability of the inclined plane problem box as a method of measuring the learning ability of the rat. *Comparative Psychology Monographs, 1,* 1–36.

Hinde, R. A. (1973). Constraints on learning: An introduction to the problem. In R. A. Hinde & J. Stevenson-Hinde, *Constraints on learning: Limitations and predispositions* (pp. 1–20). London: Academic Press.

Hobhouse, L. T. (1926). *Mind in evolution.* London: Macmillan.

Hodgson, E. S. (1977). The evolutionary origin of the brain. In S. J. Diamond & D. A. Blizard (Eds.), Evolution and lateralisation of the brain. *Annals of the New York Academy of Sciences, 299,* 23–75.

Hodos, W. (1967). The concept of homology and the evolution of behaviour. In R. B. Masterton, W. Hodos, & H. Jerison (Eds.), *Evolution, brain and behaviour; persistent problems* (pp. 153–168). Hillsdale, NJ: Lawrence Erlbaum Associates.

Hodos, W. (1970). Evolutionary interpretation of neural and behavioral studies of living vertebrates. In F. O. Schmitt (Ed.), *The neurosciences second study program* (pp. 26–39). New York: Rockefeller University Press.

Hodos, W., & Campbell, C. B. (1969). *Scala naturae:* Why there is no theory in comparative psychology. *Psychological Review, 76,* 337–350.

Hoffman, H. (1966). The hippocampal and septal formations in Anurans. In R. Hassler & H. Stephan (Eds.), *Evolution of the forebrain: Phylogenesis and ontogenesis of the forebrain* (pp. 61–72). Stuttgart: Georg Thieme Verlag.

Holmes, P. A., & Bitterman, M. E. (1966). Spatial and visual habit reversal in the turtle. *Journal of Comparative and Physiological Psychology, 62,* 328–331.

Hopson, J. A. (1969). The origin and adaptive radiation of mammal-like reptiles and nontherian mammals. *Annals of the New York Academy of Sciences, 167,* 199–216.

Hotton, N. (1976). Origin and radiation of the classes of poikilothermous vertebrates. In R. B. Masterton, M. E. Bitterman, C. B. G. Campbell, & N. Hotton (Eds.), *Evolution of brain and behaviour in vertebrates* (pp. 1–24). Hillsdale, NJ: Lawrence Erlbaum Associates.

Hotton III, N. (1980). An alternative to Dinosaur endothermy: The happy wanderers. In R. D. K. Thomas & E. C. Olson. (Eds.) *A cold look at the warm-blooded dinosaurs* (pp. 311-350). Boulder: Westview Press.

Hull, C. L. (1945). The place of innate individual and species differences in a natural science theory of behavior. *Psychological Review, 52,* 55-60.

Humphrey, T. (1966). The development of the human hippocampal formation correlated with some aspects of its phylogenetic history. In R. Hassler & H. Stephan (Eds.), *Evolution of the forebrain: Phylogenesis and ontogenesis of the forebrain* (pp. 104-116). Stuttgart: Georg Thieme Verlag.

Hunter, W. S. (1917). The delayed reaction in a child. *Psychological Review, 24,* 74-87.

Hunter, W. S. (1920). The temporal maze and kinesthetic sensory processes in the white rat. *Psychobiology, 2,* 1-17.

Hunter, W. S. (1928). The behavior of racoons in a double alternation temporal maze. *Journal of Genetic Psychology, 35,* 374-388.

Hunter, W. S., & Nagge, J. W. (1931). The white rat and the double alternation temporal maze. *Journal of Genetic Psychology, 39,* 303-319.

Hunter, W. S., & Randolph, V. (1924). Further studies of the reliabilities of the maze with rats and humans. *Journal of Comparative Psychology, 4,* 431-442.

Itoh, K., Conley, M., & Diamond, I. T. (1982). Retinal ganglion cell projections to individual layers of the lateral geniculate body of *Galago crassicaudatus. The Journal of Comparative Neurology, 205,* 282-290.

Jacobson, M. (1970). Development, specification and diversification of neuronal connections. In F. O. Schmitt (Ed.), *The neurosciences: Second study program* (pp. 116-129). New York: Rockefeller University Press.

James, W. (1890). *The principles of psychology.* New York: Dover Publications.

Jeeves, M. A., & Winefield, A. H. (1969). Discrimination reversal skills in squirrel monkeys. The reversal index and the reversal-acquisition ratio compared. *Psychonomic Science, 14,* 221-222.

Jelinek, J. (1975). *Pictorial encyclopedia of the evolution of man.* London: Hamlyn.

Jerison, H. J. (1955). Brain to body ratio and the evolution of intelligence. *Science, 121,* 447-449.

Jerison, H. J. (1961). Quantitative analysis of evolution of the brain in mammals. *Science, 133,* 1012-1014.

Jerison, H. J. (1969). Brain evolution and dinosaur brains. *The American Naturalist, 103,* 575-588.

Jerison, H. J. (1973). *Evolution of brain and intelligence.* New York: Academic Press.

Johanson, D. C., & White, T. D. (1979). A systematic assessment of early African hominids. *Science, 203,* 321-330.

Johnson, J. I. (1961). Double alternation by racoons. *Journal of Comparative Physiological Psychology, 54,* 248-251.

Johnston, J. B. (1913). The morphology of the septum, hippocampus and pallial commissures in reptiles and mammals. *Journal of Comparative Neurology, 23,* 371-478.

Johnston, J. B. (1923). Further contributions to the study of the evolution of the forebrain. *Journal of Comparative Neurology, 35,* 337-481.

Jollie, M. (1977). The origin of the vertebrate brain. In S. J. Dimond & D. A. Blizard (Eds.), *Evolution and lateralization of the brain. Annals of the New York Academy of Sciences, 299,* 74-86.

Jolly, A. (1964). Choice of cue in prosimian learning. *Animal Behavior, 12,* 571-577.

Kluver, H. (1951). Functional differences between the occipital and temporal lobes. In L. A. Jeffress (Ed.), *Cerebral mechanisms of behaviour* (pp. 147-199). New York: Wiley.

Koestler, A. (1967). *The ghost in the machine.* London: Hutchinson.

Kohler, W. (1925). *The mentality of apes*. New York: Harcourt, Brace.

Koffka, K. (1924). *The growth of mind*. London: Kegan.

Konorski, J. (1967). *Integrative activity of the brain*. Chicago: University of Chicago Press.

Koronakos, C., & Arnold, W. J. (1957). The formation of learning sets in rats. *Journal of Comparative and Physiological Psychology, 50*, 11–14.

Kosmal, A. (1976). Efferent connections of the basolateral amygdaloid part to the archipaleo and neocortex in dogs. *Acta Neurobiologia Experimentalis, 36*, 319–331.

Krantz, G. S. (1975). The double descent of man. In R. H. Tuttle (Ed.), *Paleoanthropology: Morphology and paleoecology* (pp. 131–181). The Hague: Moulton.

Krettek, J. E., & Price, J. L. (1977). Projections from the amygdaloid complex to the cerebral cortex and thalamus in the rat and cat. *The Journal of Comparative Neurology, 172*, 687–722.

Kulp, J. L. (1961). Geologic time scale. *Science, 133*, 1105.

Lacey, J. I., & Lacey, B. C. (1970). Some autonomic-central nervous system interrelationships. In P. Black (Ed.), *Physiological correlates of emotion* (pp. 205–228). New York: Academic Press.

Lashley, K. S. (1915). Notes on the nesting activities of the Noddy and Sooty terns. *Carnegie Institution Publications, 7*, 61–83. Reprinted in F. A. Beach, D. O. Hebb, C. T. Morgan, & H. W. Nissen (Eds.) (1960), *The neuropsychology of Lashley* (pp. 1–23). New York: McGraw-Hill.

Lashley, K. S. (1929). *Brain mechanisms and intelligence*. Chicago: University of Chicago Press.

Lashley, K. S. (1949). Persistent problems in the evolution of mind. *Quarterly Review of Biology, 24*, 28–42. Reprinted in F. A. Beach, D. O. Hebb, C. T. Morgan, & H. W. Nissen (Eds.) (1960), *The neuropsychology of Lashley* (pp. 455–477). New York: McGraw-Hill.

Lashley, K. S. (1951). A problem of serial order in behavior. In L. A. Jeffress (Ed.), *Cerebral mechanisms in behavior* (pp. 112–136). New York: Wiley.

Lazarus, R. (1982). Thoughts on the relations between emotion and cognition. *American Psychologist, 37*, 1019–1024.

Leakey, M. D., Clarke, R. J., & Leakey, L. S. B. (1971). New hominid skull from Bed 1. Olduvai Gorge, Tanzania. *Nature (London), 232*, pp. 308–312.

Leakey, R. E. F. (1973). Evidence for an advanced Plio-Pleistocene hominid from East Randolph, Kenya. *Nature (London), 242*, 447–450.

Leakey, R. E. F. (1981). *The making of mankind*. London: Michael Joseph Ltd.

Leary, R. W., Harlow, H. F., Settlage, P. H., & Greenwood, D. D. (1952). Performance on double alternation problems by normal and brain injured monkeys. *Journal of Comparative and Physiological Psychology, 45*, 576–584.

Le Gros Clark, W. E. (1955). *The fossil evidence for human evolution: An introduction to the study of paleoanthropology*. Chicago: University of Chicago Press.

Le Gros Clark, W. E. (1967). *Man-apes or ape-men? The stories of discoveries in Africa*. New York: Holt.

Le Gros Clark, W. E. (1971). *The antecedents of man*. (3rd Ed.). Chicago: Quadrangle Books.

Le Gros Clark, W. E., & Boggon, R. H. (1933a). On the connections of the medial cell groups of the thalamus. *Brain, 56*, 83.

Le Gros Clark, W. E., & Boggon, R. H. (1933b). On the connections of the anterior nucleus of the thalamus. *Journal of Anatomy, 67*, 215.

Lende, R. A. (1964). Representation in the cerebral cortex of a primitive mammal. Sensorimotor, visual and auditory fields in the echidna (*Tachyglossus aculeatus*). *Journal of Neurophysiology, 27*, 37–48.

Lende, R. A. (1969). A comparative approach to the neocortex. Localization in monotremes, marsupials and insectivores. *Annals of the New York Academy of Sciences, 167*, 262–276.

Lende, R. A., & Sadler, R. M. (1967). Sensory and motor areas in neocortex in hedgehog (*Erinaceus*). *Brain Research, 5*, 390–405.

Leonard, C. M. (1969). The prefrontal cortex of the rat. I. Cortical projections of the mediodor-sal nucleus. II. Efferent connections. *Brain Research, 12,* 321-343.

Leonard, C. M. (1972). The connections of the dorsomedial nuclei. *Brain, Behavior and Evolution, 6,* 524-542.

Lewin, R. (1982). How did humans evolve big brains. *Science, 216,* 840-841.

Lillegraven, J. A., Kielan-Jaworowska, Z., & Clemens, W. A. (1979). *Mesozoic mammals: The first two-thirds of mammalian history.* Berkely: University of California Press.

Lilly, J. C. (1958). Learning motivated by subcortical stimulation. The "start" and "stop" patterns of behavior. In H. H. Jasper, L. D. Procter, S. Knighton, W. C. Noshky, & R. T. Costello (Eds.), *Reticular formation of the brain* (pp. 705-721). Boston: Little Brown.

Lilly, J. C., & Miller, A. M. (1962). Operant conditioning of the bottle nose dolphin with electrical stimulation of the brain. *Journal of Comparative and Physiological Psychology, 55,* 73-79.

Lindsley, D. B. (1951). Emotion. In S. S. Stevens (Ed.), *Handbook of experimental psychology* (pp. 473-516). New York: Wiley.

Livesey, P. J. (1965). Comparison of double alternation performance of white rats, rabbits and cats. *Journal of Comparative and Physiological Psychology, 59,* 155-158.

Livesey, P. J. (1966). The rat, rabbit and cat in the Hebb-Williams Closed Field test of intelligence. *Australian Journal of Psychology, 18,* 71-79.

Livesey, P.J. (1967). The Hebb-Williams Elevated Pathway test—a comparative study of rat, rabbit and cat performance. *Australian Journal of Psychology, 19,* 55-62.

Livesey, P. J. (1968). A discrimination generalization task as a test of cognitive ability in animals. *Australian Journal of Psychology, 20,* 49-54.

Livesey, P. J. (1969). Double and single alternation learning by rhesus monkeys. *Journal of Comparative and Physiological Psychology, 67,* 526-530.

Livesey, P. J. (1970). A consideration of the neural basis of intelligent behavior: Comparative studies. *Behavioral Science, 15,* 164-170.

Livesey, P. J., Han, M. F., Lowe, H., & Feakes, R. (1972). Automated apparatus for the study of learning in monkey and rat. *Australian Journal of Psychology, 24,* 211-218.

Livesey, P. J., & Little, A. (1971). Sequential learning by children. *Journal of Genetic Psychology, 118,* 33-38.

Livingston, K. E. (1978). A casual glimpse of evolution and development relating to the limbic system. In K. E. Livingston & O. Hornykiewicz. *Limbic mechanisms: The continuing evolution of the limbic system concept* (pp. 17-22). New York: Plenum Press.

Lockard, R. B. (1971). Reflections on the fall of comparative psychology: Is there a message for us all? *American Psychologist, 26,* 168-179.

Lorenz, K. Z. (1965). *Evolution and modification of behavior.* Chicago: University of Chicago Press.

Lorenz, K. Z. (1969). Innate bases of learning. In K. H. Pribram (Ed.), *On the biology of learning* (pp. 13-93). New York: Harcourt, Brace and World.

Lorenz, K. Z. (1981). *The foundations of ethology.* New York: Springer-Verlag.

Lovejay, C. O. (1981). The origin of man. *Science, 211,* 341-350.

Lowes, G., & Bitterman, M. E. (1967). Reward and learning in the goldfish. *Science, 157,* 455-457.

Luria, A. R. (1966a). *Higher cortical functions in man.* London: Tavistock.

Luria, A. R. (1966b). *Human brain and psychological processes* (B. Haigh, Trans). New York: Harper & Row (Original work published 1963).

Luria, A. R. (1973). *The working brain.* London: Allen Lane, The Penguin Press.

McCullock, T. C. (1935). A study of the cognitive abilities of the white rat with special reference to Spearman's theory of two factors. *Contributions to Psychological Theory, 1,* 66.

Mackintosh, N. J. (1969). Comparative studies of reversal and probability learning: Rats, birds and fish. In R. M. Gilbert & N. S. Sutherland (Ed.), *Animal discrimination learning* (pp. 137-162). New York: Academic Press.

Mackintosh, N. J., McGonigle, B., Holgate, V., & Vanderver, V. (1968). Factors underlying improvement in serial reversal learning. *Canadian Journal of Psychology, 22*, 85-95.

MacLean, P. D. (1949). Psychosomatic disease and the "visceral brain." Recent developments bearing on the Papez theory of emotion. *Psychosomatic Medicine*, 11, 338-353. Reprinted in R. L. Isaacson (Ed.). (1964), *Basic readings in neuropsychology* (pp. 181-211). New York: Harper & Row.

MacLean, P. D. (1967). The brain in relation to empathy and medical education. *Journal of Nervous and Mental Disease, 144*, 374-382.

MacLean, P. D. (1970a). The triune brain: emotion and scientific bias. In F. O. Schmitt (Ed.). *The neurosciences: Second study programme* (pp. 336-349). New York: Rockefeller University Press.

MacLean, P. D. (1970b). The limbic brain in relation to the psychoses. In P. Black (Ed.), *Physiological correlates of emotion* (pp. 130-146). New York: Academic Press.

MacLean, P. D. (1973). A Triune concept of the brain and behavior. Toronto: University of Toronto Press.

McLoughlin, J. C. (1979). *Archosauria: A new look at the old dinosaur.* London: Allen Lane.

Malmo, R. B. (1959). Activation: A neuropsychological dimension. *Psychological Review, 66*, 367-386.

Mandler, G. (1975). *Mind and emotion.* New York: Wiley.

Mandler, G. (1980). The generation of emotion: A psychological theory. In R. Plutchik & H. Kellerman (Eds.), *Emotion: Theory, research and experience, Vol. 1, Theories of emotion* (pp. 219-243). New York: Academic Press.

Menzel, R., & Bitterman, M. E. (1983). Learning in honeybees in an unnatural situation. In F. Huber & H. Markl (Eds.), *Neuroethology and behavioural physiology* (pp. 206-218). Berlin: Springer-Verlag.

Meyer, D. R., Treichler, F. R., & Meyer, P. M. (1965). Discrete trial training techniques and stimulus variables. In A. M. Schrier, H. F. Harlow, & F. Stollnitz (Eds.), *Behavior of nonhuman primates: Modern research trends* (Vol. 1, pp. 1-49). New York: Academic Press.

Meyer, J. (1981). A quantitative comparison of the parts of the brains of two Australian marsupials and some eutherian mammals. *Brain, Behaviour and Evolution, 18*, 60-71.

Meyers, W. J., McQuiston, M. D., & Miles, R. C. (1962). Delayed response and learning set performance of cats. *Journal of Comparative and Physiological Psychology, 25* 515-517.

Miles, R. C. (1957a). Delayed response learning in the marmoset and macaque. *Journal of Comparative and Physiological Psychology, 50*, 352-355.

Miles, R. C. (1957b). Learning set formation in the squirrel monkey. *Journal of Comparative and Physiological Psychology, 50*, 356-357.

Miles, R. C., & Blomquist, A. J. (1960). Frontal lesions and behavioral deficits in monkeys. *Journal of Neurophysiology, 23*, 471-484.

Miles, W. R. (1930). The comparative learning of rats on elevated and alley mazes of the same pattern. *Journal of Comparative Psychology, 10*, 237-261.

Miller, G. A., Galanter, E., & Pribram, K. H. (1960). *Plans and the structure of behavior.* New York: Henry Holt.

Miller, N. E. (1951). Learnable drives and rewards. In S. S. Stevens (Ed.), *Handbook of experimental psychology* (pp. 435-473). New York: Wiley.

Miller, N. E. (1971). *Selected papers on conflict displacement, learned drives and theory,* Chicago: Aldine-Atherton.

Morgan, E. (1973). *The descent of woman.* New York: Bantam Press.

Mowrer, O. H. (1960). *Learning theory and behavior.* New York: Wiley.

Munn, N. L. (1931). An apparatus for testing visual discrimination in animals. *Journal of Genetic Psychology, 39*, 342–358.

Munn, N. L. (1950). *Handbook of psychological research on the rat.* New York: Houghton Mifflin.

Nauta, W. J. H. (1964). Some efferent connections of the prefrontal cortex in the monkey. In J. M. Warren & K. Akert (Eds.). *The frontal granular cortex and behavior* (pp. 397–409). New York: McGraw-Hill.

Nieuwenhuys, R. (1977). The brain of the lamprey in a comparative perspective. In S. J. Dimond & D. A. Blizard (Eds.), Evolution and lateralisation of the brain. *Annals of the New York Academy of Sciences, 299*, 97–145.

Nissen, H. W. (1951). Analysis of conditioned reaction in chimpanzees. *Journal of Comparative and Physiological Psychology, 44*, 9–16.

Novacek, M. (1984). Evolutionary stasis in the elephant-shrew *Rhynchocyon.* In N. Eldridge & S. M. Stanley (Eds.), *Living fossils* (pp. 4–22). New York: Springer-Verlag.

Olds, J. A. (1956). A preliminary mapping of electrical reinforcing effects in the rat brain. *Journal of Comparative and Physiological Psychology, 49*, 281–285.

Olds, J. (1958). Self stimulation of the brain. *Science, 127*, 315–324.

Olds, J. (1969). The central nervous system and the reinforcement of behavior. *American Psychologist, 24*, 114–132.

Olds, J., & Milner, P. (1954). Positive reinforcement produced by electrical stimulation of septal area and other regions of rat. *Journal of Comparative and Physiological Psychology, 47*, 419–427.

Olds, J., & Olds, M. E. (1964). The mechanisms of voluntary behavior. In R. C. Heath (Ed.), *The role of pleasure in behavior* (pp. 23–53). New York: Harper and Row.

Olson, E. C. (1971). *Vertebrate paleozoology.* New York: Wiley Interscience.

Orbach, J., & Fischer, G. J. (1959). Bilateral resections of frontal granular cortex. *A.M.A. Archives of Neurology, 1*, 78–86.

Pandya, D. N., Van Hoesen, G. W., & Domesick, V. B. (1973). A cinguloamygdaloid projection in the rhesus monkey. *Brain Research, 61*, 369–373.

Papez, J. W. (1937). A proposed mechanism of emotion. *Archives of Neurology and Psychiatry, 38*, 715–744. Reprinted in Isaccson, R. L. (Ed.). (1964). *Basic readings in neuropsychology* (pp. 87–109). New York: Harper and Row.

Passingham, R. E. (1973). Anatomical differences between the neocortex of man and other primates. *Brain, Behavior and Evolution, 7*, 337–359.

Passingham, R. E. (1975). Changes in the size and organization of the brain in man and his ancestors. *Brain, Behavior and Evolution, 11*, 73–90.

Pearson, R. (1964). *Animals and plants of the Cenozoic era. Some aspects of the faunal and floral history of the last sixty million years.* London: Butterworth.

Penny, G. R., Itoh, K., & Diamond, I. T. (1982). Cells of different sizes in the ventral nuclei project to different layers of the somatic cortex in the cat. *Brain Research, 242*, 55–65.

Pilbeam, D. R. (1978). Human origins. In D. E. Hunter & P. Whitten (Eds.), *Readings in physical anthropology and archaeology* (pp. 99–107). New York: Harper and Row.

Plotnik, R. J., & Tallarico, R. B. (1966). Object-quality learning-set formation in the young chicken. *Psychonomic Science, 5*, 195–196.

Plutchik, R. (1958). Outlines of a new theory of emotion. *Transactions of the New York Academy of Sciences, 20*, 394–403.

Plutchik, R. (1980a). *Emotion: A psychoevolutionary synthesis.* New York: Harper and Row.

Plutchik, R. (1980b). A general psychoevolutionary theory of emotion. In R. Plutchik & H. Kellerman (Eds.), *Emotion: Theory research and practice* (pp. 3–34). New York: Academic Press.

Plutchik, R. (1980c). Measurement implications of a psychoevolutionary theory of emotions. In K. R. Blankstein, P. Pliner, & J. Polivy (Eds.), *Assessment and modification of emotional behavior* (pp. 47–70). New York: Plenum.

Plutchik, R., & Kellerman, H. (Eds.). (1980). *Emotion: Theory, research and experience.* New York: Academic Press.

Polivy, J. (1980). Measuring and modifying moods: An introduction. In K. R. Blankstein, P. Pliner, & J. Polivy (Eds.), *Assessment and modification of emotional behavior* (pp. 1–7). New York: Plenum.

Pollack, J. B., Toon, O. B., Ackerman, T. P., McKay, C. P., & Turco, R. P. (1983). Environmental effects of an impact-generated dust cloud: Implications for the Cretaceous-Tertiary extinctions. *Science, 219,* 287–289.

Pollard, J. S. (1961). Rats and cats in the Closed Field test. *Australian Journal of Psychology, 13,* 215–221.

Pollard, J. S. (1963). More rats and cats in the Closed Field test. *Australian Journal of Psychology, 15,* 52–56.

Prasad, K. N. (1975). Observations on the paleocology of south asian tertiary primates. In R. H. Tuttle (Ed.), *Paleoanthropology: Morphology and paleoecology* (pp. 21–30). The Hague: Mouton.

Premack, D. (1970). The education of Sarah: A chimp learns the language. *Psychology Today, 4,* 55–58.

Premack, D. (1971). Language in the chimpanzee? *Science, 172,* 808–822.

Pribram, K. H. (1958a). Comparative neurology and the evolution of behaviour. In A. Roe & G. G. Simpson (Eds.), *Behaviour and evolution* (pp. 140–164). New Haven: Yale University Press.

Pribram, K. H. (1958b). Neocortical function in behavior. In H. F. Harlow & C. N. Woolsey (Eds.), *Biological and biochemical bases of behavior* (pp. 151–172). Madison: University of Wisconsin Press.

Pribram, K. H. (1960). Review of theory in physiological psychology. *Annual Review of Psychology, 11,* 1–40.

Pribram, K. H. (1967a). The new neurology and the biology of emotion: A structural approach. *American Psychologist, 22,* 830–838.

Pribram, K. H. (1967b). The limbic system, efferent control of neuronal inhibition and behavior. In T. Tokizane & W. G. Adey (Eds.), *Progress in brain research, Vol. 27, Structure and function of the limbic system* (pp. 318–336). Amsterdam: Elsevier.

Pribram, K. H. (1969). Neural servosystems and structure of personality. *The Journal of Nervous and Mental Disease, 149,* 30–39.

Pribram, K. H. (1970). Feelings as monitors. In M. B. Arnold (Ed.), *Feelings and emotions* (pp. 41–53). New York: Academic Press.

Pribram, K. H. (1971). *Languages of the brain.* Englewood Cliffs: Prentice-Hall.

Pribram, K. H. (1976). Self consciousness and intentionality. In G. E. Schwartz & D. Shapiro (Eds.), *Consciousness and self regulation* (Vol. 1, pp. 51–100). New York: Plenum Press.

Pribram, K. H. (1977). *Languages of the brain experimental paradoxes and principles in neuropsychology.* Monterey: Brooks/Cole.

Pribram, K. H. (1980a). Cognition and performance: The relation to neural mechanisms of consequence, confidence and competence. In *Biology of reinforcement* (pp. 11–36). New York: Academic Press.

Pribram, K. H. (1980b). The biology of emotions and other feelings. In R. Plutchik & H. Kellerman (Eds.), *Emotion: Theory, research and experience* (pp. 245–270). New York: Academic Press.

Pribram, K. H. (1981). Emotions. In S. B. Filskov & T. J. Bell (Eds.), *Handbook of clinical neuropsychology* (pp. 102–134). New York: Wiley.

Pribram, K. H. (1984). Brain systems and cognitive learning processes. In H. L. Roitblat, T. G. Bever, & H. S. Terrace (Eds.), *Animal Cognition Proceedings of the Harry Frank Guggenheim Conference, June 2-4, 1982* (pp. 627-656). Hillsdale, NJ: Lawrence Erlbaum Associates.

Pribram, K. H., Chow, K. L., & Semmes, J. (1953). Limit and organization of the cortical projection from the medial thalamic nucleus in monkeys. *Journal of Comparative Neurology, 98*, 433-448.

Pribram, K. H., & McGuinness, D. (1975). Arousal, activation and effort in the control of attention. *Psychological Review, 82,* 116-149.

Pribram, K. H., Mishkin, M., Rosvold, H. E., & Kaplan, S. J. (1952). Effects on delayed response performance of lesions of dorsolateral and ventromedial cortex of baboons. *Journal of Comparative and Physiological Psychology, 45,* 565-575.

Pritchard, P. C. H. (1967). *Living turtles of the world.* T. F. H. Publications.

Raczkowski, D. (1975). Primate evolution: Were traits selected for arboreal locomotion or visually directed predation? *Science, 187,* 455-456.

Razkowski, D., & Diamond, I. T. (1980). Cortical connections of the pulvinar nucleus in *Galago. The Journal of Comparative Neurology, 193,* 1-40.

Radinsky, L. B. (1970). The fossil evidence of prosimian brain evolution. In C. R. Norback & W. Montagna (Eds.), *Advances in primatology Volume I, The primate brain* (pp. 209-224). New York: Appleton-Century-Crofts.

Radinsky, L. (1973). Evolution of the canid brain. *Brain, Behavior and Evolution, 7,* 169-202.

Radinsky, L. B. (1975). Evolution of the felid brain. *Brain, Behavior and Evolution, 11,* 214-254.

Radinsky, L. B. (1976). Later mammal radiations. In R. B. Masterton, M. E. Bitterman, C. B. G. Campbell, & N. Hotton (Eds.), *Evolution of brain and behavior in vertebrates* (pp. 227-244). Hillsdale, NJ: Lawrence Erlbaum Associates.

Radinsky, L. (1977). Early primate brains: Fact and fiction. *Journal of Human Evolution, 6,* 79-86.

Radinsky, L. (1981). Brain evolution in extinct South American ungulates. *Brain, Behavior and Evolution, 18,* 169-187.

Rajalakshami, R., & Jeeves, M. A. (1965). The relative difficulty of reversal learning (reversal index) as a basis of behavioural comparisons. *Animal Behaviour, 13,* 203-211.

Ratner, S. C., & Miller, K. R. (1959). Classical conditioning in earthworms *Lumbricus terrestris. Journal of Comparative and Physiological Psychology, 52* 102-105.

Razran, G. (1961). The observable unconscious and inferable conscious in current Soviet psychology. Introceptive conditioning, semantic conditioning and the orienting reflex. *Psychological Review, 68,* 81-147.

Razran, G. (1971). *Mind in evolution: An east-west synthesis of learned behaviour and cognition.* Boston: Houghton Mifflin.

Rensch, B. (1956). Increase of learning capacity with increase of brain size. *American Naturalist, 90,* 81-95.

Rensch, B. (1959). *Evolution above the species level.* London: Methuen.

Riss, W., Halpern, M., & Scalia, F. (1969). The quest for clues to forebrain evolution — the study of reptiles. *Brain, Behavior and Evolution, 2,* 1-50.

Romer, A. S. (1966). *Vertebrate paleontology.* Chicago: University of Chicago Press.

Rose, J. E., & Woolsey, C. N. (1948). Structure and relations of limbic cortex and anterior thalamus nuclei in rabbit and cat. *Journal of Comparative Neurology, 89,* 279-347.

Rosen, A. J., Glass, D. H., & Ison, J. R. (1967). Amobarbital sodium and instrumental performance changes following reward reduction. *Psychonomic Science, 9,* 129-130.

Ross, D. M. (1965). The behavior of sessile coelenterates in relation to some conditioning experiments. *Journal of Animal Behavior,* Supplement 1, 43-53.

Royce, J. R. (1950). The factorial analysis of animal behavior. *Psychological Bulletin, 47,*

235-259.

Rumbaugh, D. M. (Ed.). (1977). *Language learning by a chimpanzee: The Lana project.* New York: Academic Press.

Rumbaugh, D. M., & Jeeves, M. A. (1966). A comparison of two discrimination-reversal indices intended for use with diverse groups of organisms. *Psychonomic Science, 6,* 1-2.

Rumbaugh, D. M., & Pournelle, M. B. (1966). Discrimination-reversal skills of primates. The reversal/acquisition ratio as a function of phyletic standing. *Psychonomic Science, 4* 45-46.

Sanides, F. (1969). Comparative architectonics of the neocortex of mammals and their evolutionary interpretation. *Annals of the New York Academy of Sciences, 167,* 404-423.

Sanides, F. (1970). Functional architecture of motor and sensory cortices in primates in the light of a new concept of neocortex evolution. In E. R. Noback & W. Montagna (Eds.), *Advances in primatology: Volume I. The primate brain* (pp. 137-208). New York: Appleton-Century-Crofts.

Schachter, S., & Singer, J. E. (1962). Cognitive, social and physiological determinants of emotional state. *Psychological Review, 69,* 379-399.

Schaeffer, B. (1969). Adaptive radiation of fishes and the fish-amphibian transition. *Annals of the New York Academy of Sciences, 167,* 5-17.

Schneirla, T. C. (1929). Learning and orientation in ants. *Comparative Psychology Monographs, 6*(30), 143.

Schneirla, T. C. (1943). The nature of ant learning 2. The intermediate stage of segmental maze adjustment. *Journal of Comparative Psychology, 35,* 149-172.

Schneirla, T. C. (1949). Levels in the psychological capacities of animals. In R. W. Sellars, V. J. McGill, & M. Faber (Eds.), *Philosophy for the future* (pp. 243-286). New York: Macmillan.

Schneirla, T. C. (1957). The concept of development in comparative psychology. In D. B. Harris (Ed.), *The concept of development* (pp. 78-108). Minneapolis: University of Minnesota Press.

Schneirla, T. C. (1966). Behavioural development and comparative psychology. *The Quarterly Review of Biology, 41,* 283-302.

Schnitzlein, H. N. (1966). The primordial amygdaloid complex of the African lungfish, Protopterus. In R. Hassler & H. Stephan (Eds.), *Evolution of the forebrain: Phylogenesis and ontogenesis of the forebrain* (pp. 40-49). Stuttgart: Georg Thieme Verlag.

Seligman, M. E. P. (1970). On the generality of the laws of learning. *Psychological Review, 77,* 406-418.

Setterington, R. G., & Bishop, H. E. (1967). Habit reversal improvement in the fish. *Psychonomic Science, 7,* 41-42.

Shariff, G. A. (1953). Cell counts in the primate cerebral cortex. *Journal of Comparative Neurology, 98,* 381-400.

Shell, W F., & Riopelle, A. J. (1957). Multiple discrimination learning in racoons. *Journal of Comparative and Physiological Psychology, 50,* 585-587.

Shettleworth, S. J. (1972). Constraints on learning. In D. S. Lehrman, R. A. Hinde, & E. Shaw (Eds.) *Advances in the study of behavior, Vol. 4,* (pp. 1-68). New York: Academic Press.

Simons, E. L. (1964). The early relatives of man. *Scientific American, 211,* 50-62.

Simons, E. L. (1969). The origin and radiation of primates. *Annals of the New York Academy of Sciences, 167,* 319-331.

Simons, E. L. (1976). Primate radiations and the origin of hominoids. In R. B. Masterton, M. E. Bitterman, C. B. G. Campbell, & N. Hotton (Eds.), *Evolution of brain and behavior in vertebrates* (pp. 383-391). Hillsdale, NJ: Lawrence Erlbaum Associates.

Simpson, G. G. (1953). *The major features of evolution.* New York: Columbia Press.

Simpson, G. G. (1958). The study of evolution: Methods and present status of theory. In A. Roe & G. G. Simpson (Eds.), *Behaviour and evolution* (pp. 7-26). New Haven: Yale University Press.

Simpson, G. G. (1965). *The geography of evolution.* New York: Capricorn.

Simpson, G. G. (1967). *The meaning of evolution.* New Haven: Yale University Press.

Skinner, B. F. (1935). *The behavior of organisms: An experimental analysis.* New York: Appleton-Century-Crofts.

Snyder, M., & Diamond, I. T. (1968). The organization and function of the visual cortex in the tree shrew. *Brain, Behavior and Evolution, 1,* 244–288.

Spencer, H. (1870). *The principles of psychology* (Vol. 1, 2nd ed.). New York: Appleton.

Spinar, Z. V. (1972). *Life before man.* Illustrated by Z. Burian. New York: Heritage Press (Division of McGraw-Hill), Prague: Artia, London: Thames-Hudson Ltd.

Spinelli, D. N., & Pribram, K. H. (1966). Changes in visual recovery functions produced by temporal lobe stimulation in monkeys. *Electroencephalography and Clinical Neurophysiology, 20,* 44–49.

Spinelli, D. N., & Pribram, K. H. (1967). Changes in visual recovery function and unit activity produced by frontal cortex stimulation. *Electroencephalography and Clinical Neurophysiology, 22,* 143–149.

Squier, L. H. (1969). Reversal learning improvement in the fish *Astonotus ocellatus (Oscar). Psychonomic Science, 14,* 143–144.

Stahl, B. J. (1977). Early and recent primitive brain forms. In S. J. Dimond & D. A. Blizard (Eds.), Evolution and lateralisation of the brain. *Annals of the New York Academy of Sciences, 299,* 87–96.

Stark, P., & Boyd, E. S. (1963). Effect of cholinergic drugs on hypothalamic self-stimulation response rates of dogs. *American Journal of Physiology, 205,* 745–748.

Stearns, E. M., & Bitterman, M. E. (1965). A comparison of key-pecking with an ingestive technique for the study of discriminative learning in pigeons. *American Journal of Psychology, 78,* 48–56.

Stebbins, W. C. (1976). Comparative hearing function in the vertebrates. In R. B. Masterton, M. E. Bitterman, C. B. G. Campbell, & N. Hotton (Eds.), *Evolution of brain and behavior in vertebrates* (pp. 107–114). Hillsdale, NJ: Lawrence Erlbaum Associates.

Stephan, H., & Andy, O. J. (1969). Quantitative comparative neuroanatomy of primates: An attempt at phylogenetic interpretation. *Annals of the New York Academy of Sciences, 167,* 370–387.

Stephan, N., & Andy, O. J. (1977). Quantitative comparison of the amygdala in insectivores and primates. *Acta Anatomica, 95,* 130–153.

Stephan, H., Bauchot, R., & Andy, O. J. (1970). Data on the size of the brain and of various parts in insectivores and primates. In C. R. Norback & W. Montagna (Eds.), *Advances in primatology Volume I The primate brain* (pp. 289–297). New York: Appleton-Century-Crofts.

Stewart, C. N., & Warren, J. M. (1957). The behavior of cats on the double aternation problem. *Journal of Comparative and Physiological Psychology, 50,* 26–28.

Stone, C. P. (Ed.). (1951). Comparative psychology (3rd ed.). London: Staples.

Sutherland, N. S. (1960). Visual discrimination of orientation by octopus: Mirror images. *British Journal of Psychology, 51,* 9–18.

Sutherland, N. S., Mackintosh, N. J., & Mackintosh, J. (1963). Simultaneous discrimination of octopus and transfer of discrimination along a continuum. *Journal of Comparative and Physiological Psychology, 56,* 150–156.

Terrace, H. S., Petitto, L. A., Sanders, R. J., & Bever, T. G. (1979). Can an ape create a sentence? *Science, 206,* 891–892.

Thacker, L. A. (1950). An investigation of non-instrumental learning. *Journal of Comparative and Physiological Psychology, 43,* 86–98.

Thomas, R. D. K., & Olson, E. C. (Eds.). (1980). *A cold look at the warmblooded dinosaurs. An AAAS selected symposium.* Boulder: Westview Press.

Thompson, C. R., & Church, R. M. (1980). An explanation of the language of a chimpanzee. *Science, 208,* 313–314.

Thorndike, E. L. (1911). *Animal intelligence.* New York: Macmillan.

Thorndike, R. L. (1935). Organization of behavior in the albino rat. *Genetic Psychology Monographs, 17,* 1-70.

Thorpe, W. H. (1943). Types of learning in insects and other arthropods. *British Journal of Psychology, 33,* 220-234.

Thorpe, W. H. (1950). A note on detour experiments with *Ammophila pubescens. Behaviour, 12,* 257-263.

Thorpe, W. H. (1956). *Learning and instinct in animals.* London: Methuen.

Thorpe, W. H. (1961). Experimental studies of animal behaviour: Introduction to Part II. In W. H. Thorpe & O. L. Zangwill (Eds.), *Current problems in animal behaviour* (pp. 87-101). Cambridge: University Press.

Thurstone, L. L. (1933). *A simplified multiple factor method.* Ann Arbor: Edwards.

Tolman, E. C. (1932). *Purposive behavior in animals and man.* Berkeley: University of California Press.

Tomkins, S. (1962). *Affect, imagery, consciousness.* New York: Springer.

Tomkins, S. S. (1970). Affect as the primary motivational system. In M. B. Arnold (Ed.), *Feelings and emotions* (pp. 101-110). New York: Academic Press.

Tomkins, S. S. (1980). Affect as amplification: some modifications in theory. In R. Plutchik & H. Kellerman (Eds.), *Emotion: Theory, research and practice* (pp. 141-164). New York: Academic Press.

Tuddenham, R. D. (1962). The nature and measurement of intelligence. In L. Postman (Ed.), *Psychology in the making* (pp. 469-525). New York: A. A. Knopf.

Tuttle, R. H. (Ed.). (1975). *Paleoanthropology: Morphology and paleoecology.* The Hague: Mouton.

Tryon, R. C. (1930). Studies in individual differences in maze ability. II. The measurement of reliability of individual differences. *Journal of Comparative Psychology, 11,* 145-170.

Tryon, R. C. (1931). Studies in individual differences in maze ability. III. The community of function between two maze abilities. *Journal of Comparative Psychology, 12,* 95-115.

Tryon, R. C. (1942). Individual differences. In F. A. Moss (Ed.), *Comparative psychology.* (2nd ed., pp. 330-365). New York: Prentice-Hall.

Ursin, H. (1980). Affective and instrumental aspects of fear and aggression. In M. Koukkou, D. Lehmann, & J. Angst (Eds.), *Functional states of the brain: Their determinants* (pp. 119-130). Elsevier/North Holland: Biomedical Press.

Ursin, H. (1984). Neurophysiology of behaviour. In R. S. Anderson (Ed.), *Nutrition and behaviour in dogs and cats* (pp. 139-146). Oxford: Pergamon Press.

Van Steenberg, N. J. (1939). Factors in the learning behavior of the albino rat. *Psychometrika, 4,* 179-200.

Vaughn, C. L. (1937). Factors in rat learning. *Comparative Psychology Monographs, 14,* 1-41.

Viaud, G. (1960). *Intelligence: Its evolution and forms.* London: Arrow Books.

Vogel, C. (1975). Remarks on the reconstruction of the dental arcade of *Ramapithecus.* In R. H. Tuttle (Ed.), *Paleoanthropology: Morphology and paleoecology* (pp. 87-98). The Hague: Mouton.

Von Békésy, G. (1960). Experimental models of the cochlea with and without nerve supply. In G. L. Rasmussen & W. F. Windle (Eds.), *Neural mechanisms of the auditory and vestibular systems.* Springfield: Charles C. Thomas.

Von Bonin, G. (1937). Brain weight and body weight of mammals. *Journal of General Psychology, 16,* 379-389.

Voronin, L. G. (1962). Some results of comparative-physiological investigations of higher nervous activity. *Psychological Bulletin, 59,* 161-195.

Vowles, D. M. (1961). Neural mechanisms in insect behaviour. In W. H. Thorpe & O. L. Zangwill (Eds.), *Current problems in animal behaviour* (pp. 5-29). Cambridge University Press.

Waddington, C. H. (1959). Evolutionary systems: Animal and human. *Nature, 183,* 1634-1638.

Warden, C. J., Jenkins, T. N., & Warner, L. H. (1935). *Comparative psychology: A comprehensive treatise*. New York: Ronald Press.

Warren, J. M. (1961). Individual differences in discrimination learning by cats. *Journal of Genetic Psychology, 98*, 89–93.

Warren, J. M. (1965). Primate learning in comparative perspective. In A. M. Schrier, H. F. Harlow, & A. Stollnitz, *Behavior of non-human primates: Modern research trends (Vol. 1*, pp. 249–282). New York: Academic Press.

Warren, J. M. (1973). Learning in vertebrates. In D. A. Dewsbury & D. A. Rethlingshafer, *Comparative psychology: A modern survey* (pp. 471–509). New York: McGraw-Hill.

Warren, J. M., & Baron, A. (1956). The formation of learning sets by cats. *Journal of Comparative and Physiological Psychology, 49*, 227–231.

Warren, J. M., & Sinha, M. M. (1959). Interactions between learning sets in monkeys. *Journal of Genetic Psychology, 95*, 19–25.

Warren, J. M., Warren, H. B., & Akert, K. (1961). UMWEG learning by cats with lesions in the prestriate cortex. *Journal of Comparative and Physiological Psychology, 54*, 629–632.

Washburn, S. L. (1951). The analysis of primate evolution with particular reference to the origin of man. *Cold Spring Harbor Symposium on Quantitative Biology, 15*, 67–77.

Weinstein, B. (1955). The evolution of intelligent behavior in rhesus monkeys. *Genetic Psychology Monographs, 31*, 3–48.

Weiskrantz, L. (1961). Encophalisation and scotoma. In W. H. Thorpe & O. L. Zangwill (Eds.), *Current problems in animal behaviour* (pp. 30–58). Cambridge University Press.

Wells, M. J. (1961). What the octopus makes of it: Our world from another point of view. *American Scientist, 49*, 215–227.

Wever, E. G. (1976). Origin and evolution of the ear of vertebrates. In R. B. Masterton, M. E. Bitterman, C. B. G. Campbell, & N. Hotton (Eds.), *Evolution of brain and behavior in vertebrates* (pp. 89–105). Hillsdale, NJ: Lawrence Erlbaum Associates.

Wilcoxon, H. C. (1969). Introduction to the problem of reinforcement. In J. T. Tapp (Ed.), *Reinforcement and behavior* (pp. 2–46). New York: Academic Press.

Wilkinson, H. A., & Peele, T. L. (1963). Intracranial self stimulation in cats. *Journal of Comparative Neurology, 121*, 425–440.

Williams, K. A. (1929). The reward value of the conditioned stimulus. *University of California Publications in Psychology, 4*, 31–55.

Wilson, A. C., & Sarich, V. M. (1969). A molecular time scale for human evolution. *Proceedings of the National Academy of Science, 63*, 1088–1093.

Wine, J. J., & Krasne, F. B. (1972). The organisation of escape behaviour in the crayfish. *Journal of Experimental Biology, 56*, 1–18.

Winer, J. A., Diamond, I. T., & Raczkowski, D. (1977). Subdivisions of the auditory cortex of the cat. The retrograde transport of horeseradish peroxidase in the medial geniculate body and posterior thalamic nuclei. *The Journal of Comparative Neurology, 176*, 387–414.

Wissler, C. (1901). The correlation of mental and physical tests. *Psychological Review Monograph Supplements, 3*, No 6.

Wodinsky, J., & Bitterman, M. E. (1953). The solution of oddity problems by the rat. *American Journal of Psychology, 66*, 137–140.

Woodard, W. T., Schoel, W. M., & Bitterman, M. E. (1971). Reversal learning with singly presented stimuli in pigeons and goldfish. *Journal of Comparative and Physiological Psychology, 76*, 460–467.

Woodworth, R. S., & Scholsberg, H. (1955). *Experimental psychology*. New York: Henry Holt.

Yamaguchi, S. I., & Warren, J. M. (1961). Single versus double alternation learning by cats. *Journal of Comparative and Physiological Psychology, 54*, 533–538.

Yarczower, M., & Hazlett, L. (1977). Evolutionary scales and anagenesis. *Psychological Bulletin, 84*, 1088–1097.

Yerkes, R. M. (1904). Inhibition and reinforcement of reaction in the frog *Rana clamitans*. *Jour-*

nal of Comparative Neurological Psychology, 14, 124–137.

Yerkes, R. M. (1905). The sense of hearing in frogs. *Journal of Comparative Neurological Psychology, 15,* 279–304.

Young, J. Z. (1957). *The life of mammals.* Oxford: Clarendon Press.

Young, J. Z. (1960). Learning and form discrimination by octopus. *Biological Review, 60,* 74–94.

Young, J. Z. (1962). Reversal of learning in octopus and the effect of removal of the vertical lobe. *The Quarterly Journal of Experimental Psychology, 14,* 193–205.

Young, P. T. (1961). *Motivation and emotion. A survey of the determinants of human and animal activity.* New York: Wiley.

Young, P. T. (1966). Hedonic organization and regulation of behavior. *Psychological Review, 73,* 59–86.

Young, P. T. (1968). Evaluation and preference in behavioral development. *Psychological Review, 75,* 222–241.

Young, P. T. (1973). Emotion in man and animals: *Its nature and dynamic basis* (2nd ed.). New York: Robert & Krieger.

Zajonc, R. B. (1980). Feeling and thinking: Preferences need no inferences. *American Psychologist, 35,* 151–175.

Zeman, W., & Innes, J. R. M. (1963). *Craigie's neuroanatomy of the rat.* New York: Academic Press.

Zimmerman, R. R., & Torrey, C. C. (1965). Ontogeny of learning. In A. M. Schrier, H. F. Harlow, & F. Stollnitz (Eds.), *Behavior of non-human primates: Modern research trends* (Vol. 2, pp. 405–447). New York: Academic Press.

Author Index

Subject Index

A

Ability tests (human), 157
Acanthodia, 52–53
Actinoptorygii, 94, 96
Adaptation, 9, 10, 208, 260–261
 and survival, 9, 10
Adaptive behavior, mechanisms underlying, 264
Adaptive responses, 3, 7, 14, 17, 43, 153
 adjustment in, 7, 10
Aegyptopithecus, 75, 76, 80, 86
Aelopithecus, 76
Affects: see Feelings
African Mouth Breeder, 185, 189, 195
Agama nigrocollis, 113
Aggression, 235
Agnatha, 30, 96
 brain of 50–53, 54, 108
 brain-body weight ratio, 53
 semi circular canals in, 50
Agranular corlex, 85
Alerting stimuli, 167
Alligator, 153
Alligator Mississippiensus, 178
American psychology, 8
American sign language, use with
  chimpanzies, 224
Ammonites, 33
Ammon's Horn, 110–111
Amniotic egg, 12, 31

Amoeba, 1, 39
Amphibia
 auditory system of, 54
 brain of, 92–94, 96–98, 142
 egg of, 12
 evolution of, 26, 29, 53, 249, 259
 learning in, 266
 olfactory system of, 54
 reproduction in, 31
 visual system of, 54
Amphioxus lanceolatis, 48–50, 95
Amygdala, 262
 in amphibia, 97–99
 and body weight, 106
 and emotion, 236
 in mammals, 104–106
 in marsupials, 104, 105
 proportion of total primate brain, 106
Anagenesis, 38, 153, 196
Anamniotic vertebrates, 94
Anger, 234, 240, 249
Animal behavior
 comparative studies of 151–156, 162, 163
 factorial analysis of, 160
Annelids, 41–43, 218
Aotus trivirgatus, 83, 84, 143
Anticipation: see Expectancy
Anti-drive, 254–255
Apes (Hominoids), 35
 evolution of 75–77, 83–90
 lineage, 83–90